The Baby Overland

Prologue

This book's inspiration was planted indelibly in my mind by my late Uncle James Ellis Boyd. It happened when I was a young boy – sitting on a rock formation on the bank of Swift Creek in lower Toombs County, Georgia. Just as a child, listening keenly to someone reading them a bedtime fable, I sat there entranced with my uncle's storytelling, my feet dangling in the cool stream. Uncle James told me all about a horrific event that happened on February 19, 1920, not far from where we were sitting. I became all ears!

My uncle was a magnificent storyteller and knew how to add drama and mystery to make his tales intriguing. I was enthralled as he painted a picture that apparently fascinated my young impressionable mind so much that it has lasted me a lifetime.

My grandparents' home was located near where the event occurred. That added a personal element to the intrigue. Over the years, like a boomerang, the story kept coming back to the forefront of my mind practically every time I visited my grandparents or found myself in the vicinity of their old home place. Finally, in high school, I wrote a paper about it. I continued to research the story over the decades that followed. Over time, my curiosity turned into determination and a passion for writing this book in my retirement. I wanted to tell the story of the individuals whose lives were forever affected by something that happened over 100 years ago.

A warning to my more sensitive readers: the book's main character, Lee Currie, used a lot of profanity when he spoke, which will be clearly evident by the details and instances about him that I have been able to uncover. I struggled to include this crude and offensive language in the story but chose to keep it because of its contribution to an understanding of Lee's character and his unusual actions. Profanity is common in modern fiction, on-screen, and on television, but I am not a fan unless it is fundamental to the story – which I believe it is in this case.

I would also like to apologize to any reader who feels taken aback by the attitudes of some of the characters toward women and minorities. Sadly, in 1920, sensitivity to the impact that certain words or mannerisms one normally has on the feelings of others was absent in some people, especially of the deep south. But, again, it was important to me to depict the conversations accurately in the context of how people felt and acted back then, if for no other reason but to show how far we have come with our concern for how poorly chosen words and actions can hurt others.

I would like to acknowledge the assistance of those who have helped me with this project:

Mr. Larry Threlkeld, the former Toombs County Probate Judge, and Mrs. Tina Lindsey, the current Probate

Judge, gave me access to old issues of The Lyons Progress. This local newspaper covered the events that take place in this book.

Mrs. Nancy Pittman, the Toombs County Clerk of Court, made access possible for me to newer issues of The Lyons Progress and the court records that helped with my research of the characters involved.

The late Mrs. Judy Currie Stanley, Lee Currie's niece and closest living relative, personally relayed to me the family stories she had heard about her uncle and other members of the Currie Family before she passed away.

I am also indebted to the feedback and critique of the following individuals who graciously agreed to review my first draft and offer their suggestions:

Mr. Randal Arthur – is an author of several books, including my favorite: *A Quiet Roar*.

Rev. James Boyd – my late uncle; I give him credit for originally planting in my head the seed that eventually became this book.

Mrs. Christina Griggers – my wonderful daughter-in-law, who graciously offered me helpful insights.

Mr. Willis NeSmith – the Mayor of Lyons and a voracious reader who understands the impact of significant events on a community. His wife is related to one of the principal characters in the book.

Mr. Mitch Shook – an attorney who gave me insights into the possible legal consequences of bad behavior in the 1920s. His wife Susan, also an attorney, became enthralled by the book and contributed by giving several helpful suggestions.

And finally, this book would not have been possible without the assistance of my loving wife, Debbie, who spent long hours researching the people who were a part of this story – finding newspaper accounts, tracing family trees, and providing a critical ear as I read each chapter aloud to her.

Her help was instrumental in other ways, too. For example, when I suffered from writer's block from distractions demanding my attention, she would arrange for us to go out of town and patiently sit and do research while I continued writing. She is the greatest!

"I hope you will enjoy reading this book as much as I enjoyed writing it.

Larry M. Griggers
Lyons, Georgia
December 30, 2022

Chapter 1

The pistol's unexpected report from the front passenger seat caused the driver to swerve the Model T so violently to the right that Lee Currie slid over in the back seat – almost into the lap of Fred Holmes. Lee felt himself being slammed against the door on the right side as the driver swerved back to the left. Finally, he was hammered into the back of the front seat as the driver brought the Ford to an unexpected and sudden halt. Dust enveloped the automobile while the passengers tried to compose themselves and figure out what had just happened.

"Hot damn!" Lee said, straightening himself up and leaning forward over the seat, eager to see what type of pistol it was that Clarence had just fired.

"What the hell, Clarence James! You scared the bejeebers outta me! I damn near run off the road," Lee heard Sherwood Boyd, the vehicle's driver, blurt out in excitement.

"I've been trying to hit that Rocky Creek sign for months now, Sherwood. I think I finally got it," Clarence said as he laughed aloud.

"What you finally got ... is me almost wetting myself," Fred protested from the seat directly behind Sherwood, causing Lee to laugh. Fred, at once, turned angrily toward him, "It ain't funny, Lee. We could've had an accident."

"I thought it was hilarious," Lee said and chortled. He didn't particularly like the 17-year-old youth sitting next to him. Fred was a dewdropper, a city slicker who hung around the James Farm and tagged along with Clarence, drawn to his rambunctious style like a moth to a flame. But Lee had put up with Fred because Clarence James was one of his best friends.

Firing off a round from a pistol while riding in a car didn't seem dangerous to Lee. Like a gun, for him, a car was all about controlled explosions going off in cylinders. So, to him, Clarence's surprise target practice added to the excitement of riding in a 1917 Ford Model T Touring car. It gave him an exhilarating adrenaline rush.

Lee's father, John Currie, didn't have much use for a passenger car, having decided early on that a pickup truck would be much more practical on the family farm. But there was no substitute for the thrill of being in a car going down a rough, dirt road at dang near 30 miles per hour. And he was grateful to his friend, Sherwood for suggesting to Clarence that they should come by and get him for this car ride.

"What were you shooting at?" Lee asked.

"Nothing, just shooting," Clarence replied, turning to Lee who was sitting right behind him in the back seat. "What good is having a gun if you can't shoot it?"

"Damn tootin'. That's what I say, too," Lee said.

Sherwood interrupted, "Well if the notion hits you again, give me a heads up before you fire off a round. Unless you don't care if I wreck your car here." Sherwood put the Ford back in high and slowly started down the road.

"What kind of gun is that?" Lee asked.

Clarence held the six-shot revolver up high enough for Lee and the others to see. "It's a Colt Model 1898, Lee, 45 caliber. My uncle carried this here gun in the Great War and gave it to me hisself. Finest shooting pistol I have ever seen! Wanna hold it?"

Lee's eyes flashed in agreement, and he eagerly extended his hand to hold the gun. He noticed Sherwood's disapproving look at Clarence and suspected that Sherwood didn't trust him around firearms despite their friendship. He smiled at his friend and then turned his disarming smile toward Clarence to counter the concern on Sherwood's face.

Clarence glanced at Sherwood, smiled, and then handed the pistol to Lee, declaring, "It'll be fine, Sherwood, Lee's been around guns before."

"Hell yeah!" Lee exclaimed as he held the gun and began to stare at it admiringly. "I even killed me a kraut in the Great War. The son-of-a-bitch run right up on my foxhole, and I shot him deader' n a doornail!"

Lee glanced at Sherwood, hoping he would not reveal that he had just lied to the others. He never saw combat in the Great War, and Sherwood knew it. He breathed a sigh of relief as Sherwood rolled his eyes and returned them to the road ahead.

Marveling at the pistol, Lee turned it about slowly in his hands. Fred shuffled uneasily in his seat as Lee's fascination with the gun overcame his attention to where it was pointed. Lee spun the chamber, and a live round settled with a metallic click under the firing pin.

"Hey!" Fred complained and drew back.

"Sorry," Lee responded, redirecting the gun to the outside of the car. Then, looking up at Clarence, he asked, "Can I shoot it?"

Sherwood looked disapprovingly at Clarence.

"Sure," Clarence said, ignoring Sherwood's look. "Fire away."

"No, sir!" Sherwood blurted out, slamming on the brakes again and forcing all the passengers to instinctively brace themselves to remain upright in their seats.

"Damn, Sherwood, was that necessary? We was going dang near 25 miles per hour!" Clarence complained, his eyes piercing his friend.

"If y'all gonna be shootin' guns, it ain't gonna be while I'm driving!" Sherwood said.

"Fine by me," Lee said as he swung open the car door, gun held high.

"Hang on, Lee. Let me at least get off the road," Sherwood said as he pulled over to the side of the road just beyond Rocky Creek. Lee got out and looked around. The only sign of civilization that could be seen nearby in the remote area was Rocky Creek Baptist Church up the hill. The others got out of the car and gathered on the bank by the creek.

"Betcha can't hit that turtle there," Clarence suddenly said to Lee, gesturing to a black box turtle sitting casually on a soggy, green stump in the creek's middle. Its yellow stripes, adept at keeping it well-hidden among fallen leaves, were beaming brightly against the dark water, affording a perfect target. Oblivious to the danger, the turtle calmly observed the group with a dismissive indifference.

"Aww, come on, guys," Fred protested. "That turtle ain't hurtin' nobody."

"You wrong, Fred," Lee retorted, "that there is a German turtle, and he's about to be a dead son-of-a-bitch!" Lee aimed.

Boom!

The water splashed a couple of feet from the turtle. The mildly concerned turtle leisurely scampered off the stump and disappeared into the water.

"Shit," Lee said.

Peals of laughter rang out.

Clarence stopped laughing and expressed, "Good thing that German turtle wasn't armed, or we'd be ducking and running 'bout now!"

Fred tried unsuccessfully to conceal a chuckle.

"Shut up, Fred! Don't you laugh at me," Lee said and then glared menacingly at the younger retreating man.

"Calm down, Lee. Fred ain't laughing at you! He's laughing at what I said," Clarence explained. Fred moved toward Clarence, instinctively seeking his protection, as Lee continued to glare at him.

"I'll bet that German you supposedly shot in the Great War is swimming in some pond in Germany right now just like that there turtle is swimming in that creek. Now, gimme that gun before you hurt yourself," Clarence said, extending his hand to Lee's to take the gun away from him.

Lee hesitated. He didn't think it was fair for them to judge him on one missed shot from an unfamiliar pistol. It certainly was not a bit funny. He saw that Sherwood and Fred had tensed up. Clarence gestured again for him to hand over the gun. He finally spun it around and handed it to him.

"I did kill me a German," Lee murmured under his breath and then turned to walk back to the car. He gruffly got in and settled into his seat.

"I'm sure you did, Lee. I was just teasing. You're a real badass – we all know that don't we boys?" Clarence said.

"Yeah," said Fred sarcastically, "He's a real badass, alright."

Lee again stared at Fred menacingly and began to come out of the car – Clarence pushed him back into the car.

"Settle down, Lee; he's just funning. Now, Sherwood, get this hunk of junk moving," Clarence said, poking Sherwood on the shoulder.

The Ford ground back to life and it backfired as Sherwood steered it back onto the road.

Lee stared at the rapidly passing trees. He did not like the feeling of humiliation flowing over him and ignored Clarence's efforts to engage him in conversation as they continued their ride.

"I'm ready to go home," he told Sherwood, who offered no argument and continued down Marvin Church Road toward the Currie place.

Lee continued to stare out of the window. All he could think about was getting home, getting his gun, and practicing his shooting. There would not be a reoccurrence of missing any more turtles – that was certain. There would be other opportunities to overcome their suspicion that he had not killed any Germans in the Great War. Only his friend Sherwood knew better – the others didn't, and he didn't like their assumptions about him.

If they think I can't kill someone, they would be wrong, he thought to himself.

Chapter 2

"You keep them Germans at bay, now, ya hear," Lee heard Clarence say in between his laughter, from the speedily departing car after Lee had gotten out and had begun moving toward his father's house.

"That ain't funny, Clarence!" he shouted as he picked up a rock and hurled it at the dust cloud billowing behind the swiftly disappearing Ford.

All high and mighty in his fancy car – Lee thought to himself as he walked up the steps and onto the large wrap-around porch of his pa's farm home.

"Lee, that you?" came the voice of the young lady stepping out onto the porch. Lee continued staring at the receding car for a moment and then turned to face Lilly Corey Currie.

His wife had just turned 20, and Lee thought she was beautiful; no, she was still too youthful in her appearance to be described as beautiful, "pretty" felt more appropriate. One would think she should be singing and skipping in the yard – while pushing along a rolling hoop with a stick and trailed by a happily barking cocker spaniel rather than standing on the porch as a married woman wiping her hands on her kitchen apron.

When he started courting her four years ago, just after she turned 16, he had been enchanted with her captivating looks: she was petite, with long flowing blond hair and flawless smooth skin. Now his feelings toward her were more complicated, especially after that divorce she attempted and then withdrew the previous year. He loved her, but more importantly, she symbolized having his own family and being his own man instead of being a member of his father's family.

"Who was that what brought you home?" Lilly asked.

"Clarence James and Sherwood Boyd, and some dewdropper from town," Lee responded.

"I've got you some supper ready. I cooked up a mess of catfish your step-mama caught today down on the Altamaha."

Lee did not respond to the offered menu and turned to look down the road again.

"You alright?"

"Where's my gun?" Lee said and turned to her. He noticed his wife stiffen.

"My gun, woman, where's my gun?"

"Gun?" her nervousness did not faze him.

"I didn't stutter! Where's my damn pistol?" Lee barked in a tone reserved for when he meant business. He had little patience for his wife's inquiries when he had set his mind on something, and gave her a look that threatened his wrath, should she not immediately comply.

"I think it's in your pa's gun cabinet, Lee," Lilly obediently answered, "but can't that wait? Supper's gonna get cold if you don't come on and eat. I've got fresh water in the basin for you to wash up."

Undeterred, Lee pushed past his wife and swung open the screen door with such force that it made Lilly jump back. Then, cautiously, she followed her husband into the house.

Lee instantly found the pistol – a blue steel Smith & Wesson Model 3, purchased from the Minter-Smith Hardware Store in Lyons just a month earlier.

"Where're the bullets?" Lee barked as he rambled through the drawers below the gun cabinet. "I know I've got some bullets around here somewhere, damn it!"

"I don't remember seeing any bullets, Lee, but I'm sure they sell them at the Minter-Smith Hardware store. Can we worry about that later? Your supper is getting cold."

As was characteristic of Lee, his mood changed, and his determined anger disappeared utterly.

"Can't let that happen. I'm ready to eat," Lee said as he stopped his search and headed to the kitchen.

As Lee sat down and began to fix his plate, the old hinges' squeak announced his father and stepmother's arrival at the back door.

"You're just in time, Mr. and Mrs. Currie – supper is on the table," Lilly said.

As he instinctively did, John Currie looked intently at his son for a moment to assess his current mood before speaking to him. Then, finding him in a relatively normal state, he greeted him with a familial "Hi son. You doin' all right this evening?"

Lee glanced up from the supper table briefly to acknowledge John and Lula and then reached for the catfish heaped up on a platter. "Doing alright, Pa." His eyes met his stepmother's, and he smiled, "Lilly tells me you caught this mess of fish, Lula."

Lula returned his smile and said, "They were biting today, Lee. I weren't down there no more'n an hour or so." Lula sat down, Lilly placed a plate in front of her, and John sat beside her.

"I need your help tomorrow, Lee, on about 20 feet of fence that the cows pushed over down near Marvin Church Road. Think you could help me get it back up?" John said as he began to fix his plate.

"Can't, Pa," Lee said while signaling Lilly to pour him some more tea. "Mr. Math Bell has got me a new job in Hardwick, Georgia, up near Milledgeville."

Lee frowned as he anticipated the interrogation that was coming next. He knew his father disapproved of his seeking work over a hundred miles away.

The Curries were among the most prominent and prosperous families in Toombs County, but Lee had become tired of being called "John Currie's boy." He wanted to make his own way and step out of his pa's shadow.

"Lee, I've worked hard building this farm up for you and your siblings. You'd be foolish to walk off and leave the great opportunity that is sitting right here waitin' for you...."

Lee tuned out as his father went into his oft-repeated speech about migrating to Georgia from North Carolina with nothing but the clothes on his back. John repeated the old worn-out story about how Lee's grandfather had owned a large plantation with many slaves and lost it all as punishment for enlisting in the Confederate Army, as did most of the landed gentry in North Carolina.

Lee feigned interest as his father reiterated how his grandfather's spirit broke after the war. He had to stand by helplessly as Carpetbaggers from up north – seized the plantation during Reconstruction, split it into small farms, and parceled it out to his former slaves. Lee knew these stories were sentimental for his pa, but he could not relate to the successes and failures of a grandfather who had died before he was born.

Nor could he communicate to his pa that these did not feel like his success stories. On the contrary, they belonged to his father. Through industry and a bit of luck, John Currie had gradually acquired 687 acres of prime farm and timberland in Tattnall County near the Altamaha River in the Marvin Community. When Toombs County was carved out of Tattnall, Emanuel, and Montgomery Counties in 1905, the Currie farm became one of the new county's largest and most productive agricultural operations – employing all the family members along with several sharecroppers and tenant farmers.

But none of this appealed to Lee Currie. He did not want to be a farmer, nor did he want anyone saying that his pa gave him everything he had. Instead, Lee wanted to do the same thing that his father had done – strike out on his own, with nothing but the clothes on his back, and make his own fortune. He didn't want people to look at him and think, "That's John Currie's boy." Instead, he wanted people to look at his father and think, "That's Lee Currie's pa."

His ambition to pave his path was encouraged by his mother, Vinnie. He believed her when she told him he could do anything to which he had set his mind. She had encouraged him to build his life around his new family after he had married Lilly. His mother was his rock, right up to the time she died two years earlier from the Spanish Flu at 50, leaving him without a confidant and advisor.

And now, Lee was ready to pursue the ambition she inspired. He had a new job in Hardwick and was preparing to move Lilly up there, putting him on a collision course with his pa's efforts to keep him close to home.

A counter to Lee and his father's tension was his growing friendship with Lula, John's second wife. Lula was only 25 years of age, young enough to be John's daughter, and only three years older than Lee. The rest of the family considered her a gold digger – having come from a humble past and worming her way into John's affections just over a year after Vinnie's demise. But Lee liked her and considered her more like a sister than a stepmother.

She had only been in the family for a few months, but Lula had already mastered being in the no-man's-land between John Currie and his son, and each thought she was on their side.

"Lee, your pa really could use you around here on the farm. I don't know why you are giving serious consideration to working in Hardwick. I know it probably feels like an adventure, but you have a good home here, and believe me, out here in the country is a much better place to raise a family than up there in that big city," Lula tried to convince Lee.

"What kind of job is it?" John asked.

"It's a barbershop…."

"A barbershop?" John cut him off and said, "You're turning down a job on a prosperous farm to work at a barbershop?"

Lee had sat silently during his father's plea that he stay on the farm, but with Lula seemingly taking his side, and now his father making light of his new job – he felt he needed to speak up. "I'm not just working at a barbershop, Pa.

"Mr. Harden has a pressing club also, and it's one of the biggest in the area. Times are more prosperous now that the war is over, and people can afford more store-bought clothes. And they can afford to have them cleaned and ironed. He is also doing a lot of business with the insane asylum up there. He's making a lot of money and paying me well. I'm soon going to be able to afford my own place and buy myself a car."

"A car? Already?" Lula asked.

"Yeah, I've got my eye on one of them new Baby Overland cars, and I'm going to have me one, too. You'll see."

John spoke up, "Lee, I know you think that sounds like a good thing, but I've got plenty of land here, and you can build on this property. I need you on the farm, and I can pay you enough to afford a car if that's what you've got your mind set on. It would be best if you stayed here, son. The Curries have been farming for over a hundred years. This land is your future."

Lee felt ganged up upon and bristled. "No, this is YOUR future, Pa. It's Katie's, Pratt's, John, Jr.'s, and Lillian's future. It ain't mine. I have to be on my own. I ain't cut out to be no damn dirt farmer."

"You watch your mouth, son," John Currie retorted. "There are ladies at the table!"

"It ain't like they never heard it before, and I'll say what I damn well please. I'm a grown man," Lee growled.

Lilly interrupted, "Lee, you want some more mashed potatoes? These are some of my best...."

"Shut up, dammit!" Lee stood up and turned to his father. "I'm tired of this shit hole of a hog farm, and I'm tired of being pushed around by you!" Lee threw his napkin down on the table and stormed out of the kitchen.

As soon as John started to get up, Lula held out her hand, gesturing for him to remain in his seat.

"Let me talk to him, John. He'll just get madder if you try," Lula said. John sighed and nodded his approval to his wife.

Lee had found his pistol. He was holding it in his hand while rummaging through the gun cabinet, looking for bullets, when Lula came into his bedroom.

"Son, if you will take a mother's advice, you will give me that pistol. You will be better off by it."

Lee laughed, "Oh, you think?" He aimed the pistol right at Lula and said, "Well, I happen to disagree. I'm about to put this gun to good use."

Nonchalantly, pushing the barrel away from her face, Lula calmly said, "I doubt that. Now give it to me, and I will keep it for you."

"No!" Lee said sternly. "I intend to kill John Currie if he ever bothers me again. I ain't gonna take anything off of him at all."

Lula began to cry – it unnerved Lee, instantly. He put the gun down and hugged her. "Don't cry, Lula. I didn't mean to make you cry. You been good to me. I ain't gonna bother Pa so long as he leaves me the hell alone."

"Lee, I know I ain't 'cha ma, and I would never try to replace her, but I've come to love you like you's my own son, and I want you to be happy – and so does your pa. Come on back to the supper table and let's act like family," Lula broke their embrace and wiped away her tears. Extending a hand to Lee, she pleaded, "Please come back to the table."

Lee's mood transformed to calm as quickly as it had flashed to anger during supper, "Okay, I guess we ought to go get us some more of those fish you caught before pa and Lilly eat 'em all," Lee hugged his stepmother again, and they returned to the kitchen laughing as if nothing had happened.

After Lee sat back down, John spoke up, "Lee, I'm sorry about what I said earlier – about your moving to the Milledgeville area. If you have your mind made up, you go on up there and make your way. But always remember that you have a place here if things go bad for you. And Lilly is welcome to stay here until you find a suitable place – if you like."

Lilly's brief smile at her father-in-law's offer disappeared when Lee looked at her. She said meekly, "I like it here, too, Lee. My family and friends are here. I don't know anyone in Milledgeville."

Lee shot his wife a stern look that sent a shudder through her spine. "You have lots of relatives just outside of Milledgeville, and you will make new friends. Now you are going with me, and that's that!"

Lee took another bite of catfish, and his expression showed that he had put the conversation behind him.

Chapter 3

"This here's the greatest improvement in riding comfort since the introduction of pneumatic tires, Burley, and you should be able to sell it at a profit in no time. I guarantee you there is someone in the county willing to do anything to get his hands on the wheel of this fine piece of machinery," the dealer told Burley Phillips.

"No doubt, Mr. Warthen, but as I recall, you said that same thing about that Chevrolet Series FB you sold me last year." Burley Phillips was no newcomer to the banter that marked the beginning of haggling over an automobile's purchase. "It took me three months to sell that 'fine automobile,' as you put it. I barely got my money outin' it. If'in I hadn't been using it for a jitney, I'd uh lost my shirt!"

The two old pros were no strangers to such bargaining. Ober Warthen was the local Overland automobile dealer in Vidalia, and Burley had been buying cars from him for a while now. Being a jack of all trades had kept food on the table for him and Tersia and brought them a pretty good living. The post-war boom in automobile sales had lured him into honing his skills as a mechanic. After he had saved enough to buy a car of his own, he discovered that offering his services as a jitney driver for Mr. Wilson afforded him an even better living selling cars to his jitney customers.

Burley preferred driving passengers instead of getting all greasy working on cars. Once considered a luxury purchase available only to rich folks, automobiles were getting cheaper due to new mass-production techniques, and more ordinary people could afford them. And with the Great War now over, soldiers that had returned home were looking seriously to buy an automobile.

It was a growing market, and Burley had been able to sell three cars to his riders in the last six months alone. The income from those sales freed him from spending all his earnings on necessities for him and Tersia. With his newly found fortune, he was able to buy his wife the first store-bought dress she had ever owned, and he surprised her this past Christmas with one of those new electric vacuum cleaners that were gaining popularity among the womenfolk.

But it was not all smooth sailing. Unlike the first two used cars that Burley had bought from Mr. Warthen and quickly sold, Burley had a little trouble selling the new Chevrolet, which Ober had talked him into last time. He was more cautious now and was determined to get a deal on the new Overland automobile. The next new car he bought from Ober would have to be a best-seller that he was confident he could quickly flip.

"That Chevy was a good car, Burley, and you know it. You just weren't showing it to the right buyers," Ober argued.

"No, it was the wrong car. That Chevy body is too long for our roads, Ober. Nobody wants a car with a 106-inch wheelbase around these parts. Heck, even with all this road building going on, most roads around here are still dirt and mud. You sold me a big city car, and this ain't no big city. I want to look at one of them Baby Overlands."

"I love a man that knows his cars and his customer's needs, Burley. You are absolutely right. This Baby Overland has a 100-inch wheelbase, by crackey. The car is assembled from five units only and the entire chassis assembly only requires 50 bolts! And you are going to love the mileage you get, too. They scaled down the motor to 143.1 cubic inches to make it nice and economical."

Burley frowned. He welcomed the shorter wheelbase, but an underpowered automobile would not find favor with the customers he was after. "Can't get much horsepower out of that small an engine, Ober. And like I said, our county roads ain't that good, ya know. We've got a few hilly areas in this neck of the woods, where an underpowered engine would leave a man high and dry. Maybe I better go check with the Ford dealer."

It was a bluff, of course. Burley knew the horse-trading drill. Mr. Warthen would now try to wow him by reciting the datasheet on the Baby Overland.

"Ah, well, that's where you'd be wrong, Burley. This Overland engine has 27 horsepower. The Ford Model T won't produce but 20. And the ride over those rough county roads will be very comfortable with the three-point cantilever spring suspension, and those nice leather seats – they are stuffed with genuine horsehair, you see. I took my new wife, Inez, on a ride in it, and she just loves it. Your next buyer's wife will, too. Yes, sir, the Overland is a new standard of riding comfort that all those veterans what fought in the Great War are going to want. You'll sell it in no time flat!"

"27 horsepower, huh? Hmm ...," Burley walked around the car kicking the tires and opening and shutting the doors. It was pretty solid all right and had more eye appeal than most cars he had seen around the county. The Baby Overland might appeal to the veterans after all. Most had been home long enough to set some money aside and were itching to spend it. Mr. Warthen had sold him on the car, but he didn't want the veteran car salesman to know it yet. He spotted a haggling opportunity.

"Ober, what's this?" Burley pointed to a torn section of the curtain just behind the left rear passenger seat.

"You know how easy it is for a curtain to get torn during shipping, Burley. I have a kit and can fix that up, just like new. That's an easy fix."

"Well, I should be able to fix that myself. So, I might take a chance on it, depending on how bad you want to sell it. How much?" Burley asked.

Burley knew that little money was circulating during the winter months, especially for car sales, and Ober might be eager to trade. "Well, since this will be the fourth car you've bought from me, Burley, I'm going to make you a real deal. This car retails for $1,375, but I'm going to let you have it wholesale for $975. That's $200 below my normal discount price reserved for my very best customers." Ober smiled confidently.

Burley knew the dealer still had some more wiggle room on the price. So, he fished for a bargain: "You trying to rob me, Ober? I'm not buying this car for myself. You know I intend to turn around and make a decent markup on it."

"What are you talking about, Burley? This Baby Overland is hot right now. It will easily sell retail for $1,175, and you can make $200 just like that!" Mr. Warthen said confidently and snapped his fingers for emphasis.

"If I were one of your car salesmen, you'd pay me more than that as a sales commission. So, I'll give you $850 for it right now, or you can keep it! It ain't worth a nickel more to me," Burley started walking back to his car.

"$965, and that's my final offer," Ober scowled, feeling his sale slip away.

Make it $935, and you got a deal," Burley countered.

"We go way back, my friend. Let's not quibble. How about we split the difference and trade at $950?" the dealer said and extended his hand to make a deal.

"Deal made." Burley took his hand and gave it a single shake. And with that, they struck the bargain.

"How about letting me finance this one for you, Burley? I own part of the Toombs County Bank and sit on the board. I can have them offer you a loan where you don't have to tie up your money. You can't beat that!"

Burley knew Mr. Warthen was trying to make up some of the price concession he had just given him. He had been reading the auto magazines and knew that the newly formed General Motors Acceptance Corporation was making auto loans to sell Buicks, Pontiacs, Chevrolets, Oldsmobiles, and Cadillacs. The bank was, no doubt, eager to keep automobile loans as a part of their banking business.

"I'm a bit leery of borrowing money on installment, Ober. I've heard about people having their cars repossessed if they miss just one payment. I think I can come up with the funds easily enough."

"Now, Burley, you know me better than that. Repossessions are for folks that can't manage their money. I know you are good for it. Besides, you'll probably sell this car before the first payment is due. That way, you don't have anything tied up at all. It's like having free money!" The dealer was on a roll.

"What interest rate you gonna give me?"

"Best around. It will only cost you about $5.00 a week in interest. You know it won't take more than a few weeks to sell that fine automobile. With your jitney fares and the markup on the car, you should be able to easily clear a couple of hundred dollars in a month or less."

"Deal!" Burley said and extended his hand, which Ober shook vigorously. "Maybe, as you say, I'll have it sold before the first payment is due!"

"Now that's the Burley I know – ever the optimist. Yep, there's someone in this county that will surely want this car badly. Come on in the office, and we'll get your paperwork taken care of."

Having made the sale, Ober continued his banter, "You'll love the Overland Owner's Manual. They tell you everything you need to know, including how to break it in. I've already put in the antifreeze and topped it off with gas."

Burley paid little attention to the car salesman now that he had done the deal. Instead, while Ober was talking away, he looked out the office window at the Baby Overland in admiration and thought – *that sure is a pretty car*.

I made me a good deal, he thought to himself. This car would bring him good luck; he just knew it. Tersia would be so pleased.

Chapter 4

"Who the hell gave you the idea that I would want to stay here – at this nuthouse?" Lee asked angrily, pointing his finger at the group of buildings before them. "You think I'm a lunatic or something?" John Blackstone stepped back from where the two men were standing by the car, instantly aware that even the simple task of making housing suggestions to Lee Currie was not without risks.

One of the new wings of the Georgia State Sanitarium stood majestically before them. It's beautiful Gothic architecture obscured the fact that it marked one of the entrances to a notorious insane asylum. Despite the cool air, Blackstone began to sweat at not doing more to prepare Lee for this reveal.

The Georgia State Sanitarium was initially conceived as a well-meaning effort 80 years earlier by a group of Milledgeville physicians. They tried to build a place to treat the mentally ill, but the Georgia State Sanitarium had become infamous for its extreme methods. Nevertheless, it met a great need, and when the Georgia General Assembly finally acknowledged that need and took over the project funding, the growth was dramatic. They renamed the new facility the "Lunatic, Idiot, and Epileptic Asylum at Milledgeville."

Blackstone now saw all types of opportunities for Lee to misinterpret his suggestion to rent a room here.

"They've just built some new buildings, Lee, and it will take them a while to fill them with patients. So, they've been renting out the rooms to folks like us till they need them. My father-in-law and I have rented our rooms for some time now. It's cheap and is the best deal going around, and it will tide you over until you find a permanent home here in Milledgeville," Blackstone explained as he began removing his bags from the car.

The Georgia State Sanitarium was indeed convenient to where he and Lee would be working: the Hardwick Barbershop and Pressing Club. However, despite the dual purpose of the imposing structure, Blackstone hoped that Lee would warm up to the idea that this was an affordable option.

"I don't know – it's a little big for me," Lee finally responded.

"Everything is big around here, Lee," Blackstone said convincingly. "Milledgeville was the Capitol of Georgia for six decades back in the first half of the eighteenth century. Heck, General Lafayette himself came here to visit back then."

Blackstone removed Lee's bag from the car and set it down in front of him. "This ain't nothing like your old home,

Lee, that's for sure, but it's time for you to start thinking bigger than Johnson's Corner, Georgia."

Milledgeville was indeed bigger. Even Blackstone had been amazed at the city's growth in the few months he had been living and working in nearby Hardwick, which was only a couple of miles from the bigger city. That rapid growth was due in no small part to the employment opportunities at the hospital, which was also the best customer of Mr. Harden's barbershop and pressing club. Moreover, the Milledgeville "crazy house" grew dramatically as towns across Georgia took advantage of the free admission policy to rid their communities of homeless people, the criminally insane, and those with dementia. As a result, it had grown to be the largest insane asylum in America.

The growth was so all-encompassing to the community that the Georgia State Sanitarium came to be known only as "Milledgeville." It effectively usurped the city's name, much to the other city residents' chagrin, who became the brunt of jokes as their city became well known as a place where "crazy" people lived. Blackstone had discovered early on that one of the quickest ways to start a fight with one of the locals was to mention the hospital.

"Come on, Lee, it's a good place, and mainly – it's cheap. The money you save can help you buy that Baby Overland automobile you have your mind set on."

At the mention of the Overland, Lee's countenance began to soften, and he turned to Blackstone, "Okay, let's go see what they've got."

Blackstone breathed a sigh of relief.

* * * * * *

The following day, Lee knocked on Blackstone's door –bright and early, announcing he was ready to ride to work. Lee must have liked his accommodations, as there was no longer any hint in his demeanor of any sort of dissatisfaction with staying at the Georgia State Sanitarium.

Blackstone invited Lee in as he finished his preparations to go to work. He began to regret going along with his Uncle Math Bell's desire to help Lee get a job in Hardwick, especially given they both would be working for the same employer. There was only so much of Lee's company he could stand.

Blackstone liked his employer. Although only 26 years old, Earnest C. Harden had opened the Hardwick Barbershop and Pressing Club and turned it into one of the area's most prosperous businesses. He was already expanding his business and readily agreed to Blackstone's Uncle's suggestion to hire Lee.

But Blackstone was uneasy with the arraignment. It was one thing to run into Lee occasionally back in Toombs County, where he didn't have to put up with his antics for long at a time, but this was a lot closer proximity than he desired. They were neighbors, working together and riding back and forth to work together. He also worried that Lee might return to his old habit of stealing things from his employer. If he still harbored them, Lee's larcenous habits would strain Mr. Harden's relationship with both him and his uncle.

And there was another risk – Math's arranging this job far from Lee's home and his father, ran the risk of jeopardizing Math's relationship with his neighbor, John Currie, who opposed his son being outside his control.

As they drove the short distance to work, Blackstone fished to discover how much longer he would be burdened with his rider. "With what Mr. Harden told Uncle Math he would be paying you; you should soon be able to buy your own car, Lee."

"I sure hope so, John. You can't make that kind of money in Lyons. I'm pleased to be working with Mr. Harden, that's for sure."

"Still have your eye on an Overland?" John inquired.

"Oh, hell yeah!" Lee replied. "Old man Warthen has four Overlands on his lot in Vidalia. They shore is pretty, especially that Baby Overland!"

"That's not exactly a cheap car, from what I hear. Don't you think you should be looking at some other model, or maybe a used car?" Blackstone asked.

"I can afford it with those new installment plans they been givin' folk," Lee replied.

"You sure will be the envy of everyone, Lee. I hear that car has more horsepower than a Model T Ford! You could make the trip from Lyons to here in no time at all. You gonna be working in Hardwick just long enough to make enough money to buy it, or you gonna be staying up here longer?"

"I don't spec I'll be looking to go back to Lyons nary time soon. From what I've seen so far – I think I will love it here. There is so much goin' on; it's really exciting. Besides, I got me a wife now, and we need to be on our own. I'm 22 years old, and me and Lilly are still living in my father's house. That ain't right."

Blackstone continued to hint at an eventual parting of company. "Glad to hear you are working on getting you a car, Lee. I've been having my fair share of problems with this old Ford, and I don't want this old rattletrap to be our only way to get around. Heck, I just might be needing a ride from you from time to time before long if this flivver craps out on me."

"Once I get my Overland, you will be welcome to ride with me anytime," Lee said.

Arriving at the business, Blackstone wheeled into an empty parking space in front of the Hardwick Barbershop and Pressing Club and pulled up the emergency brake. "Here we are, Lee. Right on time."

Lee reached across the back seat for his coat, popped open the door, and turned to John. "Thanks, John. You gonna give me a ride back to the Sanitarium at quitting time, right?"

"Sorry, Lee, but I'm pulling a late shift tonight, and you'll have to make other arrangements. It's just a couple of miles. You can walk or take the city trolly."

Lee gave him a fierce look, "Have you ever looked at them trolly cars running all up and down this here street? Hell, it's slam full of negros. I ain't crazy about getting on that trolly with all of them. Dammit, John, I need a ride!"

"Sorry, I just can't tonight," replied Blackstone, and immediately tried another distraction. "But don't worry, it'll just be for a little while, what with you about to get that Baby Overland."

At the mention of the Overland, the smile returned to Lee's face, and his mind appeared to go racing off in that direction, much to Blackstone's relief. "Yeah, you're right, I'll soon have my car, and I won't have to ride with nobody I don't want to."

With that, Blackstone exhaled the breath he had been holding. Lee began walking toward the barbershop. He stopped and turned to Blackstone, "But you will have to let me know before you head back to Lyons this weekend. I've got to go get Lilly and bring her back up here now that I've got us a place to stay."

"Will do," Blackstone said, as he followed Lee into Mr. Harden's shop.

* * * * * *

As they entered the stop, Mr. Harden looked up from the customer whose hair he was cutting and acknowledged their arrival with a nod.

"Good morning, Mr. Harden. Let me introduce you to your new employee. This here is Lee Currie," Blackstone said.

Harden put down his cutting tools, walked over to Lee, and extended his hand, "Good to meet you, Lee, and welcome aboard."

Lee took the offered hand and shook it vigorously, "Thank you, Mr. Harden, and I appreciate this opportunity. I aim to be the best employee you got." He continued to shake Harden's hand until the barber forcefully pulled it away.

"Well, with that kind of enthusiasm, you might just make it," Harden said. He turned toward the back, lifted his fingers to his mouth, and gave out a loud whistle. "Frank! Come, show our new employee how to work the pressing equipment." Frank waved and started coming over to where they were standing.

Lee appeared anxious to get to work, took off his Army coat, and turned to hang it on the hat rack standing by the door.

Harden halted him with a gesture, "Hang that up in the back, Lee; we need to reserve that rack for the customers."

"Sorry, Mr. Harden." Lee took down his coat and folded it across his arm.

"Not a problem, you have to learn our rules. You found a place to stay yet?" Mr. Harden asked.

Lee smiled broadly, "Hell yeah, I got a room down at the Sanitarium just yesterday."

"Watch your tongue while in my shop, young man. That kind of talk don't sit well round here," Mr. Harden warned. "This is a respectable place of business."

Blackstone's stomach tightened as he saw Lee flush red. He held his breath in anticipation; Mr. Harden might just see a full display of Lee's temper.

"I didn't mean nothing by it, Mr. Harden; it just kinda pops out without my giving it much mind. I don't mean no harm," Lee said.

Blackstone breathed a sigh of relief.

"That's okay, Lee. It ain't like I haven't heard it before. Just don't use it in the shop. It might offend the customers."

"Don't bother me none ... just men talk," said the customer in Mr. Harden's barber chair.

Mr. Harden smiled and nodded affirmatively. "It might bother my next customer, so let's not be cussing in here.

So, you found a room at the Sanitarium, huh? I thought that place was just for crazy folks. You ain't crazy, are you, Lee?"

"Naw, Mr. Harden, I ain't crazy. John here got it for me. He tells me they are renting out the new buildings' empty rooms until they get more patients. So, I got me one cheap," Lee smiled broadly.

Mr. Harden was pleased. "That's great, Lee. I know you are going to fit in just fine here in Hardwick. It's just a hop, skip, and a jump from Milledgeville, and that city has a lot more to offer than Lyons or even Vidalia. Take the Palace Theater down there on Wayne Street. Not a lot of towns have their own theater. Milledgeville is uptown and doesn't lack for nothing, that's for sure."

"My folks took me to a movie theater in Macon once. I saw one of those picture shows with Charlie Chaplin in it. He was kinda funny," Lee said.

"Ever heard of Laurel and Hardy, Lee?" the barber asked.

"Nope, can't say as I have. I just saw that one picture show; is all I done," Lee responded.

"Laurel and Hardy are more famous around these parts than Mr. Chaplin, Lee. Oliver Hardy, hisself used to work down there at the Palace Theater, not more than seven years ago, running the projectors. Why he even went to the Military School here! Now he's a big star, famous all over the world. Shoot, his ex-wife, Madelyn Saloshin, came over here and played the piano at our last homecoming – yes, sir, she sure did."

Mr. Harden was a panacea of information about all the locals, both the famous and the infamous.

Frank walked up to where they were standing, "You say this is a new employee?"

"Name's Lee Currie," Lee introduced himself as he shook Frank's hand.

"Frank, you show him the ropes and teach him right, ya hear," Harden said.

"I don't know no other way to teach, Mr. Harden," Frank said as he put his hand on Lee's shoulder and nudged him toward the back.

Lee turned his head as he walked away and said, "I'll make you proud of hiring me, Mr. Harden!" Then he headed back to the pressing room, seemingly having no interest at all in the famous son of the Milledgeville area now elevated to the silver screen.

"That's good, Lee; you do that now." Mr. Harden, disappointed that his new employee did not share his enthusiasm for the picture shows, resumed his conversation with the customer sitting patiently in his barber chair.

"His real name was Norvel Hardy, and he worked at the Palace Theater for dang near three years ..."

Blackstone turned to go to the back as Mr. Harden continued telling his story to the captive audience sitting in his chair.

"John," Harden said, stopping Blackstone in his tracks. "You keep an eye on him for me. I'm trusting you to make sure he learns our way of doing things, okay?"

Blackstone grimaced. Now he was officially Lee's babysitter. It was the kind of trouble he didn't need. "Yes, sir, Mr. Harden. I'll watch him close." Harden smiled and nodded, and Blackstone continued walking to the back.

After observing for a while, Blackstone was pleased to see that Lee was uncharacteristically attentive to Frank's instructions about using the commercial washing machines and iron presses. He was very animated by the time the three of them reached the pressing room.

Lee approached the hampers filled with the laundry to be washed and picked up a pair of trousers. "You boys are going to be my ticket to a new car, which I am going to have one day, one way or the other, by damn."

"Language, Lee!" Blackstone said quickly and glanced into the barbershop to see if Mr. Harden had heard Lee break the newly established rule on cussing. However, his boss was fully engaged in a lively conversation with his customer, and luckily, Lee's slip of the tongue had not been noticed.

"Oops, sorry," Lee said as he tossed a load of clothes into the vat and watched Frank light the fire underneath.

"You have to keep the customer's laundry separate, Lee. We don't do 'bag washing' at this store. Mr. Harden thinks it is unsanitary, and folks must agree 'cause we get a lot of customers disgusted with the other pressing clubs," Frank said. He dumped a cup of Twenty Mule Team Borax into the vat and started stirring.

Blackstone was pleased with Lee's enthusiasm for his new job. From the look on Lee's face, he was undoubtedly dreaming about owning that beautiful Baby Overland.

Maybe this will work out, after all, Blackstone thought to himself.

Chapter 5

"See you tomorrow, Mr. Harden," Lee bid goodbye as he headed out of the barbershop at the day's end. After a hard day's work, he was exhausted in his continuing effort to prove himself worthy of a raise, but the cool night air revived him. As his eyes adjusted to the dim light of the gas streetlights, he decided he was not yet ready to head back to the Sanitarium. He decided it was time to check out the nightlife of his new home city. So, he caught the trolly to downtown Milledgeville.

Lee jumped off the trolly and had only walked a block along Wayne Street when the faint sound of music drifting through the night air began to pull him in the direction of a local honky-tonk. As he approached the weather-beaten establishment, he read the words over the front door, "Patty's Parlor." Through the small windows, he could see dozens of patrons laughing, tipping glasses, and making merry. He opened the door, went in, and immediately felt excited as the full volume of the music fell upon his ears, and the smoke engulfed him. This was not a scene from his hometown. No, Lyons had nothing to compare. This honky-tonk was going to be a new kind of fun.

A few couples were on the dance floor, but most customers were huddled up at the long bar or gathered in small groups at the tables – scattered throughout the dive.

The "ladies," in bright lacy dresses, made no effort to hide their petticoats or legs discreetly. He grinned at how some of the misses were sprawled unladylike in the laps of laughing men and exhibiting few of the inhibitions that constituted the norm back home.

Lee was so enthralled with the sights and sounds – he jumped when he suddenly became aware of an arm reaching around his waist from behind.

"Easy there, sugar, a delicious stud like you shouldn't be alone in a place like this," he felt the softness of breasts pressing against his back. The voice behind him purred into his ear. "You might get eaten!"

Lee turned and looked from head to toe at the curvy female standing there, "Well then, I guess I'm lucky I have you here to look atter me," Lee said.

"And look after you, I will. I'll take extra good care of you." She put both her arms around his neck.

Lee was no amateur in the mating ritual, but this degree of sexual assertiveness surprised him. And there was no question that it was having an immediate effect on him after a tiring long day. Pressed up to him, she knew it, too. She smiled coyishly, and he blushed at this seducing sight.

She pressed her hips even tighter against his and said seductively, "Do we need to take care of that right away, or would you like to buy me a drink first?"

"Uh…what's your name?" Lee asked nervously, taken aback by her presumptive suggestion.

"Okay, conversation first – I'm Cheri. Let's have that drink." Cheri took him by the hand and led him to the bar.

"What'll ya have?" the bartender asked gruffly. The towel slung over his shoulder was filthy, and Lee almost asked him if he was interested in having Mr. Harden do the bar's laundry. Picking up a new client would get him even closer to a raise, but he decided this was not the time or place.

"Whiskey," Lee said. "And give the lady here whatever she wants."

"Make mine a Dirty Dick's Flip, Al," Cheri coquettishly whispered as Lee sat on the barstool. She pulled herself up closer to him.

"I'm going to need to see your clams, big spender," Al said to Lee, not yet affording the new "customer" the courtesies due a regular.

"Clams?" Lee said, puzzled.

"Your dough, son, your money – the drinks ain't free, ya know."

"Oh, that," Lee said. "How much?"

"That'll be thirty-five cents for yours and sixty cents for the lady. You got ninety-five cents?"

Lee scrambled into his pockets and pulled out a dollar.

"There you go," Lee said as he put the better part of a day's wages on the bar.

The bartender looked up at Lee as if determining whether there was more where that came from. Then, deciding there was, his tone turned friendly, and he said, "Coming right up."

"And what's your name, honey," Cheri cooed, now that the money had begun to flow.

"Lee."

"Butt me out of that hope chest, Lee," Cheri held up her hand to him.

Lee was puzzled by her statement. He was also completely mesmerized by this beautiful and seductive female cuddling up next to him. "What?" He asked.

"You do smoke, don't you ... Lee?"

"Yeah."

"Well, then butt me, sweet cheeks," Cheri smiled.

Now realizing the meaning of the unfamiliar phrase, Lee fumbled in his pockets for his smokes. Finding the pack, he extended it to her clumsily.

"Now dear, you are a gentleman, are you not? You don't want me to have to take it out of the pack myself, do you?" Cheri purred.

"Oh, I'm sorry," Lee said as he taped the pack on his finger, and a cigarette fell to the floor.

"Damn!" Lee said and tapped his pack again, gingerly this time, allowing a lone cigarette to pop out. He held it up at her chin awkwardly.

Cheri looked at him and smiled, which triggered a tingling on his skin. Then she gently placed her hand under his and raised the pack higher. Seductively, Cheri put her lips on the cigarette butt, never taking her eyes off his. She pulled it from the pack and gazed lazily at him.

Heart racing wildly, Lee looked back at her, furtively searching for clues as to what he was supposed to do next.

"Lee?" she asked in a soft, questioning voice.

"Lee?" she repeated. His gaze drifted up to her eyes.

"Yeah?" the word almost didn't come out.

"You gonna give me a light, honey?" she said softly, confident she now had complete control of the man sitting next to her.

"Oh, yeah, sure," Lee replied as he fumbled in his pocket for a match. Striking it with his thumbnail, he nervously held the flame near her cigarette tip.

Cheri wrapped her fingers around his shaking hand, steadying him, and pulled the match toward her cigarette, lighting it. The match's soft glow illuminated her face ever so slightly, with the shadows from her eyelashes dancing around in the match's flickering light. In his aroused state, Lee thought she was the most beautiful woman in the world. His marriage to Lilly drifted completely from his consciousness. He held the match there – unmoving as the flames burned precariously close to his fingertips.

Pursing her lips in a manner that triggered an avalanche of chill bumps down his arm, she sensuously blew out the match.

Thin whips of smoke waffled from the cooling matchstick for a moment. Lee couldn't take his eyes off her. Finally, composing himself, he shook the extinguished match and dropped it to the floor.

"Thanks, Lee," she said as she took a long drag from the cigarette, tilted her head to one side, and blew the smoke away from him.

Al placed their drinks on the bar. Lee was transfixed on Cheri, undone by the cascading buzzing sensation he felt all over his body. A deep breath failed to quieten this "Cheri effect." Glancing around, he felt suddenly embarrassed that everyone in the bar probably knew that he was in an aroused state. He nervously gulped some whiskey.

He watched as Cheri also raised her glass to her lips and sipped. He found himself staring at the lipstick traces imprinted on the glass' rim as she lowered it again. He fell into a burning pit of desire for her.

Lee had heard of places like this in big cities. Then, finally, it dawned on him that Cheri was a working girl and not just someone drawn to his charm. But the time for thinking about what to do had passed. Raw passion was now in control, and it mattered not to him that she had successfully hooked him. Then, as if sensing that her mark was ready, she looked straight into his eyes.

"Why don't we go get a wiggle on, Lee." It was not a question. It was a directive, and Lee had no resistive power to disobey.

"Yeah, why don't we do that," Lee agreed dreamily.

Cheri took another drink from her glass and set it down on the bar. She winked at Al and took Lee by the hand. Lee quickly chugged the rest of his drink and looked at his nickel change from the drinks lying on the bar.

"You can keep the change," he said, evoking Al's glare as they stepped away.

"Well, thank you very much, big spender!" Al snorted as he pocketed the nickel and moved on to his other customers.

* * * * * *

"Room 5," said the man behind the desk at the stairs' base. She turned to Lee, "You need to settle a little matter with him, sweetie."

"Huh?" Lee replied and looked in puzzlement at the man behind the desk.

"$3.00, Bud," the man said casually.

It was all the money he had saved over his living expenses that week, but Lee dug into his pocket and put the demanded fee on the counter. Gathering the money, the man handed Cheri a key, a clean towel, and a hand cloth.

"Thanks," she said matter-of-factly to the man, and then, turning her head, she said invitingly to Lee, "Come on, honey."

She retook his hand, and Lee followed her dutifully up the stairs, moving to the side to allow another painted lady and her most recent customer to descend past them. Lee turned to look at the "John" and was momentarily distracted, but Cheri tugged at him and said, "No dallying, honey. We have business to attend to."

Lee stepped to the side at the top of the stairs to allow another couple to pass. He was in new territory now. However, he and Lilly had been married for over two years, and he was perfectly aware of what was about to happen. Lilly was not aggressive in their foreplay or lovemaking. What Lee was now feeling was new for him – a strong feeling of satisfying an urge. It felt good. Cheri was definitely guiding events, but he felt empowered.

The clatter of the key going into the keyhole set Lee's heart racing even faster, and his breathing deepened. She had released his hand and bent over to unlock the door. He reached around her and cupped her breast.

"No, Lee, not here in the hall," she resisted as she gently pushed his hand away. The door opened, and she pulled him into the room.

* * * * * *

Lee stepped aboard the trolly and breathed a sigh of relief that he and the operator were the only ones riding at the late hour. He didn't want to try and hide his still blushing cheeks from strangers or have them trying to read his expressions, of which he had not yet regained control.

The required trolly fare consumed his last nickel, and he settled onto a bench near the back of the craft. Broke – he stared blankly at the floor. The experience of the evening was like no other in his life. Even though it had left him penniless, the spontaneity of the moment and the instant gratification he got from this whimsical unplanned sexual tryst had given him a rush generally reserved for the domain of opiates.

Rumbling along, feeling the sway of the trolly car to and fro, he began to relax. He realized, to his chagrin, that with all his savings now gone, the Baby Overland was even further from his reach, but the adrenaline rush of instantly getting what he wanted was intoxicating and overshadowing all his thoughts. Where there is a will, there is a way, and if he wished to possess a Baby Overland car, then, one way or the other, he was going to have one, just like he had wanted Cheri, and then he had her. The wind blowing his hair as he drove that Overland would feel as good as Cheri's hair cascade over his face as they consummated their business earlier.

In due course, the trolly arrived at the Sanitarium. Lee disembarked and waived to the operator as the trolly moved away and disappeared into the night. Then, he turned to walk to the front door of the building where he was staying.

"You there," a voice bellowed from the night behind a flashlight brightly shining in his eyes. "What are you doing here?"

Lee threw up his hands to ward off the light. "Hey, watch the light."

"What's your name, and what's your business here?" the man asked with that air of authority usually possessed by a policeman or security guard.

"Lee Currie, I'm renting a room here."

"Stay right there a minute," the voice demanded as its owner checked a list.

"You checked in last night, did you?" the voice asked.

"Yeah, that's right, last night," Lee responded.

"Okay, I see you here. Sorry, but I have to check these things out. I'm the Chief of Police here at the Sanitarium."

"Good to know," Lee responded nonchalantly.

"Look, you don't need to be coming to your room this late at night. People are trying to sleep, and I'm trying to make sure we don't have any inmates running about bothering folks."

"Sorry, it was my first day, and I was trying out the nightlife – seeing what kind of town this Milledgeville is," Lee said.

"Well, I can hardly blame a man for wanting to do any of that, but I might warn you to stay away from Patty's Parlor off Wayne Street. Those ladies will leave you without a penny in your pocket before ya know it, and they ain't clean. They will put something on you that Borax won't wash off," the Chief advised.

"Thanks for the warning, Chief; I certainly wouldn't want to be caught in that place," Lee lied.

"You have a good evening now, ya here. If you need anything, my name is Alex Hawkins. See ya around."

"Good night, Chief Hawkins," Lee said.

* * * * * *

Lee's room had access to something he had never seen before: a shower down the hall. Despite his father's relative wealth, they had no electricity at the farm and washed from a washbasin. They had a basin in this room but given what the Chief had just said about the place he had visited earlier; he was ready to avail himself of that shower.

The superintendent had shown him how to operate it and warned him not to take too long else he might find himself all lathered up and out of hot water. He also needed to be courteous to others who might want to use the shower. But given the lateness of the hour, it was doubtful that anyone else would be showering tonight, so there was no need for him to conserve. He took his time adjusting the water to the right temperature. For the first time in his life, he was enjoying the sensation of standing under heated water, cascading over his body. It felt great and convinced Lee further that he wanted to enjoy everything modern living could provide.

By the time he had toweled off, returned to his room, and dressed for bed, exhaustion finally overcame him. As his racing mind began to calm and he drifted into that twilight that comes just before sleep, he began to think about Cheri.

I hope that woman didn't have no diseases, for God's sake, he thought to himself and uneasily drifted off to sleep.

Chapter 6

"Come on, if you're riding with me," John Blackstone called out through the door.

Rap, rap, rap, he knocked. "Lee?"

The door opened.

"You don't have to bang my door down, John; I'm ready," Lee turned to get his traveling bag.

"Well, hurry it up then; I want to get to Toombs County before late," Blackstone said as he headed for his automobile. Lee followed, locking the door behind him.

"You boys headed home for the weekend?" Chief Hawkins called out as Lee tossed his bag into the back of the car.

"This is my home now," Lee said defiantly. "I'm going to get my wife and bring her back here."

"Well, that's just fine, Lee, but you be sure to tell the super that you're going to have somebody else staying with you. There's an extra charge for that, you know." The Chief tipped his hat and continued his rounds.

Lee grumbled, and Blackstone, not wanting Lee to say something to the Chief that would delay their departure, spoke up, "You keep an eye on Mr. Bell for me while I'm gone, would you, Chief?"

"My pleasure, John," the Chief answered, not looking back.

Lee was not happy about his continuing money problems.

"Extra charge – just what I need. How the hell you 'spose to get ahead in this place?" Arriving back in Toombs County to pick up his wife penniless, with nothing to show for all his work, was not a good start.

"Everything costs more in big cities like this, Lee. The system is stacked against us poor working stiffs. The only people prospering in this here economy are rich folks and thieves, and both are cut from the same cloth."

"You got that right," Lee said. "But I'm going to have my share, no matter what I gotta do to get it."

Blackstone made a lot of allowances for Lee's ramblings. Lord knows he had to put up with his boasting and dreams of grandeur during each of their trips back and forth to Milledgeville, but there was something about Lee's tone this time that troubled him.

Blackstone thought to himself, *He's a young child in a man's body*. John Currie had doted on him way too much over the years, but deep down, Blackstone knew that he probably would have done no different had he a son like Lee. As he thought more about it, he admired John Currie's devotion to his errant offspring.

They left Hardwick and headed south toward Irwinton. Blackstone worried about the possible complications of Lee's bringing Lilly to where they were. That was asking for trouble. Barely two years had passed since she had filed for a divorce, and the marriage may not yet be stable enough to withstand separating her from her family support system. Wimberly Brown, her attorney, and John Currie's good friend, had told him that Lilly had yielded to pressure from her in-laws and not gone to the court hearing when the divorce came up. The case was dismissed, and the couple started living together again, but it continued to be a tumultuous relationship. Blackstone believed that the only thing holding it together was their living with John Currie and Lee's stepmother, who had a knack for keeping the young man's temper in check.

Bringing Lilly to Milledgeville would likely remove those restraints, and Blackstone feared that he and his Uncle Math would wind up in the middle of Lee and Lilly's spats as the peacekeepers, or worst still, have to provide Lilly with a sanctuary when Lee went on one of his tirades. It was not an attractive prospect.

"Would you look at that puny sick cow," Lee said, brandishing his Smith & Wesson and pointing it at a malnourished cow in a pasture they were approaching. "What da ya think, John, should I put him out his misery?"

"Put that away, Lee! Guns make me nervous. Do you always carry that thing in your pocket?"

"All the time. Ya never know when you might need it," Lee said.

"Well, let's not be shooting any cows from my car, Lee, and I don't like you waiving it about like that. Put it away!"

Lee laughed. "Hell, I wasn't gonna shoot that cow; I ain't got no bullets – no how."

How easily Lee was distracted, Blackstone thought. A moment ago, his mood was dark, and he was worried about his finances. Now Lee was ready to shoot a sickly cow. It was baffling, but one thing was clear, Lee Currie was not right in the head, and here he was, riding in Blackstone's car with a gun in his pocket. Being a jitney driver for a crazy man, bullets or no bullets, was something he needed to end as soon as possible.

Blackstone finally relaxed as Lee nodded off to sleep, relieving him of the discomfort of having to carry on a conversation. Thankfully, the well-maintained road from Milledgeville to Dublin allowed him to make a pretty good time. With some luck, his passenger might sleep the rest of the way home.

* * * * * *

Lilly was already standing on the porch when Blackstone drove up in the Currie yard to drop Lee off. As cars were rare in this part of the country, if one approached, it always drew the home occupants out to the porch to see who it was.

"See you Monday," she heard Lee say as he stepped out, retrieved his bag from the back seat, and waved as

Blackstone pulled away. She noticed that Blackstone stuck his hand up in the air in a wave but did not look back.

"Have a good trip, honey?" Lilly said.

"Tolerable. I slept most of the way. You got anything to eat? I'm starving."

"Come on in. I'll fix you something."

Lilly tried to feel glad that her husband had returned, but it was getting more difficult. She remembered the excitement she felt three years ago when he asked for her hand in marriage, and how happy her father was at the prospect of her marrying into a family like the Curries. But it had not been easy being Mrs. Lee Currie. Worse yet, no children had yet come from the marriage.

A woman her age without offspring was not well received in the community. If she could get pregnant, it would give her a new lease on life and a new outlet for those mothering instincts she was currently using exclusively on the man-child that was her husband.

Lee made small talk as he ate his supper, mostly telling how much he hoped to make working for Mr. Harden. Lee went on and on about wanting to buy that cursed Baby Overland when so many other things had a higher priority in her thinking. When Lee had his mind set on something, there was nothing that could change it.

Lilly tried to appeal to Lee's fixation on the car once more. "Lee, if you stay here and work with your father, you would probably be able to buy that Overland much sooner, don't you think? After all, we wouldn't have the expense of having to keep up our own place, you know?"

"Nope, we are going to Milledgeville, Lilly. I've got a good deal going on up there. Besides, we need to be on our own. I'm sick and tired of taking orders from Pa. It's you and me now ... "Lee looked directly at her, and she saw his face hardened. "... and you will go where I say you will."

Having failed once more to dissuade him and sensing his anger rising, she moved on. "More chicken?"

"Naw, I'm full as a tick and ready to go to bed," Lee said as he wiped his mouth, dropped the table napkin, and stood.

"Why don't you wash up first, honey," Lilly said flirtatiously.

Lee's limited powers of understanding were quite sufficient to surmise what that meant. His wife was rarely "in the mood," and her hinting at an encounter perfectly suited him. "Sounds good, Lilly. Heat me some water."

Lilly drew some water and put some fresh wood shavings on the embers still smoldering in the cookstove from supper. "I'll have you some wash water in a little bit, Lee; you just get comfortable."

Later, as Lilly undressed and got into the bed with her husband, she said a little prayer that the Lord would let her conceive that night. The thought of having a baby growing inside her excited her in a way Lee's lovemaking could not. The size of Lee's manhood and his mastery of the Kama Sutra were underwhelming, and she got little satisfaction when she had to perform her wifely duties. However, it was not sexual satisfaction that she was after this time. Lilly Currie wanted a baby and was ready to do whatever it took to get one.

* * * * * *

Lee left the house the next morning to help his father put out some fence posts. He was smiling and in good spirits, having bedded Lilly again that morning. She seemed insatiable. *I must be a stud*, he thought to himself as he got into his father's truck, and they headed out.

Later Saturday night, Lilly retired to the bedroom soon after supper, beckoning him once again to join her. By Sunday morning, he had made love to his wife four times. Lee had never seen Lilly be so passionate. He thought having his wife in Milledgeville would be great, and he was looking forward to a new start with her there.

"Lilly, why aren't you packed? John will be here soon to take us back to Milledgeville," Lee asked.

Lilly had been contemplating this moment all weekend. She didn't want to leave the Currie farm. If she could just delay her departure long enough to find out she was pregnant, then she could argue that it would not be good for the baby if she made a long journey to a new and strange home. She was ready to launch her plan to stay with John and Lula a while longer.

"Lee, honey, you need to give me a few more days to get things in order. First, I've got to visit all my relatives and tell them bye. After that, who knows when I will see them again, what with Milledgeville being so far away? I also don't have anything to wear in a big city, and I'll need to make some clothes. I know you can't afford to buy anything right now. I just need more time to get everything arranged," she paused and watched nervously for his reply.

Lee welcomed this suggestion. He had been worried about his financial situation. He was flat broke and didn't want Lilly to know that just yet. He knew there would be food to buy as soon as they arrived in Milledgeville, and then there was that extra rent Hawkins had told him would need to be paid. He needed to make more money before bringing Lilly into the picture.

"I understand, Lilly. You do what you gotta do, and I'll come back to get you in two or three weeks. How's that sound?" Lee asked.

Lilly let out a little girlish squeal, "That's perfect! You are so sweet," she hugged him. "I'll get your things packed and fix you some food for the road."

"Throw some extra food in there for John, will ya?"

"Of course, honey, anything you say."

Lilly turned to prepare Lee for the trip back and practically skipped into the bedroom to get his things. Lee slowly exhaled.

That worked out just perfect, he thought to himself.

* * * * * *

Lee had been gone for three weeks when Lilly felt a sharp pain in her pelvic area as she was making up the bed. Had her diligence paid off when Lee last came home from Milledgeville? Had she finally conceived, and was this the way it felt?

Now feeling an urge to void herself, she went to the bathroom. The burning sensation she was feeling quickened her breathing. Something was not right. She began to shake when she saw the yellowish discharge. She decided to call her Aunt Sarah. She would know what to do.

* * * * * *

Dr. Hall put away his stethoscope. His troubled look sent Sarah Smith's heart racing.

"Am I pregnant, Doctor Hall?" Lilly asked him.

Dr. Hall looked up at Sarah and stood up from the bed where Lilly was lying.

"I wish it were so, Lilly, I do. I know how badly you want a baby, but you are not pregnant."

"Then what is it, Doctor," Sarah asked. She and Dr. Hall had been friends for a long time, and she knew that look. It did not bode well.

"I won't mince words, Lilly. You have gonorrhea, and we need to treat it right away."

Sarah immediately saw the puzzled look on her niece's face.

"Gonorrhea – what's that, Dr. Hall?" Lilly asked.

"It's a venereal disease, Lilly."

"A venereal disease ... I'm ... I'm not sure I know what that is, doctor," Lilly said innocently.

"You catch it through sexual intercourse with someone who has it," Dr. Hall responded grimly.

"But ..." Lilly dropped her eyes in embarrassment, "But I haven't had relations with anyone but Lee." Tears began to swell her eyes.

Sarah sat on the bed and hugged Lilly, "It didn't come from anything you did, honey. It's that husband of yours. He's been unfaithful."

Lilly was thunderstruck. For a moment, she trained her gaze on Sarah and then the doctor as if waiting for one of them to tell her she was dreaming. Then she began screaming uncontrollably. "No, no, no!" She cried out, shaking violently.

Sarah cradled her more tightly as Dr. Hall hastened to find a syringe in his bag.

"Lee didn't give me a baby ... he gave me a venereal disease ... that son-of-a-bitch!" Lilly began flailing her arms as if trying to get away from her aunt.

"Hold her arms," Dr. Hall said as he sat on the bed.

Sarah held her niece tightly as Dr. Hall injected her with a sedative. In just a moment, Lilly calmed and then went limp. Sarah gently laid her back down on the bed.

"She'll sleep for several hours," Dr. Hall said. "This is awful news she has absorbed, but we have to get her to my office as soon as possible. Bring her in first thing tomorrow, and I'll get her treatment started."

"Can it be cured, Dr. Hall?" Sarah asked.

"Yes, we have some very effective treatments, but the disease affects different people differently. She will survive, but it could have some serious ramifications."

"Ramifications?"

"I'm afraid so ... it could render her barren."

"Barren?" Sarah's gaze slowly moved from the doctor to her niece as the dreadful words sunk in.

"I'm afraid so. It could mean that she can never have any children."

Sarah continued to look at her young niece, now facing the prospect of being childless for the rest of her life due to her husband's philandering. She tried to suppress a feeling of relief that Lilly might never have to bear Lee Currie's child.

Sarah stroked Lilly's hair, "Poor, poor girl. She hasn't done anything to deserve this." She stood up and extended her hand to Dr. Hall. "Thank you for coming doctor. I'll bring her to your office in the morning."

"I'll see you then, Sarah."

The doctor stood up and snapped shut his bag. He looked down at the sleeping girl and shook his head.

"So young… "he said and turned to walk away. He hesitated and turned back.

"Lee will need treatment, too," he said.

"That's his problem, Dr. Hall, that's Lee Currie's problem."

Dr. Hall nodded, sighed, and walked away.

Chapter 7

"Isn't that Solomon Corey's truck?" John Blackstone said to Lee as they drove up to the farmhouse, having driven from Milledgeville for the weekend. It had been three weeks, and Lee was now financially ready to get his wife and take her back to their new home.

"He's probably here to spend some time with his daughter before she leaves for Milledgeville," Lee replied.

"Makes perfect sense. It's a bit of a trip for Solomon to drive from his home in Register on poor roads. Do you 'spose he's planning on spending the night?"

"Mor'n likely, and that's okay. Pa's got plenty of rooms for company," Lee responded.

Turning into the lane going up to the house, John saw Sarah Smith step out on the porch. "Lilly's Aunt here too? Well, this is a regular family reunion. You don't suppose they are all here to try and talk you out of taking Lilly up north, do you?"

"They'd be barking up the wrong tree if they tried," Lee said confidently.

John pulled up to the gate in front of the house, set the brake, but left the car running. He didn't want to walk into the middle of a family kerfuffle.

They both turned at the sound of John Currie's truck approaching the house.

"That's pa," Lee said.

Everyone delayed their greetings while John pulled his truck into the wooden shelter, turned off the fuel tap, and waited to allow the automobile to burn the last of the gas from the line. Leaving it open would completely drain the tank in the gravity-fed system. John was a stickler for taking good care of his vehicles. Years ago, when he bought his first automobile, Mr. Warthen had told him when not to leave fuel in the line, as it would foul the carburetor.

Impatiently, the group waited while John's engine consumed the last fuel in the line, shuttered, and loped to a starving finish. Finally, John stepped out of the truck and made his way to the front porch as quickly as his arthritis would allow.

As he rounded the corner of the house, Solomon called out. "Evening, John. Evening, Lee. Evening, Mr. Blackstone. Hope you folks a' doing good."

John Currie nodded but was troubled by the look on Sarah's face. He turned to John Blackstone.

"John, thanks for bringing Lee from Milledgeville."

"My pleasure, Mr. Currie, but I need to be getting on. Don't cotton too much to night driving on these roads. If you don't mind, I'll be taking my leave," Blackstone said as he turned to go to the car.

"I'll see you Sunday, John," Lee called out as John got in his car and drove away.

John Currie turned to his other guests, "Didn't expect you to come a callin' Solomon ... Sarah, good evening to you both. What brings you out this way?"

Sarah was in no mood for small talk. "We've got a big problem, John. It's your boy – he's messed up bad this time."

"Slow down, Sarah! What's he done?" John shot a sharp look at his son, looking for a protest, but Lee dropped his head and said nothing.

John noticed Solomon turn to look at Sarah and his eyes sternly told his sister-in-law that she had said enough. "Hang on, Sarah, you let me handle this," he turned back to John. "Lilly has been having some female problems, John. Dr. Hall came by this afternoon and saw her."

"Female problems, my eye," Sarah said. "Your boy done give my niece the clap!"

"Sarah, you go back in the house right now, you hear me! This is men's business, you git, now!" Solomon pointed to the screen door.

Sarah hesitated. "Men's business, that's the problem, men's business, indeed," she turned and went inside, slamming the door behind her.

"What's this all about, Solomon?" John asked, puzzled.

"You'll have to excuse my sister-in-law, John. You know how women get easily excited about things."

"She said Lilly had the clap. What's she talking about?" John asked.

"I'm afraid that's what Dr. Hall says. He asked Sarah to bring Lilly to his office in the morning for treatment."

John turned to his son. "Lee, what the hell is going on here?"

Lee kept staring at the ground.

"Lee, you tell me what you've gone and done, and I mean right now. Don't you lie to me, boy!" John Currie said, his anger intensifying.

"It must have been that whore up in Milledgeville, Pa. That's why I need Lilly up there; man's gotta have his fun, you know."

John slapped his son across the face, staggering him backward. Fire flashed in Lee's eyes, and he instantly bowed up and clenched his fists. Solomon quickly stepped off the porch and stood between them, facing Lee.

"Lee, you best calm down now. Your pa is not too happy with you, and neither am I. You've done Lilly wrong." Solomon said.

"That don't give him the right to hit me," Lee said.

"He's your father, Lee. I spec that gives him the right," Solomon replied.

"I'm a grown man," Lee protested.

John was furious. He pushed Solomon to the side where he could face his son, "You're a married man, too, Lee. And a married man don't go whoring around on his wife. You was raised Christian, son. Not only have you broken one of the Ten Commandments, but you have infected your wife with a whore's disease. You've brought shame and dishonor on our house and Mr. Solomon's house as well," John moved toward his son again, and Solomon restrained him.

"What's been done, been done, John. All's ahead is to figure out what to do now."

As angry as he was at his son's indiscretions, John now feared for his son's marriage. Solomon had talked his daughter out of divorcing Lee two years earlier. Lilly's father believed strongly in the Holy bonds of matrimony, but would Solomon still support the union after the flesh's weakness had dishonored the marriage? He looked at Solomon with angry but tearful eyes as if pleading for guidance in dealing with his son.

Solomon saw the misery in John's eyes and spoke up, "Men are gonna be men, John. I've been around Lee long enough to notice that he's got very little power to resist temptation. When he sees something he wants, he goes after it. That's what happened up in Milledgeville, probably. Some saloon harlot just tempted him, and his wife wasn't there to stop it."

"Yeah, that's just what I said. If Lilly had of ..." Lee tried to say before his father cut him off.

"Dammit, this is not Lilly's fault! YOU cheated on her! Now, what are you going to do to make it right?" John shouted.

Solomon again tried to quieten everyone, "John, Lilly is pretty upset with her husband. I think it best they don't see each other until things calm down. So, our first order of business is to get her treated. And you too, Lee, if you gave it to her, that means you have it, too," Solomon said.

"I had some early sign, but it ain't run on me for a week. I'm over it. I sure don't want to go see no doctor. Doctors been poking and prodding on me all my life. I ain't got no use fer 'em," Lee said.

John had not taken his eyes off his son. He should have put his foot down and never allowed Lee to go to Milledgeville, or anywhere else, for that matter. His son was too undisciplined to be away from him for an extended period. He might be a grown man on the outside, but he was still an immature little boy on the inside.

"Can Sarah take Lilly with her, Solomon?" John asked, still glaring at his son.

"Now wait, Pa, Lilly's my wife and ..."

"Shut up, boy! I spec she ain't got no desire to be around you right now, husband or no," John said.

John turned to Lilly's father and said, "Ain't that right, Solomon?"

"We'll take her with us, John. Lee, don't you worry none about your wife. I know how to take care of my daughter," Solomon said and turned to the house.

"Solomon," John called out. Solomon stopped and turned. "I'm really sorry about what Lee's done to your daughter. She's a fine Christian girl, as sweet as they come. She don't deserve this."

"John, you were there at the wedding. I gave my daughter to your son, for better or for worse. He's done her wrong, but by the Lord's grace, he will be forgiven, and he'll make this right. I have every confidence it will work out," With that, Solomon Corey turned and walked into the house.

John was not so confident about the future of the marriage. However, he knew Solomon's motivation. Solomon was a poor farmer and wanted more for his daughter than he could give her. Marrying into the Currie family assured him that she would have a better life than he could give her or his other daughters.

John was also aware that Solomon had been able to talk Lilly out of divorcing Lee once before, but infidelity and bringing a whore's disease into the marital home? He turned to his son.

"Lee, go hitch up the mule and go to Clarence James' house. Ya'll are good friends, and he will let you stay with him till we figure this thing out."

"I'll go to Clarence's, Pa, but I'm going back to Milledgeville this Sunday. I've got to be at work on Monday, or Mr. Harden will fire me for sure."

"Damn Mr. Harden and damn that job, Lee! If you hadn't been in that din of inequity in the first place, none of this would have happened. If you had one lick of sense in that thick skull of yours, you would see that this is a sign from God Almighty Himself that your place is right here, boy!"

John saw his son struggling with his thoughts but finally giving in to his father's will, "I'll go to Clarence's for now, Pa, but come Sunday, I'm going back to Milledgeville," Lee said and headed for the barn.

John watched with trepidation as his son walked away. Tears welled up in his eyes. He completely believed the devil had gotten God's permission to test him just as he tested Job. He prayed for his redeemer to come, and he prayed for his son.

* * * * * *

"You come on in here, Lilly, we've got a bed ready for you," Raymond Smith said as he met Lilly, Sarah, and Solomon in the driveway of their Lyons home.

"I don't want to put anyone out, Uncle Raymond," Lilly said as she stepped out of her father's car.

"Sallie Kate will double up with Bertie Mae and let you have her bed, Lilly. It's no trouble; it'll be just like when you used to come to spend the night with us when you were growing up. We're just glad you're here among family," Raymond comforted his niece as he took her bag from the trunk.

"That's right, honey, you're welcome to stay here as long as you need to," Sarah added.

The five children of Sarah and her husband Raymond spilled out the door onto the porch and surrounded Lilly, jumping up and down.

As the children greeted Lilly excitedly, Sarah fully understood the dismayed look on her niece's face. She and Lee had been married for over two years and were still childless, and her latest effort to conceive had turned out to be a disaster.

"You children give Lilly a chance to breathe, now. Git back in the house," Sarah said as she tried to herd the noisy children back inside.

Lilly began to cry, and one of Sarah's daughters wrapped her arms around her. "What's wrong, Cousin Lilly?" Sallie Kate said as she looked up at her.

Sarah took her daughter by the shoulders and pulled her away from Lilly, "You leave her be, Sallie Kate. Your cousin is not feeling well. Ya'll git back in the house, now. Every one of you is barefoot, and here it is, the dead of winter!" Sarah herded her brood toward the house as Raymond carried Lilly's bags through the door.

"If you got everything under control, I'm going to head back to Register," Solomon said as he put his arms around his tearful daughter. "Lilly, don't you fret none. Everything is going to work out fine. The good Lord has a plan for you, and this is just a temporary setback. Trust in him, honey."

"Thank you, Pa. It means a lot that you came all that way to see about me," Lilly kissed her father on the cheek and managed a smile.

Sarah choked back her own tears as she saw Solomon wipe away a tear from Lilly's eye, "That's what family's all about, honey. You get Raymond to call anytime you need me, night or day."

"I love you, Pa," Lilly said.

"I love you too, honey," Solomon said as he turned to walk to his car.

"Let's get you inside, Lilly. You and I are going to have us a good family talk about that sorry husband of yours," Sarah said as she gently took her niece by the arm and walked her to the door.

* * * * * *

Sarah slipped into the bed and drew up to Raymond for comfort. She was exhausted, having talked for several hours with her niece.

"How's she doing?" he asked.

"She's resolved to leave him, and I support her decision wholeheartedly, Raymond. I hope you don't try to persuade me any differently."

"Her father doesn't believe in divorce, Sarah."

"He's going to have to get used to it. Lee Currie ain't right in the head, Raymond. Sooner or later, he will hurt her, and I don't mean giving her no disease either. He's gonna really hurt her."

Her husband did not respond immediately. He seemed to be deep in thought. Finally, he spoke, "I'm afraid I have to agree with you, Sarah. Lee's a hard case and needs a strong hand to keep him controlled. Lilly isn't a match for his temper, and Lord help her, she is likely to be a frequent target of his outbursts."

Sarah was relieved that her husband would not fight her on this. "She needs our help, Raymond."

Raymond sighed, "I'll make an appointment with Wimberly later this week after Dr. Hall treats Lilly. Wimberly filed the divorce papers last time. I'll tell him the marriage is still not working out."

* * * * * *

"I believe I can get the divorce on the docket for February 18th, Raymond. Given what you have told me, Lee's giving his wife a venereal disease is indisputable proof of infidelity, and there is no way Lee can defend his actions.

It should easily go through this time," attorney Wimberly Brown told Lilly's Uncle.

"You sure this is what you want, honey?" the lawyer turned to Lilly and asked, looking concerned.

Lilly said slowly, "Yes, my marriage is over."

"Don't you worry about a thing, Lilly. I'll take care of it. If Lee doesn't protest it, you probably won't even have to appear in court. There's a good chance that you will never have to see Lee Currie ever again."

Raymond got up and helped Lilly to her feet, "Thank you, Wimberly."

"It's my pleasure to be able to help Lilly out, Raymond. Don't fret about it another minute."

Lilly stepped out of the lawyer's office and headed for the car. Raymond hesitated and turned.

"I wish that was the end of it, Wimberly, but Dr. Hall has told us that poor Lilly may not be able to have any children on account of this disease Lee gave her. You make sure that divorce goes through, you hear me? It's got to go through."

"It will, Raymond. It will. And I'll probably be able to get her some alimony. I'm sorry that I can't fix Lilly's medical problems in court, but I can see to it that she can put Lee Currie behind her and move on with a little financial support."

"I knew you could make it happen. Thanks, Wimberly," Raymond said as he left the attorney's office.

Chapter 8

"Does a Mr. Lee Currie work here?" the well-dressed gentleman asked Mr. Harden, who was busy shaving a customer.

"In the back," the barber said, gesturing to the shop's rear without interrupting the blade's smooth flow across his customer's cheek. The man walked to the back and up to one of the workers.

"Lee Currie?" the man asked. The worker shook his head and pointed to Lee, standing by one of the pressing machines. Lee stopped what he was doing and looked up as the man approached him.

"Is your name Lee Currie?"

"That's right," Lee said suspiciously.

The man handed Lee an envelope and tipped his hat. "Then these papers are for you. Good day, sir," he turned and left.

Lee looked at the envelope, puzzled. In the upper left-hand corner, addressed to him, was written, "Wimberly E. Brown, Attorney-at-Law." Apprehensively, he opened it.

"Shit!" Lee blurted out in a loud voice, attracting the attention of his two co-workers.

"What's that you got, Lee?" one of them asked.

"That bitch is divorcing me," Lee blurted out. "I've got to be in court in Lyons on Wednesday!"

The two workers looked at each other and, without hesitation, returned to their work. Having worked with Lee long enough, they were aware of his volatility and, thus, did not want to engage him.

Neither was Lee interested in talking about it. He pulled his apron, threw it on the workbench, walked to the barbershop's front, and approached Mr. Harden.

"I got to go, boss. I got trouble back in Lyons, and I have to get there by Wednesday."

"Trouble, you say?" Mr. Harden inquired.

"Nothing I can't handle." Without waiting for his employer's permission to leave work, Lee walked out the door.

* * * * * *

"It's Tuesday, Lee. I can't do it... not this early in the week."

Lee frowned upon hearing John Blackstone turn down his request for a ride to Lyons – another reason he badly needed a car of his own.

There was no way to get home except to hire a jitney driver, which would further deplete his funds. Lee could feel his anger rising. This divorce severely interfered with his plans, and he smelled a rat. He was sure Lilly's aunt was behind this and had put her up to leave him after that gonorrhea business.

Damn the luck! If my wife had been in Milledgeville with me, I wouldn't have needed to go whoring in the first place; Lee thought as the jitney driver pulled out on the road that would take him back to Lyons, with a brief stop in Register, Georgia.

* * * * * *

No sooner than Lee had come by to show him the papers, Solomon Corey knew he had to stop this divorce. He got in his truck and drove 34 miles straight to Sarah Smith's house in Lyons.

When the women get involved in these domestic matters, it goes to hell in a handbasket, Solomon Corey thought to himself as he got out of his truck and stepped up on the porch. He rapped hard on the front door, which Sarah soon opened.

"Come on out here. I got something to say to you," Solomon said.

Sarah grabbed her shawl from by the door and stepped out on the porch. She wrapped it tightly around her as protection from the chilly air and the even greater chill in her brother-in-law's words.

"You had no business sticking your nose into their marriage, Sarah. That was for Lee and Lilly to work out. You've gone and done it now."

Solomon Corey was not at all happy with his sister-in-law's meddling in Lilly's affairs. Although Lee was not an ideal husband, finding another spouse with the resources of the Currie family in Toombs County would be next to impossible, especially if she was a divorced woman. As if her poverty and possibly being barren wasn't enough to keep most suitors at bay, eligible bachelors around these parts would view a young divorcee as "troublesome." Leaving Lee would doom her to a deprived life, and he was not about to let that happen.

"Go get my daughter and bring her out here on the porch – right now!" he commanded.

Sarah's expression showed that she knew she had gone too far with her brother-in-law. She averted his glare, turned, and went into the house to get her niece.

The porch swing grunted as Solomon sat down hard on it. He needed to calm himself before talking to his daughter. He was beyond upset that Sarah had taken advantage of Lilly's naïveté. Solomon had to counter that, leveraging his standing as her father to appeal to that place where he believed women lived most of the time – in her heart.

"There's my girl," Solomon softly said as Lilly walked out the door. He stood and embraced her.

"Come, sit with me, angel. Sarah, you leave us be. I need to talk to my daughter alone," he commanded. Sarah went back inside and shut the door. Lilly sat on the porch swing beside him.

"Before you start, Pa, my mind's made up. There's no use in your trying to talk me out of it," Lilly made a feeble attempt to stop what was coming.

"Sarah has said her piece, Lilly. Now it's my turn. You listen to your father. What you are trying to do is a bad idea, angel."

Solomon Corey laid out his case for why Lilly should not end her relationship with Lee. He reminded her of the sanctity of marriage and how being a "divorced woman" would probably destroy her chances of getting a good husband in the future.

"Lilly, I did the best I could to raise you right, where you would make someone a good wife. You know I'm not a wealthy man. I have nothing of value to leave you and your siblings. I don't want you to struggle all your life like I have."

"But you don't understand, Pa; I may never be able to have any children because of what Lee's done," Lilly began to cry. Solomon put his arms around her and patted her on the back.

"You don't know that for sure, honey. If God wants you to have children, then you will have children. You need to leave that in His hands.

"But think about your situation for a minute, my angel. If you can't have children, what other man would want a barren woman? Like it or not, Lee is all you've got, and he is more obligated to you now than ever. It would ruin him in this community if folks knew he made you barren and then left you. No, my sweet, he's morally obligated to take care of you now, and that's what I want for you," Solomon said, stroking her hair as she cried softly.

Solomon could see that Lilly was weakening, but it was clear that Sarah had been filling her head with nonsense. She continued to plead her case, "It's not just that, Pa; what if he hits me again? You know how quickly he flies off the handle."

"I won't ever allow him to hurt you, Lilly. If he lays a hand on you, he will have to deal with the rest of your family and me. And John Currie won't allow him to mistreat you either; you know that."

"But he wants to take me to Milledgeville, Pa. How you gonna protect me there?" Lilly protested softly.

"There ain't no place on earth too far to go if my little girl is in trouble. Don't you worry none," Solomon pulled his daughter closer to him.

Lilly went silent. Solomon had answered every argument she presented, and he sensed that he had overcome the grip her aunt's reasoning had on her. Solomon pressed his advantage.

"One more thing, Lilly; divorces are ugly affairs. The judge will require you to testify in open court about your reasons for wanting to leave Lee. With a prominent family like the Curries, there will be many witnesses and maybe even a newspaper reporter there. Do you want the whole community to find out that Lee gave you this horrible disease and that you may be barren as a result? If all that comes out, it will make you an object of pity in the community. You could become the subject of gossip for as long as you live."

"I don't want that," she said in a whisper.

"Then drop this divorce action, angel. It's the wrong thing to do," Solomon said as if it were his closing argument.

Lilly said nothing for a long minute.

"Okay, Pa, I'll drop it," Lilly surrendered.

"That's my girl!" Solomon said and hugged her.

Lilly pushed away from him and sat up straight. "Wait, the hearing is tomorrow!"

"Don't you worry about it one little bit. I'll handle everything," Solomon stroked his daughter's hair once more, and she settled back into his comforting embrace.

"Everything is going to be alright, honey," Solomon assured.

* * * * * *

"Hear ye, hear ye, the hour of convening having arrived, the Toombs County Superior Court is now in session, the honorable Judge Robert N. Hardeman presiding. All rise!" the bailiff said loudly and pompously as the judge entered the courtroom and seated himself behind his desk.

"You may be seated," Judge Hardeman said as he rapped his gavel. A low rumble sounded in the courtroom as the

lawyers, court officials, and spectators sat down in unison.

"Call the first case. The Clerk will read the docket," the judge directed.

"Mrs. Lee Currie v. Lee Currie, action for disillusion of marriage, your Honor."

"Are the parties ready?" the judge asked routinely.

"Wimberly Brown, your Honor, counsel for the Plaintiff. My client should be here any minute."

"T. Ross Sharpe, your Honor, for the Defendant. My client, Mr. Currie, is present, and we are ready to proceed."

"Mr. Brown, was your client not notified of the time to be here?" the judge asked.

"She was, your Honor. I fully expected her by now. Something unexpected must have come up. Uh, I move for a continuance ...," Mr. Brown said.

T. Ross jumped up, "Your Honor, I object to any delays in this proceeding. My client has come all the way from Milledgeville at great personal expense to answer the subpoena sent to him by this court at Mr. Brown's request.

"Mr. Currie is strongly opposed to this action and ready to show the court why you shouldn't grant this divorce. Now I don't know where Mrs. Currie is, but what Mr. Brown is characterizing as 'something unexpected' is more likely to be that she has had a change of heart!"

"That's an assumption not supported by evidence," Brown objected.

"Ah, but I do have evidence, your Honor. Mr. Solomon Corey, Mrs. Currie's father, is with us here in the courtroom and is ready to testify under oath that he talked with his daughter just last night, and she does not want to end this marriage," Lee's attorney continued.

"No need to swear anyone just yet ... That true, Mr. Corey?" the judge asked.

"Objection!" As he stood up quickly, Mr. Brown said, "I'm sure the court would prefer to hear that from Mrs. Currie's lips, your Honor."

"Don't presume what the court would prefer, Mr. Brown. Your client's absence from these proceedings is sufficient evidence for me to dismiss this case, but I'll hear from her father nonetheless," Judge Hardeman said sternly.

Mr. Brown sat down, and Solomon Corey slowly stood up, "My daughter no longer wants to end her marriage, your Honor."

"Thank you, Mr. Corey; you may sit down," the judge said.

"Your Honor, the Defendant moves that the case be dismissed where this couple can resume their marriage and get on with their lives," T. Ross immediately proposed.

"Your Honor, Mr. Corey was not sworn, and we've heard no evidence ..."

The judge rapped his gavel. "Sit down, Mr. Brown. Plaintiff is not present to plead her case. I need no further evidence than that. If she were committed to this divorce action, she would be here, and if Mrs. Currie is not committed, she has no one but herself to blame for the outcome. The defendant's Motion to have the case dismissed is hereby granted," Lee jumped at the gavel rap.

"That it?" Lee asked his counsel.

"That's it," T. Ross said as he stood and began to gather up his papers.

"Well, alrighty then," Lee said gleefully. He followed his attorney out of the courtroom, winking at a hapless Mr. Brown as he passed.

Chapter 9

"Clarence, can I get you to carry me to Vidalia? Pa's got the truck," Lee Currie asked his friend as he got off his horse.

Clarence James laughed. "Well, it must be mighty important for you to ride that nag all the way over here. That there horse is on her last legs, Lee."

Lee was in no mood for levity. "Can you take me or not, dammit?"

The two young men had grown up together and been friends and neighbors almost all their lives. Lee felt comfortable around Clarence and could always depend on him to come through in a pinch, like right now. Clarence didn't have a lot of friends that lived nearby. Lee enjoyed his company, and they had a long history together. Clarence also had come to know him well enough to avoid irritating him, and Lee appreciated how quickly Clarence sensed his mood and halted his teasing.

"Just kidding, Lee. Sure, I can take you. Give me a minute to finish up a couple of things and tell ma." Clarence turned and went into the house.

Lee walked his horse to the barn and tied her in front of a hay bale. Clarence's willingness to take him to Vidalia was a welcome change from depending on other people with whom he was not such good friends.

Lilly's filing for divorce again was a wake-up call. He needed to get her away from her family and up to Milledgeville as soon as possible. It had become more urgent than ever that he talk to Mr. Warthen about one of those Baby Overlands.

Hearing Clarence crank up his old Ford truck, Lee patted his horse on the rump and walked briskly out to the shed to where the vehicle was sputtering to life.

"Climb in," Clarence called out over a backfire from the Ford.

"You sure this hunk of junk will make it?" Lee quipped as he stepped up into the truck.

"Hey, beggars can't be choosers," Clarence said. "It'll get us there, don't you worry!"

Lee laughed as the Ford's gears agonized loudly at being wrestled from their slumber, and the truck jerkily lunged to life.

"If I'm a guessing right, I figure you're going to Vidalia to buy a car. That right?" Clarence inquired as they made their way, slipping and sliding down the muddy dirt road. The rain of the last two weeks had grounded all but the most daring of drivers.

"Yep, that's right. I've got my mind set on buying me a new Baby Overland," Lee said, looking straight ahead.

"A Baby Overland ... wooeee! That's a fine piece of machinery. How you figuring on paying for a car like that?"

"I'm figuring on Ober Warthen giving it to me on one of those new installment plans folks been talking about. My job in Milledgeville's paying pretty good, and I've got to have a way to go. Besides, I need to get Lilly up there with me."

"I hear that Lee, and it makes perfect sense. Lots of folks are buying cars these days. Seems like all those boys that drove around all those military vehicles in the Great War now think they can't get along without their own vehicle."

"Yep, I know I need one, that's for sure. I think it will make a big difference to Lilly, and, besides, having to bum rides back and forth to Milledgeville ain't working out for me. I don't like riding that trolly up there back and forth to work every day."

The two men continued talking all the way to Vidalia. Clarence drove straight to Mr. Warthen's dealership.

"Need me to hang around?" Clarence said as he pulled to a stop and set the emergency brake.

"No need, Clarence. I'm going to get a Baby Overland before the day is out. You go on back to the farm. I appreciate the ride."

"Any time, Lee. Good luck with squaring things with Lilly and good luck with Mr. Warthen. I can't wait to see what you get, so you be sure to bring it 'round," Clarence said.

The gears ground and grumbled again as he put the Ford in first and lurched forward. He waved as he drove away, and Lee waved back. There was more grinding as he quickly shifted into second.

"That Clarence James?" Mr. Warthen said as he came out to greet his newly arrived customer.

"Yep," Lee said.

"He needs to learn how to start that car off in second gear. That first gear is just for uphill starts or when he's fully loaded. He keeps that up, and he's going to need to bring that Ford into my shop for some repairs to the transmission," the dealer proposed.

Lee turned to greet the salesman, "I'm Lee Currie, Mr. Warthen."

"Ah yes, Lee Currie. I know your pa well. How is Mr. John doing?"

"He's fine."

"What brings you to the car lot today, Mr. Lee? You looking to buy a new car?"

"Yes, sir, I am."

"What did you have in mind?"

"I've set my mind on one of those new Baby Overlands."

"Great car and great choice, Lee! Unfortunately, I sold my last Baby Overland to Burley Phillips just a few weeks ago. Can I interest you in one of these new Fords instead?"

Mr. Warthen gestured to several bright, shiny cars lined up on his lot.

Lee was crestfallen. He never considered for a moment that the Overland dealer would not have the car he wanted in stock.

"No, I've got my mind set on a new Baby Overland. When will you have some more?"

"They are hard to come by, Mr. Currie, I'm sorry to say. I put in an order for two more just over a month ago, but the manufacturer wrote me that they wouldn't deliver them till sometime around the end of March."

That is five weeks away! Lee thought.

Mr. Warthen continued, "Well, if your mind's made up, I can't help you, Mr. Currie. You sure you don't want to look at one of these other cars? That new Ford Model T center door sedan is selling like hotcakes. Everybody around here loves that car!"

"No, damn it! I want the Baby Overland!" Lee was beyond disappointed. He was getting angry.

"I like a man who knows what he wants," the adaptable salesman quickly replied. "Let me see what I can do. I might be able to get one sooner than that. How's about I get word to your pa as soon as I find out something. That work for you?"

"Who'd you say bought that Baby Overland?" Lee asked, ignoring Mr. Warthen's question.

"Burley Phillips; say, come to think of it, Burley has been known to sell the cars he buys from me to interested parties. You might want to talk to him about it."

"Where does he work?"

"He's a jitney driver for Mr. R. S. Wilson's Jitney Service."

Without a word, Lee turned and set off toward Mr. Wilson's Jitney Service.

"Come on back if you change your mind about one of these other cars!" Mr. Warthen called after him.

* * * * * *

"Anybody know where I can find Burley Phillips?" Lee asked upon arriving at Mr. Wilson's Jitney Service.

The owner looked up at the young man who had just stepped into his office. "He's got a fare to take two men to Pembroke and won't be back till late. But, if you need to go somewhere, we have plenty of other drivers available."

"No, thanks. I've got business with Mr. Phillips. When do you expect him back?"

He promptly answered, "He'll be back late this afternoon, around 6 o'clock, I suspect."

Lee nodded and walked out of the office. It was close to 9 in the morning, and there was some time to kill. He set off to the east down the railroad tracks. He knew most of the merchants in Lyons and didn't care too much about trading with Vidalia businesses.

It would only take him about an hour and a half to walk the six miles. He was overdue for a shave and a haircut and could go to his regular haunt, the Lyons Hotel Barber Shop at the Elberta Hotel. Next door, he could also pick up some bullets for his gun at the Minter-Smith Hardware Store. That would give him plenty of time to return to Vidalia before Burley returned.

Walking along the railroad tracks, Lee lost himself in thoughts about the Baby Overland – how the heads would turn when folks saw him driving it. It was a beautiful car, and he would be the envy of everyone. Lilly would just love it, which would help smooth things over where they could finally put that divorce business behind them. He also would be able to finally show his pa that he could make it on his own. *Yes, sir, everyone will sit up and take notice once I get that car.*

His train of thoughts was moving down the tracks so rapidly that it took the second honk of a horn nearby to attract his attention. He turned to look for whoever was blowing at him. He saw a car with "For Hire" in the front window pulling off on the side of the road closest to him.

"Lee Currie! It's mid-February, you dang fool! What you trying to do, catch your death of cold?"

Lee recognized the driver as Lloyd Jones, who was about Lee's age and lived a little over four miles from his pa's farm. Their friendship went back for seven or eight years. Tall and lean, with jet-black hair and brown eyes, Lloyd had a city boy's pale skin and slim look. Lee had no idea that he had rejected the farm life and gone to work in the city.

"Hey, Lloyd! You a jitney driver now?" Lee asked as he walked down the railroad embankment and over to the car.

"Hell yeah! Been at it for over a year. I'm working for Mr. Wilson in Vidalia. Where ya goin'?" Lloyd asked as Lee approached the car and propped his elbows on the car window.

"Headed down to Lyons."

"Well, I'm headed over that way myself, Lee, and I ain't making no money deadheading this car. Hop in."

"I ain't got the fare, Lloyd. Been down on my luck."

"You got a dime, don't you? I'll just charge you what Mr. Wilson charges me. You can't beat that, my friend!"

Lee reached into his pocket and pulled out a dime. He handed it to Lloyd, smiled, and stepped to the car's side.

"I'm much obliged, Lloyd. I was getting chilled to the bone," he said as he stepped into the car and shut the door.

There were rarely any cars or wagons on the narrow, dangerous dirt road leading to Lyons, but Lee noticed Lloyd glancing back for traffic, probably out of habit. The car purred as he steered the vehicle back onto the road.

"That's a different sound for an automobile, Lloyd. I haven't seen one of these. What is this you're driving?" Lee asked.

"It's a Studebaker Special Six ... just came out a couple of years back. Sweet engine, and it's got hydraulic four-wheel disk brakes, Lee. It'll stop on a dime, paid extra for that."

"I see where it's got a spare wheel on the back, too."

"I wouldn't go to all the places I have to take people without one, Lee. The roads in this county are just plain awful."

"You got that right; they ought to do something 'bout the roads now that more people have cars. I'm in trade for one myself."

"Really, what are you looking to buy, Lee?"

"I'm aiming to get me one of those Baby Overlands."

"That's a nice piece of machinery. Burley Phillips works as one of Mr. Wilson's drivers, too, and he just bought one – nice car."

"Yeah, nice," Lee smiled. He was already beginning to anticipate how much he would enjoy the bragging rights on a car he didn't yet possess.

"I wish I had Burley's knack for quickly selling the cars he buys to one of his riders. That Overland is kinda pricey, but I doubt he'll have it very long before someone comes along and takes it off his hands."

"Probably not," Lee said in a low tone. He ran his fingers over the revolver in his pocket.

"Where you want me to drop you off, Lee?"

"Take me to the Minter-Smith Hardware Store, if you don't mind."

"Don't mind at all. I keep the car near there for folks to find me when they need to go to Vidalia."

"I'll need to go back this afternoon between 5:00 and 5:30. You gonna be around then?"

"Not sure. It will depend on the fares I get between now and then."

"Well, look for me if you are down here 'round then; I'll want to catch a ride back to Vidalia with you."

Lloyd stopped across from the Minter-Smith Hardware Store. Lee opened the door and stepped out.

"Much obliged, Lloyd. I hope to see you this evening."

"If I don't see you then, you tell your pa I said hello," Lloyd said. Lee shut the door, and Lloyd smoothly shifted into gear and waved as he drove away.

Lee watched him drive away, fidgeted with the revolver in his pocket again, turned, and headed toward the hardware store.

* * * * * *

"Good morning, Mr. Lee. What can I do for you?" Cecil Smith said. He was the store clerk and a nephew of the store manager, Mr. William Thomas Ivey. Lee knew him from his being a member of Marvin Church, and Cecil knew John Currie's entire family. Yet, despite this familiarity, for some reason unknown to Lee, Cecil had never tried to befriend him at the various church socials and homecomings.

Lee pulled the Smith & Wesson Model 3 revolver out and placed it on the counter, "Cecil, you got any bullets that will fit this here gun?"

The clerk picked it up and rotated it in his hands, scrutinizing it.

"38?" Cecil asked.

"Yep. I bought it right here last month. You must have been out that day," Lee said. "As I understand it, that there's the same type gun that was carried by Jesse James, Billy the Kid and John Wesley Harden."

Cecil continued to look at the gun. He breached it and held it up to his eye, looking through the openings in the cylinder.

"I believe them boys preferred 44 caliber, not 38," Cecil lowered the gun and put it on the counter.

"Just give me the damn bullets, Cecil," Lee barked, upset at being called a liar.

Cecil turned and picked up a 38 cartridge box and put it on the counter next to the gun.

"I didn't mean to offend you, Lee. How many you need?"

"How much for six of 'em," Lee asked.

"I can sell you a half dozen cartridges for a dime or this whole box of 50 for 75 cents."

Lee pulled out a dime and put it on the counter. Cecil counted out six shells and handed them to Lee, who started to put one in a chamber.

"Whoa there, Lee! Store policy doesn't allow you to load that thing in here," the clerk said nervously.

Lee smiled and put the cartridges in his left pocket and the pistol in his right. "Don't wanna break no store rules." He turned and headed out of the store, bumping into Mr. William Ivey, the store manager, as he exited.

"Sorry, mister" Lee pronounced and walked out of the door.

* * * * * *

Mr. Ivey tipped his hat to Lee and followed him with his gaze as he was leaving. "Who was that?" He asked Cecil.

"John Currie's boy; you know him."

"Seem to be in a mighty big hurry, what'd he buy?"

"Some pistol cartridges."

"Pistol cartridges, huh? From what I've heard about him, I don't think I would trust him with a pistol," the store manager said.

"From what I know about him, I'd have to agree with you. He's a little hot-tempered," Cecil responded.

"A hot temper and gunpowder don't mix well, in my book," Mr. Ivey said.

* * * * * *

Lee felt empowered as he walked down the wooden sidewalk toward the Lyons City Power Plant. The police had a shooting range not far from there that would allow him to test out his pistol and work on his aim. *The next turtle I shoot will be scattered into a dozen pieces, that's for sure*, he thought.

It was about a three-minute walk to the shooting range. Lee scooped out a handful of soil in the dirt mound backstop and sat a bottle up in the indention. Then, stepping back about twenty paces, he turned, took out his pistol, and loaded the six cartridges. As most gun battles were much closer than this, he reasoned that close combat should pose no problem if he could hit the target from this far away.

BAM!

The shattering of the bottle brought a smile to Lee's face, but that smile quickly turned upside down when he realized he could not cock the gun for a second shot. The tips of the bullets were preventing the cylinder from rotating.

"Dammit!" Lee exclaimed. He could not see what was preventing the cylinder from rotating. It dawned upon him that he had been sold a lousy gun.

"Dammit, dammit, dammit!" he stomped the ground in rage and pointed the gun in vain at the target area, frustrated that he could not fire again.

"Dammit!" He repeated once more. Exasperated, Lee unloaded the five unfired rounds from the gun, put them back in his left pocket, and returned the gun to his right. He started the trek back to the hardware store, cursing under his breath.

Cecil was still on duty when he entered the site again. Lee walked briskly over to the clerk and snarled. "This damn gun you sold me is a piece of shit!"

"Hold on there, young man. We're not going to be having any cussing in this store," Mr. Ivey interrupted as he walked over.

"Cecil, the back stock room needs to be swept," the store manager said. Cecil nodded and quickly hurried away from the counter.

"Now, tell me your concern calmly and without any profanity, young man," Mr. Ivey said.

Lee took the gun out from his right pocket, laid it on the counter and said, "This gun you sold me fired one round and wouldn't fire anymore."

Mr. Ivey picked up the gun and studied it carefully. Verifying it was empty, he pointed it off to the side, cocked, and let it dry fire. He did it again and again.

"There's nothing wrong with this gun, Mr. Currie."

"The hell it ain't, the chamber won't spin like it's sposed to."

"Watch your language, Mr. Currie; I won't ask you again. Now, it just rotated fine while I was trying it."

"You ain't tried it with the bullets in it."

Lee forcefully cast the five unspent shells on the counter. Instinctively, Mr. Ivey reacted by moving his hand to the edge to catch one of the cartridges that was about to spin off to the floor.

"No need for anger, Mr. Currie. If we sold you the wrong ammunition, we'll make it good." The store manager picked up a round, dropped it into the chamber, and then looked at the bullet's tip.

"Ah, I see your problem. These bullets are not designed for use in this make and model gun. Let me see if we've got ammunition that might work."

Mr. Ivey looked at the labels on several boxes and then carefully studied the gun again.

"We acquired those guns as army surplus last year. They are not a standard weapon, and my clerk just made an innocent mistake. Most manufacturers stamp the caliber of the bullets they are designed to fire on the gun's body, but this one was made quickly during the Great War and didn't have standard markings," Mr. Ivey explained while turning the gun in his hands under the overhead light and peering carefully at it. "That is why we have offered these guns for sale at a greatly reduced price."

"Have you got the ammunition to fit it or not? I've got to get back to Vidalia by six," Lee retorted impatiently.

"Be patient, Mr. Currie, I will have to try each brand I have one at a time."

After several minutes and several tries of different ammunition, Mr. Ivey turned to Lee.

"I may have to order you some ammo made especially for this gun, Mr. Currie. I just don't have anything that will fit it."

Lee could feel his irritation growing. "You don't have anything I can use till then?"

"The closest I have to what you need is a 32 caliber Winchester round. Unfortunately, it's still a smidgen too long, about $1/8^{th}$ of an inch or maybe $1/16^{th}$, I would guess."

"Is there anything you can do to make it fit?" Lee asked.

"Well, I could trim off the balls a bit, if you don't mind them being flat. Be mindful it might affect the accuracy."

"Yeah, I've got a little bit of sense; go ahead and do it," Lee said.

"Okay, but I'll be just a minute. Gotta get a file from the back. Why don't you take a look around the store while I do that? You might see something you need."

"How about I go get a shave and a haircut next door while you do that?" Lee proposed.

"You go right ahead," Mr. Ivey said, handing the gun back to Lee.

"You don't need that?" Lee asked.

"No, I've got the measurements now. We'll get these trimmed and bring them over to you at the Hotel Barber Shop."

Lee's expression changed to a smile. "Now, we're talking."

* * * * * *

The Lyons Hotel Barber Shop was Lee's favorite barbershop in the county, and William Carl was his favorite barber. When he was a child, his pa used to take him there on his infrequent trips to town to get his hair cut. He enjoyed the mirrors that stretched from wall to wall on the two long sides of the room. They were like the hall of mirrors he once entered as a child when the circus came to town. When he looked at one of the mirrors, he would see dozens of increasingly smaller diminishing reflections of himself trailing off.

Two customers surrounded an old wood-burning heater in the far-left corner with hands outstretched over the radiating warmth.

Lee shut the door behind him, and all the men in the shop glanced his way briefly and then resumed what they were doing. Mr. Carl, who was on duty, surrounded by an unswept circle of hair on the floor, straightened up from being bent over shaving Barney Brown, a clerk from the drug store across the railroad tracks. He smiled and looked up to acknowledge his regular customer entering his shop.

"Come on in and enjoy the heater, Lee; I only have two customers ahead of you," the barber said.

Lee nodded and walked directly to the old heater. The other two customers greeted him and made room for him. He extended his hands and rubbed them together over the heated air waffling from the top surface. Barney raised up slightly from his reclined position in the barber chair to see who the newcomer was. Mr. Carl pushed him back down in the chair.

"You hold still now, Barney. I just honed this blade this morning, and it's razor-sharp," the barber said, chuckling.

One of the men by the stove, Dave Bryant, continued his conversation with the others gathered around the heater before Lee came in. "How are your customers reacting to that new Prohibition Law that took effect the first of the year, John?"

John Clifton turned and spit into the nearby golden spittoon. "You mean my former customers, don't ya? Dang government done shut us down."

"I hate to hear that. Y'all had that liquor store for what now, maybe thirty years or more?"

"Ever since they incorporated Lyons back in 1897, Dave. We were the first liquor store to get a license from the city, and for the first twenty years, we were the only ones selling liquor legally. We even survived when those other two liquor stores opening up, but this dang prohibition has done put all three of us out of business," John said, shaking his head.

"Dad-blame shame, that's what it is. Alls the heck they are doing is making the moonshiners richer," Dave said.

Lee spoke up, "Yep, there's money to be made now in moonshine."

The two men looked at Lee, seeming to him to be deciding if they would allow him in their discussion. Just as he felt his anger start to rise, Dave finally responded, "I'm thinking about taking that up myself, and if I catch one of those revenuers coming around my still; well, let's just say I've got an itchy trigger finger." All the men laughed in unison.

Lee continued to rub his hands together while staring at the heater. He leaned over to open one of the vents a little wider to increase the heat.

The barber stepped on the barber chair lever, bringing Barney to an upright position. "There you are – clean as a whistle. That will be twenty-five cents for the haircut and fifteen cents for the shave." He wiped the shaving cream from Barney's face and tossed the cloth over his shoulder. Barney gave him forty-five cents, adding a nickel for a tip.

"Thanks, Barney!" Mr. Carl said. Ringing up the fee in the cash register and pocketing the nickel.

As happened when each newcomer arrived, all conversation ceased, and everyone in the barbershop turned to look at the door as Cecil opened it and stepped in. He scanned the room and spotted Lee.

"Here they are, Mr. Lee. All trimmed up for you," Cecil said, walking over and extending his hand with five cartridges in it.

Lee took the cartridges and held one up to the light coming in the transom windows above the door. The ends had been carefully filed off flat.

"Mr. Ivey took off about 1/8 of an inch. He assures me they should allow the cylinder to rotate now without a problem," Cecil continued.

"These are just right," Lee said, still gazing upward at the bullet he was holding.

"Did you want any more?"

"Yes," Lee reached in his pocket and pulled out another dime. He gave it to Cecil, "Go get me some more."

"A full dime's worth?"

"Yep, that should do it," Lee said as he put the five cartridges in his left pocket.

"Who's next?" Mr. Carl called out as Barney stepped out of the chair and gave the barber two bits.

"You go ahead," one of the two customers said to Lee. "We're in no hurry."

"Thanks," Lee said as he stepped over to the barber's chair and sat down.

"Shave and a haircut, Lee?" Mr. Carl asked?

"Just a haircut today, William," Lee said as Mr. Carl stepped on the pedal, and the chair leaned back to a reclined position.

Lee closed his eyes and relaxed. He was aware of the gun's pressure in his right pocket, and he could feel the bullets in his left. He felt newly empowered.

Chapter 10

If Lloyd Jones ever made it back to Lyons, Lee did not see him. He had waited an hour past when he should have left and was now in a hurry. As he made the long six-mile walk from Lyons to Vidalia, he became even more determined to have that Baby Overland Burley Phillips had bought from Mr. Warthen. He needed it, and he had a right to it. One way or another, he would trade for it, which would put an end to his transportation problem.

Approaching the outskirts of Vidalia, Lee could see the town's lamplighter extending his long pole to touch a burning wick to the gas lights. The distant dim light they offered, reflected off the steel rails and, drew a straight line of light pointing to his destination.

He arrived at Mr. Wilson's Jitney Service at 7:20 p.m. In the office, Mr. Wilson's countenance was faintly illuminated by the steady glow of the oil lamp sitting on the desk. He appeared to be writing in his ledgers. Lee spotted his old friend Nathaniel Haskins coming around the corner from the direction of Mr. Meadows's cotton warehouse and walked over to him.

"You walkin', Nathaniel?" Lee asked as they approached each other.

"Why, hey, Lee. Yeah, I'm walking. My car's broke down."

"The hell you say?"

"Fraid so. Don't ever buy wire wheels if you have a Ford, Lee. You will get in bad if you do. I had to let Mr. Meadows know that I couldn't take him home this evening. He likes for me to take him home every day. Don't that beat all? He could easily afford his own car, but he tells me he's too old to learn how to drive. Frankly, I think he's too tight with the coin to buy himself one," Nathaniel said, and they both laughed.

"Of course, it suits me just fine that he needs me to drive him! He pays me a little bit, and I get to stay on his good side with my job and all."

Lee nodded and smiled.

"You had supper yet? I'm on my way to the restaurant right down there by the Bank of Vidalia. Come on and go with me. They have stew beef tonight, and they always have a good mix of vegetables. If we hurry, we can get there before they close up."

"I appreciate the invite, Nathaniel, but I'm not hungry."

"Well, alright, then. I'll talk to you later, Lee." Nathaniel turned and headed toward the restaurant.

Lee squinted his eyes as the lights from an automobile briefly fell upon him. Then they widened as he recognized the car to be a Baby Overland. Goosebumps ran up his arms, and his heart rate began to elevate in anticipation.

Burley Phillips got out of the car and walked to Nathaniel, just fifteen or twenty steps away. Lee could not take his eyes off the car.

"Bout time you got back, Phillips," Nathaniel teased.

"Dang rain has got the roads messed up all the way to Pembroke, Nathaniel. I started to spend the night down there rather than fight the ruts coming back. I'm all tuckered out!"

"Come to the restaurant and let me buy your supper. That will make you feel better."

"No, I appreciate it, but I'm sure Tersia has supper fixed, and waiting for me. I'm beyond ready to head home, kick back, and put my feet up."

"Before you go, you got a cigar on you? I'm fresh out," Nathaniel asked.

"No, but the drugstore's right down there. Let me buy you one in celebration of my big Pembroke fare."

The two men walked down the street and stepped into the drug store. Having overheard their conversation, Lee was confident they would be in the store for a while. He slowly walked over to the Baby Overland – his breathing deepened as he approached the car of his dreams. The reflection of the light from Mr. Wilson's oil lamps on the car's surfaces seemed to be emanating from the metal itself as if the Overland was glowing.

He ran his hands over the leather seats admiringly and touched the wheel as gingerly as if it were a sacred relic.

Slowly, he walked around the automobile. He had never been this close to a Baby Overland. He touched the parts to validate that it was real and this close to him. The car was magical. It was beyond metal, leather, wood, and cloth and seemed a breathing thing – living beauty personified.

He didn't just like the car. Lee Currie was bonding to it. He wanted desperately to sit in it, drive it away, and call it his own.

"Nice car, huh?" Lee jerked his hand back as if caught with it in a cookie jar. He was so indulged in the survey of the car that he had not noticed Burley's return from the drug store.

"Very," Lee said in a breathless whisper, still staring at the car. "This is the most beautiful automobile I've ever seen in my life."

"Yeah, she's a beauty, alright, bought her just a few weeks ago from Mr. Ober Warthen. Still breaking her in."

Lee extended his hand. "Name's Lee Currie."

"Burley Phillips," Burley responded. The two men shook hands.

"I overheard that you just returned from Pembroke. I know you must be tired, but do you think I could get you to take me to my home in Johnson's Corner? I need to get there tonight," Lee asked.

Burley took a deep breath, "Well, Mr. Currie, I'm tuckered, but I'm not one to turn down a fare from a fellow man in need. Listen, I've been on the road all day, and I need to go home and get some supper first. Do you mind waiting for just a mite?"

"No, I don't mind at all. You go ahead. I'll be right here waiting for you," Lee said.

* * * * * *

Burley Phillips was bone-tired by the time he walked into his home. He called out to Tersia, who he could see in the kitchen, to let her know he was coming into the house. Burley took off his overcoat and hat and practically fell into his favorite chair. The comfortable padding was a welcome relief to his backside after the hours he had spent in the car going to Pembroke over what can only be described as horrible roads.

Burley took out his tin of Prince Albert and gingerly packed some of the crimp-cut tobacco into his pipe bowl. Overpacking the tobacco made it too hard to puff it; he had mastered the packing technique long ago. Burley held the match to the tobacco, drew in a breath to light it, shook out the match flame, and tossed the charred stem into the nearby fireplace. Closing his tired eyes, he slowly inhaled the aroma of the tobacco drifting from his pipe. He opened them again, settled back into his chair, and picked up the Vidalia Advance from the side table.

"You want to eat at the table, or would you rather I bring it to you?" Tersia called out from the kitchen.

Lowering the paper, he welcomed the more casual option, "I'll take my supper right here in this chair, sweetheart, and I'll be thanking you for asking."

Burley placed the newspaper aside, leaned back, inhaled another puff of his pipe, and closed his eyes again. The tobacco slowed his mind, and he could feel himself relaxing even more as his lungs delivered the stout dose of nicotine. It was the perfect way to end a day. Smoking was something to be relished, and pipe smoking was designed for men in no hurry.

He grinned as he thought about his friend and co-worker Nathaniel Haskins' first attempt to smoke a pipe. He had puffed away like the engine on a freight train and had spent the next half hour in the privy puking his guts out. *Proper punishment, I'd say, for not showing tobacco the appropriate respect.*

He opened his eyes after hearing Tersia set a cup of coffee down beside him.

"Ah, you are a saint, woman," he said as he picked up the cup and took a sip.

"I'll have your plate in a moment, dear. I had to heat it back up. I had no idea when you would get back from your trip to Pembroke," Tersia said and returned to the kitchen.

"I've got to go out again, I'm afraid," Burley said, raising his voice, so it would carry to the kitchen.

"Oh no, Burley," Tersia said as she came back into the living room. "I can tell you are exhausted. You don't normally work the night shift. Why you?"

"The customer asked me in person, Tersia, and I am getting a strong impression that he is interested in the car I just bought. If I can turn that around quickly, I can get you that new Boss Oven down at the hardware store."

"No, Burley, I still haven't figured out how to work that vacuum cleaner you bought me on Christmas, and besides, there is nothing wrong with my oven. My mother baked in that oven, and it suits me just fine."

"I just want you to have the best, dear. I won't be gone long. It's just a run down to Johnson's Corner."

Tersia smiled and took her husband's plate out of the oven. She put it on a tray and took it to him. Burley sat up and raised his arms as his wife sat the tray down in his lap. She took the cloth napkin from her arm and tucked it into his blue shirt.

"How did I get so lucky to have a wife like you!" he said to her.

"Well, it didn't hurt none that you were the most handsome boy in my school!" she winked at him and smiled.

Burley winked back. As she returned to the kitchen, he thought of how much he might ask for the Baby Overland. That Lee Currie fella badly wanted to buy it from the look on his face back at the jitney stand. He just had to make sure he didn't ask for too much. Ober Warthen had sold him the car for $950 and told him that it usually retailed for $1,175, and he had only had it a few days. It was practically new.

I'll start him off at $1,150 and not go a penny under $1,100; he thought as he took another bite of his supper.

"Will you be a wanting seconds? I need to clean up the kitchen," Tersia called out after a few minutes.

Burley pulled out his Waltham gold pocket watch and saw that it was 8 p.m. He needed to head back soon to pick up his fare. "No thanks, honey, I need to be leaving now. I don't want to keep the fare waiting too long. I'll see you later tonight."

Tersia returned from the kitchen and wiped her hands on her apron, "You be careful, dear. The roads are wet and muddy from all that rain we've been having."

"I drove to Pembroke and back on some of the most treacherous roads I've ever seen. I'm sure driving to Johnson's Corner won't kill me," Burley laughed as he donned his overcoat and put on his hat. He tapped out the tobacco ash from his pipe into the ashtray and slipped the pipe into his pocket. Then, checking to confirm he had enough money to make change for any denomination Lee might give him for the ride, he kissed Tersia and stepped out the door.

* * * * * *

Lee was still sitting outside Wilson's Jitney Service as he had promised, waiting as Burley returned. Burley pulled up in front, leaned over, and opened the right rear door, which swung open to the rear.

"Sorry, it took so long. My wife had to reheat my supper. Jump in."

Lee stepped in and shut the door. Being actually inside the Baby Overland made his chill bumps return. He closed his eyes and took a deep breath, taking in the smell of the leather seats.

"Smells good, don't it," Burley said. "Nothing like the smell of a new automobile, no sir – there's a footrest bar on the floor back there for your comfort."

Burley put the car in gear smoothly without a single transmission grind, and the Overland moved onto the road as if it had a mind of its own and knew exactly where it was going.

For the thirty- or forty-minutes Lee had to wait at the Jitney Service for Burley to return, the Baby Overland occupied his thoughts. Sitting in it now, going down the road, gave him a feeling he couldn't describe. He grabbed the passenger pull-up bar on the back of the front seat and pulled forward to survey the car's controls. Everything about the dash was fascinating to him – the fuel gauge, the amperes indicator, and the speedometer. He noticed that the odometer only showed 152 miles, probably from Burley's Pembroke trip earlier in the day. Burley was telling the truth; the car was practically brand new.

"Ever seen a dash like that?" Burley asked.

"Never, she's a real beauty," Lee responded.

The controls were not all that different from his father's truck, gear shift, spark advance, throttle advance, choke, and fuel mixture. He was sure he could drive it with no problem. He could already see himself as the owner of the car. Burley Phillips seemed an imposter, sitting in HIS seat in front – an interloper who could never feel about the car the way he felt. Burley Phillips did not deserve THIS car.

Lee's eyes fell on the "For Hire" sign in the window. That would be the first thing to go after he took possession of what should be his. He would not be carrying passengers for hire; no, this car was for him and Lilly and their friends in Milledgeville, of which there would be plenty as soon as people saw him driving this car.

"Can you go down the Dixie Highway? I need to pick up some whiskey," Lee said.

"Sure, it's your fare; we can go whichever way you want," Burley replied.

"Then take me in the direction of Mr. Simmons Alexander's gin house. Ben Singleton will have some whiskey I can buy," Lee said.

"Ben Singleton, you say?" Burley asked.

"Yeah, he's a darkie that lives down there, just across Cobb Creek."

"Good to have a place where you can buy booze these days, what with the prohibition and all," Burley said.

As they drove toward the south end of Toombs County, Lee continued to admire the Overland. He reached out and ran his fingers over the back of the front seat, the fabric curtains, the back seat, and the fabric top.

"You do know this car is for sale, right?"

"I do. Mr. Warthen told me you frequently sell your jitney cars to passengers who take a liking to them," Lee responded.

"Oh, you know Mr. Warthen? I've practically been one of his salesmen for years. Taking a jitney ride in a car you are thinking about buying is a great way for folks to try out the cars and see how they ride before committin', you know? He lets me have them a little above his cost, and since they have already been used a bit, I sell them below what he is offering them for new. I make a little money, and you save a little. You might say it's kind of like him paying me a commission for selling these cars for him."

"Sounds like you got a sweet deal working. How much you wanting fer it?" Lee went right to the point.

"I'm glad you ask, Mr. Currie. Except for that drive down to Pembroke this morning, this car is practically brand new. Mr. Warthen was asking $1,175 for it, but I'll let you have it for $1,150. How's that sound?"

"Sounds like too much to me. My pa's been buying vehicles from Mr. Warthen for years. I could probably talk him down some more if I traded with him directly."

"Well, how much you willing to give for it then?"

"I'm thinking $950 sounds good to me."

Burley laughed, which was not the right thing to do with Lee Currie. "Heck, I thought you wanted to buy this car," he said, which unsettled Lee all the more. "Tell you what I'll do. I'll take $1,100 for it, cash money, and it will be yours."

"I don't have that kind of cash. Can you offer me one of those installment plans?" Lee asked.

"I'm a jitney driver, not a banker. It's cash or no deal," came Burley's reply.

Lee's disappointment was turning into rage.

Just then, Burley drew the car to a stop. Lee looked out, curious as to why the driver had stopped so suddenly. The headlights revealed that the wooden bridge spanning Cobb Creek was impassible due to the recent rain's rising waters.

"I was afraid of that," Burley said. "We are not going to be able to get across the creek."

"Never mind about the whiskey. Just go ahead and take me on to my pa's," Lee said.

"Sorry 'bout that," Burley said and turned the Overland around.

As soon as they were again underway, Lee pointed at a small road to the right, "Turn there!"

"You sure? That don't look like no well-traveled road, and with all the rain we've been having ..."

"This is the way, and the roads are fine!" Lee said sternly.

"Okay, have it your way, but if we get stuck, you will have to pay to get us a tow," Burley said as he turned into the lane.

Just off the road ahead was the Cobb Creek Baptist Church. As they approached it, the road seemed to run out. Burley brought the car to a stop.

"Looks like you're wrong, Mr. Currie. I don't even see a road, and I'm pretty sure I can't go any further this way."

Lee's heart was racing. Phillips had indeed come to the end of his road. *That son-of-a-bitch is driving my car*! Lee thought. He put his hand in his right pocket and tightened his grip around the Smith & Wesson pistol.

"Where to now?" Burley asked.

Lee pointed off to Burley's left with his left hand. "Don't know how I could have missed that road. Isn't that the Cobb Creek Baptist Church over there?"

Burley turned to look in the direction Lee was pointing.

Lee pulled the revolver from his pocket, put it right behind Burley's left ear, and fired at point-blank range. Burley's back stiffened, and he sat up straight as if the bullet had missed. Lee thought about firing again, but then Burley trembled and slumped backward. His head lolled unnaturally over the back of the seat, with his eyes wide open. Almost immediately, blood began to flow from his mouth and the wound in his head.

Lee was unnerved by the death stare in Phillips' eyes. Blood was oozing from the wound in his head in a rhythmic pulse from a still-beating heart.

"Shit," Lee said aloud. "This son-of-a-bitch is bleeding all over my damn car!"

Lee put the revolver back in his pocket, grabbed the dying man by the shoulders, and heaved him over into the back seat, letting him fall onto the floorboard in front of him. He stepped out and slammed the door. Backing away from the car and staring at it, Lee felt goosebumps run down both arms. He stood there for a long minute.

Finally, he went around to the driver's side and opened the door. Nothing now stood between him and the beautiful car in front of him. All that remained standing in his way of being the proud new owner of a Baby Overland automobile was to get rid of the body on the back floorboard. He opened the door and sat down in the driver's seat.

He slowly placed both hands on the steering wheel and began to shake, not a shake of fear, but a shake of pure exhilaration at finally having something he had wanted so badly. Lee sat there for several minutes, enjoying the endorphins that were flowing through his brain. Then he turned and looked in the back seat. He felt himself getting angry at Burley Phillips for bleeding all over his car.

"I got to hurry up and bury this son-of-a-bitch," he said aloud as he put the Overland into gear, turned it around, and headed toward his pa's farm.

Chapter 11

The Overland was finally his! Lee could do with it whatever he desired – go anywhere he wanted to go. Now it was entirely under his control, it seemed he had become the car, and the car had become him.

Lee struggled to contain his excitement while driving north up the Dixie Highway. He liked everything about the Overland. Such a beautiful conveyance; it was like nothing he had ever seen, much less driven. So long a wait, and now, it was his!

He was irritated with the night's darkness as it diverted so much of his attention to driving, and away from being able to admire the interior and the beautiful dimly illuminated dashboard. Nevertheless, Lee could not get enough of the car. He felt pure joy and complete elation for the first time in his life.

His mind raced through the possibilities now open to him. He could take Lilly to Milledgeville; she could drive him to work and then take the car to do her shopping. Yes, it would solidify her love for him. He would have to teach her how to drive it, of course, and take care of it. *That's what the head of a household does,* he thought and smiled.

Those awful days of hitching a ride with John Blackstone between Lyons and Milledgeville were behind him. Perhaps for the first time in all these years, Lee felt all grown up and no longer dependent on his father.

Pa won't be able to tell me what to do anymore!

It wasn't just a desire to be on his own that was the genesis of his euphoria. A part of him wanted his father to finally be proud of him for showing he was man enough to strike out on his own and support his family. After all, wasn't that determination part of the Currie family legacy? Isn't that what his father did when he came to Georgia?

Securing the Baby Overland was his first overt step into the future – his future. THIS was how you measure success! Adrenaline flooded into his bloodstream again, and his excitement grew to the point that he was shaking. It was as if he was out of his body and looking down at himself riding in that beautiful car, not believing his good fortune. He managed the automobile's control mechanisms with his whole being, his foot depressing the gas pedal, his left foot at the ready to push the clutch, his hands firmly gripping the steering wheel. He carefully guided the craft down the road and around the curves like a pilot, confidently turning a great ship's helm.

Lee scanned the dash, noting the speed, the gauges indications, the darkness in the rearview mirror, and the headlights' glow on the road ahead. Nobody was driving this car but him, and it was his driving skill – HIS – keeping the vehicle in the center of the country lane and headed toward a destination of his choosing. He smiled yet again.

But his smile faded as the dead man's body bleeding on the rear floorboard of his car again crept into his consciousness. He needed to attend to that business as soon as possible.

Lee turned right on the road that led to Johnson's Corner. *Pa keeps a shovel in the gin that I can use to bury that bleeding son-of-a-bitch,* he thought.

He drove by Mr. Ed Parker's farm. He could imagine his neighbor standing in the yard, following the Overland enviously with his eyes as it whizzed by, wondering who in the community could afford such an excellent conveyance.

Arriving at Johnson's Corner, Lee turned south toward his father's farm. It was late, but his father might still be awake. He couldn't risk being spotted until he had disposed of the body on his back floorboard. Turning the headlights off, he slowly drove up to the home place. The pitch black of the moonless night presented no hindrance to him, as he knew the farm intimately. He unerringly pulled up directly in front of his father's gin house.

I'll need a shovel, Lee thought as he slowly rolled to a stop. Keeping his mind focused on the immediate task of disposing of the body proved difficult as his thoughts kept returning to the car. How smoothly the brakes halted the Overland's forward motion without the squeaking that emanated from his father's old truck when the brakes were applied.

So far, so good, he thought as he got out of the car and approached the gin storage building. He cursed under his breath as the hinges complained of being disturbed with loud squeaks, freezing him in his tracks. The door was old, and the hinges rusty. Opening it would be tricky.

Apprehensively, he squeezed out of the partially opened door and strained his eyes to look up at the house. No lanterns came on, and thankfully nobody seemed to be stirring. Breathing a sigh of relief, he slowly opened the door and reentered the gin, feeling his way. His pa had sent him to the gin house often enough for tools that he knew precisely where the shovel would be stored, and, sure enough, both the hoe and shovel were right where he remembered. He took them, stepped back out of the gin, and turned to look at the door. Leaving it open would avoid any further noise and facilitate returning the tools later without having to open that squeaky door again.

Lee laid the tools on the body crumpled on the back floorboard to prevent any damage to the rubber mat. *You're bloodying up my car*, he thought to himself, *but at least you are useful for something.*

Lee eased back into the driver's seat, again engaged the Overland's gears and slowly eased back onto the road, holding out the door and not shutting it just yet so as not to alert the sleeping Curries in the main house. He turned his lights back on but waited until he turned west on the next road down from the house to shut the door. Light would not alert a sleeping person, but he reasoned the odd sound of a car door being shut just might be enough to arouse them.

He drove a short way and then turned north on the road going by the house where he had spent so much time at his old babysitter, Novella McRae's feet, listening to her tell him and his siblings all those exciting stories that fired his imagination as a young man. Lee had warm memories of playing in the yard and being cared for by the old Crow Indian woman John Currie had brought with him from North Carolina to look after his children.

At the bend in the road, he turned onto an old throwed-away road that his pa had stopped maintaining some time back. Then, being careful to avoid the limbs that might scratch the Overland, he inched his way along the rough road about a hundred yards and well out of sight of the main road.

Right here is going to be your final resting place, Phillips! He thought to himself as he stepped out of the car.

He retrieved the hoe and shovel and walked into the area illuminated by the headlights.

This ditch will do nicely, Lee thought and began the task of digging a hole on the side of the old road.

He dug with purpose. The quicker the jitney driver was in the ground, the sooner his problems would be behind him. Then, he could begin a new life as the owner of a Baby Overland – gainfully employed, happily married, and ready to assume his rightful station as a contributing Milledgeville community member.

That Overland will turn heads for sure! Lee thought. He could imagine driving down Milledgeville's streets, his beautiful wife by his side, with people stopping to stare and sometimes pointing to the car to alert others to look as he was driving by. The folks in Milledgeville would not know his history. They would not think that this was some privileged son whose pa gave him everything he had. No, to them, HE would have earned his keep by working at the Hardwick Barbershop and Pressing Club, HE would be thought of as possessing the charm necessary to win his beautiful wife, Lilly, and his ownership of the Overland would be the final proof that he was at last – a man!

Alternately using the hoe to break up the hard dirt and the shovel to cast it aside, the hole he was digging grew slowly in length and depth. After digging a couple of feet down, he tossed the tools aside and stepped out of the makeshift grave.

Staring down at his handiwork, he smiled, delighted that he would soon be rid of Phillips. He then looked at the car directly into the headlights abating the darkness and, for the first time, noticed the faint outline of the car's signature sculpture – the hood ornament.

That beautiful ornament proudly announces that this is the finest automobile in the world.

Lee turned his head to continue gazing admiringly at the hood ornament as he walked to the car's side and casually opened the rear door.

He was startled and jumped back when Phillips' arm fell out. *Come on, Lee, the man's dead as a doornail*, he said, trying to reassure himself, but his apprehension grew when he heard what sounded like a gurgling grunt as he pulled the body from the Overland, and it flopped to the ground.

Lee jumped back, pulled his gun, and aimed it at the body lying motionless before him. *Dammit, you son-of-a-bitch, why won't you die!* A long minute passed before he lowered his weapon, convinced Phillips was no longer a threat to him.

Pocketing the pistol, he grabbed his victim's arms and pulled him to the side of the makeshift grave. Dropping the body beside it, he silently congratulated himself for correctly judging the dimensions of the hole. It appeared Phillips would fit perfectly well.

Let's see what you got on you, Lee thought as he crouched and rifled through Phillips' pockets. He found a watch, a pipe, matches, and coins. *Dammit, I know you got some money somewhere*, Lee said aloud, continuing his search. Finally, his face lit up when he found a roll of bills. *Hot damn! I knew it*! Lee exclaimed as he held the roll of money up in the headlights. Then his smile faded as he discovered that it was just dollar bills on the inside with a few fives on the outside.

What's this shit? Lee said aloud as he stood up, counting the bills. He had heard his pa talk about car traders, with their big talk when making a deal, trying to make people think they had more money to trade with than they had.

He stood up and kicked the side of the body. *You crooked car salesman son-of-a-bitch!*

Lee pocketed the money roll and grabbed Phillips again, pushing him right up to the side of the hole he had just dug and, with a grunt, rolling him into the hole.

His early accolades for his handiwork were premature. The grave was not quite wide enough for the body to lie flat, and instead, it came to rest on its left side, the right shoulder only six inches below level ground. Lee frowned at the prospect of pulling the body back out of the hole and digging it deeper. *No, this will have to do.*

Standing up with his hands on his hips, he looked around in the darkness. Yes, he was way off the beaten path, well out of sight of prying eyes. He satisfied himself as to the grave's adequacy. *It's just six inches under for you, Mr. Phillips, not six feet, but who's counting?*

Lee kneeled and shoved Phillips' right arm down, almost under the body. He stood up again and stared down emotionless. After a moment, he picked up the shovel and started filling the hole.

As he surveyed his handiwork later, he was a bit concerned that he had buried Phillips' right shoe heel just an inch or two down. Would animals detect the smell and dig him up? Would the rain run down the side of the road and uncover him?

Hell, quit ya worrying. Ain't nobody gonna find him, he finally convinced himself and placed his tools carefully into the back floorboard of the Overland. He stared again at the makeshift grave in the soft glow of his headlights. *Lousy luck, Phillips, to be buried unceremoniously like this out in the woods, but you brought it on yourself. Rest in peace, you old son-of-a-bitch, and don't worry. Nobody will ever disturb you out here.*

He felt fully empowered as he reentered and started the car, HIS car now. He took the gun out from his pocket and put it in the driver's side door pocket.

Driving down the road, unburdened by the unwanted passenger in the back floorboard, Lee relaxed and even smiled. Returning slowly to his father's gin house to replace the shovel and hoe, he was careful to slowly close the squeaky gin door. *How 'bout that, not a peep this time, it's done!*

Chapter 12

It was approaching midnight, and Lee was exhausted from both the arduous task of burying the man he had killed and the high levels of adrenaline-charged energy he had expended since he left Vidalia. He turned his thoughts to where he would put up for the night.

His Uncle Dave Wright's place was less than a mile away. He had stayed there many times before. Uncle Dave was married to his mother's sister, and he and Aunt Nancy seemed very fond of him. They would not be upset by his appearance at this late hour on their doorstep nor inclined to consider his late-night visit unusual enough to tell anyone about it.

However, what might puzzle them and possibly lead to unwanted questions would be his arriving this late at night in a new car. Lee concluded it would be best to leave it behind for now. Turning off the Overland's headlights, he set out to walk the short distance to his uncle's home. Pausing a few feet away from the car, Lee looked back. *It will be fine here,* he convinced himself, and again began walking in the darkness.

Lee knew the terrain well and was undaunted by the moonless night. He blew into his hands to warm them as he walked briskly in the chilly February air. He arrived at his Uncle Dave's house in no time and knocked on the door.

Lee walked to the edge of the porch and peered through the cloth bedroom curtains. He was relieved to see his uncle's faint outline rising out of bed and lighting a lantern. He returned to the front door, and shortly after that, his uncle opened it.

"Lee, what in tarnation are you doing out this late and on foot? Is everything alright with your pa?" Dave Wright asked, peering left and right out the door as if expecting someone to be with him.

"I had a friend drop me off, Uncle Dave, and I'm fine ... just a little chilled is all," Lee answered.

"Well, get on in here and let me start a fire to warm you up," Dave pushed open the screen door to let Lee in. Lee squinted as his uncle held the lantern up to his face.

"Boy, you are flushed. You ain't got a lick of sense being out this late in this cold. You'll catch your death," Dave lectured.

Lee watched as his uncle added a couple of logs to the central room fireplace and stirred up the still glowing embers underneath the logs. He was confident they would ignite the new wood and warm them both in short order. Dave stepped over to the extra bedroom and opened the door. He returned, stirred the fire a bit, and then he and his uncle pulled their rockers up closer to the fireplace's opening and looked expectantly into the dancing flames that had already begun chasing away the chill.

"We should be pretty comfy here in a minute. If I had knowed you were coming, I'd already had a fire lit and left the door open to the extra bedroom. I'm afraid it's going to be a mite chilly in there," Dave said as he added some kindling to assist the embers in getting the fire going.

"Beggars can't be choosers, Uncle Dave; I'll be fine. Besides, I'll bet Aunt Nancy has seven or eight of her famous quilts on that bed," Lee replied.

Dave chuckled, "Yep, you know your aunt well, Lee. She is the main organizer of the Marvin Church quilting bee. She has every storage area in this home stuffed with quilts, and there's a couple of dozen more stored in the attic. That woman does love making quilts. But I think it's high time she stops making quilts and starts selling 'em!"

"I don't think it's the making of the quilts she loves, Uncle Dave. I think it's listening to all the gossip from the ladies that come to the bee," Lee said, and both men chuckled in agreement.

They continued to palaver for about a quarter-hour when Dave said, "Well, I've got an early start waiting for me in the morning, so I'll turn in. What are you doing tomorrow, Lee?"

"I'm in a trade early tomorrow, Uncle Dave."

"Oh? What you tradin' fer?" Dave queried.

"I'll letcha know, iffin it works out. I don't want to jinx it by talking about it," Lee deflected.

"All righty then," Dave got up, added another piece of wood to the fire, and put the grating in place to prevent embers from escaping the hearth. "I'll be saying goodnight then. See you in the morning." He nodded to Lee and left the semicircle of amber light surrounding the fire.

"Nite, Uncle Dave, and thanks for puttin' me up."

Lee sat there by the fire, thinking about the Overland and how it was at this very moment silently standing guard in a moonless night over a makeshift grave.

Thunder rumbled in the distance, and a new concern caused the hair to stand up on the back of Lee's neck. That thunder could mean rain, and he had buried the body in a ditch. Running water in that ditch could quickly erode the loose earth around that fresh grave and spell trouble for him. He might need to take extra measures to secure the site in the morning.

And then there was Tersia Phillips. She would have been worried about her husband not returning home last night. He had to think up something to keep her from sending out folks to look for Phillips.

Sleep began to overcome Lee, and he headed to bed. He would think about all that tomorrow.

Chapter 13

The first light of morning was loudly announced by Dave Wright's rooster and echoed by several others from distant farms. Lee was not asleep, however, having tossed and turned all night. Sweeping aside Nancy's heavy quilts, he rose to a sitting position. During the night, a plan had materialized in his head to solve the problem with Tersia Phillips, who did not yet know she was a widow.

Phillips was known to be a wheeler and dealer of automobiles. It would not be unusual for him to leave town for a few days to deliver a car to a new purchaser. If he disappeared and never returned, folks would look for him where he supposedly delivered the vehicle. They would not suspect foul play back in Toombs County if they never found him. *Yes, it could work*! He convinced himself. He would drive to Claxton and send Tersia a telegram, making it appear it was from her husband saying he would be out of town a few days.

Set now to his purpose, Lee got dressed and went to the wash station to wash his face.

* * * * * *

Dave Wright woke up at the crack of dawn, still concerned. Despite Lee's assurances the night before that all was well, his instincts told him something was indeed amiss.

He was sensitive to the frequently shifting moods of his wife's nephew and felt protective of him. Having gone through a troubled childhood in the shadow of John Currie, one of the county's most successful farmers, it seemed to Dave that Lee tried too hard to be perceived as a man of substance. Unfortunately, the boy was going through life playing with a deck short a few cards.

Dave's feelings for the boy motivated him to encourage Lee at every opportunity to learn new things and try different jobs, which was quite a challenge, given Lee's short attention span. He also had made it known to Lee that he was always welcome to stay at his home, and the boy was indeed a frequent guest, especially when he and his father got into one of their violent exchanges.

That another family fight had probably taken place was the first thing that came to his mind when Lee arrived the night before, but Lee was not wearing his customary scowl that signaled a spat with his father. He was acting strangely, as if he had something big on his mind. Dave needed to find out what was going on.

The fire blazed back to life after he added a few more logs and stoked it with the fire poker. He splashed some water on his face from the basin on the wash shelf and headed to the kitchen to start cooking. Breakfast would provide an excellent opportunity to question Lee and hopefully determine what was bothering the young man.

Dave peeked into his nephew's room and saw Lee wipe his face and hands and toss the towel to the water shelf rather than hanging it back on the dowel rod as he usually did. Lee quickly combed his hair as if in a hurry to leave, and Dave frowned. Something was definitely off.

While he turned to flip the eggs sizzling in the frying pan, he heard the front door slam.

What in tarnation? That boy's already gone! Dave thought to himself, puzzled. Nancy joined him in the kitchen and pushed him gently away from the stove.

"Here, honey, making breakfast is my job," she said as she opened the fire door and put some more wood in the stove. "Was that Lee I saw leaving?"

"Fraid so," Dave answered.

"That's not like him to skip breakfast," Nancy added as she broke open an egg in the frying pan.

"I know, Nance, he's got me befuddled."

"Don't recall him coming over that late before; what in the world could be going on with him?" She asked.

"Haven't figured it out yet, Nance. He seemed kinda normal, but that's what's confounding me. Coming in that late, I fully would expect him to be upset about something, but he was calm, unnervingly so. He might have been a tad preoccupied, but he was not upset," Dave responded.

"Think he was coming from his pa's?" Nancy asked.

"He said no, and I believe him. Since he moved to Milledgeville, Lee's visited his pa very little, like he's trying to prove himself before he goes back to see John," Dave said.

"So, what do you think he's up to?" Nancy asked, showing concern.

"I don't know, I was hoping to try to find out over breakfast, but he scooted out," Dave answered. Dave's concern had grown into worry.

"Did he tell you where he might be going?" she asked.

"Said he had to go to Reidsville – but he's on foot. Something ain't right, I tell ya."

"Lee is a hard one to understand, Dave, and you may as well let it go. You know how hard it is to get him to change course when he gets his mind made up."

"Yeah, something's got him distracted, alright. I just wish I knew what it was."

"It probably don't 'mount to much; you know how he can get in a stir about something most folks wouldn't make a fuss over. In any case, what's important to Lee ain't none of your concern. Now sit down and eat your breakfast."

Begrudgingly, Dave sat down. Nancy put his plate in front of him and joined him. He took his wife's hand and bowed his head.

"Lord, bless this food to the nourishment of our bodies and us to thy service and be with Lee today as he deals with whatever it is on his mind. He needs your guiding hand, Lord. Protect him from the evil one. In Jesus' name, amen."

"Have you got one of your premonitions, honey?" Nancy asked, with a worried look on her face.

"It's probably nothing, but I've watched your sister's boy grow up, and he don't think like the rest of us. It's been a struggle for him to find his way. His pa has kept him on such a short leash."

"Well, can you blame him? John Currie had his hands full with Lee from the first day that boy was born. You remember John having to contend with the teachers' notes about Lee fighting with the other children?"

"That's just boys being boys," Dave replied, feeling himself getting defensive.

"And was it boys being boys when he broke into old man Shumake's store?" Nancy continued, on a roll now.

"What normal child would go in and steal little old things, like candy and tobacco, that wasn't worth nothin' and give them to anybody he come across?" She asked.

"Come on, Nancy, what was he, like maybe eight years old when that happened?" Dave was practically whining. Nancy reached out and took his hand.

"Dave, I know you love Lee, just as I do, but you can't get that involved in the world that exists in his head. You'll drive yourself crazy!"

"Is that a car I hear?" Dave interrupted and went to the window to peer outside. "Jesus Christ, it's Lee, in what looks like a brand-new car!"

Dave opened the door and headed out on the porch as Lee drove up. Nancy peered out of the window in astonishment. It was the prettiest car she had ever seen.

Lee stopped quickly at the gate and smiled as the dust caught and briefly engulfed the car. He pulled back on the brake handle as if he had been driving the car for years.

"Dang, Lee, where did you get this automobile?" Dave asked, stepping off the porch and walking up to the gate. Less than ten minutes had passed since his nephew had left his home walking, and now he had returned in a beautiful car. What was going on?

"It's that car I was telling you about last night, Uncle Dave. I can tell you now, being as I've done the deal, it's a Baby Overland – freshly bought and a good trade, too. She's a beaut, ain't she," Lee responded.

Dave noticed that he didn't answer his question. "Nancy's got breakfast on the table, Lee. Come on and have a bite with us. You can tell us all about it."

"Maybe later, Uncle Dave, like I told you yesterday, I gotta go to Reidsville," Lee said.

"Reidsville? C'mon Lee that can wait. You gotta eat," Dave made a futile last effort to urge Lee to come inside.

"Another time, Uncle Dave, I gotta go to Reidsville. Come go with me." Lee asked.

"Lee, you know I can't leave the farm with all I have to do," his uncle replied.

"You work too hard, Uncle Dave. You're going to miss riding in this great car, but I'll take you for a ride later," Lee said as he released the brake.

Dave was completely perplexed. He opened his mouth to say more but then closed it. Lee backed up, put the car into first gear, and sped off, the car tires throwing rocks as he went. He waved in the air without looking back.

Dave gave his wife, who had stepped out on the porch, a bewildered look.

"That boy sure is full of surprises today," Nancy said as she rubbed her hands together. "It's freezing out here, come back inside before you catch your death."

Dave continued to stare at the disappearing cloud of dust.

"Something ain't right, Nancy, I tell you something just ain't right."

"Dave, it ain't your problem. Now git in here."

Dave slowly lowered his head and turned to the porch.

"I'm coming," he said.

* * * * * *

The Overland gleamed in the daylight hours. Lee took in its every curve and feature, now splendidly revealed in the sun's brilliant illumination. The engine's purring was just faintly audible over the wind whistling by the fabric of the top canopy.

His first daytime drive of the car rekindled the pure joy of his driving it the night before. The dashboard, barely discernible in the amber lights' faint glow last night, was magnificently gleaming in the day's revealing light. The gas gauge registered almost full.

Thanks, Phillips, for filling it up for me, he thought to himself. Having to stop for fuel would be an inconvenient disruption of his ride – his long ride in his new car, which he wanted to go on forever.

Lee congratulated himself. He had cleverly misled his uncle that he was going to Reidsville while his real destination was the Telegraph office in Claxton. There, Lee planned to send Phillips' wife a telegram to make her think her husband had sold the car to a man in Jacksonville and was going down there to deliver it. That way, when he didn't return, the authorities would go looking for him down there. Clever!

The blood in the car was another problem. He needed to wash it out but doing so around here would arouse too much suspicion. Claxton would have some gas stations that would let him wash his car out, for sure. But that blood in the fabric of the Overland might not come entirely out. He needed a good story for that.

I'll tell anyone who sees the car that I run over a deer, he said aloud and then quickly frowned. How would running over a deer get blood IN the car? He suddenly realized he was driving too slowly, having lost his concentration on the road. He sped up. *Pay attention, dammit, this is important*! He said to himself.

Then it hit him. If he accidentally ran over someone's hog, he would have to pay for it and remove it from their property. *Bled like a pig*, folks always said, and lots of blood was just what he needed. People would believe that story.

Lee turned south onto Marvin Road. It was daylight now, and he dared not go by his father's place, as he was sure to be spotted. Instead, he would drive down to Marvin's Church and turn left to Claxton by the back route.

As he passed Winfield Sutton's place, fortune smiled on him. On the side of the road was a calf, casually grazing on the lush grass. An opportunity has presented itself, and Lee pulled quickly off the road and struck the hapless calf, killing him instantly. As he pulled away, he could hear a scraping sound.

Damn! He said aloud as he pulled over to the side of the road. The calf's impact had bent the right fender of the Overland and it was scrapping the tire. After a few tugs on the thick metal, he was able to get it back into place. Unfortunately, the paint had flecked off at the crease. Lee frowned at the damage to the Overland and then smiled. The dent was just the proof he needed. Lee got back into the car and continued driving toward Marvin Church.

＊＊＊＊＊

What in tarnation? Winfield Sutton thought to himself as he heard a thud and a calf bleat. Looking up toward the gate to his cow field, he saw one of his calves trashing on the ground. Winfield thought the big car slowing down looked like a Ford. As the driver got out of the car and walked around the front, he recognized him.

That's Lee Currie, and he done kilt one of my calves! Winfield ran toward the gate, shaking his fist.

He saw Lee get back in the car. *Is he going to come to square up with me over this calf?* Winfield wondered. But Lee just sped off down the road as if he had not seen him.

That boy ain't right, and he's gonna git somebody kilt, Winfield thought, as he finally arrived where the calf lay, still kicking. He stared down at the poor creature for a minute. From the calf's head's odd angle, he knew the impact of the car had broken its neck. Finally, the kicking stopped.

He's done for, the exasperated farmer sighed and turned back toward his home. He had no desire to confront Lee Currie about the calf. He'd see John Currie at church on Sunday and would take the matter up with him.

Chapter 14

After five short weeks, Robert Fussell was getting very comfortable with his new job as a clerk telegraph operator at the Western Union Telegraph Office in Claxton, Georgia. His late grandfather, Byrd Fussell, had fought with five different Georgia Militias in the War Between the States. He had encouraged him when he was just a young lad to seek a job with the railroad, as the War had proven the future value of rapid transportation. Even after he had grown up, he remembered his grandfather's urging. So, when the Abbeville station agent told him about an upcoming opening for a telegraph operator in Claxton, he busied himself learning Morse Code and reading everything he could about telegraph offices.

His perseverance landed him the Claxton job, and the 27-year-old relocated there. Mr. M. H. Mulkey, the station agent for the Seaborn Air Line Railway and manager of the Western Union Telegraph Office, was scheduled to leave the company for a new job in a different location later in July. Robert knew he was looking for a successor, so he strove to master all the office tasks and, after only five weeks, could send code at 30 words per minute. The young man felt confident that he was a prime candidate to replace Mr. Mulkey.

Robert was so engrossed in sending dots and dashes over the telegraph line to Savannah that he involuntarily jumped when the bell over the door to the telegraph office announced that a customer had just entered. He glanced to his left to see a young man dressed in an army overcoat, walking up to the counter.

Mr. Mulkey, whose desk was situated where his back was to the counter, also heard the bell. He rose and walked over to the counter window.

"Can I help you?" he asked the new customer.

"Can I send a telegram from here to Lyons?" the customer asked.

"Sir, we can send a telegram to just about anywhere in the world! Welcome to the Western Union Telegraph Office. My name is M. H. Mulkey, and I'm the station agent here. The gentleman working the key over there is Mr. Robert Fussell."

Robert nodded at the customer, who gave him a disinterested smile. There was something about the man's dark piercing eyes that unnerved him.

"Pleased to make your acquaintance," the man said. Robert noticed that the stranger did not offer his name in return. "I've never sent a telegram before. How's this work?"

"Well, it's easy. There's a stack of blank telegram sheets and pencils right on that table over there. Just fill in the blanks showing who you want to send it to and where you want it sent. Then write out your message, and we'll be happy to send it for you," Mr. Mulkey said and turned to sit back down.

Lee Currie walked to the table against the wall opposite the counter of the Claxton Telegraph Office. He had never sent a telegram before and was in unchartered waters, but he knew what he wanted to do. First, Lee had to make it appear to Phillips' wife that her husband had gone somewhere in another state, like Florida, and would be gone for a week. Then, he reasoned, when Phillips didn't return, they would go looking for him in that state instead of on his pa's farm where he had buried him the night before.

What was that son-of-a-bitch's full name? Lee questioned himself. He knew his last name was Phillips, and he had heard his name when he introduced himself the evening before at Mr. Wilson's Jitney Service.

T. E. ... R.E. ... B.E. ... What was his damn name? Lee decided to go with "R. E." on the theory that Phillips was probably named after the same General in the War Between the States who inspired John Currie to call him Lee.

He took one of the forms and touched the pencil thoughtfully to his tongue while he tried to read the instructions.

"I don't understand all this stuff in the boxes at the top," he said over his shoulder.

"Oh, don't worry about that – it's for us to fill out. Just start at the 'To' line and fill it out from there," Mr. Mulkey responded without looking up from his desk.

Lee didn't know Phillips' wife's name, so he wrote "Mrs. R. E. Phillips" beside the word "To." Then he paused again, staring at the blank form. The right words just would not come to him.

A couple of minutes passed, and he became self-conscious after seeing Mr. Mulkey looking over at him. Lee positioned himself where the station agent wouldn't be able to tell he was struggling.

Lee couldn't get his thoughts together. He tried to write something, paused, then tore up the form and threw it in the trash. A second attempt also found its way to the trash.

Finally, Lee wrote, "Honey, I'm not coming home tonight. I've sold a car to a man in Jacksonville and am going to take it down there and catch the train back. I'll be gone a few days. Don't worry about me."

Then he thought to himself, *Hell, I don't know if he calls his wife "honey" or not*! He again tore up the message and tossed it into the trash. Glancing back, he saw the station agent staring at him. Annoyed, he turned around to his telegram.

The less I say, the better, Lee tried to convince himself, but his mind remained as blank as the yellow paper staring back at him.

Having noticed the sound of his customer's third failed attempt hitting the trash, Mr. Mulkey spoke up and offered, "Whenever you get it ready, let me know, and I will check it and collect for it."

"Alright," Lee responded. "I'm 'bout done."

Lee tried a fourth time, "I sold my car to a man I took for a jitney ride today. He is from Jacksonville. He wants me to drive it down there for him. I'll catch the train and be back home sometime next week. Signed: R. E. Phillips."

Lee did not want to create any more suspicions. It would have to do. He announced, "I'm ready."

Mr. Mulkey laid down his pencil and slowly rose from his seat. He met Lee at the counter and took the telegram from him. Lee watched him intently as he read what Lee had written.

"Mr. Phillips, you are sending a telegram to your wife, not a letter. Unlike mail, we don't charge you by weight; we charge you by the word. You need to shorten this up, or it's going to be quite expensive."

The agent had taken the bait and assumed he was Phillips. Lee smiled at how well his plan was coming together.

"I'm not too good with words, Mr. Mulkey. Didn't get much book learning in school," Lee said.

"Don't worry about it, son; that's what we are here for," the agent said. Mr. Mulkey made several suggestions, with

Lee nodding his head in approval each time. Finally, after several revisions, the telegram read, "Sold my car to man from Jacksonville and going to drive through for him. Be home next week."

"Well, now, you whittled it down to a splinter," Lee said.

"Well, I've been doing this for a long time. Let's check it over one more time. Hmmm, the destination is blank. Where did you say you want to send it?"

"To Lyons," Lee replied.

"Alright," Mr. Mulkey wrote in the town. "To Lyons, it is." He counted the words, "That will be sixty cents, Mr. Phillips."

Lee reached into his pocket and fished out a crumpled-up dollar bill. He handed it to the agent. He had taken the dollar from his victim of the night before. Lee smiled at the irony of Phillips effectively paying for this deceptive telegram to his wife.

Mr. Mulkey opened the drawer under the counter and put the dollar in the appropriate tray. He picked up the change and carefully counted it back to Lee.

"Your fee for the telegram was sixty cents. This nickel makes sixty-five cents, this dime makes seventy-five cents, and this quarter takes us up to your dollar."

"Thank you, sir," Lee said as he pocketed the change, turned, and left the building.

Mulkey checked the station clock and wrote: "9:50 AM" on the telegram.

"I'm already on the line with Savannah; you want me to go ahead and send it now?" Robert asked.

"Might as well. That fella's wife will be worried about him if we don't."

Robert tapped the message into the telegraph sounder key and got the acknowledgment back from Savannah, showing it was received and relayed to Lyons at 9:57 AM. He wrote that on the telegram.

"Weird bird, that one," Robert said and slapped the telegram on the spike stick holding the sent telegrams.

* * * * * *

Lee breathed a sigh of relief as he got back into the Overland. The task of throwing Mrs. Phillips off the scent was behind him, and he could finally put the body buried in Toombs County out of his mind and begin enjoying the car. The next order of business was to get it cleaned up and ready to show off. Washing out the blood at one of Claxton's service stations wouldn't attract as much attention as it would in Lyons.

Driving up to a Standard Oil Service Station, he told the attendant that he needed to clean something out of his car.

"You want me to detail it for you, sir? Only one dollar," the attendant asked.

"No, it's just a little bit. I can do it if you don't mind. Is there a charge for that?" Lee asked.

"Naw, the water's free, and I ain't gonna charge you for the cleaning supplies. You'll find them over against that 'er wall; help yourself," the attendant said and returned to his work on the car he was servicing.

The dried blood washed off the leather seats easily and from the rubber mats on the floor, where it had thickly pooled, but it was stubbornly resisting his efforts to remove it from the fabric on the back of the front seat. The dark stains brought him unwelcome flashbacks of Phillips bleeding after being shot. Being constantly reminded of the car's former owner by his bloodstains staring at him every time he got in or out of the vehicle was not what he wanted. He made a mental note to ask one of the ladies he was about to visit what he could use to get the bloodstains out of the fabric.

As he was putting away the water hose, bucket, and brush he had been using, Lee suddenly panicked. He had told the telegraph agent that the telegram was to go to Lyons, but Mrs. Phillips lived in Vidalia! Lee had to return to the telegraph office right away. Jumping in the car, he accelerated quickly, throwing rocks at the station attendant.

"Hey, you bunghole! At least buy some gas!" the attendant yelled, shaking his fist at the inconsiderate freeloader speeding off in the distance.

* * * * * *

Damn that bell! I'm never going to get used to it, Robert thought as the opening door struck the bell hard. He was puzzled to see that the young man in the army overcoat had stepped back inside but said nothing as he walked up to the window.

It seemed like a full minute passed before Lee asked no one in particular, "Has my telegram gone out yet?"

"Yes, it is gone," Robert answered.

"Where did you send it?" Lee asked.

"To Lyons, just as you told Mr. Mulkey earlier," Robert replied.

Upon hearing his name and realizing the recent customer was back, Mr. Mulkey, who had been studying a dispatch from the railroad headquarters intently, turned to look at him.

"Hello again, Mr. Phillips. Is there something wrong?"

Robert's alarm grew as Lee paused for a minute and looked furtively around the room as if he was unsure what to do next. Lee shook his head to signal "no" and started for the door. But instantly, he stopped and wheeled around, "I made a mistake. I meant for that telegram to go to Vidalia."

There was just something about Lee's manner that unnerved Robert. Something was amiss. How could a husband not know where to send his wife a telegram? And why was he getting so nervous? Robert aggressively abandoned his usual deference to Mr. Mulkey.

"We sent it like you told us, sir. If you want it to go to Vidalia, you will have to write out a new telegram and pay for it."

Lee's face went crimson, and Mr. Mulkey, who had been trained that the customer was always right, immediately cut in. "You'll have to forgive my telegraph operator, Mr. Phillips. He's a bit overworked today and has forgotten his manners. We can make this alright without your having to write another telegram and pay sixty cents again. It was just a mistake, after all. We all make them. Let's set this right." Mr. Mulkey turned to retrieve the message from the spike stick. He returned it to the counter.

"You say you want it to go to Vidalia?" he asked.

"Yeah, that's right, Vidalia," Lee said and glanced malevolently at Robert.

"We'll take care of it, don't you worry. Your wife will get the message right away, and you can be off on your trip to Jacksonville without further ado," Mr. Mulkey said; in the calm voice Robert had seen him deploy when a customer was unruly. He wrote something on the telegram and handed it to Robert.

"Robert, tell Savannah to send Lyons a service message asking them to disregard the message they just received for Mrs. Phillips and then ask them to resend it to Vidalia."

Robert begrudgingly took the telegram from Mr. Mulkey's extended hand. He saw where his boss had scratched out "Lyons" on the telegram and wrote in "Vidalia." He looked up at Mr. Mulkey as if to protest and saw his boss widen his eyes, signaling that he needed to calm down.

"Yes, sir," Robert said and started tapping out the message to Savannah on the telegraph sounder.

Mr. Mulkey turned back to Lee, "All taken care of, Mr. Phillips."

"Thanks, Mr. Mulkey. Unlike some folks around here, you're a real gentleman." He glared at Robert, then turned and was out the door.

"That could have gotten ugly, Robert," Mr. Mulkey said after Lee had left.

"Something stinks about this telegram," Robert said suspiciously, without interrupting the steady stream of dots and dashes he was tapping into the sounder. "I don't believe for a minute that was Mr. Phillips."

"I don't care who he was, Robert. We don't question the customers. Your reaction was out of line. That's the first time I've seen your temper flare like that."

Robert winced at the scolding and continued to send the message. Savannah acknowledged that the new instructions had been received and carried out.

"Okay, it's done," Robert reported gruffly.

"Good. Now, why don't you settle down and pour yourself another cup of coffee? Put Mr. Whatever-his-name-is out of your mind. You have lots of other telegrams to send this morning."

"Something bad is going to come of this. I can just feel it," Robert added.

"Mayhap, but it's none of your affair. And don't you forget that when I leave for Peoria, Illinois, in July, they will need a new station agent. You need to work on your people skills if you want my recommendation for you to replace me when I retire."

Robert sat straight up, and a chill ran down his spine. He decided Mr. Phillips was no longer significant in the grand scheme of things. He got up and headed toward the coffee pot.

Chapter 15

Once Lilly's family feasts their eyes on this new car, they will convince her to forget all about this damn divorce business. I know her pa is on my side. The others will come around too, just you wait!

Lee was supremely confident as he drove the Baby Overland north of Claxton to Bob Kerby's house. Bob's wife, Anne Jane Nevill Kerby, was Lilly's mom's sister. Aunt Anne was one of Lee's favorite in-laws, and he enjoyed a good relationship with her.

Lilly's mom had died the year after she and Lee were married. Her two aunts had stepped up to the plate and afforded her guidance and support to make the marriage work. Lee felt her Aunt Anne was the most accepting of the union of the two. He felt Anne could be very persuasive in getting the rest of the family to convince Lilly to put the business of his infidelity behind them.

* * * * * *

Back at the Standard Oil Station, the bloodstains had stubbornly resisted all his scrubbing and remained as unsightly dark spots on the Overland's upholstery where Burley had bled profusely. But Lee felt confident he had established a good cover story by running over Mr. Sutton's calf that morning.

Just four miles from Claxton, Lee spotted Bob and Anne Kerby, his wife's aunt, and uncle, approaching him in a wagon. A cloud of dust enveloped Lee as he braked to a sudden stop by the wagon.

"Hey, Uncle Bob ... Aunt Anne!" he said.

"Lee, what in tarnation you doin' here?" Bob asked.

"I come to see you and Aunt Anne, Uncle Bob."

Bob looked over the car admiringly, "Well, we glad you did, Lee. Hey, that's a nice car. Whose is it?"

"This here's my car, Uncle Bob. Just bought it. Whadda ya think?" Lee said boastfully.

"It's beautiful, Lee," Anne said. "I ain't never seen a car that purdy."

Lee beamed. "Yep, she's a beaut, alright. Where y'all headed?"

"Gotta pick up some supplies in Claxton. I'm gonna stop at Jim's to pick him up first," Bob answered.

"That's great. I can go there, too. Aunt Anne, you want to ride in this brand new car with me?" Lee asked.

Anne turned excitedly to her husband, "Oh, Bob, can I?"

Bob peered down into the car and squinted his eyes, "I don't know, I don't trust them infernal machines, and you might be a mite too young and restless in that new car of yourn. And what are them dark stains on the seats? Them bloodstains?"

Lee tested his excuse for the bloodstains, "Yeah, ain't that the damnedest? Brand new car, and already I done ruint it some. I ran into a damn hog no sooner than I bought it. The hog's owner was madder' n hell. Had to pay him $11 to calm the son-of-a-bitch down. He told me I had to get that dead hog off his property, so I put 'em in the car, and the damn thing bled all over the place," Lee explained.

"Watch your tongue, Lee. I don't cotton to that kind of strong language around my wife," Bob cautioned.

"Sorry, Unk. I guess I'm still just a bit upset about messing up my new car."

"Well, I can sure understand that. Under the circumstances, we'll let it slide this time," Bob nodded his assent to his wife, and Anne anxiously jumped down from the wagon, ignoring her husband's extended hand to help her. She sprinted around the back of the wagon and then slowed down as she approached the front of the car, letting her fingers glide along the curves of the Baby Overland as if touching a real baby.

"Oh, Bob, isn't it beautiful!" Anne exclaimed. She looked intently at the door, "It ain't got a handle. How do I open the door?"

Lee reached across the car and opened it for her, "It opens from the inside, there you go, hop in."

Anne touched the leather admiringly, ran her fingers across the seat, then hopped in.

"Tough break on a new car, getting it all stained up like that," Bob said.

"Don't I know it," Lee said. "It was bleeding all over the car."

"What did you do with it?" Bob asked.

"I just drove down to the creek and throwed it in."

"Throwed it in the creek? That's a waste of good pork," Bob said.

"I know, I know, but it just wouldn't stop bleeding in my car, and I had to get rid of it," Lee stated.

"I heared that. That's a mighty pretty car to be getting all bloodied up," Bob responded.

Anne was rubbing her hands on the seats in awe. She took in every feature of the dashboard. She had only been in a few automobiles, and none came close to the beauty and wonder of this one.

"You going to spoil her, Lee. Next thing you know, she'll be adder me to get a car too," Bob said.

"$1,150, and you can have one just like this one," Lee said haughtily.

"Iffin I had $1,150; I'd be buying ole' man Jones property next to mine, not buying no new car!" Bob laughed.

"Well now, don't you be showing out in that thing. I wouldn't want anything to happen to my Anne," Bob retorted.

"I'll get her to Jim's in one piece, Unk. Heck, it ain't but just half a mile to his place. What could go wrong? See you there," and with that, Lee spun the vehicle around quickly, spooking the horse.

"Whoa, Nellie, whoa now," Bob said, pulling back on the reins as he watched Lee speed away. *Yeah, yeah, what could go wrong? Damn fool will kill my wife, iffin he ain't careful*, he thought to himself.

He slapped the reins, and the horse started trudging on down the road. He craned his neck and strained to see the road in the billowing dust cloud behind Lee's rapidly disappearing car.

* * * * * *

Jim Kerby unloaded another bag of trash from the wagon and threw it in the fire pit he had dug in the field.

"Lord, how does a family produce so much trash?" he asked out loud.

Sally, the family mule, turned her head lazily toward him as if to answer.

"It ain't been more than a month since I last had to burn a load. Seems like everything you buy today has got to be individually wrapped in something too flimsy to use for anything else. Wasn't like that in my pappy's day," he said, seemingly to the mule, which blinked and patiently listened for a keyword that might signal a sugar cube coming from one of his master's pockets.

The distant cloud of dust heralding a fast-moving vehicle caught his eye. Wasn't that the same car going north that had just come by his place a few minutes ago? Straining his eyes, he recognized Anne in the passenger seat, but he couldn't make out the man driving the car. He took his rake and pushed the trash toward the center of the burning fire in the pit. Stepping up into the wagon, he surveyed the fire and assured himself it was under control.

No wind today; it'll be fine, he thought to himself as he slapped the reins across the mule's behind. "Giddy up, there, Sally. Let's go'd de house."

* * * * * *

Jim pulled the wagon into the barn, unhitched Sally, and put her out to pasture, all the while glancing over to the empty car sitting out in the lane by the front gate to his house. Apparently, whoever was with Anne had gone into the house with her.

He'd never seen that car before it came speeding by earlier today, and it was way too nice to be the property of any farmer he knew, but Anne had been riding in it, so it had to be somebody familiar.

Bob was supposed to be on his way over to ride to Claxton for supplies. Now here was his wife Anne riding up in a car. Not sure what was going on, Jim approached the vehicle and peered inside.

The front door of his house swung open, and Lee stepped out, followed closely by Anne.

"Howdy, Mr. Kerby," Lee said as he bounded down the front porch steps.

"Well, hey, Lee," Jim responded, "This here your car?"

"Yep," Lee replied as he lovingly put both his hands on the driver's side door. "It's mine; it's all mine. Ain't she a beaut?"

"Ain't never seen a prettier car 'bout these parts, that's fer sure," Jim said as he looked the Overland over.

"Looks like you done bent it up some," Jim said as he observed the bent fender.

"Yeah, I have abused it a bit. Accidentally ran over and killed a hog over near my pa's place."

"He says he put the hog in the car, and it bled all over his seats," Anne volunteered.

"It did. I drove down to the nearest creek and throwed the hog in," Lee said.

Jim looked into the car again. "Mighty big waste of good pork," he said, repeating the words his brother said earlier. "Dang, if it didn't make a mess, Lee, that's a shame. Such a nice new car."

"I can get those bloodstains out with cornstarch," Anne offered from the porch. "How 'bout I make up a paste to rub on it. When it dries, the stains should come right out. Vinegar will work too, but it smells a little until it fully evaporates."

Jim nodded his familiarity with the old remedy for removing bloodstains. "Whatever you do, you need to do it soon. If blood stains are allowed to set for 24 hours, it's hard to get them out."

"I'd be much obliged iffin you would do that for me, Aunt Anne," Lee said.

"I'll be right back," Anne said as she turned and went back inside.

Bob finally arrived in the wagon. He pulled up next to the Overland.

"Quit gawking at that car, Jim, and don't go dreaming you can afford anything like that. Git on up here; we need to be a headin' to Claxton," Bob said.

Lee reached into the car and retrieved the hat he had taken from Burley Phillips. "Fellows, here is a hat I found this morning. If one of you can use it, you may have it."

"What size is it," Bob asked.

Lee looked at the band of the hat. "Number seven."

"I can wear that," Jim said. "Where'd ya find it?"

"I found it this morning on the road between Claxton and Pembroke," Lee lied and then winced at his response. He had not been anywhere near Pembroke, but neither man questioned what he had just said from their expressions. Lee breathed a sigh of relief.

"Well, there ain't no way to figure out who lost it, so it might as well be yourn," Lee said, and he tossed the hat across the car.

Jim made an easy catch and looked at his new possession. "Looks like it's got a few splotches of that er's pig's blood on it," he said.

"Sorry about that. It's been rolling around in the floorboard," Lee explained nervously.

Jim took out his pocketknife, flipped it open one-handed with a seasoned farmer's expertise, and scrapped off the blood splotches.

"There ... didn't even nick the felt. It's good as new," Jim said as he tried on the hat.

"Looks like a nice fit, brother," Bob said.

"Yep, fits me like a glove, thanks, Lee," Jim replied.

"Think nothing of it. Only the best for the brother of one of my in-laws," Lee said.

Bob looked into the Overland again.

"If those are your purses in there, you might ought be careful leaving your money lying around like that, Lee. That nice a car might attract some thieves," Bob said.

Lee picked up both purses and stuffed them in his pockets. "You're right, Uncle Bob. I've got to get used to this car attracting attention. That's fer sure."

"Come on, Jim, if we leave now, we should make it to town just in time to go by Mary's Diner for dinner," Bob said.

Jim nodded and turned to Lee, "Me and Bob are going to eat in town. You want to join us?"

"I appreciate the offer, but no, thanks. I need to stick around for Aunt Anne to do her thing with that cornstarch treatment on those bloodstains," Lee answered.

"Suit yerself then. I'm sure Ellen will be happy to fix you some lunch, iffin ya hungry," Jim said as he pulled up to the wagon seat and sat down next to his brother.

"I might just take you up on that, Mr. Kerby. Eating Miss Ellen's cooking sounds mighty fine," Lee said.

"You heading back home later, or you needing a place to stay tonight?" Bob asked.

"Iffin you're offering; I'm taking you up on your hospitality, Uncle Bob. I've got some visiting I want to do with Lilly's family. I want to talk to her sister Minnie and her pa. They's good folks, and I haven't seen 'em in a while. Besides, I'm a wanting to show them this here new car once Aunt Anne helps me clean it up a bit," Lee concluded.

"My home is your home, Lee. You're welcome to stay the night. I'll see you when you get done with your visiting," Bob said.

"Thanks, Uncle Bob! See ya then," Lee replied.

Bob shook the reins and urged the horse toward Claxton. The wagon moaned and creaked as the horse strode down the road, the metal-rimmed wheels tossing up flecks of rain-soaked earth as the wagon rolled away from the house.

* * * * * *

Lee sat in the swing on the porch of Jim Kerby's home while waiting for his wife's aunt to finish making up the batch of cornstarch paste. He had crossed his legs at the ankles and was gently pushing the swing back, then letting gravity pull it forward again. He held on to the chain attached to the front of the armrest and let his eyes follow it to where it joined with the chain connected to the armrest's back. His gaze followed the chain to the eye bolt in the crossbeam protruding from the house.

A young dirt dauber emerged from its mud home, which was firmly attached where the crossbeam met the house's siding. He watched it struggling to get out as he swung back and forth and marveled when it spread its wings, shook them as if spinning the crank of a new automobile, and took flight after a few moments.

How lucky they are to go from birth to flight in a matter of minutes, Lee thought. He envied the wasp for its quick progress in its life's journey.

I, too, have taken flight, just like that wasp. I am finally free!

The swing's calming motion took his mind to a place of relaxation, and he was pleased with his decision to visit his in-laws as the first order of business. Seeing him with his new car, knowing he had an excellent job in Milledgeville, and sensing his new confidence, they would surely encourage Lilly to get over her anger about that gonorrhea business. She would then eagerly come with him to live a new life in Milledgeville.

More than reconciling with his wife, he was now enjoying the fact that he was his own man. There would be no more kowtowing to the great and respectable John Currie, walking in his shadow, or being referred to as "John Currie's boy" by the townsfolk.

He didn't go overseas to fight in the War to End All Wars, but he had now killed a man. Yet, strangely, that act of putting Phillips down made him feel powerful and grown-up, as if he had taken the dead man's life force into his own.

I'll bet my father never killed anyone, he bragged to himself.

He sat lost in his thoughts as the swing emitted its repetitive creaking sound while swinging gently to and fro.

Anne emerged from the house carrying a washbasin holding the corn starch paste, a horsehair brush, and several cloths. She motioned for him to help her with the task. The swing kicked backward as he jumped out of it and then swung obliquely side to side as he bounded down the steps.

Anne directed Lee on applying the cornstarch and chatted endlessly about how her husband was forever getting blood on his overalls and how well the mixture did its magic and removed the stain before it set. She chided him for waiting so long to attend to the blood removal and expressed a hope that it would work on the fabric of the Baby Overland.

Lee smiled as he watched Anne humming contently and stroking the seats of his car so affectionately. He reminded himself that both Anne and Lilly had lived a simple existence and had never seen anything as fascinating as this Baby Overland automobile. If only Anne's reaction is a preview of how Lilly will react, he thought to himself as his smile widened.

They chatted away while the cornstarch dried and hardened, then she took the horsehair brush and went to work. To the delight of both, most of the bloodstains came out. A few areas still showed traces of a stain, but Lee was pleased to see the traces of Phillips' continuing hold on the vehicle disappearing. It was his car now – completely.

"That turned out pretty good," Anne said. "Let's go get some dinner."

Lee stared admiringly at the seats for a moment, then tossed his cloth into the washbasin.

"I'm right behind you," he said. He glanced over his shoulder at the Baby Overland.

Yep, it's mine now – all mine.

Chapter 16

It was a good meal that relaxed Lee. The previous day's stresses and restless night finally caught up with him, and he had a powerful urge to sleep.

"Mind if I take a nap, Miss Ellen? That fine meal is a wanting to be digested, and a bed is calling me," Lee asked his hostess.

"Of course, Lee. You can use Jim's room," Ellen said.

"Can you wake me up at 1:30? I've got a lot of visiting I want to do this afternoon," Lee asked.

"Sure, I'll get you up. Now you just lie down in there and make yourself comfortable," Ellen proposed.

Lee removed his shoes and stretched out on the bed. He looked through the bedroom window at Anne sitting in the swing on the front porch. The swing's gentle back and forth motion hypnotically took all the worries from his mind, and in just a few minutes, sleep overtook him.

* * * * * *

"Jump up, Lee. It's 1:30, and you wanted me to wake you."

Lee's eyes opened to the sound of Ellen's voice.

"Thanks, Miss Ellen." Lee swung his feet off the bed and started putting on his shoes. "That was just what I needed."

Lee's mind shifted its focus to his next stop, George and Maggie Smith's house. Maggie was one of Lilly's younger sisters, and her influence over Lilly was undeniable. Her husband George had always been nice to him and hopefully would support his efforts to get Maggie on his side.

"Thank you again, Miss Ellen," Lee said as he made his way onto the porch and down the steps. The seats of the Overland had dried completely from the cornstarch treatment and looked almost new again. Even the dark area where Burley Phillips' blood had pooled was hard to see. He cranked the engine and began to pull off.

"Bye, Lee, and thanks for the ride this morning," Anne shouted, still in the swing, waving to him as he pulled off.

Lee waved back.

It was only about ten miles to the Smith home but over some wagon roads not designed for an automobile even when they were dry. Lee limited his speed to 10 miles per hour, and even then, he had to leave the road entirely on several occasions to avoid the deep rainwater-filled pools. These were no problem for a horse-drawn wagon, but they threatened to engulf and stall the Overland engine.

After an excruciating hour that seemed much longer, Lee arrived at his destination around 2:30 p.m.

Cars being a rarity near his farm, George Smith had heard the car coming for over a mile, and he and Maggie were standing on the porch when Lee arrived.

"Well, hello, Lee; what brings you to these parts?" George asked.

"Hey George," Lee answered, smiling. "Hey, Maggie!"

"Hello, Lee," Maggie answered coldly. From the expression on Maggie's face, it was clear to George that she and Lilly had been talking, and he suspected it would take some doing to overcome the cold shoulder Lee was getting.

George stepped off the porch and walked up to the gate just as Lee set the emergency brake. Lee left the car idling, letting the smooth engine noise work its magic and impress his in-laws.

"It looks like you got you a new Ford."

"Nope, not a Ford," Lee responded teasingly.

"What is it, then?" George asked.

"It is a new Baby Overland," Lee answered proudly.

"An Overland, huh? Never heard of one of those; where'd you get it?" George asked as he ran his hand over the door and felt the upholstery.

"I bought it in Milledgeville," Lee lied.

"Milledgeville? Isn't that where you're working?"

"Hell, yeah. Making good money at Mr. Harden's barbershop and pressing club over in nearby Hardwick."

"You must indeed be doing good to afford this baby; what'd ya give fer it?" George asked.

"$1,150," Lee offered, repeating Phillips' original asking price.

"Woo-we, that's a right smart of money, Lee. More'n I can afford, that's fer sure."

Lee smiled proudly. "Well, hell, jump in, and let's take it for a spin."

"Come on, Maggie!" George obligingly said over his shoulder as he ran around the front of the car and got in. She appeared reluctant at first to Lee, but then it seemed she was taken away by her curiosity, and she followed George into the back seat.

Lee noticed George looking all about the interior. He was glad there was no longer any need to explain the distracting bloodstains. That was trouble he didn't need.

George whistled. "Damn, Lee, I ain't never seen no car like this!"

"Wait till you feel the 27 horsepower it has," Lee bragged, putting the car in gear. George laughed with glee as the Overland accelerated up Nevils Daisy Road. It rocked from side to side as they went through a washed-out area. Maggie let out a small scream.

"You okay back there?" George asked.

"I'm fine; I just wasn't ready for that. You tell Lee to be more careful," Maggie said.

George turned to his brother-in-law, "Keep a sharp eye out, Lee. You almost upset the missus. The county don't do much to maintain the roads. We've been pretty much keeping 'em up ourselves, but during the winter, especially with all this rain and cold and no need to go anywhere, it just don't seem to be worth the bother."

"This Overland's got a pretty good suspension system, George. I just have to avoid driving into water that might splash up on the engine and drown her out."

The Baby Overland did its magic on both George and Maggie, and soon the three of them were engaged in a lively conversation about the car and Lee's new job. The subject of Lilly's infection had not come up, much to Lee's relief. Better to impress Lilly's sister with how well he was doing now than to get mired down in his previous bad behavior.

Lee found a wide spot in the road, turned the car around, and stopped. "Wanna drive her?"

George held both hands out in front of him as if to ward off an evil spirit. "Oh, no. I couldn't afford the repair bill if anything were to happen. Besides, nobody has ever taught me how to drive a car. I've only ridden in Mr. Johnson's farm truck a couple of times at most. You remember my neighbor Mr. Johnson, don't you?

"You know how it is out here in the Nevils community. Most everybody is still riding on horseback or in a wagon or a buggy. Some even consider these automobiles to be a public nuisance," George said and laughed.

"Do you consider it a public nuisance, Maggie?" Lee turned and asked.

"I think it's awesome," Maggie giddily replied as she rubbed her hands over the upholstery.

Lee wondered what it was about soft upholstery that was so appealing to women. He hoped it would have the same effect on Lilly.

Lee turned back to watch the road in front of him. He was pleased so far at Maggie's reaction. She was laughing and no longer frowning at him. It appeared his mission here was a complete success. It was time to move on to the next sister, Minnie Brannen.

"George, can you ride with me over to Minnie's house? I don't know where she's living since she got married, and I haven't seen her in a while. I want to see if she'd like a ride in my new car," Lee said.

"I haven't got time, Lee. I am trying to plow a little," George answered.

Maggie jumped in, "Aw, come on, George, let's take him to Minnie's. She has never ridden in a car like this. I'd hate for her to miss out on this opportunity."

Lee tried to suppress a smile. His plan was working out far better than he could have hoped. There was no longer any doubt; what he had to do to get the Overland was well worth it.

"All right, if you want me to go, I'll go over there with you," George said.

"Sure, you don't want to drive it?" Lee asked, feeding George's evident excitement.

"No, I'm fine. You're doing all right by the driving of this thing."

Chapter 17

Minnie Brannen pushed open the front door, summoned by the unusual sound of an automobile horn, and spotted a car coming down the lane. She wiped her hands on her apron and curiously peered into the distance to discern who could be the fancy contraption's owner. Most of the women she knew were married to sharecroppers, and few had farm trucks. Fewer still had automobiles.

However, her husband, George Brannen, owned his farm, which, to her father Solomon Corey, made him a good catch for one of his three daughters. Minnie knew her father had been fully supportive of their union and did not object when George asked for her hand, despite her being the tender age of 14. Here it was less than a year after the marriage, and she believed she was already pregnant, having missed her last period.

Minnie propped up the straw broom she was using to sweep off the porch. She still could not recognize who was in the approaching automobile. Unknown company coming without her husband being home was disquieting. As it became clear that one of the car passengers appeared to be a woman, she relaxed a bit.

As they drew nearer, she first smiled when she recognized it was George Smith and her sister Maggie in the car; however, her smile disappeared when she saw Lee

Currie was driving. Being around her sister Lilly's philandering husband was an encounter she did not want to have.

Minnie had gotten the entire lowdown from her Aunt Sarah on how Lee had recently given her sister the clap. Despite her father Solomon's urging against it, she had joined in the general agreement among the sisters that Lilly should leave Lee. That pact had been stable, or at least she thought it was before seeing the joyful look on Maggie's face as Lee pulled up to the fence that fronted their home.

As if to add insult to injury, Lee pulled the emergency brake, smiled broadly, and blew the horn, prompting Minnie to put her hands to her ears.

"You stop that, Lee Currie! You'll scare the chickens, and I won't get any eggs today," Minnie snapped.

"Just wanted you to hear how the horn of a fine automobile sounded, Minnie. I meant no harm," Lee said and chuckled.

Maggie spoke up, "Oh, Minnie, you have got to come ride in Lee's car. It is more fun than you can imagine. On some of the better roads coming over here, he got it up to 30 miles per hour!"

Minnie was surprised at how her sister was acting, seemingly oblivious to how Lee had cheated on Lilly, "Maggie, you ain't getting me in that thing at 10 miles per hour, much less 30, thank you very much. And what are you doing riding around with Lee Currie, after what he did to our sister!"

"That's all over, Minnie," Lee said. "Lilly decided she wanted to stay married to me, and the divorce suit was dismissed by Judge Hardeman on Wednesday."

"So, you say, but I ain't 'bout to believe that till I hear it from Lilly's mouth," Minnie said dismissively.

Maggie dropped her eyes from Minnie's as if finally remembering their pact. George jumped in, "Minnie, let's not get in between a man and his wife. Remember what your pa said – that's for them to work out. Now, don't be silly. Lee is a good driver. You come on down here and get in this car right now."

Minnie's curiosity and George's insistence caused her to weaken a bit. "I've got washing to do, George. Some of us have chores, you know. If my husband comes out of the fields and finds his clothes are not ready for Sunday church day after tomorrow, I'll never hear the end of it!"

Maggie jumped in, "You have all day Saturday to tend to the washing, Minnie. How often do you have an opportunity to go riding in a car like this? You know the Corey women's husbands don't have no cars as nice as this one. Come on and ride with us."

"I ain't a mind to go no 30 miles per hour, Maggie Smith," Minnie protested weakly.

"I promise I won't go that fast, Minnie," Lee ensured.

Maggie was right. Lee's family did have lots of money, and Lilly would not have to struggle like she and her sister were struggling. Her husband was hardworking but having something takes a long time when you start with nothing.

"Okay, if you and your George are gonna keep pestering me 'bout it. Let me leave my George a note," Minnie said and turned to go into the house. Inside, she peeked through the window. She had reservations about going on a ride with Lee Currie, but Minnie could see that her sister was excited and having a good time. She didn't want to be a stick-in-the-mud, and she had never been in a car like that. Minnie quickly penned a note to her husband, removed her apron, and grabbed her shawl. She decided to comb her hair a bit and put on some rouge. There was no sense being seen in one of the only automobiles in Bulloch County looking like you had been washing clothes. She stepped out of the house, closed the door behind her, and stepped slowly down the front porch steps.

"Let her sit upfront, where she can see better," Lee said to his front-seat passenger.

"Good idea," George said. "I need to see if it feels as good in the back as it does in the front anyway."

"There are other good reasons you need to sit back here with me, my little lamb skin," Maggie teased.

"I'm your huckleberry," George said.

Minnie saw George wink at Lee, who winked back, and crawled over the seat, flopping into the back seat with his head falling into Maggie's lap to her girlish giggles.

"You crazy animal!" Maggie exclaimed.

"How come I'm sitting in the front?" Minnie asked.

"You don't think for a minute I'm going to let you sit in the back seat of an automobile with my husband, do you, Minnie? This man has my brand on 'em," Maggie said, to howls of laughter from everyone in the car.

Minnie turned to Lee, "Don't you scare me now, Lee Currie. I've been riding wagons and buggies all my life, but I have been curious about these here automobiles. Don't you be turning me agin 'em, you hear me?"

"You'll think I'm a hearse driver, Minnie," Lee said, smiling at the irony of his having used the car as a temporary hearse to transport Burley Phillips to his burial site. He put the car into reverse.

Despite being a married lady, Minnie was still a young teenager, and the automobile did excite her. She could not hide her glee. Before he gave her sister the clap, Minnie had a crush on Lee. She was 11 when Lee and Lilly were married, and Lee was the most handsome man she had ever seen. She wanted to be mad at him for his mischief with other women other than her sister, but the feeling of freedom offered by the wind blowing through her hair made it difficult to be angry at anyone.

She held both hands out the window as the Overland glided over the dirt roads of Bulloch County and diverted the chilly air into the car's body where she could deeply inhale it. She closed her eyes and took a refreshing breath.

"Stick a cork in that polar bear's arse, Minnie – damn!" George said, immediately wincing as Maggie slapped him on the wrist.

Minnie pulled her hands back in the car and grinned toward her brother-in-law in the back seat, who had his hand just a little too far up his sister's skirt for mixed company.

"You bad boy!" Minnie said.

"Eyes forward, little sister," Maggie said, giggling.

They rode for over an hour all over Bulloch County, stopping several times when they would see someone they knew outside.

Minnie kept curiously glancing back at George and Maggie. It was clear that George was enjoying more than just the automobile ride. The car brought out a wild side of Maggie, and he took advantage of every minute of it.

"Lee, iffin a car like this can add this much spirit to my lady here, well, maybe it's time for me to start saving up my money! Come here, you sweet thang you," George said as he pulled Maggie toward him.

"Not in front of Minnie, George; you stop it now," Maggie said and giggled.

There was something on the floorboard that caught George's eye. Following his gaze, Minnie looked down behind the seat. "Is that a pipe?"

George reached down and picked it up. It was indeed a pipe, and a Prince Albert tin was beside it. "Well, lookee here at what I found ... a pipe and some tobakee! Lee, you don't smoke. What's this here pipe doing back here?"

"The man I bought it from left it behind. You can have it if you want it," Lee said.

"Well, okie, dokie, I think I'll smoke some," George said.

"Aw, honey, do you have to light up that stinky thing?" Maggie cooed with a disappointed look.

George winked at her, "It gets me excited, honey!"

He tapped out the tobacco to fill the bowl of the pipe. Flipping the lid of the tin shut, he struck a match on his shoe and lit it up. George took a deep draw and blew it out in the front seat's direction, causing Minnie to waive the smoke frantically away from her nose.

"George! Blow that ding dang smoke out the side," Minnie protested.

George laughed and turned to Maggie. "It tastes good, honey. Even better when it's on my lips, come here and see." He puckered up, shut his eyes, and moved toward his wife.

"I'd just as soon lick an ashtray when you light one of those things up, George. If you want any of these lips, you'll douse that stupid thing," Maggie pouted.

George laughed and emptied the pipe bowl out the car's side. "You happy now?"

"That's my sugar," Maggie said and put her arms around him.

Despite her earlier prohibition, Lee showed Minnie what the Overland would do and even got the car up to 30 mph on one stretch of well-maintained road near Statesboro. No reminders of the speed limitation came from her. Minnie loved every minute she was in the Overland automobile. It was a lot smoother ride than could be had in the fanciest buggy in which she had ever been and certainly a lot smoother than she experienced going to town in a wagon.

She was never going to have it this easy. It was only fair that at least one of the Corey girls got to have a pampered and fun life, and if that awful disease had made her sister barren, well, there was something to be said for not having another kid arriving every year in the fall.

Minnie was disappointed when Lee finally drove her back home. She made her farewells, and George jumped back into the front seat. As they went away, Minnie thought, *I'm really happy for Lilly. Lee's not so bad a husband, after all.* She turned and walked up the porch and entered the house.

* * * * * *

All the talking and laughter proved that Lee's mission to restore relations with Lilly's family was working. He was having a good day.

"Be sure to take that pipe with you; it's yours," Lee told George.

"All right, I appreciate it, brother. Can I have this tin of tobacco, too?"

"Sure, I'm not a pipe man myself. You make good use of it," Lee said.

"I'm bad about biting my pipes, so I'll put me a bit of string around the stem to protect it," George said.

"I hope you get a lot of enjoyment out of it," Lee offered.

As George and Maggie were getting out of the back seat, Lee asked his sister-in-law, "You think your pa is home about now?"

"He should be. He stays pretty close to home these days, 'ceptin he needs to make a trip to the hospital in Glennville tomorrow to see my stepmom. She's been real sick, you know."

"Sorry to hear that," Lee said.

"I speck he might appreciate your taking him in this car since it is a lot faster than going by wagon," Maggie replied.

"Good idea; that will give us some good talking time," Lee said.

The young couple waved at Lee as he rode off toward Register to the home of Solomon Corey, Lilly's father.

George and Maggie lingered on the front porch and watched Lee drive away.

"You know, Lee can be a lot of fun to be around when he's in a good mood, and that new car has sure got him flying high," George commented.

"Yep. he's a hoot all right when he is in a good mood. I just hope, for Lilly's sake, if she takes him back, that dark side doesn't raise its ugly head again," Maggie added, staring at the receding cloud behind the Overland speeding off in the distance.

"They will do fine. We all got a dark side that comes out every now and then," George said as he turned to his wife. "And we got a sexy side that comes out every now and then, too. Come here, woman."

Maggie giggled and broke for the front door, with George in close pursuit.

Lee hurried down the road toward Solomon Corey's home. He knew that Mr. Corey had been very supportive of his marriage to Lilly. Just two days before, he had talked Lilly out of divorcing him, just as he had done two years earlier when she first tried to leave him during their honeymoon year. Lilly's pa was indeed his ally and could be the key to getting Lilly's entire family firmly in his corner. With her family telling her to make nice to him and the Baby

Overland showing her how prosperous she could be in their marriage; he was sure to get their union back on track.

It was going to work; he just knew it.

Chapter 18

Lee felt confident as he drove to his father-in-law's house in Register. While it was true that Solomon had rescued his relationship with Lilly twice now, he needed his help yet again to get fully back in the family's good graces. He needed the help of all the family in convincing Lilly to go to Milledgeville, and he certainly didn't want the family members talking bad about him behind his back.

His time driving George, Maggie, and Minnie around had been a success, but the essential convert he needed was still ahead. He had purposely but inconspicuously driven by Solomon Corey's house several times during their ride, hoping his father-in-law might be near the barn or in one of his fields and see him riding with his daughters.

At around 7:00 p.m., the sun dropped below the horizon, and Lee turned on the lights of the Overland. Knowing Solomon was in the habit of going to bed early urged him to drive faster. However, ferrying Burley Phillip's body the night before over the poorly maintained muddy roads had taught him the folly of overdriving the lights of the Overland, and he dared go no faster.

The light coming from Solomon's front living room caused him to give a sigh of relief as he pulled into the front yard. No sooner than he had stopped, turned off the lights, and killed the engine, the front door opened, and his father-in-law appeared, holding an oil lamp before him. Lee swallowed hard.

"Who's that come a calling on me at this hour?" Solomon called out, peering around the oil lamp.

"It's your son-in-law, Mr. Corey. It's Lee Currie."

"Lee? What are you doing here? Is something wrong with Lilly?" Solomon asked anxiously.

"No, Mr. Corey, nothing's wrong. I apologize for visiting you so late. I came by earlier, but it looked as if you weren't home."

"So, that was you speeding by here this afternoon like some maniac. I was here, not that you could have known, fast as you were going," Solomon said sternly.

"Those daughters of yours were egging me on, Mr. Corey. They was encouraging me to go fast. I'm sorry I missed you."

"My daughters? I don't appreciate you driving that fast with them in that car. Well, no matter. Come on in, Lee. It's cold out, and I've got a fire going."

Lee strode up the porch steps, shook his father-in-law's hand, and followed him inside. If there was any pent-up anger in Solomon's countenance about his giving Lilly a venereal disease, it was not evident.

Lee and Solomon talked for over an hour. Lee was relieved that there was no doubt that Lilly's father supported him and Lilly getting back together. During the divorce proceedings, Solomon spoke up and told the judge that Lee and Lilly needed to get on with their life together. Lee's earlier apprehension gave way to the comforting realization that Solomon was a poor farmer with eight children, and three of them were daughters that needed husbands.

This was one time that Lee was glad to be John Currie's son. As he looked around the modest dwelling where Lilly and her sisters grew up, he began to appreciate the stark contrast between this humble abode and meager farm and the Currie family's larger and more prosperous one. It was evident that his family's circumstances had motivated Solomon to support the continuation of the marriage to ensure his daughter's financial security.

"I understand that you might be looking for a ride to Glennville tomorrow to see Mrs. Corey in the hospital. That right?" Lee asked.

"Yep, Bob Kerby is going to take me in the buckboard," Solomon said.

"I can get you there much faster in my car, Mr. Corey if you'll let me. I'd like to drive you over there. It'll give us a chance to talk some more," Lee said.

"That sounds good, Lee. I'm curious what it would be like going for a ride in that car, that's for sure, but I'll have to get word to Bob where he doesn't make a trip over here for nothing."

"That's no problem. I'm spending the night with him. I can tell him," Lee said.

"Okay, that'll work out good. Goin' in your car will let me do my visiting and git back early enough to tend to some chores I'd otherwise have to put off. Can you come get me early? Anne has promised to fix breakfast for Bob and me. I wouldn't want to miss out on her cooking," Solomon asked.

"Sure 'nuff can. I'll come to get you about daylight," Lee said.

After another quarter-hour or so, Lee said his goodbyes. He was smiling as he drove back to Bob's house.

The Kerby's were still up, but it had been a long day, and they didn't talk long. Lee turned in for some much-needed sleep. It had been a productive day for him, and he was feeling good about his chances of reuniting with his wife. Most of her family was now supporting him. He slept soundly that night.

* * * * *

Lee did not need an alarm to wake him up at the crack of dawn Saturday morning. He arose, washed his face, dressed, and then drove to Solomon's home. Despite the cold, his father-in-law was waiting for him on the front porch.

Lee was looking forward to giving his father-in-law a ride to the hospital. The drive would be a further opportunity to seal the deal and firmly recruit his father-in-law as his chief ally in getting Lilly comfortable about coming back to him. People were more easily persuaded when you showed them a little kindness during times of sickness and distress. They were talking and laughing as they arrived at Bob's house.

"Working people would have been up long before now," Solomon loudly announced as they entered the house.

Anne and Bob both began to stir.

"It's a Saturday, in the dead of winter, Solomon. Today is one of the few lazy days we have on this farm," Bob groaned as he wiped the sleep from his eyes.

"There ain't no lazy days for a real farmer," Solomon teased.

"Good morning, Mr. Corey," Anne said as she put on a thick pink robe and stepped into her slippers. Lee smiled as he saw her glance in the mirror and quickly run a hairbrush through her hair. Ah, the vanity of women, he thought.

"You ready for that breakfast I promised?" Anne asked.

"Brought a big appetite with me, Anne," Solomon answered.

Lee held his hands out before the glowing embers in the fireplace of the main room.

"That fire is going to need kicking up a bit," Solomon remarked as he looked for firewood.

"I'm afraid I'll need to go fetch some more wood," Bob said.

"You weren't kidding about being lazy," Solomon chuckled.

"I can get it if you want to finish getting dressed," Lee offered.

"No, I've got it, Lee, but I'll need to feed the chickens too, so you two early birds just grin and bear the chill for a bit," Bob said as he bundled up and headed for the door.

Anne came from the bedroom and headed for the kitchen. "Good morning, Lee. You're up mighty early. You headed out already?"

"I'm taking Mr. Corey here to see Jeanette in the hospital in Glennville," Lee said, following her to the kitchen.

Lee watched Anne as she put some paper under the kindling in the stove firebox, lit it, slid the ventilation slide to the right, and opened the damper.

"Oh? I thought Bob was going to take him," Anne said as she blew out the match, waved it to cool the ember, and tossed it into the ash bucket. She added some water from the well-bucket to the coffee pot and set it on the stove's top.

"I can get him there quicker, and it will give us a chance to talk," Lee responded. He pulled out a chair at the dining room table and settled into it to watch her prepare breakfast.

Anne's sister Elizabeth had been Solomon's wife. She had died on November 27th two years earlier, and Solomon had married Jeanette Smiley from Tattnall County in June of the following year.

"She probably won't know you are there, I'm afraid. She's bad sick, Lee. I have been praying for her to recover every day. Poor Mr. Corey lost my sister a couple of years ago, and now Jeanette is bad sick – only eight months into their marriage," Anne said in hushed tones, where her brother-in-law could not hear her in the next room.

The kindling had already begun to brightly burn when she added a larger piece of wood, regulated the damper, and slid the vent over. The stovetop heated quickly. She effortlessly and skillfully began cracking eggs with one hand on the side of the frying pan. He loved the sizzling sound they made as they slid out of the shell and landed on the cast iron skillet.

"Bob and Solomon like their eggs scrambled. That okay for you, Lee?"

"Like 'em best that way," Lee answered.

Bob entered the kitchen with a load of wood and placed it in the wood box. He slapped his hands together to knock off the wood particles, then spread them out, palms facing the stove.

"Brrrrr, it's colder than a witch's tit in a brass bra out there!" he said.

"Bob!" Ann scolded as she continued to scramble the eggs. Lee chuckled.

"Well, it is cold," Bob smiled and said as he sat down at the breakfast table.

"Don't sit down just yet. Go stoke up the big fire like you promised and warm yerself in yonder with Mr. Corey if you don't mind, while I finish cooking you boys some breakfast," Anne said, playfully pushing him out of her way.

Bob slapped her on the backside.

"Bob!" Anne giggled, "You behave!" she turned and added some bacon strips to the frying pan.

"Come on, Lee. Let's get out of Anne's kitchen and let her do her magic."

Lee followed Bob into the main room, sat down, and watched him stir the remains of last evening's fire. The smoldering embers leaped back to life as soon as Bob added some fresh oak. Bob poked it about to position the wood just right, placed the poke to the side, and settled himself into his rocker. He took out a pipe from the side table, sprinkled some Prince Albert tobacco in the bowl, lit it, drew a long puff, and blew it out slowly. The fire's light gave an amber cast to the smoke as it spread slowly and randomly toward the ceiling.

"Tobacco?" Bob offered the red tin to Solomon.

"Don't mind if I do," Solomon responded and took out a pipe from his overalls.

Solomon offered tobacco to Lee.

"Never took it up, Mr. Corey," Lee responded.

Bob looked at him questioningly but then turned back to the fire and took another puff.

There was something about smoking that just seemed proof of manhood, but Lee had never acquired a taste for it. His lungs just rebelled whenever he tried to master the unnatural process of deliberately inhaling the acrid smoke from burning tobacco. His pa would berate him for not taking up the habit when so much of their farm income depended upon their tobacco crop, so, not smoking was another way to protest his father's domination. He was okay with being the only man he knew besides his best friend, Clarence James, who didn't smoke.

"I know what you are doing, Lee," Bob said reflectively, staring at the flickering flames.

Lee looked at him with a puzzled look.

"Lilly's done left you over that business with that tart up in Milledgeville, and you're trying to get Solomon here to help you get back into her good graces."

Lee was speechless. Was his plan that obvious?

Bob turned to him. "Don't deny it, Lee. Me and Solomon figured that out right away, which wasn't hard, given that the womenfolk have been squawking about it ever since they found out you gave Lilly the clap."

Lee blushed, unprepared for this frank talk in front of Lilly's father. "It was just a one-night stand, Uncle Bob. It didn't mean nothing. If Lilly had come with me to Milledgeville, it would never have happened," Lee whined.

Solomon added, "I must defend my son-in-law on that one, Bob. A man ought not be left by himself too long aftern' he's had a taste of married life. Especially a young man. It's just asking for trouble."

Bob chuckled, "Afraid I'll have to agree with you there, Solomon. We men can't be trusted, and the womenfolk know it. Even at my age, Anne watches me like a hawk at church to make sure none of those lonely widows turn my head."

Lee laughed nervously. He was not expecting this assistance from Bob with Solomon.

"Looks like Solomon here understands the situation, Lee. Us menfolk must stick together when one of us errs. She'll come around. Her pa has always been a powerful force to all his daughters."

"Well, I'm most grateful," Lee said, breathing a sigh of relief.

"Breakfast is ready!" Anne called out from the kitchen.

* * * * * *

Lee and Solomon took turns hugging Anne and thanking her for breakfast before they stepped out onto the porch into the chilly February air.

As they walked over and got into the Overland, Lee said, "That Anne sure cooks a mighty fine breakfast."

"That's for sure," Solomon agreed as he sat down and pulled the car door shut. "Her mother raised her to be a good wife. As it says in Chapter 2 of Titus, 'And so train the young women to love their husbands and children, to be self-controlled, pure, working at home, kind, and submissive to their own husbands, that the word of God may not be reviled.'"

"You both come from good stock there, Mr. Corey," Lee responded. He smiled at the thought of his father-in-law recalling a Bible verse that bolstered his case even more. He suspected that Solomon was mulling over in his mind what he was going to tell Lilly to get her to come back to her husband.

"And I can see your good influence on Lilly. She's making me a good wife."

Lee backed the car up and turned it toward Glennville. His father-in-law's responses when Bob brought up the infidelity this morning and the Bible quote he recited as he got into the car convinced him that Solomon was firmly in his corner.

"Are the roads better to go through Daisy or Claxton?" Lee asked.

"I don't think I'd recommend taking this nice car through Daisy, Lee. You better stick to the Claxton Road. The county keeps it maintained a bit better," Solomon offered helpfully.

"Well, it's well-nigh over thirty miles to the hospital, but we should be there in just over an hour," Lee said.

Solomon shook his head in amazement. "That's just hard to believe, Lee. Going to Glennville in a buggy is easily a four-hour ride if you give the horses a decent rest along the way. In Bob's wagon, with them mules, it takes us at least five hours one way."

"Yep, this here car is definitely the way to go," Lee offered.

As they rode along the bumpy dirt road, Lee noticed that Solomon looked the car over with that awe that comes when one's ideas about transportation are in the process of being updated by modern technology. He turned around to check out the back, and his eyes came to rest on the stains on the fabric. Lee could read his father-in-law's thoughts.

"Yeah, I know, I've already abused it a bit, hauling a hog in here," Lee responded.

"A hog? What in tarnation?" Solomon asked.

"I ran over him by accident, and the man what owned him demanded I pay him $11.00 for it and get it off his property, son-of-a-bitch."

"Language, Lee. I don't cotton to that kind of talk."

"Sorry, Mr. Corey, my tongue gets ahead of my manners sometimes when I'm riled up."

"So, this is a bloodstain?" Solomon asked. "You can hardly tell it."

"Anne helped me clean most of it out yesterday afternoon with some cornstarch."

"What'd you do with the hog?" Solomon asked.

"It wouldn't stop bleeding, so I throwed it in a creek," Lee answered.

"I wouldn't of done that, waste of good meat," Solomon said, marking the third time Lee had heard that admonition.

Lee's father-in-law continued to survey the car. Lee was sure Solomon had never been in a conveyance like the Overland. Most likely, horses and mules had been the primary means for him to get about all his life. This car probably was a marvel he never thought he'd live to see. Lee could sense it as Solomon's eyes came to rest on the car's side pocket next to Lee's left leg.

"Those side pockets good for storing anything?" Solomon asked.

Lee took the gun from the side pocket and waved it in the air proudly, "Yep, it's where I keep my gun, Mr. Corey. It's a blue steel Smith & Wesson Model 1917. I got it from the Minter-Smith Hardware Store in Lyons just last month. What do you think?"

"I think you better stop waving it around and concentrate instead of driving this car!" Solomon said.

Lee returned the gun to the side pocket, smiling.

"Lee, you had better be careful how you tote a gun without what you got a license to carry it. It's a violation of the law," Solomon said.

"I carry the license, Mr. Corey. Don't worry. I'm all legal," Lee lied.

As they arrived on Claxton's outskirts, Lee pulled out the pocket watch he had taken from Burley's body and checked on the time.

"We're here in Claxton already, Solomon," Lee said, using his father-in-law's first name now that he knew he would help him get Lilly back.

"That's a nice watch, Lee, that new?" Solomon inquired.

"Just got it Thursday," Lee said truthfully. "It's a lot more precise than my old watch."

Lee flipped open the back with his thumb and held it up where Solomon could see it. "Lookie here, Mr. Corey, it's got all them jewels that make it more accurate. The man what I got it from said it had 18 of 'em," Lee extended the watch toward Solomon.

Solomon held up his hand, warding off the offered watch, "I wouldn't be knowin' nothing 'bout watches. Never found the need to carry one myself. Ole Clarence, my rooster, tells me when to get up, and Millie, my cow, tells me when it's time to milk. Between them and the sun, the good Lord makes sure I know what time it is."

Lee put Burley's watch back in his pocket and took out his watch from his other pocket. "But watches are really helpful. You can have my old watch if you want it."

"No, thank you, Lee. Like I said, I've made it this far without one, and I don't want to have to worry with one now," Solomon refused politely.

Entering Claxton, Lee pulled the car into a gas station to fill up. He pulled out the money he had taken from Burley.

"Can I get you a Coca Cola?" Lee asked.

"Well, thank you, Lee. I'll take a Hires Root Beer if they have it; otherwise, an RC Cola would be nice," Solomon said.

"Comin' right up," Lee said as he exited the car and went into the station. He was very pleased with himself. No doubt, Solomon could see that Lee was doing well, what with this new car, a new gold watch, and all. He had purposely pulled out the roll of money to impress upon him his success with his new job in Milledgeville.

It was also increasingly apparent to Lee that Solomon fully believed that Lee could provide Lilly with those nice things he couldn't afford for his wife or children.

The attendant came out and wiped his hands on a very greasy shop rag, "How can I help you fellas today?"

"Five gallons will do it," Lee said.

The attendant nodded and started pulling the long lever that pumped gas into the glass cylinder mounted on the pump. As it reached the five-gallon mark, he stopped, put the nozzle in the Overland, and started dispensing the gas. Afterward, he returned the nozzle to the pump's side, replaced the gas cap, and turned to Lee.

"Let's see, that'll be $1.50 for the gas, twelve cents for the two drinks, and a nickel for the Moon Pie. That comes to a total of $1.67, mister," the attendant said.

"Here you go," Lee said, pulling two dollars from his money roll. The attendant reached down to the coin handler on his waist and clicked out a quarter, a nickel, and three pennies.

"Thank you, sir. Y'all have a nice day now. Stay warm!" He turned quickly and trotted back to the warmth of the gas station.

"A Moon Pie," Solomon said, pleasantly surprised. "I had a nice breakfast, but I can always make room for one of these.

"That's quite a money roll you got there, Lee. You ought not to be flashing that around. Somebody will be done knocked you in the head and taken it from you."

"Yeah, I know; Uncle Bob has already warned me about it. I do need to be more careful," Lee said, pleased that Solomon had noticed the money.

"You must be doing all right at your new job, huh?" Solomon asked.

"Oh, yes I am. How do you think I was able to buy this car? I'm making good money now," Lee replied.

Solomon took a bite from his moon pie. Lee was confident that his father-in-law felt good about having married his daughter off to a member of a good family. He was optimistic that Solomon would help convince Lilly that she needed to forget about her attempt to leave her prosperous husband.

They chatted nonstop as they drove to the hospital in Glennville, mostly making small talk about farming, Georgia politics, and the weather.

Anne was right. She had told Lee that Jeanette was severely sick. Mrs. Corey did not acknowledge either of them when they entered her room at the hospital, but the doctor told Solomon not to worry, that she would pull through. Still, it was evident that Jeanette's sickness upset the man who had already lost one wife to disease. Unlike their drive over, silence prevailed as they drove back to Register.

Chapter 19

"Lee Currie, you git right back in that shiny new automobile and get the hell off my property," Lee heard Sarah Smith shout from her front porch. As he emerged from the Overland, he found himself looking straight down the barrel of a double-barreled shotgun.

Lee nervously took off his cap. "My business is with Lilly, Mrs. Smith. Will you tell her I'm out here, please?"

"Lilly ain't got no desire to see you, Lee. Now git before I blow you to kingdom come!" Sarah said, pulling back both hammers of the shotgun.

Lee held up his hands defensively, "Now, Mrs. Smith, you calm down. I ain't gonna harm her, and I got every right to talk to her; she's my wife!"

"You lost your rights to call her that when you screwed that whore in Milledgeville and gave Lilly the clap, you son-of-a-bitch! On account of you, she may never be able to have children. I ought to cut you in half where you stand!" Sarah intimidatingly leaned forward, with the shotgun still pointed at him.

"Lilly! Lilly! YOU IN THERE!" Lee shouted desperately.

BLAM!

Leaves flew everywhere as Sarah discharged the shotgun into the tree above Lee's head. Lee hit the ground and covered his head.

He raised his head and looked at her, "Damn it, woman, you scared the crap out of me!"

The screen door flew open, and Lilly came running out. "Don't shoot him, Aunt Sarah!" She stood behind her aunt, looking nervously over her shoulder.

Sarah was still pointing the shotgun at Lee. "You better git from here before you git shot. She ain't wantin' to talk to you or have anything else to do with you. She's divorcing you."

"No, she ain't, not no more. Judge Hardeman dismissed her divorce this past Wednesday," Lee responded.

"I ain't listening to any of your lies, Lee Currie. Get off my property!"

The faces of Sarah's five kids, Alma, Junior, Wallon, Sallie Kate, and little Bertie Mae, spilled out onto the porch in their nightclothes, drawn by the shotgun blast.

"Lilly, please, let me talk to you a minute, just a minute; you owe me that," Lee pleaded.

Sarah kept standing between Lilly and Lee, "I said to git, and you need to git, Lee."

Raymond Smith came rushing out on the porch. Immediately assessing the situation, he wrestled the shotgun from Sarah. "Have you lost your mind, woman? Get back in the house!"

Raymond turned to the children and shouted, "ALMA ... JUNIOR ... WALLON ... SALLIE KATE ... BERTIE MAE ... BACK IN THE HOUSE, NOW!" The children banged into each other in their mad rush to go inside.

"I ain't leaving this porch 'til that bastard leaves this property," Sarah snarled.

"I just want to talk to my wife, Mr. Smith. I just want to talk. I ain't here to cause no trouble. I just want to talk's all," Lee said plaintively.

"Over my dead body," Sarah surged forward again, and Raymond restrained her. "Talking's done!"

"Sarah, he wants to talk. They's still married, and this is betwixt them. Now you get inside!" Sarah did not move. "Now! I ain't telling ya again!" Raymond said.

Sarah stared at Lee menacingly but still did not move. Lee lowered his head back down to the ground submissively.

"Sarah," Raymond said gently but authoritatively, "Go back inside like I told you. They'll be alright. I'm not going to let anything happen to your niece."

Sarah glared at her husband for a long moment. Measuring his firm resolve, she then looked back at Lee. "Alright, I'm going inside, but he ain't taking her from this house, Raymond Smith – he ain't taking her; I mean it now." With that, she turned and stormed into the house.

The door slammed behind her. Lee looked up humbly, saying nothing. Seeing that Sarah was no longer a threat, he slowly stood up and brushed himself off.

Lilly looked up, too, then back down. Lee could see that she was visibly shaking, and he suspected it was not from the February chill.

"It's alright, Lilly; I just want to talk, that's all," Lee said to his wife.

"Lilly, you want to talk to him, Honey? You don't have to iffin you don't want to. It's your call," Raymond said gently.

Lilly moved to the porch swing and sat down. For a moment, she said nothing. Then she looked up and said, "I'll talk to him, as long as he stays in the yard. I don't want him touching me."

Raymond turned to Lee, "You going to have to talk this out on her terms, Lee. You agree to that?"

"Yes, sir, Mr. Smith, whatever she wants," Lee said, spinning his cap nervously between his fingers.

"SARAH, BRING LILLY A SHAWL," Raymond called out.

In a few moments, Sarah appeared at the door and glared at Lee as she handed her husband the shawl. Raymond nodded to her, nudged her back inside, and closed the door. He gave the shawl to Lilly.

"Thank you," Lilly said, wrapping the garment around her shoulders, still staring down at the porch.

"Lee, I'm going to leave you out here to talk like two adults. I want you to respect Lilly's wishes that you stay out there in the yard," Raymond turned to Lilly.

"Lilly, Honey, I'll be right inside. If you need me, you just call out or knock on the side of the house, and I'll be back out here lickety-split. You understand?" Raymond asked

"Yes, sir," Lilly said weakly.

"You sure now?" Raymond asked.

"Yes, sir. I'm okay. I'll be fine," Lilly looked up at him and smiled.

Raymond turned again to Lee. "You behave, Lee Currie." Then he turned and went into the house.

* * * * * *

There were no insect sounds in the chilly February air. There were no cars or horses, or neighbors sitting on their porches talking. No sounds were coming from inside the house as Sarah and Raymond were sitting in the living room, carefully listening for raised voices. There was nothing but the deafening sound of silence.

"Well?" Lilly finally said.

Lee said nothing.

"You gonna talk or ain't cha?"

"I knew what I was going to say on the way over here, Lilly, but now, I ain't got no words."

"Well, you better come up with some, or I'm going back inside. It's cold out here."

"Why didn't you come to the courthouse last Wednesday," Lee asked.

Lilly was silent for a long minute, leaving Lee to speculate nervously on what she was thinking.

"Pa talked me out of going through with the divorce."

Good old Solomon, Lee thought to himself. He decided to press his luck, "You sure it was your pa? Or was it something else?"

"Like what?"

"Like, maybe that you still love me a little bit?"

"Lee, you gave me the clap!" Lilly started to cry.

"Ah, Lilly, don't start crying now. That ain't gonna help nothin'," Lee said as he moved toward the steps.

"You stay in that yard, Lee Currie, or I'll scream," Lilly said between her sobs.

Lee immediately stepped back, "I'm back in the yard, I'm back, don't scream, Lilly, I'm back in the yard."

"How could you do that to me? The doctor told me I may never be able to have children now."

"Doctors don't know everything, Lilly. Lots of women have had that shit before, hell, they say it's all over Lyons."

"Not among decent women, it ain't," Lilly said as she continued to cry. "It's a whore's disease, Lee, and you gave it to me – TO ME! Your wife!"

Lee didn't know what to say. He couldn't understand the medical hoopla over this clap business. But he knew he wasn't the first person to catch it and wouldn't be the last.

He thought about the Overland. He walked over to it and took on the countenance of a used car salesman making a pitch.

"Honey, look here at this car I got for us. It's a 1920 Baby Overland automobile. It's got 27 horsepower, and I've had it up to over 30 miles per hour. You ought to let me ..."

"Lee, you gave me that awful disease. and now you are talking about a car, like me not being able to have children ain't nothing! Are you listening to me?"

Lee hung his head. "I'm sorry about that, Lilly, I'm really sorry, and I'm trying real hard to make it up to you. I got us this here car and ..."

"We probably won't be able to have a family, Lee. I don't give a damn about that stupid car; you've ruined me!" Lilly started crying again.

Lee began to spin the hat in his fingers and looked at Lilly and then the car, then back at Lilly, then the car again.

"But I thought you would like the car, Lilly. It's a Baby Overland," Lee said, almost whimpering.

"A baby Overland, a BABY Overland!" Lilly stood up. "Well, I'm glad you have a baby Overland because it's the only baby you are ever going to get from this marriage!" Lilly sat back forcefully in the swing, which yawed wildly and hit the side of the house.

Raymond opened the door and peered out, "Lilly, is everything alright?"

Lilly looked up, wiping away tears, "I'm sorry, Uncle Raymond, I didn't mean to hit the house with the swing. I'm okay."

"Remember what I said, Lee. You behave now," Raymond said, as he looked first at Lee, then back at Lilly. Then he stepped back inside and pulled the door shut again.

Lee was nonplussed at how women were so perplexing and challenging to predict, much less control. He didn't know what to do. The Overland, the car of his dreams, the car he had killed someone to get, seemed to have no effect on Lilly.

He tried a different tactic, "Honey, I know you will be happy up in Milledgeville. I've got a good job with Mr. Harden, and the room at the Sanitarium is great. John Blackstone's wife is up there too. Y'all be best friends, and they've got two kids. You could be like an aunt to them ..."

"Lee, I don't want to be an aunt to somebody else's kids. I wanted my kids, our kids!" Lilly put her face into her hands, sobbing again.

"Well, damn. Okay, I done messed up, I know that, but there ain't nothin' I can do about it now. Hell, lots of people don't have kids. We could even adopt some. It'll be okay. You'll love Milledgeville; it's got a theater that shows movies, and a dance hall, and ..."

"Yeah, I know about your dance hall, alright," Lilly said sarcastically.

"Shit, I can't say nothing right, but dammit, Lilly, I want you with me up in Milledgeville. We're married, goddammit, we got married in a church, with a pastor and everything, and the Lord's blessings. We took vows, Lilly!"

"You use the Lord's name in vain and then talk about his blessings on our marriage in the same breath? And your marriage vows didn't stop you from laying with that whore, did it? No, it didn't. You violated your vows, and now you want me to honor mine?

"You don't own me, Lee. And I ain't ready to go with you to Milledgeville. I may have agreed to stop the divorce, but I'm not sure I will EVER be ready to go with you anywhere. I just got to think about this, that's all, and I ain't sure what I'll be deciding. But one thing's for sure. I ain't ready to be living with you right now," Lilly said determinedly.

Despite the warning from Raymond, Lee could feel his anger rising. Lilly was his wife, and her place was with him. He took a step onto the porch.

"Dammit, Lilly, you are my wife, and you need to stop this nonsense and come with me, NOW!" Lee shouted.

Lilly screamed.

The front door bolted open, and this time it was Raymond with the shotgun. He pointed it right at Lee. Sarah stepped out onto the porch behind Raymond, glaring at Lee.

"Lee, I told you to behave. Now I'm going to have to ask you to leave my property," Raymond said firmly.

Lee thought about the gun in the car. He would have an excuse for killing these people now, and it would be self-defense, for sure. He turned and went quickly to the car.

But Raymond followed him close behind right up to the car, standing just a few feet away, shotgun aimed right at Lee's head, giving him no quarter.

He's got the drop on me this time, Lee thought.

"Alright, I'm going," Lee said as he cranked up the Overland, backed out, and stopped for a moment.

Raymond did not lower the gun.

"Lilly, your place is with me, and don't you ever forget it," Lee shouted.

"You go to hell, Lee Currie!" Sarah yelled.

"Git on, now, Lee. It's time for you to go," said Raymond calmly.

Lee floored the Overland, and dirt flew from the tires as it sped away.

* * * * * *

"My life is over," Lilly cried as she buried her head in Sarah's chest.

"No, baby girl, you just got your life back," Sarah said as she stroked her niece's hair.

Raymond Smith lowered the shotgun. He watched the taillights of the Overland fade from view.

"No good is ever going to come from that boy," he said as he turned, walked up the steps, and put his arm around Lilly.

"Come on, girl, the excitement's over. Let's go inside and get you warmed up again."

Chapter 20

There was no use returning to Sarah Smith's place to talk to Lilly again today. Lilly had made it clear the day before that she wasn't going with Lee back to Milledgeville. He was beyond discouraged and beyond angry. Lee had descended into a deep dark depression now that his plan was completely falling apart. Most hurtful was that despite all he had done to secure it, Lilly wouldn't even look at the Overland. Everything had just gone to crap.

He was now beginning to worry about losing his job with Mr. Harden at the Hardwick Barbershop and Pressing Club. He didn't ask his boss for any time off to go to court, and he had been gone almost a week. He couldn't afford to spend any more time coaxing Lilly. He had to go back and make sure he was still employed.

He had no choice now but to put Toombs County behind him. If there was any hope of changing Lilly's mind, it would have to be a problem for a different day. His biggest concern now was explaining his extended absence from work to his employer.

Maybe Math Bell, who had helped him get the job with Mr. Harden in the first place, might be able to come up with a good excuse. Math usually returned to Toombs County on the weekends and was likely at his son-in-law John Blackstone's home right now.

The Overland's tires squealed as he sharply turned the vehicle onto the Dixie Highway and headed toward the south end of the county.

* * * * * *

"Is that someone coming down the lane?" John Blackstone asked.

He got up from the rocker in front of the fireplace and went to the window. He pulled the curtains to one side and peered out. "Yep, I see headlights, for sure," he said. He let go of the curtains, went to the door, stepped outside, and shuttered as the frigid February air greeted him.

Math Bell followed him to the porch and squinted at the approaching headlights with that healthy curiosity that accompanies life in the country with few visitors at night and even fewer automobiles. "That ain't no car I recognize."

Blackstone recognized Lee driving the vehicle as he recklessly pulled up in front, almost knocking down the mailbox. Lee cut the engine and turned off the lights. Blackstone heard a ratcheting sound as Lee pulled up the emergency brake handle.

"It's Lee Currie," Blackstone said. He gave his father-in-law a troubled look. This late arrival probably spelled trouble they didn't need.

Lee got out and waved as he approached the steps.

"Why Lee Currie, what you doing in that new car?" Blackstone asked, pretending to be upbeat about seeing Lee.

Lee stopped on the steps and turned around to the car, "Ain't she something? That there is a genuine 1920 Baby Overland automobile."

"Well, you got your Overland at last, just like you said you would. But you haven't been working long enough to afford this. Your pa help you buy it?" Blackstone asked sarcastically.

Lee flashed crimson. "Hell no, I bought it myself."

Blackstone looked at Math Bell again, raising his eyebrow in disbelief that Lee Currie could afford a bicycle, much less a car, all the while trying to hide his expressions from Lee. He knew better than to crank him up with a truth challenge.

"Well, it's a mighty fine car, Lee. I'm happy you are doing so well at the Barber Shop," Math said.

Lee stepped up to join them on the porch. "Well, you see, that's what I'm here to talk to you about, Mr. Bell."

Blackstone stepped back and opened the door, "Well, it's too cold out here to be doing any talking. Y'all come on inside, and we can talk by the fire."

Math stepped in through the open door. Blackstone reflexively grabbed it as the spring began to pull it shut behind Math and held it open for Lee to enter, moving his hand in a sweeping motion while slightly bowing as if Lee was royalty.

Math Bell stepped into the kitchen and returned with another chair for the new guest. Everyone sat down, and for a moment, the only sound to be heard was the fire crackling.

"What's on your mind, Lee?" Math asked.

"I'm worried about my job, Mr. Bell. I left suddenly without Mr. Harden's permission when this damn business with Lilly come up, and I've been gone for nearly a week. I'm afraid he's gonna fire me when I go back up there."

"Did Lilly get her divorce?" Blackstone asked.

"Nope," Lee said. "She didn't even show up for the hearing, and Judge Hardeman threw her case out."

"That was earlier this week, Lee; you could have gone back to Milledgeville after the court date, right?" Blackstone asked.

"No, I couldn't. I had more business to tend to. I've been trying to get Lilly to go back with me to start our lives up in Milledgeville out from under my pa's shadow. But she ain't wanting to go with me, especially with that bitch of an aunt of hers running her mouth agin' me," Lee retorted.

"Which aunt?" Blackstone asked.

"Sarah Smith!" Lee snarled.

"Lee, Mr. Harden is a good Christian and strong on family. I'm sure he won't be a holdin' it agin' you to be trying to keep your family together," Math said.

Blackstone looked again at Math Bell and sneered out of Lee's sight. Lee's infidelity had gotten him into this trouble with Lilly, and he wasn't feeling sympathetic at all. In all seriousness, he wished Math had never vouched for Lee to get him that job in Milledgeville in the first place, bringing him front and center into their lives. Lee was a bad seed, but Math had a soft spot for him because of the older man's respect for John Currie and his perception that Lee was not right in the head.

"I hope you're right, Mr. Bell, but if you're not, would you be willing to speak to Mr. Harden on my behalf?" Lee asked.

Behind Lee, Blackstone mouthed "NO!" to his father-in-law.

"Of course, Lee. When are you going back up there?" Math asked, ignoring his son-in-law's pleadings.

Lee's face brightened. "I can leave in the morning! I can even take you guys back tomorrow in my new car, iffin ya like!"

Blackstone was now frantically mouthing, "NO! NO! NO!" to his father-in-law and shaking his head behind Lee.

"That's mighty generous of you, Lee," Math said.

Blackstone groaned. "Uh, Math, that might not work; I've got to take my wife and our two little rambunctious children back. It would be a long uncomfortable ride with the six of us in one automobile, don't you think?"

"Nonsense, John," Lee retorted. "My Overland is a lot bigger than your car, and it's got plenty of room. Besides, they is small kids. We'll be fine!"

Blackstone sighed. He just couldn't get shed of Lee, no matter how hard he tried. But Math's mind apparently was made up.

"Can you be here by eight in the morning, Lee?" Math asked.

"You bet, Mr. Bell," Lee said and stood up. "I just got me a few errands and some packing to do. I'll be here at eight sharp."

The others stood and tried to keep up as Lee shook each one's hand vigorously.

"Thank you, Mr. Bell, thank you!" Lee said as he opened the door and backed out, waving as he went.

"Thank you!" he shouted out once more as he jumped in the car and sped off.

* * * * * *

Lee's good mood soured as his thoughts returned to Lilly while he drove away from Blackstone's place. Math Bell's willingness to talk to Mr. Harden about his job had lifted his spirits, but it could not overcome his disappointment that Lilly hadn't immediately jumped back into his arms upon seeing his new car.

I've done everything for her – everything. I even killt fer her, and she still doesn't want to come back to Milledgeville with me, he moaned. What more could he have done?

It's that bitch of an aunt what's turned her agin' me, Lee thought to himself as he flushed red with anger. He had left no stone unturned to get the support of her family. Lee had managed to get her father, Solomon Corey, and her sisters, Maggie and Minnie, firmly in his corner. He was also confident that her Aunt Anne supported the marriage, but Lilly was staying with her Aunt Sarah in Lyons, and Sarah was violently against Lilly's going back to him. He just hadn't figured on Sarah being the one remaining a stumbling block to his plans to reunite his family.

As he entered the city limits of Lyons, Lee put his hand on the Smith & Wesson in the side pocket. I ought to kill the bitch; he thought as his finger found its way to the trigger. He pulled the gun out and rested it on his lap.

But killing Sarah Smith would not be easy. Killing Burley Phillips was a different matter; what with their being alone and out in the country, away from prying eyes. Lilly's Aunt Sarah would be home with her husband, Raymond, and Lilly.

Lee drove slowly by the home of Raymond and Sarah Smith on Lanier Street, clutching the pistol. He could see the light on in the living room. That shadow on the curtains, it had to be Lilly, yes, it had to be. His heart almost stopped.

He drove further up the Dixie Highway, his depression deepening. Just out of town, he pulled over to the side of the road. He put the gun behind his right ear and cocked it. *Maybe I ought to just take this here gun and shoot myself right behind my right ear, right where I shot Burley Phillips. I could mix my blood with his in this cursed car. That would show her how much she done messed up my life.*

For a long moment, Lee sat there, gun to his head, shaking with rage and breathing rapidly. Then he slowly put the gun back in his lap. His breathing returned to normal. His eyes went down to the weapon; he kept staring at it for a long moment. Nope, that ain't gonna help nutin'. She'll come around. She'll come back to me. Without me, she ain't nobody. She was as poor as dirt when I met her, and she ain't got nothing but me right now. She'll come to her senses as soon as she thinks about it some more. She'll come round for sure.

Lee let the hammer down, returned the gun to the side pocket, and turned the car around. As he drove by the Smith's house a second time, he was determined not to slow down or even turn his head, but Lee couldn't resist the urge to look carefully at the house as he drove by. Seeing no one in the windows, he continued on his way.

* * * * * *

Lee was restless, uneasy, and bothered. Impulsively, trying to regain control, he turned the Overland onto the road to Vidalia. The cloak of darkness enveloping him assuaged any fears of being seen in his victim's residence city. He didn't know why he wanted to drive through Vidalia. He didn't know right now why he was doing anything. He was just restless. Maybe, in some twisted way, returning to his victim's domain while driving what used to be Burley's car, which was now HIS car, would be a victory to restore some of the self-esteem this Lilly business had taken away from him.

He drove by Wilson's Jitney Stand, where his victim had worked. He stared hard at the corner where he had stood four nights ago while watching Burley walk with Nathaniel Haskins into the drug store to buy a cigar.

Lee thought he saw Nathaniel looking at him as he was driving by. He turned his head straight ahead and sped on. *It is dark; I'm sure Nathaniel didn't recognize me or this car*, Lee thought. "That was stupid, Lee," he said aloud to himself.

Lee continued driving aimlessly through Vidalia. *These are the same streets Burley Phillips carried passengers about, not knowing that his life was about to end*, he thought. Lee felt uneasy with this new curiosity about Burley. In a way, he didn't like the feeling, but he also felt empowered by the knowledge that he had taken another man's life. Driving about his territory seemed to be a way of capturing his victim's power.

He turned down 1st Street, where he thought Tersia Phillips lived. Would she be sitting by her fire, wondering when her husband would return from Jacksonville? Would the unknowing widow be pulling back the shades, looking for the ghost that was now Burley Phillips? What would she tell the Chief of Police when the week alluded to in the fake telegram had ended without her husband's return?

Lee turned back on the dirt road that would take him to Lyons. He would go to Clarence James' place and spend the night with his old friend. What had been done to Burley Phillips could not be undone. Water under the bridge, spilled milk, a mule gone from the barn. It was not to be worried about anymore. *I'm over it*, he thought as he turned on the road to Johnson's Corner.

Lee heard a distant roll of thunder as it began to sprinkle, and he thought to himself – *rain, this is good; I will get to test the windshield wipers.* A distant flash of lightning briefly revealed the faint outline of clouds, and just as quickly, Lilly, Nathaniel, and Tersia disappeared from his concerns.

Chapter 21

The crow of Clarence James' rooster did not actually awaken Lee Currie. He had long been awake and had turned his head toward the window in anticipation of the rooster's announcement of the day's arrival. The pattering of rain on the tin roof, like the feet of soldiers marching up a hill taken in battle, prevented sleep from restoring him.

His mind was marching along with those imaginary soldiers. He had buried Burley Phillips' body in a shallow grave by the same side of the road where the water flows after a rain, like the one that had kept him from sleeping soundly last night. A new fear now entered his mind. Did the rain wash up Burley's body? Was his corpse lying on that throwed-away road half exposed and half-buried? He had to know.

* * * * * *

The sound of the Overland in which Lee had arrived the night before grinding to life roused Clarence James from his bed. As he lay there uncertain of what was going on, he heard the automobile start down the road without the recommended delay to allow the engine to warm up in the cold February air. He got up and stepped over to the window just in time to see it headed away.

"Where is that crazy boy off to this early in the morning?" He asked himself out loud. But Clarence had known Lee long enough to know better than to try and fathom his motives. He tousled his hair and crawled back into the warm bed.

* * * * * *

Lewis C. Edenfield heard an automobile's sound in the distance, let go of the teat he had just squeezed, and leaned over where he could see around Esmeralda, his father's milk cow.

Isn't that Lee Currie in that car? He thought to himself. *Yep, that's Lee;* he confirmed as the car got closer. Enough of the sun had peeked over the horizon to illuminate Lee clearly. *I wonder where he is going in such a hurry at this hour*, he thought, as Lee, traveling east, turned south onto an old throwed-away road.

"Hmmm, nobody ever goes down that road, but it's his pa's property, so I guess it's his business," he muttered out loud. Esmeralda turned her head back toward him as if she was mildly curious about the cause of the interruption of her milking.

"I know, Esmeralda, I know. That boy's a strange one, for sure," Lewis said as he returned to his milking and skillfully squirted another stream of milk into the pail.

* * * * * *

Lee slowly pulled up to where he had buried Burley the night before, cut the engine, and looked around nervously. He breathed a sigh of relief – nobody was in sight. He got out and walked over to the makeshift burial site. Sure enough, rainwater had been flowing over the grave, but his choice of the top of a hill for the burial site had worked to keep Burley Phillips' remains well concealed. The rain had little velocity flowing over the grave, and only scant erosion occurred.

Nevertheless, Lee felt the grave needed further concealment. Looking around, he spotted a log about seven feet long nearby. Straddling the log, Lee grunted and pulled it backward, over to one end of the grave. Looking behind himself to make sure he aligned the log with the grave, he dragged it over the entire length of where Burley's body lay and dropped it.

Lee gathered some pine boughs and spread them out about the log. *That's too many,* he thought to himself and tossed some of the pine boughs aside.

He stepped back a few steps and surveyed the site. *That's it, Mr. Burley Phillips, your final resting place; nobody will ever find you now.* He slapped his hands together to knock off the dirt and brushed them against his pants. The deed was done. He got back in the Overland and headed toward John Blackstone's home.

* * * * * *

Lee arrived at the Blackstone place at 8 a.m., just as Mr. Bell had requested. They were all ready to go, and one of the children jumped into the front seat between Lee and Mr.

Bell. The other clamored into the back seat between her mother and father.

"Everybody all set?" Lee asked.

"We're as ready as we'll ever be," John Blackstone said from the back seat.

"Well, alrighty then. I've got to stop by Durden's Store to gas up, and we'll be on our way," Lee said. The gears ground as he put the Overland into first gear – and they were off.

Mrs. Blackstone and Math had their hands full, managing the excited children. They kept crawling over the adults to peer outside. Neither had ever been in a car like the Overland before, and this was, for them, an awe-inspiring adventure.

After fueling up at Durden's Store, Lee turned on the big road south of Lyons to Marvin's Church and headed for Cedar Crossing.

"Wouldn't it be better to go through Lyons or Vidalia, Lee?" Math asked.

"No, I like this route," Lee replied.

"Through Cedar Crossing?" Math asked.

"Yep," Lee replied.

"You going the long way, Lee. The shortest route is to go by Lyons, up to Swainsboro, on up to Wadley, and then to Milledgeville," Math insisted.

"No, Mr. Bell, this way has got better roads and will get us there quicker. We'll go to Mt. Vernon and then to Soperton and then make our way up to Milledgeville. It's much faster this way," Lee explained.

"Well, alright, have it your way. You're the driver, and we're just passengers," Math said, settling back into his seat, eyes on the road ahead.

"I'll get us there before sundown, don't you worry none, Mr. Bell," Lee said confidently.

Lee smiled. He didn't have Lilly with him, but he was finally on his way back to Milledgeville and away from Toombs County. He would worry about Lilly later. Right now, he was confident that Burley Phillips was no longer a concern. In about a week, Mrs. Phillips would start to worry, and the law would likely look for her missing husband down in Jacksonville, Florida, following the lead in the phony telegram Lee sent in Burley's name.

By the time they stopped in Dublin for lunch, Lee had laughed and carried on with his passengers as if none of the events of the past several days had ever happened.

He was safe and about to begin his new life in a new city.

Chapter 22

"I'm going to skin that negro alive when I see him," John B. Rushing angrily muttered to himself as he latched the gate to the fence surrounding the barn, apparently left open the day before by his inattentive field hand.

Mabel, his milk cow, was nowhere to be seen.

"It's dang near 9 o'clock. Mabel will be letting me know any minute where she is when her bag begins to ache from all the milk she'll be carrying," he continued to mutter. As if on cue, the cow bellowed way in the distance toward John Currie's farm.

Rushing grabbed the short mane of his mule, Jubilee, swung up upon his bareback, and urged him forward. At the edge of the field, Jubilee gingerly stepped down the slight incline, hesitantly jumped the small ditch, and came to a trot on an old throwed-away road.

It was the car tracks that first caught Rushing's attention. He thought the road had been abandoned for some time, yet there they were. They appeared fresh as if someone had been down the road in a car that very morning. Rushing slowed Jubilee and began to survey the road ahead of him carefully.

It was clear that somebody had stopped where Jubilee was approaching, and Rushing halted the mule with a "whoa." He slid off the side of the animal and bent down to look more closely. Indeed, there were fresh tracks of a small shoe in the sand, still wet from last evening's rain.

"Someone has been here this morning, girl," Rushing said to Jubilee, who looked at him with a puzzled look as if to remind him that Mabel was still the greater priority.

Rushing observed the log on the road's side where the tracks led and was lying parallel to the road rather than across, as you usually see the trees lie when they fall into the roadway.

Rushing's curiosity turned to suspicion. He tossed the pine boughs away and examined the log. The sand under it should have been dry, but it was wet from the light rain the night before. *This log was put here this morning*, he thought. *Someone had buried something here before last night and returned this morning to conceal it! What the heck?*

Neighbors looked out for one another, and Rushing was concerned that someone was up to no good coming onto John Currie's property. There were no crops in the field, and hunting season was long past, but some teenagers could be doing a little sparking. In any event, Mr. Currie should be told about it.

As he continued to look around, there was more sign of the heavy log being dragged to where it now lay. Rushing followed the sign and found the dry area where the log was during last night's rain.

The cow bellowed again, still distant, and Jubilee whimpered at him to remount where they could continue their search. Rushing climbed back up, and the mule, well accustomed to these frequent hunts for errant cows, continued toward the cow. Pulling on the reins, Rushing turned the mule and looked back at the log. *I need to check this out later,* he thought to himself, *and I'm going to need help.*

Rushing gigged Jubilee into a trot in the direction of a neighbor's house. Sensing his master's newly acquired sense of urgency, the intelligent mule readily obliged. In a matter of moments, he arrived at the Wolfe farm, where he saw Bennie Wolfe and his younger brother, Hoke, out in a field. He enlisted the help of both to help him find and retrieve Mabel.

* * * * * *

With Mabel safely back in the barn, John Rushing thanked the Wolfe brothers and began the cow's long overdue milking. Rushing's mind, however, was not on what he was doing, and Mabel mooed at him to urge him get on with it and relieve her from her pain. Rushing accelerated his milking, but his mind was elsewhere. He was trying to decipher the unusual situation on John Currie's property. His curiosity compelled him to go back and check it out further. As a courtesy to his neighbor, he had to let somebody on the farm know about his concerns. You didn't go-getting into a neighbor's business without alerting them first.

To the great relief of Mabel, the milking was completed. Rushing let her out into the gated field and remounted Jubilee to go find someone to secure permission to go on John Currie's property. He was determined to investigate the mysterious site to see if something lay buried there.

Rushing didn't recognize the man plowing in the nearby field, but he suspected he was one of Mr. Currie's field hands.

"Good morning to ya," Rushing said as he approached the field hand.

"Mornin'," the man replied as he halted the mules, took off his hat, and wiped his brow. Plowing was sweaty work, even in February, but the ground had to be prepared for the spring planting.

"Tell me, mister, have you seen a car down there on that throwed-away road this morning?" Rushing asked.

"Can't say as I have," the man replied.

"Any chance you were plowing here yesterday?" Rushing asked.

"No, I'm just plowing today," the man replied defensively.

Rushing extended his hand down to the man. "Excuse my manners. John Rushing's the name. I live across the branch there."

The man shook his hand, "Alan Dukes, pleased to meet you."

"Might there have been anybody plowing here yesterday, Alan?" Rushing asked.

"Jacob has been plowing this field. He would have been here all week. Why do you ask?" Alan replied.

"I'm a mite puzzled about something I seen down in that direction, there," Rushing said, gesturing to the old throwed-away road. "Where is Jacob now?"

"Some of Jacob's people done up and died, and Mr. Currie asked me to finish up this field."

Alan tied the reins to the mule to the plow and walked over to him. "What's got you so puzzled?"

"I think somebody buried something yesterday on that old throwed-away road down there. I saw some fresh sign of the earth being disturbed, and there were some new tire tracks.

"Ain't nobody been using that road for a while, and that would be kinda odd. Might be nothing, but it's got my suspicions up. I think I need to let Mr. Currie know where he can look into it," Rushing said.

"Well, Mr. Currie has gone to town right now. Not sure when he's going to be back," Alan said.

"You reckon I can borrow one of Mr. Currie's field hands to help me dig whatever it is up?"

"Most of the hands are working elsewhere this time of the year. I don't think anyone is available, but I can help. You really think something is buried down there?"

"I think so," Rushing answered, glancing toward the road. "I ain't fer certain. It sure appears that a fresh hole has been dug and filled up," Rushing said.

"A fresh hole, you say?"

"I think so. I appreciate your offer to come go with me yourself. You can tell me what you think," Rushing said as he dismounted the mule. He and Alan started walking toward the road leading the mule behind them.

By the time the two men reached the burial site, they had gotten well acquainted. Rushing tied the mule to the fence, jumped over, and slid down the hill to the road, with Alan right behind him. Alan slowly approached the area.

"Don't that look like someone buried something there?" Rushing asked.

Alan looked carefully at the sand and the log lying upon it. He began to walk around the log.

"Try not to step on those tracks!" Rushing said, and Alan halted his forward motion and stepped back.

"Well, would you look at that? It appears to be a shoe track, small-sized, looks like," Alan said.

"Someone has definitely been here this morning and buried something under that log," Rushing's speculation had turned into certainty. He was beginning to get alarmed.

People buried their pets and even larger animals all the time, but whoever had buried something that morning had tried to conceal it. That was not normal behavior.

"Alan, how 'bout you take Jubilee down there and across the branch to Attis Wright's house? Ask him to bring a shovel if you will," Rushing said.

Both men realized this was serious, and Alan immediately turned and scaled the incline between the road and where Rushing's mule was tied. He mounted Jubilee, who readily accepted the new rider and, at Alan's urging, began to trot towards the Wright house.

Rushing was uncomfortable staying behind. He feared foul play was afoot as he continued to stare at the disturbed soil in front of him.

He bent down and tossed the pine boughs aside, then stood up. Should he wait for someone to arrive before going any further? Leaning over, he looked beneath the log. Yep, the ground under there was wet, he thought. He moved around to where the log had been before being dragged to where it now lay. Rushing carefully avoided the tracks neither he nor Alan had made. The ground there was dry, which convinced him that someone had moved the log from the dry spot to where it now was.

Rushing sat down on a nearby stump and waited.

* * * * * *

Jubilee's approach brought Rushing back to his feet. Alan was talking to a couple of men. That was good; the more, the merrier. He recognized Attis Wright and his brother, Bud Wright, as they got closer. Bud had a shovel.

"Morning, John," Attis greeted him. "Alan here tells me you've found something unusual out 'cher. What' cha got?"

"I don't know, Attis, but it's pretty clear to me that someone is up to some mischief. I think they buried something right here some time earlier and then drove out here this morning in a car and put that there log on the filled-in hole to hide it," Rushing said, gesturing to the log. "Some of the footprints are leading over to where that log was before. Look at how the weeds over there are dry, and the sand underneath the log is wet," Rushing said pointing to the weeds.

"What' cha make of it?" Bud asked.

"I hate to say, Bud, but iffin you ask me, I think there might be a body buried there," Rushing suggested.

The other three men looked at Rushing incredulously, then at each other, then, almost in unison, down at the log.

"The hell you say," Attis said.

"I don't know what else to make of it, Attis. Look at the size of the disturbed area under that log. There's no weeds there, just that log. I tossed away several pine boughs that someone had put there to make it look all natural. That there looks like a makeshift grave to me," Rushing said with conviction in his tone.

"Let's don't be jumping to no crazy conclusions, John. Somebody may have come down here to bury their pet dog," Bud said.

"Out here on this remote road? People bury their pets in their backyard, not out here – away from everything. And why go to so much trouble trying to conceal the site? I tell you, there is a dead man down there," Rushing said convincingly.

Now alarmed, Attis jerked the shovel roughly from Bud's hands. "Only one way to find out. You two move the log," he directed.

"Be careful not to step on those shoe prints," Rushing said, gesturing to the tiny shoe prints near the site.

Rushing moved to one end of the log, and Alan moved to the other. They picked it up and tossed it over into the ditch.

"If it's a body, you best be careful with that shovel. We don't want to jam it into whoever's face it is. Messing the body up would be hard on the family," Bud said.

Attis moved to one end where the log lay and gently pushed the shovel with his foot into the ground.

"Damn, Attis, be careful, for Pete's sake," Bud urged.

Attis dropped the shovel. "Well, get down there and help me dig by hand then, Bud if you are so concerned about it being a corpse."

Bud dropped to his knees and dug where Attis had removed a shovelful of sand. The three other men closed in around Bud, peering down. They dug about five inches into the dirt and stopped suddenly.

"Oh, my God! That there's a shoe heel!" Bud said as he sprang to his feet and took several steps backward. "It IS a grave!"

All four men stared down at the exposed shoe heel. For a long minute, nobody said anything.

"John, go take my mule and ride to my house. I've got a telephone. You call Sheriff McLeod and round up any more neighbors you can find," Attis said gravely.

"But we need to dig him up and see who it is," Rushing protested.

"Somebody's done kilt this man and buried him here. That makes this a murder, John, and the business of the law, not us. We done gone as far as we can, now git!" Attis said.

Rushing turned and ran to the mule, almost leaped upon him, and sped off toward Attis Wright's house.

"Damn, Bud, who would kill someone and bury him on Mr. Currie's property?" Attis asked.

"I don't know, but it is out of our hands now," Bud said, staring at the exposed shoe heel. "This here's a matter for Sheriff McLeod."

Chapter 23

Sheriff George McLeod frowned when he arrived at the location he'd been given over the phone. There were several cars, wagons, and horses gathered on the road. He turned on his red light and worked his way carefully down the old farm road. As he arrived at the scene, he stared disapprovingly at all the people gathered there. David Wright stood next to Lewis Edenfield, and they were engaged in a lively discussion. As he pulled up, he winced at how the men were walking all over his crime scene.

John Rushing approached McLeod's car. "We're glad you're here, Sheriff; the body's over there. Come quick!"

More accustomed to a murder scene than these farmers, McLeod methodically gathered his clipboard and hat. He stepped out of the car, carefully put his hat on in an authoritative manner, and ran his fingers along the brim.

"I want all you men to step away from the grave and come over here," Sheriff McLeod said sternly. "And please try not to step on any of my evidence."

They all dutifully and carefully moved to McLeod's vehicle.

"You can see his shoe heel, Sheriff," Bud offered excitedly.

"We moved the log the killer put on the grave," Attis added.

"There were pine boughs on top of the log, Sheriff," Alan added.

McLeod's brow furrowed at how this "helpful" bunch had already disturbed his evidence. He held up his right hand, "Slow down, fellas, slow down. If there is a man buried there, he ain't going nowhere. Now, who found the body?"

Rushing stepped forward, "That'd be me, Sheriff."

"What were you doing on Mr. Currie's land, John?" McLeod asked as he started making notes.

"A field hand of mine left my barnyard gate open, Sheriff, and my best milk cow Mabel run off. I normally milk her in the morning. I can't ever depend on that man ..."

McLeod interrupted him, "John, just tell me how you found the site, please."

"Well, I could hear Mabel down this way, and I stumbled upon this body trying to find her," John replied, gesturing to the burial site.

"What aroused your suspicions?" McLeod asked. He couldn't rule out the possibility that the person reporting something like this might be the killer, but he hid his suspicions with a seasoned lawman's aplomb.

"Well, it was the fresh sign of the dirt being disturbed that caught my attention, Sheriff. Nobody uses this road anymore, but there were fresh tire tracks from an automobile and signs that somebody with a small-sized shoe had been walking around the grave," Rushing explained.

"Show me," McLeod said as he and Rushing walked over to the gravesite. Several men started to follow them but stopped in their tracks as the sheriff turned and glared at them.

Rushing looked around uncertainly and then turned a full circle scanning the ground. "I don't see 'em now, Sheriff. It looks like we done stepped all over 'em, but they were small-sized shoe prints, I can tell you that."

Sheriff McLeod sighed. "Damn," he mumbled under his breath.

Rushing walked over to where the log was before it had been moved and lit up, "Over here, Sheriff. Here's some of his footprints. I think this is where he got the log."

McLeod carefully stepped over to where Rushing was standing.

"What are you thinking, John?" McLeod questioned. He knew the answer but had not yet ruled Rushing out as a possible suspect and wanted to let him talk.

Rushing was in the spotlight and enjoying it. "The log was lying on the grave over there when I got here, yet the sand underneath was wet from last night's rain. That log was moved from here to over there by the killer this morning," Rushing said enthusiastically.

"And you know that to be true, how?" McLeod asked.

"Well, it rained some last night, Sheriff. The grass here is dry. That means that sometime after the rain, probably this morning, somebody moved that log." John smiled, pleased with his forensic reasoning. The men gathered at McLeod's car drew closer.

"Y'all stay over there, you hear me!" McLeod warned, this time with an authoritative voice. "You have practically destroyed my crime scene already." The men returned to the car, mumbling to each other.

McLeod's suspicions about Rushing began to subside. The killer would not help explain these clues after going to so much trouble to conceal the makeshift grave earlier. "Let's not get ahead of ourselves, John. We gather evidence first and try to figure out what it means later. Now, show me those tire tracks."

Rushing showed McLeod the tracks, and McLeod retrieved a ruler from his car. He studied the tracks and carefully measured the distance between the treads, making more notes as he did so. He turned to the men standing by the car.

"Okay, I need one of you to dig him up. Any volunteers?"

Lewis Edenfield quickly stepped forward. "I'll do it, Sheriff."

"I'll help him," Attis raised his hand.

McLeod nodded, and the two men approached the gravesite and started digging with the shovel.

"Put that shovel down. It doesn't look like the body's buried very deep. Use your hands," McLeod said.

A few minutes of enthusiastic digging later, the two men had removed most of the loose sand and loamy soil from around the top of the body, which was only about five inches down, as McLeod suspected.

The victim was lying on his left side in the grave in what appeared to be an overcoat. As they got the sand and dirt out from around the body, Lewis looked closely at the right side of the man's head.

"Sheriff! He's got a bullet hole in 'em!" Lewis exclaimed.

"Lots of things make holes, Lewis. Let's not jump to conclusions yet," McLeod said as he squatted and peered down. Sure enough, there were powder burns on the victim's neck, and the hair was singed around the small hole behind his right ear. This man had been shot at point-blank range.

"Y'all step back; you're blocking my light," McLeod told the two men.

McLeod took out his pen and picked at the blood caked with dirt at the wound. Fresh blood immediately oozed out of the exposed hole. The victim had not been dead very long.

"Let's get him out of there," McLeod said. "Be easy with him."

"Y'all come help me lift him out," Lewis called out to the others, who gathered around the grave. Together, they raised

the body and laid it carefully on the ground.

Lewis brushed the dirt off the man's face, and his eyes widened. "Sheriff! I know this man!"

"Who is it, Lewis?" McLeod asked.

"That there's Burley Phillips! He's a jitney driver for old man Wilson over in Vidalia."

The men gathered closer.

"He's right, Sheriff. I recognize him, too," David Wright said.

McLeod noticed immediately that David Wright seemed troubled. His eyes followed David as the man turned and walked back toward McLeod's car, appearing deep in thought.

"That bullet done passed through his head, Sheriff. It's just broke the skin here beside his left eye socket," Lewis said. "But that ain't the worst of it."

"What?" McLeod asked, his attention returned to the body.

Lewis drew in a deep breath as if it was difficult for him to tell McLeod what he had just seen.

"Damn, if he ain't got dirt in his nostrils, Sheriff. Some son-of-a-bitch done buried him while he was still alive!"

The men began to murmur among themselves. McLeod bent over and looked carefully at the nostrils of the dead man. He inserted his pen partway in one, lifted it to open it slightly, and peered closely.

"Well, I'll be dammed," he stood and put the pin back in his shirt pocket.

"Looks like you are dealing with one sick son-of-a-bitch, here," Lewis said.

McLeod looked down. The unfortunate victim had been shot in the back of the head and then buried while he was still alive. This had just become a case he wanted desperately to solve. Whoever did this needs to hang!

"Attis," McLeod called out. "Get that sheet out of my trunk and put it in the back seat." He turned to the others standing around, all looking down silently at the body of Burley Phillips. "You men there, pick him up carefully and put him in the back seat of my car."

"Shouldn't we go through his pockets, Sheriff?" Lewis suggested.

"Might not be a bad idea, Lewis. Go ahead, if you're not too squeamish about it," McLeod said.

"Don't bother me none, the man's dead, and we need information," Lewis said as he began searching through Burley's pockets. He pulled out a matchbox with two matches in it and a dirty pocket-handkerchief.

"You can tell he must have been working on a car, Sheriff. There's automobile grease on this handkerchief," Lewis said as he handed the items to McLeod. "He's got on two pairs of pants. Shall I look in the inside pair?"

"No, don't bother. I can understand wearing two pairs of pants in this cold, but nobody puts anything in the inside pockets when they are wearing an extra pair of pants. Find anything else?"

Lewis held up his hands, with palms open, then stood up. "That's it, Sheriff."

"Alright, thanks for doing that. Now you fellas move him to the car, please."

McLeod went to his cruiser's hood. He placed the matchbox, matches, and handkerchief on the hood, studying them. Then he got a bag from the car and dropped the items in it.

The men carefully and reverently picked the body up and placed it in the back seat of the cruiser. McLeod appreciated how they appeared to be treating it with extra special care to acknowledge that the man, when alive, had suffered enough, and now his corpse deserved respect.

"Where you taking him, Sheriff?" Rushing asked.

"Protocol requires that I take him to Dr. Youmans, John. It's his job as coroner to do a full examination, being as this is now a murder investigation. I want to establish the time of death and learn anything else I can about how this man died.

I'll need some help managing the body, so I need for you to go with me."

Rushing nodded and got in the vehicle, carefully resting the head of Burley Phillips in his lap. Lewis shut the door on the other side.

McLeod was still watching David Wright, who had acted suspiciously earlier and was now standing near the car's hood. McLeod further noticed that he did not help the others move the body. He seemed to be lost in thought and disturbed.

"David?" McLeod asked.

David looked right at him, "Yes, Sheriff?"

"I'm going to need some help getting him out of the car at Dr. Youman's office, David. Why don't you ride with me and John."

McLeod reasoned that something was definitely bothering David Wright, and it wasn't just his recognizing the victim. David moved reluctantly to the car's passenger side, opened the door, and got in. McLeod noticed that he glanced back at Rushing holding Burley's head in the back seat and then turned around and stared at the floor.

McLeod took one more look at the now-empty grave. Lewis Edenfield walked over to him.

"Sheriff, I don't know the connection to this crime, if any, but when I was milking this morning, I saw Lee Currie drive by my place going in this direction."

"Oh? What kind of car was he driving, Lewis?"

"It was one of them Overland automobiles, Sheriff," Lewis was almost panting.

"You sound positive. You know the car?"

"I do, Sheriff, I do. It looks just like that Baby Overland Burley has been driving all month as a jitney. I noticed it because it was a lot nicer automobile than he normally buys."

"Thanks, Lewis, that's very helpful. You keep this information to yourself. I don't want a lot of rumors starting up about the Currie boy. You understand?"

"My lips are sealed, Sheriff," Lewis said as he made a zipping motion across his mouth.

McLeod walked over, got into his vehicle, and let out a deep sigh. His mind was racing now that Lee Currie's name had been linked to the murder. He was a mixed-up and violent young man, but he didn't know if he was capable of a crime like this. He also was David Wright's nephew by marriage, and that might explain David's unusual behavior earlier. He looked up at Attis Wright, standing by the car, waiting for further instructions.

"I'll have some more questions later, Attis. Tell all these men to leave this area and not mess up any more of the evidence. A terrible crime has taken place here, and we will not stop until we find out who killed Mr. Phillips."

"You need to do just that, Sheriff. The good Lord would not let such a heinous crime go unpunished. I'll be here when you need me. Go catch the bastard what did this," Attis said.

Sheriff McLeod looked up at him. "Oh, we will, Attis, we will."

* * * * * *

Sheriff McLeod, John Rushing, and David Wright rode along in silence on Marvin Church Road. As soon as McLeod turned toward Lyons, he began exploring what was troubling Wright.

"Okay, David, something's bothering you. Want to tell me what's on your mind?"

David was silent for a long moment. "I knew Burley, Sheriff. Seeing him kilt and buried alive like that, well, it has just upset me."

McLeod's instincts told him that the delay in David's response followed by a perfectly reasonable answer was contrived, and something else was bothering David.

"Yeah, that was enough to upset anybody. A man would have to either be very callous or not right in the head to kill a man like that and bury him out in the middle of nowhere."

Again, that moment of silence. "I guess we have some folks like that in this county, Sheriff."

"True that David, but not very many, thank God. I've seen many killings in Toombs County, but one like this is rare."

McLeod's instincts told him that David knew something he wasn't ready to reveal. He knew him to be a good man, a hard-working carpenter, and a faithful Christian. He didn't suspect that David could have done this terrible deed, despite his only living just over a half-mile from where they had found Phillips, but his instincts told him that David knew more about this crime than he was admitting. McLeod decided to go directly to where the evidence was leading.

"Lewis saw your nephew Lee Currie near the crime scene this morning, David. Know anything about why he would be over around this area?"

David froze, and his hands started shaking, which McLeod noticed instantly.

"If you know something, David, you best be telling me. Concealing evidence of murder is a serious crime. You don't need that kind of trouble."

"What makes you think I know anything about it?" David asked nervously.

"Son, I've been a lawman for enough years to know when somebody is hiding something from me. Now you need to come clean. What was Lee doing in that area?

"He's family, Sheriff," David said, struggling to maintain his composure.

"I know. And I also know that Lee ain't right in the head. Whoever did this was probably not right in the head either. Now, I'm asking you again, do you know what Lee was doing in this area?"

David took a deep breath and exhaled it slowly. His hands stopped shaking. When he could hold his thoughts no longer, it was as if a dam had burst.

"He came to my house Thursday night 'bout midnight and spent the night with me. He was on foot. He left early the next morning and returned in about ten minutes with an automobile I had never seen before. He told me it was a Baby Overland and he had just bought it. Then he left about daybreak. Told me he was going to Reidsville and tried to get me to go with him, but I had chores and couldn't."

McLeod took in what David had just told him. Lee had arrived at David's house late at night on foot and left early to retrieve a car. He had returned in ten minutes, just enough time to walk the half-mile or so to the site where Burley Phillips' body was buried and return in the car. This morning Lewis Edenfield had seen Lee near the site in a vehicle like the one Burley was driving, and there was a fresh sign that the murderer had returned to that site to conceal the body further.

Lee Currie had just become his prime suspect.

"Why did he spend the night with you, David?"

"He and his pa fight all the time. It was not uncommon for him to come to stay at my place when they were on the outs."

"Had he been fighting with his pa that night?"

"No, or iffin' he had, he didn't let on. He said a friend dropped him off, but I don't remember hearing no other car."

"Tell me about his appearance," McLeod prodded.

"Well, Lee said he was chilled when he came in, but he looked flushed to me, despite the cold outside. I accepted that a friend had probably dropped him off up on the crossroads near here, and he had walked a spell."

"Could be. What'd y'all talk about?" McLeod asked.

"Not a whole lot. It was late, and we didn't talk but about fifteen minutes or so. My next day was going to start early," David said and paused again. It was clear to McLeod that he was struggling with ratting out his nephew.

"This is not the time to hold back, David. Go on."

"Mostly, he talked about being in a trade for a new automobile. He wouldn't tell me that night what it was, on account of he thought it might jinx the deal. The next morning, when he came back with it, he told me he owned a brand-new Baby Overland."

"In ten minutes?"

"Yeah, that didn't make any sense to me either. I tried my best to get him to stay and eat some breakfast. Nancy had fixed up some bacon and eggs, and it would have given me a chance to find out some more about it, but he was in an all-fired hurry to get on the road. Before I could plead any further with him, he had said his goodbyes and was gone."

"I'm afraid I'll need to bring him in for questioning. Do you know where he is staying? Is he still living with his father?" McLeod asked.

"No, Math Bell helped him get a job a few weeks ago up in Milledgeville with some barbershop and pressing club, according to what he told me. Math's son-in-law, John Blackstone, works up there, too, and helped get Lee a room. He was real excited about it," David answered.

"Do you know where he is staying?" McLeod asked.

"He's staying in that nuthouse up there," David answered.

McLeod gave him a strange look. "The Georgia State Sanitarium?"

"Yeah, but not as a patient. They keep adding patient rooms to that huge facility, and it ain't nearly 'bout full. They rent out the empty rooms on a short-term basis. Folks get a good rate and can stay there till the hospital needs the room for a new patient. That's all Lee told me about it," David answered.

McLeod was troubled. Lee Currie had to be brought in for questioning, which would greatly upset his friend John Currie, Lee's father.

"I sure hate this for Mr. Currie. If Lee killed Burley Phillips to steal his car, he'll hang for it, which will probably destroy his old man. John has struggled with that boy from the day he was born," McLeod said.

"You don't know the half of it, Sheriff. I love Lee like he was my own son, but he has the mind of a child. He has been in and out of trouble all his life. If he was anyone else but Mr. John Currie's son, he would have already been in prison by now."

"John Currie is one of the finest citizens in Toombs County, David. But it is not uncommon for great families to have at least one black sheep among them, and Lee would seem to qualify. Still, this is going to break John's heart if it turns out to be true."

"It ain't going to just break his heart. There will be a trial, and if I know John Currie, he will sell everything he has to get Lee the best lawyers money can buy. I'm afraid this is going to destroy the Currie family."

"I know you are part of that family, and I appreciate how difficult this is for you, David. I hate to see families have to go through a trial like this. I just hate to see it."

"I guess justice has to be done," David said sadly.

"From someone reluctant to tell me about this a few minutes ago, you now sound like me," McLeod said.

"I guess I'm resigned to it, Sheriff. I have worried about Lee all his life. I'd hoped he would grow out of his immature ways, but he didn't. Sometimes he would even scare his Aunt Nancy with his quick temper. She loves him, but she insisted I stay close when he was around. Lee's fights with his pa had damn near come to blows on many occasions.

When he would come to stay with me, he would rail on about how his pa was suffocating him and not letting him do what he wanted to do. But Mr. Currie had to keep him on a short leash for his own protection."

"I'm afraid he gave him too much slack this time," McLeod said and sighed.

* * * * * *

Sheriff McLeod pulled up behind Ideal Pharmacy in Lyons. Dr. Youmans had his practice in the back of the store, and his nurse quickly answered the bell. McLeod explained why they were there, and the doctor came up and motioned for them to bring the body inside.

Dr. Youmans gave directions as Wright and Rushing carefully moved Burley's body from the car to the examination table in the doctor's office.

"Dr. Youmans, please call as soon as you have completed your report," McLeod said.

"It shouldn't take more than a couple or three hours, Sheriff," Dr. Youmans responded.

McLeod turned to Wright and Rushing and said, "I need to go by the office, make a few calls and a few visits. I'll get one of my deputies to take you men back home. Do you mind?"

"I'm fine. You do what you need to do. It takes precedence over anything I had planned," Wright replied.

"I'm good, too," Rushing said.

"Thanks, I appreciate it."

Dr. Youmans spoke up, "Sheriff, could you leave one of these men to help me with managing the body?"

"I'll stay," Rushing volunteered.

"Thanks, John. Let's go, David," McLeod said as they left the doctor's office.

McLeod drove to the jail near the courthouse where his offices were located. He asked David to wait in the lobby and beckoned for Aldon Odom, one of his Deputies, to follow him into his office.

"Aldon, I need you to run Mr. Wright back to his home in Johnson's Corner for me. In about three or four hours, Dr. Youmans will call. I will then need for you to get his report and take John Rushing home. He's there helping the doctor," McLeod said.

"You left in a mighty big hurry after that call this morning. What's up, Sheriff?" the deputy asked.

"Somebody killed Burley Phillips, a jitney driver out of Vidalia, and buried him on John Currie's farm. My primary suspect right now is Lee Currie," McLeod said.

"Somehow, that don't surprise me none, Sheriff, that boy's bad seed," Aldon said.

"No, he comes from a good family. But he is just one of those misfires practically every family has," McLeod lamented. "Anyway, I don't want you talking about the case to him or anybody else. I haven't contacted the widow yet, and I don't want wind of this to get out. I've seen people lynched for less than this, and I don't need a mob on my hands. You warn David when you drop him off to keep his mouth shut," McLeod instructed.

"Respected as Mr. John Currie is around these parts, I spec he is just as anxious as you to keep this quiet, Sheriff, but I'll remind him anyhow."

"Thanks, Aldon."

McLeod wanted to call Mr. Wilson at the Jitney Service in Vidalia to ask when he last saw Burley and find out who his last rider may have been. He asked his secretary to get him on the line. A few moments later, Martha signaled he was holding.

"Good morning, Mr. Wilson. Sorry to bother you so close to dinnertime," McLeod said.

"Morning, Sheriff, no bother, except the normal consternation that accompanies a telephone call from the High Sheriff of Toombs County. How can I help you?"

"I'm in the middle of an investigation, Mr. Wilson. When was the last time you saw Burley Phillips?"

"Strange you should ask that, Sheriff. He was scheduled to work for me this weekend and up and took off to Jacksonville, Florida, without telling me. Created an enormous scheduling problem for us, I can tell you that. We will have a little discussion about it when he gets back.

"Burley can't make up his mind whether he is a jitney driver that works for me or a car salesman that works for Mr. Warthen. We are going to have a little prayer session over it, and he's going to have to decide that once and for all," Mr. Wilson said, in the rambling manner of an old man who loves an opportunity to tell a story.

"You say he went to Jacksonville?"

"Well, that is what his wife Tersia said. I called her last Friday afternoon late when he didn't show up for his afternoon shift. I had to call in Nathanial Haskins to work, and he had family coming in from out of town. He asked me for the ..."

"Mr. Wilson, I'm sorry to interrupt, but I'm in a bit of a hurry. When did Tersia last talk to him, do you know?" McLeod asked.

"Sorry, Sheriff, I do know how to make a short story long, folks tell me. Tersia said she saw him last Thursday night when he come home to take his supper. She said he left after eating and didn't come home that night, and she was beginning to worry, but he often makes long out-of-town trips, so she didn't think much about it. Then she got a telegram Friday afternoon saying he had sold the car to a man from Jacksonville, Florida, and was going to deliver it to him. Said he be gone a week or so."

"You say she got a telegram?"

"That's right, or at least that's what she told me when I called."

"What type of car was Burley driving?" McLeod asked.

"One of the best-looking cars I've seen in a while. More expensive than most of the cars Burley buys and probably out of the price range of his typical customers, most of whom struggle to afford a Model T, much less a car like that ..."

"Mr. Wilson ..." McLeod interrupted.

"Oh, there I go again. I'm sorry, Sheriff. He had recently acquired one of them Overland automobiles from Mr. Warthen. Got a real deal on it, but, as I said, it was still a little expensive for most of his customers. I was giving him a hard time about it and ridiculing his business sense a bit, but he seemed confident he would find someone who would fall in love with it and take it off his hands. Sometimes he can flip 'em pretty fast," Mr. Wilson said.

"Do you know who his last passenger was on Thursday?" McLeod asked.

"I had already gone for the day, but Nathaniel was here and would have entered it into the log for me. Hang on a minute."

Despite being a seasoned veteran, Sheriff McLeod could feel his heart pounding. If Lee Currie was Burley's last passenger, that would seal his case.

Mr. Wilson picked up the telephone. "Says here that it was Mr. John Currie's boy, Lee, what booked his last fare of the day, Sheriff. Says he took him to his father's place. I don't see any more entries where he made any more trips that night, but Thursday nights are always kinda slow. Anything else I can do for you?"

"No, you've been very helpful. I appreciate this information. It will help me with my investigation," McLeod said.

"That's the second time you have called it an investigation, Sheriff. Has something happened to Burley?" Mr. Wilson asked.

"It's just routine right now, Mr. Wilson, nothing to concern yourself about."

"Well, okay, but if you see Burley before I do, tell him he's got a balling out awaiting him when he gets back here."

"You have a good day, Mr. Wilson," McLeod said, without responding to the impossible request he had just received.

"You, too, Sheriff. Nice talking to you," Mr. Wilson said and hung up.

* * * * * *

George McLeod was not looking forward to his next task.

"Martha, I can't remember the name of the pastor of the North Thompson Baptist Church. Would you look it up and get him on the line for me? I think he may have sent me an invitation to a revival recently," McLeod instructed his secretary.

The worse part of his job was notifying the family of the deceased. Each family reacted differently after receiving a death notice. Tersia's pastor would be better prepared to handle her reaction and comfort her. Martha signaled that the Reverend was on the line, but she failed to give him his name. He would have to wing it.

"Good morning, Reverend; how are you this morning?" McLeod asked

"I'm doing fine, Sheriff. I trust you are calling to tell me you are coming to the Revival next month. All the county elected officials are going to be there, and I'm counting on you being in attendance, too."

"I'm still trying to work it into my schedule, Reverend. I'll let you know," McLeod answered.

"Please do. I know we are not your regular church, but you are sheriff over the whole county, and you need to visit us, too, when you can."

"I promise," McLeod lied.

"How can I help you this morning?" the Reverend asked.

"I'm afraid I have some bad news about a member of your congregation, and I need your help," McLeod said solemnly.

"Oh no, who died?" It was clear he was accustomed to receiving similar calls.

"Burley Phillips, and under terrible circumstances. Someone murdered him," McLeod broke the news.

There was a gasp on the other end of the line. "Oh Lord, not Burley, such a good man and a valuable member of the Vidalia Quartet. He was going to sing with them in the upcoming Revival. Oh, sweet Jesus, I don't know how we are going to replace him, such a good man," the preacher said grievously.

"I am so sorry to be the one telling you this, but I would like for you to go with me to tell Mrs. Phillips. I don't know her personally, and I think it would go better with her if you were there to comfort her."

"Of course, I consider it my duty. Oh my, this will devastate Tersia. She is also such a good person and a strong member of our congregation. This news will crush our whole church family."

"I'm going to catch a quick dinner down at the Elberta first and then drive up. Can I pick you up about 1:30?" McLeod asked.

"I'll be ready. Just come by the parsonage. I'll be there."

"If you don't mind, Reverend, would you be able to drive over there in your vehicle? I won't be able to stay long, and she might need you to help her notify her family and friends. Could you do that?" McLeod asked.

"Of course. It might help if I went by and picked up her mother, Mrs. Rebecca Willis. She can help me console her. I'll meet you there at 1:30."

McLeod hung up and sighed. He was glad the Reverend had so readily agreed and would be staying with Tersia. He did not want to stay around and field a lot of questions about what had happened to Burley. Fear was also growing in him about how the Phillips family would react. He needed to get Lee Currie in custody as soon as possible.

* * * * * *

Telling Tersia Phillips that her husband had been murdered was one of the hardest death notices he had ever given. She was beyond consolation, but it was a relief in one sense. She did not have the presence of mind to ask about the details. She just kept crying and asking what she would do without him and how she would tell the family. He was grateful her mother and the Reverend were there to console her.

McLeod told her how terribly sorry he was for her loss and promised to find the killer and bring him to justice. Then he made his goodbyes and left the hard work of putting her back together again to her mom and the good Reverend.

Driving back to the office, McLeod looked at all the houses on 1st Street, where Tersia lived. Plenty of folks to form a lynch mob here, he thought to himself. I've got to move fast on this and prepare for the worst.

Chapter 24

McLeod drove back to the office. As he walked briskly by Martha's desk, he signaled his secretary to follow him.

"I need you to type me up a warrant on Lee Currie for the murder of Burley Phillips," McLeod said, settling into his desk and arranging papers.

Martha stared at him blankly, then asked, "John Currie's boy?"

"I'm afraid so. Keep it under wraps. Lee is in Baldwin County, and I'm going to have to call the sheriff up there to have him arrested. Get me Sheriff Terry on the line," McLeod said.

"My, my, my, this is terrible news," Martha said as she turned slowly and went to make the call.

"Oh, and I will need for you to call James Mallard and tell him to be on standby to go with me to get Lee when they arrest him," McLeod directed.

"That hot-headed wannabe sheriff's deputy? You sure?" Martha questioned.

"I know, but he's cheap and readily available, and I'm afraid I'm about to go over the quarterly budget with what's coming. And tell Carl that I will need for him to go with us to drive my car back. James and I will bring Lee back in the car we believe Lee may have stolen from his victim," McLeod said.

After about ten minutes, she signaled that Sheriff Samuel L. Terry was on hold.

McLeod nodded to her and picked up the telephone, "Hello, Sheriff."

"Hello to you, Sheriff. To what do I owe this honor?" Terry responded.

"I'm afraid you have a fugitive in your county that I believe may have killed one of our citizens, Sam. I need for you to have him arrested and hold him for me. I'm in the process of getting a warrant now," McLeod answered.

"Sorry to hear that, George; what's his name?"

"Lee Currie, son of a prominent farmer down here with a history of trouble. I'm led to believe he ain't right in the head."

"Pretty bad murder?"

"Reminded me of how John Wilkes Booth shot President Lincoln. 'Ceptin he shot the victim behind his right ear and not his left. It did have in common with Lincoln's assassination that it didn't kill him instantly. But it is more heinous in that Lee appears to have buried his victim alive. The deceased had dirt in his nostrils."

"Damn, that's some bad business. If that gets out, you gonna have a lynch mob on your hands," Terry said ominously.

"Been thinking about that already. I've got to call some people who have helped me in the past when I've been short-handed."

"Better draw up a plan to have him moved somewhere if it comes to that. Want us to keep him up here?"

"No, if I have to move him, we have an arrangement with Chatham County."

"Sounds good. Where do you think we'll find your perp?"

"I have word that he's staying at one of those rental rooms at the Georgia State Sanitarium. May be living near a man from here by the name of Math Bell or his son-in-law John Blackstone. Math got him the room. Currie's got a job up there at a barbershop in Hardwick. It's only been for a few weeks," McLeod said.

"That'd be the Hardwick Barbershop and Pressing Club. I know it well.

"It might be disruptive to Mr. Harden's customers to arrest him at the barbershop. Best to catch him this afternoon when he arrives at the Sanitarium, out in the open. I'll call Alex Hawkins; he's the Chief of Police at the Sanitarium. Alex makes it his business to know all the patients and all the renters staying there," Terry said.

"Call me when you have him in custody, Sheriff. I'll be coming up there to get him right after," McLeod said.

"If Alex arrests him after work, it will probably be between 5 and 6 o'clock. You'll likely want to wait till tomorrow."

"Your probably right. I'd rather transport him during the daytime anyway. I think he will be driving a stolen Baby Overland. I'll want to pick that up and bring it back with me for evidence and to eventually restore it to the victim's family," McLeod said.

"I'll send you a wire when we arrest Lee, and we'll warehouse the car till you get here. The road commissioners fuss about the cost of these long-distance calls. You must have a better bunch than I have to deal with," Terry laughed.

"Naw, ours is just as bad, but I don't pay them much attention. I'm a duly elected Constitutional Officer, and they are required by law to fund all my necessary operations," McLeod said.

"Necessary, that's the keyword. My commissioners believe a telegram works just as good as a telephone call and don't cost near as much. Hell, the last long-distance call I made, they only reimbursed me for what a telegram would have cost. Sons-a-bitches," Terry laughed again and then continued, "It's the world we live in, and they do control the purse strings – for the most part. We'll get your man, Sheriff, don't you worry."

"Thanks, Sam. I owe you one."

"I'm sure you will have plenty of opportunities to repay me, George. Since they built the State Sanitarium up here, I've gotten to know just about every sheriff in Georgia on a first-name basis!" Terry laughed.

McLeod laughed as well. "That probably explains why they are so fussy about the long-distance calls. I don't envy you none. Thanks for handling this for me."

"Don't mind a bit. That's what we're here for. We have to look out after each other. I'll get him."

"I appreciate it, Sam. Talk to you later."

"Keep an eye out for my telegram," Terry said as he hung up.

* * * * * *

"Alex, I need you to arrest someone for me," Sheriff Terry told the Chief of Police at the Sanitarium.

"Good afternoon, Sheriff. Who do you need for me to bring in?" Alex responded.

"His name is Lee Currie. You know him?"

"Yes, I know him. Moved into one of the rental rooms a few weeks back, but I haven't seen him for, oh, probably a week now. I think he went to his folk's place in Lyons."

"I have reason to believe he may have come back to town this morning. Toombs County has issued a murder warrant on him. He's believed to have killed a fella by the name of Burley Phillips down there, so be careful. He's likely to be armed, and I understand from Sheriff McLeod that he's not a stable fellow, mentally, that is."

"Seemed perfectly normal when I first met him. Had to warn him about coming in so late, but he took it well. I'll be careful."

"Thanks, Alex. Let me know when you have him in custody. I'll need to notify Toombs to come to pick him up. Oh, and please secure the Overland he's driving. I suspect it has some key evidence in it."

"I know the drill, Sheriff. I'll be in touch."

* * * * * *

Alex Hawkins began his rounds at the Sanitarium, looking earnestly for the Baby Overland Lee Currie was reportedly driving. He had gone by the barbershop and pressing club earlier and did not see the car there, so the chances were slim that Lee would come in to work this late. He would soon be arriving at the Sanitarium.

As dusk approached, he parked his patrol vehicle near the entrance to the rooms where Lee, Math Bell, and John Blackstone were staying. He didn't have to wait long. Around 5:30 p.m., the Overland turned into the parking lot, and four adults and two children spilled out of it, appearing to be happy to be at the end of a long journey. Alex exited his vehicle and walked over to the Overland.

"How you folks doing this evening?" Alex asked.

John Blackstone spoke up. "Getting along fine, Chief. Good to see you again. Has everything been quiet while we were gone?"

"Yep, pretty peaceful. Mr. Currie, I've noticed you've been gone about a week now. I was starting to wonder whether you were coming back."

"Had some court business to take care of this trip, Chief. Took longer than I expected," Lee replied.

Alex noticed that Lee looked down, avoiding eye contact. Lee's demeanor fit the mold he had been trained to detect. He continued to reduce the distance between them.

"Exactly what type of court business did you have in Lyons?" Alex asked as he moved even closer to Lee.

"Don't see where that's any of your business, Mr. Hawkins," Lee said curtly.

Alex swiftly moved between Lee and the other passengers. "That's where you're wrong, Mr. Currie," Hawkins drew his revolver and pointed it at Lee. "Math, John, y'all need to move those children away from the car. Me and Mr. Currie here have got some business to take care of," Alex commanded.

"Ora Bell, get the girls inside, right now." Blackstone sternly ordered his wife, who was already gathering them up and pushing them toward the Sanitarium entrance.

"What's this about, Alex?" Math inquired.

"None of your concern, Math. You and John mind your affairs and move away. Lee Currie, you are under arrest for the murder of Burley Phillips. Now turn around and put your hands behind you!" Alex ordered.

"Murder! What's he talking about, Lee?" Math asked anxiously.

"He don't know what he's talking about, Math. This is bullshit. I ain't kilt nobody," Lee growled.

"Turn around and put your hands behind you, Currie. I ain't telling you a third time," Alex said, more menacingly this time. He moved even closer to Lee.

Alex was fully alert and ready for anything Lee might do. He could tell Lee's blood was getting up because he had started shaking. But Alex knew he had the drop on him, and if we went for his gun, all the bystanders were out of the way. Lee slowly turned around and put his hands behind him.

Alex took a pair of handcuffs from his belt, holstered his weapon, and cuffed Lee. Sheriff McLeod had warned him that Lee might have a gun, which was why he drew down on him. Alex quickly slapped his pockets around, looking for a weapon. He didn't feel anything.

"You gonna regret this, Alex. When my pa finds out what you have done, he'll have your job," Lee threatened.

"Your father's name don't mean shit up here, Mr. Currie. You are in Baldwin County now, and you're going to jail. Now come along, right peaceful like," Alex said as he took Lee by the arm and led him to his police cruiser.

"Call my pa, John, tell him these damn fools have arrested me for no good reason," Lee called back over his shoulder.

"You'll see your pa soon enough, Mr. Currie. In the morning, Sheriff McLeod is coming after you and this car you stole," Alex opened the back door to the cruiser, held his hand over Lee's head, and sat him down roughly in the back seat.

"Murder, stolen car," Math Bell muttered incredulously, staring at the car and then Lee in the police cruiser's backseat. He looked at the police chief, "Chief Hawkins, I have known this man all his life. There must be some mistake here."

"He's got a warrant out on him, Mr. Bell. They'll have to sort it out in Toombs County," Alex said.

"He's not making a fuss. Are the cuffs necessary?" Math asked.

Alex hesitated. Lee was unarmed and angry, but he had not resisted his arrest. Alex bent down to unlock the cuffs, and Lee turned his back toward him to accommodate the release. After being freed, he rubbed his wrists and took a knife out of his pocket. Alex stepped back and put his hand on his revolver.

"Don't get excited, Chief. I just thought you might want this for safekeeping," Lee extended the unfolded knife toward him.

Alex warily reached forward, took the knife away, and put it in his pocket.

"See, Chief? I'm a peaceful fellow, just like Mr. Bell says. I ain't kilt nobody, and I don't want to cause you any trouble," Lee said calmly.

The officer was struck by how quickly Lee could change from hot to cold. A moment earlier, he was sure that Lee would have gone for his gun if he hadn't drawn down on him right off. And now, Lee Currie seemed like a perfectly mannered good citizen. He shut the door and walked back over to the Overland. Math and John were still standing there, stunned. Alex opened the door and started looking through the car.

"Chief, do they really think Lee killed somebody?" Blackstone asked.

Alex stood up with Lee's pistol in his hand, retrieved from the side pocket of the Overland. "Yep, they do, and there is one bullet missing from this gun I just found in this car. There're bloodstains here, too. Someone's tried hard to remove them, but they're here."

Blackstone and Math both came closer and looked into the car.

"He told us he had run over a hog and put him in the car while he was still bleeding," Math said.

"What did you expect him to say, Mr. Bell? The man he is alleged to have killed was shot in the head in the driver's seat. This bloodstain pattern is consistent with that type of wound. He wouldn't sling a hog, probably weighing a couple of hundred pounds, over the driver's seat. And I find it hard to believe that he put a bleeding hog in his newly acquired car in the first place," Hawkins said as he stuck Lee's revolver in his pants pocket, took the keys from the Overland, and shut the door.

"But there ain't no use in speculating. That will be evidence for a jury to decide. I'll send someone to move this car to the warehouse after you get unpacked. Don't remove anything that's not yours," Alex ordered.

"We've got everything of ours already, Chief," Blackstone said.

"Okay, good enough. I'm sorry if I upset your children in any way, John. Mr. Bell, I can sense you care about Lee. I'm sorry about all this," Alex shook hands with both men.

"You're just doing your job, Chief. You don't owe us an apology," Math said in quiet resignation. He turned and began walking to the building with his head down.

"My father-in-law has tried to help Lee every way he can, Chief. But I have worried about him coming up here with us from the get-go. I was especially worried about bringing Ora Bell and the kids to live with me. I hate to say it, but it's kind of comforting seeing him locked up in the back of your cruiser," Blackstone said.

"If he is convicted for that murder, you won't be bothered with him ever again," Alex said.

"That won't be an unwelcome outcome, Chief," Blackstone said.

The two men exchanged glances, confirming their joint speculation that Lee Currie's fate had been sealed.

The officer tipped his hat at Blackstone, turned to return to his police cruiser, and drove away with Lee in the back. Lee waved cheerfully at Blackstone, who raised his hand reactively to return the wave and then seemed to catch himself and lowered his arm. In the rearview mirror, Alex watched Blackstone standing there staring as he was driving away, then he saw him turn to go to his room.

* * * * * *

Math's door was open, and Blackstone stepped inside.

"I told you he was going to be trouble, Math, and I knew he didn't have the money to buy a car like that. But for him to have killed someone to get it, well, even I didn't see that coming."

Math Bell shook his head. His heart hurt for how his good friend, John Currie, would take this bad news. Lee Currie had the mind of a child and stubbornly went after anything he wanted, even those things he could not afford.

But to have killed someone to get something he wanted? No, that could not have been foreseen. This was not going to end well.

* * * * * *

"Telegram for Sheriff McLeod," the telegram boy announced loud enough for Sheriff McLeod to hear him. He looked up to see the boy walking briskly up to Martha's desk.

"I'll take it, boy," he heard her say as she handed him a penny tip in return. The boy touched the brim of his cap, tipped it to her, and said, "Thank you, ma'am!" Pocketing the tip, he bounced out of the office as quickly as he had entered.

"That from Sheriff Terry?" McLeod called out from his office.

He saw Martha quickly get up and walk into his office. "Looks like it is." She handed it to his outstretched hand.

The sheriff read the telegram in earnest. "They've got Lee in custody, and they've got the Overland secured in a warehouse. Let Carl and James know we will be leaving to go get him as soon as they can get here."

"I've started a file on Mr. Currie. You want me to add that telegram to it?" Martha asked.

The sheriff handed the telegram back to her. "Please, and I'll need that warrant to pick Lee up. You got it ready?"

Martha returned to her desk, picked up a folder marked "Lee Currie," put the telegram in it, and returned to the Sheriff's office.

"The warrant is in there – all signed and legal, Sheriff," she said as she handed it to him.

You're the best, Martha. Remind me to put you in for a raise when we do next year's budget," McLeod said.

"What, that raise you've promised me for the last three years? I'll be gray before I get that," Martha laughed.

"I'm going to get you that raise, don't you worry. Oh, I just remembered, have one of the deputies ride out to Mr. Ober Warthen's car lot, and alert him we will be bringing that Overland by this afternoon for him to identify. And tell the deputy to find Thomas Phillips, Burley's brother. They need to tell him that we have recovered his brother's Overland and will be returning it to the family after we have had a chance to examine it."

"Will do, Sheriff," Martha said as she returned to her desk.

McLeod took in a deep breath. He was about to be tested, and he knew it. Lee Currie was the son of one of Toombs County's most prominent farmers and a good friend. John Currie was a highly respected man in the community. Lee's killing a Vidalia resident in such a heinous manner would not sit well with the citizens there. It might be wise to call the Vidalia Chief of Police, J. R. Love, to give him a head's up about any possible civil unrest that might fuel a lynch mob.

He was also worried about his budget. The commissioners had cut his funding to the bone, and his staff was inadequate to prosecute this type of murder investigation and trial.

More importantly, this was an election year, and how he handled this trial might turn him out of office. It was trouble he just didn't need.

Chapter 25

James Mallard and Carl McLeod soon arrived at the Sheriff's Office. The sheriff was glad to see them because they had a long day ahead of them.

"Y'all had breakfast?" McLeod asked.

"Of course – I knew you'd want to leave early," Carl said.

"Me, too," James said, excited to be included in this transfer of a suspected murderer.

"Want me to drive, Pa?" Carl asked.

"No, I'm good. But I'll need you to drive this car back on the return trip," McLeod said.

"Whatever you need me to do," Carl said as everyone got into McLeod's cruiser.

"What route you gonna take, Sheriff?" James asked.

"We will take the road to Macon and then cut over to Milledgeville. It's better roads, and we can make better time."

The gears ground as McLeod pulled off and began his journey to take them to Milledgeville. Given the recent rains and the stop in Vidalia, it would probably require at least four and a half hours to make the hundred-mile trip, just barely allowing them enough time to get back to meet Mr. Warthen at his dealership.

No sooner than they were underway, James spoke up eagerly, "Tell me what we got on Lee, Sheriff."

McLeod had been contemplating the ride back with Lee and James Mallard. Different scenarios for questioning him had kept him awake last evening well into the wee hours, but he didn't feel tired, what with the adrenalin currently coursing through his veins. Foremost in his mind was the challenge of keeping the cop wannabe Mallard in check, but, then again, having an amateur with him could work to his advantage.

There were limitations on what a sheriff, as an officer of the law, could legally ask a suspect in custody. But the rules for civilian volunteers were a bit laxer, as they were not trained in the higher standards of acceptable questioning tactics. McLeod had decided to fill Mallard in on enough facts to keep their conversions going in the direction he wanted.

"Not much to tell right now, James. We know from Mr. Wilson at the Jitney Service in Vidalia that Lee hired Burley Phillips to take him to John Currie's place last Thursday evening. Somewhere along the way, we think Lee shot him point-blank in the back of his head, behind his right ear. The bullet went clean through his brain, stopping just under the skin beside his left eye socket. Lee appears to have buried him on his pa's farm while Burley was still alive," McLeod said.

"Damn," James said in a low breath.

"Yeah, pretty brutal," McLeod continued, "Lee was spotted coming back to the scene yesterday. The evidence seems to indicate that he returned to conceal the spot better where he buried Burley earlier. Shortly after Lee was spotted, John Rushing found the body while looking for a stray cow."

James interrupted, "Was John the one who spotted Lee at the site?"

"No, it was Lewis Edenfield who spotted him, but John musta just missed him, given what we know 'bout his movements," McLeod answered.

McLeod could feel James' excitement without having to turn to look at him in the back seat.

"Well, what say I bend the truth some and tell Lee Mr. Rushing spotted him at the site. How'd that be?" James asked excitedly.

McLeod thought for a moment. Telling a lie to a suspect to trick him into making an admission might be legally risky if an officer did it, but James might naively ask it without legal consequences.

Being careful not to encourage the questionable query, McLeod said, "I'll let you decide on that one should the opportunity to put it to him come up."

McLeod continued, "Alex Hawkins, the Chief of Police at the Georgia State Sanitarium in Milledgeville, arrested him last night at 5:30 in the evening when Lee returned there from Lyons. It appears Lee had given Math Bell, John Blackstone, John's wife, and John's two children a ride up there where they are also staying."

"What was Lee doing in Milledgeville in the first place?" James asked.

"Mr. Bell got him a job at a local business in Hardwick where Blackstone works."

McLeod added, "Hawkins told the Baldwin County Sheriff that there were bloodstains in the car that someone had tried in vain to clean. Lee told Blackstone that the stains were from where he ran over a hog and carried the animal off the owner's property.

"I'm hoping we'll learn when we get there that the Chief found a gun on Lee or in the car," McLeod paused and looked over his shoulder at James to emphasize how damming that evidence would be.

James' mouth was wide open, "That'd make it a slam dunk case, Sheriff. That Lee Currie is one step closer to the hangman's noose."

"We are going to have to be really careful, James. John Curie is one of our most prosperous and respected farmers, and knowing how he dotes on that boy, he will undoubtedly wind up hiring the best lawyers in the county to defend him, probably Giles & Sharpe. We are going to have to collect all the evidence we can find and talk to as many witnesses as possible," McLeod stated.

"What type of additional evidence you think we need, Pa?" Carl asked.

"I want to interview Mrs. Phillips as soon as she gets her husband buried and has a little time to deal with the worst part of her grief. I need to find out what Burley was wearing that night, what he may have said about where he was going, and what personal items he may have had with him. A jitney driver is normally going to have a watch and a money purse with him, and I need to see if she can confirm he had those items. No doubt, she can also confirm that Burley had a hat."

"You think Lee took that stuff?" Carl asked.

"We found none of those items near the body, and the killer may have taken them with him, and if he did, I want to find them," McLeod said.

McLeod was feeling good about the hard evidence possibilities. He had mulled over all the potential evidence in his head and could almost visualize the crime unfolding.

McLeod continued, "She also told Mr. Wilson that she received a telegram, appearing to be from her husband, telling her he was going to Jacksonville for a week or so to deliver the car to a buyer. I want to see that telegram and find out exactly from where it was sent. Burley was already dead by the time his wife received it. I suspect Lee may have sent it to throw everyone off."

McLeod paused and thought about the evidence he needed to gather. He was not staffed for this or funded, so it would fall on him and volunteers like James Mallard to put in the extra hours.

"We also need to trace Lee's whereabout after he shot Burley. His Uncle, Dave Wright, said he came to his house about midnight to spend the night and left early the following day. Lee told him he was going to Reidsville. If that's true, he may have sent the telegram from there.

"Everyone that Lee talked to in the five days between when he allegedly killed Burley and was arrested needs to be interviewed. We have got to develop an iron-clad case," McLeod said.

James appeared to be beyond excited. "Well, this is going to be the biggest murder case ever to come up in Toombs County, that's for sure!" James leaned up and put his arms on the front seat's back, "Maybe I can get him to talk on the way back from Milledgeville, Sheriff."

"We've got to be careful, James. If we don't follow proper protocol when we talk to him, a good lawyer will have our evidence thrown out," McLeod warned.

James sat back, "I know, I know, we can't threaten him or offer him any type of reward, right?"

"It will certainly go better for us if he volunteers the information. But that may not be all that hard. Sometimes, people who get caught are anxious to tell their side of the story, and Lee is widely known as a braggart. If he does go to talk, just give him his head and don't ask any leading questions. Chit chat with him, friendly-like, and let him talk at his own pace. Act like you are in awe of him. Remember, he must tell us everything freely and voluntarily."

McLeod continued, "We've got to uncover his motive and determine if he planned this killing, you know, like it was premeditated. He's a big talker, and if we're careful, he might tell us exactly how he did it without realizing he's confessing to capital murder.

"His lawyers are probably going to claim self-defense. Maybe they will assert that it was an act of rage after an argument over the jitney fare or some such excuse. We need to look for motive and deliberate actions. If Lee planned this thing and then attempted to cover it up, it would clearly show he knew what he did was wrong. We've got a lot of investigating ahead of us, including finding out why he buried the body the way he did and why he sent that telegram."

"You think he sent the telegram?" James asked.

"Who else? It had to be him, and if we can prove it, or if by some streak of luck, he admits to it, well, then the solicitor has him on murder one. At any rate, you just act intensely interested in what he's saying. As I said, he's a braggart. Hopefully, he will get to talking and hang himself."

"I've been around suspects during questioning before. I think I know the drill," James said, somewhat defensively.

"James, I know you think you know the drill, and I appreciate your help, but you are not a trained police officer. I'm taking a big chance having you come with me on this trip. I don't need you messing up my case against Lee. You let me do the major questioning and just play along and ask friendly, supportive questions."

"Don't worry about me, Sheriff," James answered.

McLeod was not reassured, but on the other hand, James might just work out to be just the right man to get Lee to open up. If McLeod did most of the talking and asked most of the questions, Lee might clam up knowing he was talking directly to the county's top law enforcement officer. On the other hand, if James, a civilian, was the one taking to Lee, especially if he showed a lot of interest, it might just get Lee to open up and tell all.

"You watch me closely while you are talking to him, James. If you see me turn my head ever so slightly, stop doing what you are doing till I can get the conversation back into safe territory," McLeod warned.

"Got it, Sheriff," James gleefully answered.

* * * * * *

Sheriff Samuel L. Terry greeted the officer contingent from Toombs County with a hearty handshake to each during the introductions.

"I 'spect you fellas are tired from the trip. How long did it take you?" Terry asked after ushering them into his office and gesturing for them to take seats.

"Four and a half hours, Sheriff. The roads were a bit wet and muddy," McLeod answered.

"Yep, we've had a right smart of rain, that's for sure. The county has been pretty good about dragging the roads around here, but they can't do too much with this mud. Did y'all go through Dublin? The roads are better that way."

"We went through Swainsboro and Wrightsville this time, but that might have been a mistake. We'll go through Dublin on the way back if you think it's better that way. Besides, we gotta stop off at Vidalia, and Dublin's more on the way," McLeod answered.

Terry settled down into his chair and lit a pipe.

"Smoke?" he offered.

"No, thanks, we're good," McLeod answered for all.

"It's a bit early, but if you are a wantin' some dinner, I can have my cook rustle you up some grub," Terry offered.

"No, thanks, but I sure would welcome some coffee, Sheriff; iffin you got some brewed," McLeod said.

"I can do better than that," Terry answered. "Bessie brought in some donuts with her this morning, and they are the best. I'll get her to bring you some. All three of you want coffee?"

All nodded.

James jumped in eagerly, "That's mighty hospitable of you, Sheriff. I love donuts."

"Bessie!" Terry called out. "Bring these men here some coffee and some of those delicious donuts you brought in this morning."

Bessie, a rotund, middle-aged black lady, suddenly appeared in the doorway, wiping her hands on an apron tied around her ample waist.

"Comin' right up, Mr. Sam," She responded as she did a headcount and then turned to the kitchen.

"Was it that chief of police at the sanitarium who made the arrest?" McLeod asked.

"Alex Hawkins? Yep, Alex got him as he was returning to his room. Told me he didn't put up any significant resistance other than mouthing off a bit," Terry said, then laughed.

"Lee even handed him a pocketknife he missed when he patted him down and put him in the car. He seemed real jolly about it all, but he's been complaining ever since we locked him up about the accommodations. I think that boy might have led a sheltered life. Don't appear to be used to this."

"He's the son of a prominent farmer, Sam, and has indeed lived an easy life, but he never quite grew up and has been in and out of trouble all his life, despite his father's best efforts to rein him in. Unfortunately, he's made a giant leap from his past shenanigans with this suspected murder. If it turns out he's guilty, I'm afraid he messed up big this time."

"I know you told me yesterday on the telephone that Currie shot his victim point-blank in the back of the head and buried him while he was still clinging to life, but you wouldn't think him capable of such meanness from the demeanor we've observed so far. He talks to the other prisoners and guards as if he knowed 'em all his life. Seems completely oblivious to the trouble he's in."

"I think that's part of the problem, Sam. The boy don't seem capable of grasping the notion that there are consequences to his actions. He's been known to steal things and have his pa make it right with his victims."

"Unfortunately for him, a human life is not something he can take when he wants."

"Nope, he can't. He doesn't know it yet, but I'm afraid he's gonna learn it soon enough."

"You building a case for murder one?"

"That's the solicitor's decision, but I think it will easily pass muster for that. And for that reason, it has me worried. This is going to be a highly charged trial, Sam. Could affect the election later this year."

"Heard that."

Bessie brought in a tray with three coffees and a plate full of donuts. "I know you menfolk are gonna love deese. It's my mamma's recipe."

"If they taste as good as they smell, I know I'm going to love 'em," James said as he reached for a donut.

"Appreciate it, Miss Bessie," Carl added.

"Have you got any cream?" McLeod asked.

"Sho do, young man, be right back," Bessie said and returned to the kitchen. In a moment, she brought a small carafe of cream.

"Thank you, ma'am," McLeod said as Bessie gave a big smile at the unusual display of manners coming from white folks and returned to the kitchen, pleased she had decided to bake donuts for today.

"Must be nice to have a large enough jail to have a full-time cook on hand," McLeod said enviously.

"Oh, she's not hired help. She's into spiritual healing, herbs, and potions. We busted her for practicing medicine without a license, and now she's one of our trustees working off her sentence.

"I prefer prisoners working off their sentences to hired help. Even on the off chance that the Commissioners were somehow supportive of a permanent position, the more people you have on the payroll, the greater a headache it is to keep up with 'em all. Even now, I feel like a danged full-time administrator. I don't get to do much serious law enforcement anymore. I got deputies and trustees in charge of every aspect of my operation. I'm just a dang manager –

a glorified paper pusher – that's all. I miss being out in the field."

"Well then, I guess I don't envy you, after all, Sam," McLeod laughed.

The men continued talking while they enjoyed their coffee and donuts. They compared the challenges of being the sheriff of a big county to being elected in a smaller jurisdiction like Toombs, and they talked about some other cases they were handling. McLeod asked how much he owed them for serving the warrant on Lee and housing him overnight.

"This one's on Baldwin County, George. You can return the favor sometime, should I even need help down your way."

"Can't thank you enough, Sam. It goes without saying that I look forward to returning the favor.

"Are you worried about your re-election, Sam?"

"I've been here since 1906, George. Fourteen years and three elections. I had some opposition the first time I ran, but nobody's come out agin' me since then, so, no, I ain't worried. But it sounds like you might be a bit on edge 'bout yours, are you?"

"Well, this is my first term, and this murder trial could cause me some real problems if it doesn't go right. Like I told you earlier, Lee's part of a large prominent family in lower Toombs County, and the victim comes from a well-known family in Vidalia. There's gonna be people mad at me no matter how this thing goes, I'm afraid. I just hope they don't carry their anger to the polls."

"What are your plans if they turn you out of office?"

"They won't kick you out, Pa. You've been a good sheriff," Carl injected anxiously as the consequences of this case dawned upon him for the first time.

McLeod took a long sip of coffee, "That don't matter in politics, Carl. It is a rough and tumble business. I told you that when you decided to follow your pa into law enforcement."

"Well, if they don't re-elect you, I'm leaving, too," Carl said.

McLeod laughed, "I spec you won't have much choice, Carl. If I get defeated, your being my son will probably mean that you are on the chopping block of whoever beats me. That's also the way politics work. To the victor go the spoils."

"Seriously, George, what are your contingency plans?" Terry asked again.

McLeod hesitated. He enjoyed talking to another sheriff about county politics' uncertainties and having contingency plans, but Terry was not the only audience for this conversation. He could feel his son's growing anxiety.

"Been talking with the feds about possibly becoming a U. S. Marshall at the end of my term. They are showing some interest in my joining them."

"Whoa, that should be a nice salary bump and some steady employment for a while. And there's not much turnover among the federal marshals," Terry said.

McLeod smiled and nodded. He had the federal job in mind when he ran for sheriff in the first place. Working for the federal government offered much better benefits, and it avoided the expense of having to run for office every four years. Besides, being a former sheriff looked good on a resume and provided some excellent experience for the marshal's job. However, he had never discussed his ambition in front of Carl before, and he could tell from his son's expression that he had just caught him by surprise.

"Reckon, they will have room for me there, too, Pa?" Carl asked.

"Maybe, never can tell."

"If you find yourself unemployed, Carl, you come see me. I can always use a good deputy," Terry said and slapped Carl on the shoulder.

McLeod noted that reassurance from his fellow sheriff didn't help his son's spirits very much and said, "But if I do get on with the feds, you can bet I'll be looking to bring my son and best deputy along with me!"

McLeod stood up. "Let's get Lee Currie off your hands, Sheriff."

Terry stood up, too. "Sure thing, George. I've notified Chief Hawkins over at the Sanitarium that you will be coming for the Overland. He said he would get it all gassed up and ready to go."

"Can't ask for better service than that, Sam. I appreciate it," McLeod said.

"Heck, by coming this early, you saved me from having to feed him dinner," Terry laughed and then turned to pick up an evidence bag containing Lee's gun. He handed it to McLeod. "Hawkins found this gun in the Overland. You'll find the bullets very interesting, George. Apparently, they were too long for the cylinder, and somebody filed them off to allow it to rotate. That makes them real unusual. It looks like one round's been fired. If the bullet your coroner pulled from the victim matches this gun's rifling and shows sign of being filed off, too, well, you have a compelling piece of evidence there."

McLeod took the gun from the evidence bag, opened the cylinder, and took out a round. Sure enough, the bullet had been roughly trimmed by hand to allow for the cylinder's rotation. This evidence was more than just a break in the case. This could be irrefutable evidence that the gun found in Lee's possession was the same weapon that killed Burley Phillips. He smiled at Terry, put the bullet back in the cylinder, snapped it back into place, and returned it to the evidence bag.

"Here's Hawkins' affidavit stating that he took the gun from the car. I've signed the section that shows he turned it over to me, and now I've turned it over to you. That should prove the chain of custody," Terry handed the affidavit to McLeod.

"And here's one for the car," Terry said as he gave him a second affidavit.

"Looks like providence has been kind to me, Sam. Thanks."

Terry took a ring of keys from his desk drawer and led the way back to lockup. Lee spotted them as soon as the sheriff unlocked the outer cellblock door.

"Sheriff McLeod! Bout time you got here. I need you to get me out of this damn stinking place. They got roaches here like you ain't never seen before. And I'm powerful hungry. I couldn't eat that slop they call breakfast this morning. I'm ready to get the hell out of here," Lee Currie said.

"Hello, Lee, nice to see you, too," McLeod said.

"Step back away from the door, Currie," Terry said as he approached the cell door.

Lee held both hands in the air and stepped back. "Glad to oblige, Mr. Lawman, sir. Whatever it takes to get the hell out of this dump."

Terry unlocked the door and turned to McLeod, rolling his eyes. "I'm gonna have to cuff him while taking him out, George. He's a bit unpredictable."

McLeod handed him his handcuffs.

"Aw hell, Sheriff, not them damn things! We got a long ride back to Lyons," Lee protested.

"You can talk to your sheriff about taking 'em off later, Currie, but to get out of this building, they are going to have to be on you. Now turn around," Terry commanded.

"This is bull crap. Y'all treating me like I'm some kind of criminal, and I ain't done nutin," Lee continued to protest, but he turned around as instructed and put his hands behind his back.

Terry cuffed Lee, turned him around, and passed him to McLeod. "He's all yours, George. Good luck carrying him back to Toombs County."

"Thank you, Sam. And thank you for your hospitality. I look forward to your coming to Toombs County where I can repay the favor," McLeod said.

"Can't say as I've enjoyed your hospitality worth a damn, lawman," Lee said.

"Come on, Lee. Let's get you on the road," McLeod said and quickly pulled him toward the exit.

James grabbed another donut as they passed by the tray. "Enjoyed meeting you, Sheriff!" He waved at Terry and followed Lee, McLeod, and Carl out the door.

"You too, James. Y'all take care," Terry said and waved back.

* * * * * *

Sheriff McLeod and his entourage drove to the Sanitarium, where they found Chief Hawkins standing in front of the main entrance beside the Overland. The Chief greeted him and turned over the keys.

"I suspected nothing good would come of that one, Sheriff McLeod. I must admit; I'm glad to be shed of him," Hawkins said.

"Did he leave anything behind we need to pick up?" McLeod asked.

"Just a few clothes, some shoes, and toiletry items. They are in the trunk. Did Sheriff Terry give you the gun?"

"Yes, I have that," McLeod shook Hawkins' hand. "I appreciate your making the arrest. You done us a huge favor. And thanks for taking care of the car."

"No problem, Sheriff. You watch him close now," Hawkins said and turned to return to the Sanitarium.

McLeod opened the door of the cruiser to let Lee out.

"Get in the Overland, Lee. You'll be riding in it back to Lyons."

"Hot diggity damn!" Lee Currie said in a loud voice and jumped in the Overland's front seat after Sheriff McLeod unlocked his handcuffs. "Am I glad to get out of them damn cuffs! Gimmie the keys to my Overland, and let's git out of here."

"Don't think so, Lee. I'll be doing the driving," McLeod turned and extended his cruiser keys to Carl, "See you back in Lyons, son. You take care of that cruiser; the taxpayers don't have any patience for our abusing a county vehicle."

"I'm just gonna follow you, Pa, in case you have any car trouble," Carl said and got into McLeod's cruiser.

Lee reluctantly got out of the front seat and moved to the back. "Well, if you insist, Sheriff, it is a fun car to drive. Now how about takin' me back to my room at the Sanitarium and leaving me with my car? I got to go to work tomorrow, or Mr. Harden will fire me for sure."

"Fraid not, Lee, your stuff is already in the trunk, and I'm taking you back to Toombs County," McLeod said as he climbed into the Overland's front seat and started the engine.

"Come on, Sheriff, I ain't done nuttin'."

"This murder warrant says otherwise, Lee. I gotta take you back to stand trial."

"Murder warrant? Dammit, Sheriff. I ain't kilt nobody."

"Then you don't have nothing to worry about. If you're innocent, we should be able to get this cleared up pretty quick."

"Yeah, but in the meantime, who's gonna help me get my job back, and my car?" Lee asked angrily.

"We have to let this business run its course, Lee. Now just settle back and relax. We have a long ride ahead of us."

"Alright, if'n you're hell-bent and determined to go on this snipe hunt, I guess there ain't 'nutin I can do about it, but dammit, you got to feed me first, I'm starved!"

James added, "I could use some grub, too, Sheriff."

"You just ate three donuts, James," McLeod said.

"That was just a snack, Sheriff. Me and Lee's ready for some real food, right, Lee?" James chirped. McLeod smiled as he was already trying to establish himself as Lee's friend for the trip back.

"I heard that, real food. Them Milledgeville jailers didn't have none of that back in that jail. That's for sure, and they sure as hell wouldn't let me have any of them donuts," Lee said.

The sheriff pulled into a nearby café; Carl pulled up and parked next to them, and the four men had a meal. Lee laughed and talked as if utterly oblivious to the murder warrant in the sheriff's pocket.

That was working right into McLeod's plan. He wanted Lee to relax in hopes that he would open up later. He made small talk with him, asking Lee how he liked his new job and what he thought of Milledgeville, being careful not to discuss the case just yet.

McLeod paid the bill with a county check and pocketed the folded-up receipt. They turned toward Scottsboro, with Carl following in the cruiser behind them.

They had engaged in idle talk for five or six miles before the sheriff concluded it was time to get into the case.

"Lee, where exactly did you get this car?" McLeod asked.

In his rearview mirror, McLeod saw James turn to his left in the back seat, presumably to better engage Lee. He could clearly see Lee in the mirror, and he immediately noticed that Lee was thinking hard about his answer.

"I bought it from some strangers," Lee finally said.

James jumped right in, "How much you give fer it?"

"A hundred dollars," Lee said without thinking further.

"A hundred dollars! Why this new car probably sells for ten times that much nowadays? You got a real steal," James said enthusiastically.

"Yeah, a real steal," Lee repeated. McLeod noticed him wincing after he answered, probably because he just realized that his made-up number was way off the mark.

The sheriff tried hard to hide his elation. Lee had both claimed ownership of a car he had stolen and just lied about how he acquired it. He listened intently for what Lee was going to say next.

But Lee went silent and seemed reflective as if he was trying to work out his story of how he got the car. He wished he could coach James on how to follow up on Lee's answers, but their rudimentary signal system only had a provision for James to stop questioning, not to continue.

"You sure don't come across a deal like that every day. Did you pay cash fer it?" James finally asked.

"No, I give a note," Lee answered.

"A note? Who to?" James pressed.

Lee grew irritated. "Hell, I don't remember their names. It was strangers that I traded with."

The sheriff turned his head over slightly, and James immediately stopped questioning, getting the signal right away. McLeod could sense the tension in the prisoner sitting behind him. He didn't want James to interrogate Lee. McLeod hoped to establish a rapport instead, to get Lee to relax and talk voluntarily. They rode on for two or three miles, and the sheriff decided which question he would ask next.

"Lee, that was the worst thing that has ever happened in Toombs County," McLeod said.

"What?" Lee asked immediately.

"A man being killed and robbed," McLeod answered.

"Who?" Lee asked.

"Burley Phillips. They say the killer buried him on an old throwed-away road on your pa's property and took his car, a Baby Overland, just like this one," McLeod answered.

Lee froze and then started shaking. McLeod noticed this change in his demeanor. There was utter silence for a long minute before Lee spoke.

"I don't know nuthin' about that," Lee finally said.

James jumped right in with his lie, "Well, Lee, there ain't but one thing or nobody wouldn't of suspicioned you of knowing anything. But this morning, a log was put on the grave, and if a man hunting cows hadn't seen you ..." James said.

Lee interrupted, "Who was that?"

"That man will come up later on," James answered.

McLeod watched Lee in the rearview mirror as frequently as he could without being noticed. Lee seemed lost in thought; his countenance went calm as if he had worked it out in his head.

"I knowed that Phillips was kilt." Lee said.

McLeod was ecstatic. They had just discovered the body yesterday morning, and few people knew that it was Burley Phillips. Lee had just said the name of his victim.

"That's right; he was," McLeod said.

"Well, I didn't kill him," Lee said.

"Was there an argument?" James asked.

"No, there weren't no argument," Lee answered.

"Then there weren't no trouble betwix' Phillips and you?" James asked.

Lee was confident now, "No, narry a bit. Everybody was peaceful like, and there weren't no fussing."

"Well, Lee, if you didn't kill him, who did?" McLeod asked.

Lee dropped his head and thought for a long moment.

"I'll tell you exactly how it happened, Sheriff; I ain't got nuttin' to hide. I was up at Wilson's Jitney in Vidalia and ask Phillips to take me to my pa's place."

McLeod's pulse quickened as Lee continued, "There was two men already in his car, and he said he was taking them out towards pa's. So, I got in, and we set out to Lyons and then turned on the Dixie Highway to go south.

"We got down to about where you turn left to go to Johnson's Corner, and one of them men said he would like to buy some whiskey. He asked me did I know where he could get some."

Lee's words were now flowing fast and freely. Both James and the sheriff were listening intently.

"There are a lot of bootleggers in lower Toombs County, that's fer shure. What did you tell him?" James inquired.

"I told him that I knew a colored man just over Cobb Creek that sold good whiskey, and he might could get some there."

"What'd he say?" James asked.

"He told Phillips to keep on going down Dixie Highway where he could get some whiskey – said he'd pay the extra fare. Phillips said, 'okay,' and we kept on going past the turnoff to Johnson's Corner," Lee answered.

"Were you able to buy some whiskey?" the sheriff asked. If Lee answered "yes," he would have another count to charge against him, buying liquor illegally.

"No. When we got to Cobb Creek, the road was flooded from the rains, and Phillips didn't want to go over the bridge," Lee answered.

"So, what'd you do?" James asked.

"I told them I knew another colored man named Jesse Carter what lived on this side of the river that might also have some whiskey for sale. I told Phillips how to get there, and we drove down this little road a bit afore I told him to stop, and I would go the rest of the way on foot," Lee said.

"Why'd you do that?" McLeod asked.

"Well, iffin' a car full of men a come a driving up in Jesse's yard, he might take them for revoneurs and take to shootin'! I told them to wait, and I would step up there and see if I could get some whiskey," Lee answered.

"Good thinking," James said.

"I walked on up the lane and called out to Jesse, but it looked like he weren't home. I walked around back and didn't see him anywhere abouts, so I walked back to the car.

"While I was gone, one of those men done killed Phillips, I reckoned, 'cause he was lying there on the ground, and I knowed he was dead. I said to one of the men, 'Well, what did you do?' He wouldn't answer me, so I went off in the branch and sat down on a log," Lee said and fell quiet for several moments.

"Well, did you just keep sitting on that log?" James asked.

"No, adder a while, I went back up there, and Phillips had been moved," Lee answered.

"Moved? Where did they move him?" James asked.

"I don't know where they carried him to or anything about it. They was trying to crank up the car, but they couldn't. Finally, they told me, 'There is the car; you can have it,'" Lee answered.

"So, this car ...," James started a question.

"Yeah, I know this was his car, but them men gave it to me," Lee answered.

McLeod took a deep breath. Lee had just contradicted himself. He had told them earlier that he bought the car for $100, and now he was saying the men in his made-up story had given it to him. Lee also admitted it was Phillips' automobile. He was about to ask another question when James seemed to have read his mind and asked it instead.

"So, you didn't buy the car then?"

Lee seemed puzzled for a bit, as if he had just remembered the contradiction with his earlier statement. He said, "Oh, yes, I bought the car."

James pressed him, "Well, where did you buy it?"

"At Reidsville."

"When?" James asked

"The next day," Lee answered. His story was going all over the place. McLeod smiled.

James remembered what McLeod said earlier and decided to use that information, "Well, didn't you tell your Uncle Dave Wright that you were going to Reidsville the next day in this car?"

McLeod glanced at James to signal that he should stop the line of questioning. Lee's story was falling apart, and the sheriff didn't want him to clam up. He wanted to give Lee a moment or two to get it back together in his head and start talking again. The more Lee said, the deeper he dug the hole for himself.

"Yes," he finally answered after they had driven down the road for a bit.

James continued to press. It was clear that Lee was making up his story as he went, as the inconsistencies were glaring.

"Where did you go from there?" James asked.

"To Claxton," Lee answered.

McLeod's face lit up as he congratulated himself for bringing James along. He was getting all manner of admissions out of Lee, and now his questioning had placed Lee in Claxton. Perhaps the telegram was sent from there instead of Reidsville.

Just as he was trying to figure out how to ask Lee about the telegram, James blurted out, "Claxton? Well, now ain't that a coincidence. Mrs. Phillips got a telegram from Claxton supposedly, from her husband, who was dead at the time, telling her he had sold the car and would be home in a few days."

A chill ran up McLeod's spine. He again turned his head to signal James to stop this line of questioning.

"No, not in a few days," Lee answered.

McLeod was thunderstruck. James had tricked Lee into correcting him when he said "a few days" in his bungling premature statement. The telegram author said Phillips would be back from Jacksonville in a week, not a few days. Lee had as much as admitted it was him who composed the telegram.

"Look, y'all trying to pin this thing on me, but those men killed Burley Phillips, and I saw him lying dead on the ground!" Lee retorted.

"But this is Phillips' car, and you took it," James said.

"Yeah, I know this was his car, but it was those men what stole it from him, and then they gave it to me," Lee said.

The sheriff had enough evidence to convince a Grand Jury to return a true bill on Lee Currie for the murder of Burley Phillips. He had heard Lee admit that he had hired Phillips to take him to John Currie's place. He had further revealed that he saw Phillips was dead. Lee had just as much admitted that he knew about the telegram content – and he had admitted that he knew the car he was driving belonged to Phillips.

There were many leads to run down and gather additional evidence, but he had all he wanted from Lee right now. He did not want to jeopardize his case by asking too many questions before Lee secured himself a lawyer.

He turned and looked at James, which implied that the questioning was done for now.

* * * * * *

Little more was said between the parties as they drove to Lyons. About a mile and a half on the other side of Vidalia toward Soperton, Lee blurted out,

"Damn, Sheriff, I'm about to pee in my pants!"

McLeod pulled over to the side of the road and turned off the car. He needed to stop, as well. A bumpy dirt road and a full bladder just didn't mix. All three men stepped to the side of the road and relieved themselves. Carl, who was following behind in the sheriff's car, pulled over as well, immediately surmising the purpose of the stop. He also availed himself of the opportunity to empty his bladder.

The sheriff could not help but notice that Lee was having trouble and winced as his flow started as if it was burning him.

"You alright, Lee?" McLeod asked.

"Yeah, I'm fine. Ever since I had the clap a while back, it's hard as hell to get my water going. Aggravating, that's what it is," Lee said.

The men finished their business and got back in the Overland, but the sheriff could not get it started. Lee leaned up in the seat and looked at the dashboard.

"You didn't advance the spark, did you? You don't have to do that after it is warmed up, you know," Lee said helpfully.

"I don't think it's the spark. It won't turn over at all," McLeod said.

"Dead battery?" James asked.

McLeod turned on the lights. "Carl, are the lights on?"

Carl walked in front of the car.

"Yep, the lights are strong," Carl said.

James offered, "You didn't turn the key off, did you, Sheriff?"

"Nope, the key is in the switch, and it's turned on," McLeod answered.

"Can't help you, Sheriff. It looks like we're stuck," Lee said and sat back in his seat.

"Carl, we are not far from Vidalia. You go on ahead to Mr. Warthen's place and see if he can come see what's wrong with the car," McLeod directed.

"Okay, Pa. You want me to come back?" Carl asked.

"No need. Get the chain out of the trunk of my car and leave it with us. If Mr. Warthen can't get it going, I'll ask him to pull us to town," McLeod said.

Carl fetched the chain and put it in the back trunk of the Overland. He waved as he pulled by them, headed for Vidalia. Lee waved back.

"Wonder who the hell lives up there, Sheriff?" Lee said, gesturing to a nearby farmhouse.

McLeod noticed how Lee's demeanor was now bright and cheerful as if he was unaware of the trouble he was in, and they were just out for a drive in the country. There was something not right about this young man. He seemed to have a childlike exuberance about him at times, and at other times he would seem dark and foreboding, like Dr. Jekyll and Mr. Hyde fella he had read about in school years ago.

"Robert Lewis Stevenson," he mumbled.

"What's that, Sheriff?" Lee asked.

"Oh nothing, I just remembered a book I once read," McLeod answered.

"Don't care too much for books myself. Ain't nuttin' in 'em I much need nohow," Lee said.

They made small talk for a while. McLeod stayed away from the facts of the case. He wanted to become more familiar with how Lee's mind worked and get some insight into how he could have committed such a heinous crime – killing a man in cold blood and burying him alive. Looking at Lee now, it didn't seem the man riding with him was capable of such callous murder. Yet, at times, it did.

But how valid were either of the "confessions"? After all, with two different versions of that night's events, Lee appeared to be making stuff up. Were either of the two versions the true story? Or was what happened still unknown? McLeod couldn't fathom what was running in Lee's head.

"I've been wondering about one more thing …" James started.

"James, quit asking so many damn questions. Lee's probably exhausted, and Mr. Warthen will be here any minute," McLeod said and shot James a look that clearly signaled that the sheriff didn't want any more questions asked. He didn't want to taint this confession Lee had just freely made.

Just then, Warthen topped the hill and pulled to the road's side across from them. McLeod got out of the car.

"You men stay here," he directed.

Warthen met him in the middle of the road.

"Thanks for coming out, Ober. We couldn't get it started," McLeod said.

"That the man who killed Burley?" Warthen said as he looked over the sheriff's shoulder to the car.

"He's just a suspect right now, Ober. He's innocent 'til proven guilty," McLeod answered.

"There are lots of folks in Vidalia what are ready to hang him, Sheriff. Burley has a lot of family there. There's talk of a lynching party," Warthen warned.

"He's gonna have a fair trial and, if found guilty, the state will hang him for them," McLeod said.

"Yeah, I know how justice works, Sheriff, but there are a lot of mad folks that don't have the patience for the law to take its course. Poor ole Mrs. Phillips is beyond consolation, and I'm not too happy about it either. Burley was one of my best customers," Warthen said.

"Losing a loved one ain't ever easy, Ober. It's especially bad when folk is murdered. I hope this doesn't get out of hand," McLeod said.

"Well, let me take a look and see if I can get you men back on the road," Warthen said and started moving toward the car. McLeod stopped him.

"I want you to pay particular close attention to the car, Ober, and make damn sure it is the one you sold to Burley. Try not to be too conspicuous to Lee as you are doing it. He's a bit unpredictable," McLeod said as he turned to accompany Warthen to the Overland.

"Hello, James," Warthen said as he approached the car.

"Hey, Ober. Good to see you. This here's Lee Currie. Lee, this here's Ober Warthen; he sells cars," James said.

"Oh, I know Mr. Currie. I talked to him a few days ago about buying a car. I see you got that Overland you were wanting, Mr. Currie," Warthen said.

Lee took his offered hand and shook it, "Yep, but the sheriff here it trying to take it from me, Mr. Warthen."

Warthen opened the driver's side door, and McLeod noticed how he hesitated as he saw the dark stains on the upholstery.

"It's just hog blood, Mr. Warthen. I cleaned most of it off. It won't get on you," Lee offered, apparently also noticing Warthen's hesitation.

Warthen looked up at Lee warily, who was smiling back at him. He got in and looked at the dash.

"Here's your problem, Sheriff. The Overland has an automatic cut-out, and when you push the switch on, it will drop off. You just have to push this little button here, and it should start back up," Warthen said and then pushed the button. The car cranked right up.

"There you go," Warthen added.

"That's it? I feel a little silly about making you come all the way out here for something as simple as that," McLeod said.

"It's a safety feature that Overland put on this car. It trips up most people who aren't familiar with it. I normally explain it to a new owner before I let them leave the car lot," Warthen said and got out of the car.

"Gosh, Sheriff, I could have told you that, iffin you had of ask me a while ago. I didn't know you hadn't pressed the button. It's as plain as day what it does. I thought you had some other problem," Lee said.

McLeod looked at Lee suspiciously. He wouldn't be surprised if Lee had not told him about the button on purpose.

"Let me make sure you don't have any other problems," Warthen said as he walked around the car. He bent over to look at the dent in the right front fender.

Lee suddenly leaned over James, then called out the passenger side window to Warthen standing outside, "That's where I run into the hog I kilt."

Warthen smiled back at Lee and nodded his head. Then he turned to the sheriff to make eye contact and continued walking around the car.

"It looks good to me, Sheriff. I don't think there is any danger that bent fender will hit the wheel," Warthen said.

The sheriff followed him to his car.

"Can you confirm that's Burley's car?" McLeod asked.

"No question 'bout it, Sheriff. It has the same tag number. I also saw where Burley had patched the curtain in the back. It was torn during delivery, and I offered to fix it for him, but he said he could fix it."

"I'll need you to come by the office later this week and let me take your statement, Ober. I appreciate your coming out here like this."

Warthen walked toward his car and then stopped and turned, "I heared he buried Burley alive. That's a real bad one you got there, Sheriff."

"Bad news travels real fast in this county, I'm afraid. I hate it for the Currie family. John Currie is one of the finest men I know. This ugly business is going to break his heart."

"Yep, I speck so, just like Tersia's heart is broken right now. This has forever changed a lot of people's lives. That's for sure," Warthen turned and stepped into his automobile. He extended his hand to the sheriff through the window.

"I don't envy your job right now, George. Good luck."

"Thank you, Ober. I'll need it," McLeod responded and returned to the Overland.

"Friendly enough chap," Lee said after McLeod got into the car.

"Yep, Mr. Warthen is a nice man," McLeod said.

"Well, it's been over four hours since we ate up there near Milledgeville, and I'm so hungry I could eat the south end of a northbound mule. When we gonna eat again?" Lee asked cheerfully.

"Soon enough," McLeod said as he put the Overland into gear, pulled back onto the road, and headed toward Lyons.

Chapter 26

Sheriff McLeod had not been looking forward to it but was bound by his official duties and friendship for John Currie to notify him that he was holding his son in custody – charged with murder. Before daylight Thursday morning, he left to go to the Currie farm to catch him before anyone else could tell him about the trouble his son was in. This was not going to be easy.

As he approached the farm, he saw his old friend standing in the front yard by the road, and a bad feeling started forming in the pit of his stomach. He pulled into the yard and stepped out of the cruiser.

"Morning, Sheriff, you are out and about mighty early. What brings you to my neck of the woods?" John asked as he extended his hand to McLeod.

"Good morning to you, too, John. I hope you're doing well. I've just got a little business to discuss." McLeod answered as he shook the offered hand. Getting started was going to be the challenging part. He didn't want to just blurt it out.

"A little business, huh? Well, it's not healthy to talk business on an empty stomach. You're just in time for breakfast. Lula is fixin' up a batch of hoecakes and cane syrup."

McLeod welcomed the invitation. A cordial atmosphere of eating together might better set the stage for the bad news he was about to deliver. "That sounds inviting, John; I could use a good ole country breakfast."

"Well, come on in then," John said and turned to gather some wood stacked on the porch.

"Let me help you with that," McLeod said as he gathered up several pieces and followed John into the house.

"Who's that with ya, honey?" Lula called out from the kitchen.

"It's Sheriff McLeod, Lula. Set an extra plate for him, please. He's going to join us for breakfast."

Lula came into the living room, wiping her hands on her apron, "Well, what a surprise. Good morning, Sheriff," Lula said as she hugged the sheriff. "Family doing well?"

"Everybody is doing fine, Lula. You sure I'm not imposing?"

"Heavens no, I'm used to folks coming by at eatin' time, and I always fix a little extra. None of my men will ever go unfed if I have anything to do with it. Come on in and let me serve you some vittles."

Lula began telling the sheriff all manner of news about her neighbors and friends, and McLeod welcomed the chatter. It gave him time to think about the best way to break the news of Lee's arrest. Gradually, he became aware of

John's growing curiosity. He had clearly begun to sense that this was no casual visit.

They finished their meals, thanked Lula, and went into the living room. John gestured to a chair, and McLeod sat as his host tossed a couple of fresh wood pieces into the fire. Bright amber sparks angrily swirled into the air in protest of being disturbed.

"I guess you have been busy with Superior Court last week," John offered to give the hesitant sheriff a conversational opening.

"Just the normal mischief, John, stealing cows, fistfights settling old disputes, and dealing with automobile problems. There is more horsepower in those new cars than most people know how to handle. They are running into people's things and each other right regular."

"Well, if court was that routine, you want to tell me what brings you all the way out here to see me?" John asked, his curiosity finally having exceeded the need for warmup conversation.

McLeod took a deep breath. He had found no good opening to break the bad news and braced himself to just start talking.

"John, your boy's in big trouble. I've got him locked up in my jail."

John did not look surprised. "I suspected as much when you came out here this early. What's he gone and done now?"

"It's bad, John."

"Mary Shelly once wrote that nothing is so fearful as the expectation of evil tidings delayed, George. The sooner you tell me, the better. Let's have it."

"It looks like he's gone and killed a man," McLeod said, swallowing hard. He braced himself for an unpleasant reaction.

John was silent for several long and uncomfortable moments. "Who do they think he's killed?"

"A jitney driver from Vidalia name of Burley Phillips. We dug his body up from a makeshift grave day before yesterday." McLeod said, marveling at how calm John appeared. It was as if Lee's father knew this day would come and had mentally prepared himself for it a long time ago.

"What makes you so sure that Lee done it?"

"I have a witness who saw him driving the dead man's car near where we found the body. The evidence suggests that Lee took the car after he killed him. Lee claimed he had bought the car. We had Lee arrested in Milledgeville, and he had the car with him."

"Having a man's car doesn't mean he killed him," John Currie said defensively.

"The suspected murder weapon was in the car, with one round fired. There also was a lot of blood in it."

John poked at the fire. For the first time, McLeod was able to read his friend's emotional state. John's hand was shaking as he stirred the embers.

"Where'd they find the body," John asked.

"Not far from here. It was on an old throwed-away road."

"Not far from here?"

"Yes, I'm afraid it was on your property, John."

"Damn," John Currie said in a low breath.

"I'm sorry, John. I know this comes as a shock. I can't tell you how badly I hate having to be the one to tell you," McLeod said.

John sighed. A long minute went by, and he continued stoking the fire.

"You think he done it, Sheriff?" John said, without looking up.

McLeod hesitated before answering. He didn't want to crush Lee Currie's father, nor did he want to give him any false hope.

"It doesn't look good, John. The evidence against him is growing. While we were bringing him back from Milledgeville, he admitted that he had hired Phillips to take him to your place. He also admitted that he knew he was dead but claimed that two men who were riding with them killed him."

"That sounds plausible," John said.

"I admit that it does, but then he said they gave him the car, even though it wasn't theirs to give. Later, when we pointed out how that conflicted with his earlier statement that he had bought the car, he changed his story once again."

"That's all well and good, George, but I didn't ask you all that. I asked if you think my son killed that man," John Currie said sternly and solemnly.

"I'm afraid all the evidence points to that conclusion, John," McLeod said slowly.

"George, I don't care about where all the evidence points, dammit. I'm going to ask you for a third time. Do YOU think he did it?"

McLeod swallowed hard. After a moment, he said softly, "Yes, John, I think he did."

Soft or not, McLeod could tell that his words hit John Currie hard. His head dropped as he shifted his gaze from the fire to his feet.

The sound of Lula washing the breakfast dishes in the kitchen finally broke the long silence that followed. John looked up toward the kitchen.

"I'm glad that Lee's mother Levency did not live long enough to hear this terrible news, but it's gonna be hard for his stepmother to hear. She's grown very fond of my son and feels just as protective as I do of the boy."

John poked the fire again, and a swirl of glowing embers fought for the chimney flue. "I don't know how either one of us is going to be able to help him now."

"I'm sorry, John," McLeod offered. Being the bearer of this horrible news was just as hard as he had imagined, and it was weighing heavily upon him.

"Can I see him?"

"Of course. Any time."

John got up in a manner that signaled McLeod that the visit was over.

"George, I appreciate your coming out here personally to tell me about this. I know you have deputies for that. You're a good man. I'll be down later today to see him."

"I spec you'll be needing to get him a good lawyer, John," McLeod said as he stood to leave.

"T. Ross Sharpe goes to my church. His pa and I go way back. I guess I'll be calling on him and Enoch Giles to represent my son."

McLeod nodded his head. He expected as much. Giles & Sharpe was the best law firm around.

The two men walked out to the sheriff's cruiser. They shook hands, and McLeod opened the door. He looked back at John Currie, now slumped as if he was bearing the world's weight on his shoulders.

"I'm really sorry, John. I hated to have to tell you this."

"You're just doing your job, George. I can't blame you none for that."

McLeod got into his car and shut the door. As he started the engine, John stepped up to the window.

"They gonna try to hang him, ain't they," John said. It was not a question. McLeod winced upon realizing that his old friend had tears in his eyes.

"Giles & Sharpe are good attorneys, John. They are the best in the county. If it is humanly possible to spare Lee the noose, those men will come closer to doing it than any other lawyers you could find."

"I've worried about that boy all his life, George. I think the good Lord brought him into this world to punish me for my youthful sins. I've already lost one child. Carry Bell was only 15 when she died six years ago, and it made me even more protective of my six living children, but I have given Lee more of my time and attention than any of the others. I have always believed that if I could help him straighten up and live a normal life, then it would be a sign that God had forgiven me, but now this."

"God is not punishing you, John. I don't believe all that business about God punishing children for the sins of their fathers. You've done right by Lee. Don't fault yourself for what he may have done."

John nodded and turned away. He began ambling back toward the house. McLeod watched him slowly ascend the porch steps and go inside. Tears came to his own eyes. This murder had devastated the families of both the victim and the perpetrator.

He put the car in gear and headed back toward Lyons.

* * * * * *

T. Ross Sharpe admired the new chair his senior partner, Enoch Giles, had just bought for him. It fit him like a glove, and the rich leather smelled of success. Only 26 years of age and five years out of Mercer University, and now here he was – a full partner with one of the most highly regarded lawyers in Toombs County.

Giles, a native of Florida, was incentivized to come to Lyons by Mr. Robert Musgrove Garbutt, half-owner of Garbutt & Donovan Manufacturing Company. Mr. Garbutt was in the timber business and had operated a big lumber mill in Lyons for years. He was also a railroad baron. He and Mr. William Owen Donovan owned the Garbutt & Donavan Short Line Railroad, a lumber and freight railroad that ran from Lyons to the Georgia and Florida Railroad at Oak Park, Georgia.

Mr. Garbutt was the wealthiest man in Lyons and relied heavily on Giles for all his legal needs. This one client paid most of the firm's bills, but since establishing his law office, Giles also represented the two biggest banks in the county.

He represented the Citizens Bank of Vidalia – a growing concern. He was even more invested in the Toombs County Bank in Lyons, serving as its president and as a bank director. The firm was doing well. Giles was 27 years T. Ross' senior and had graduated from the prestigious Bradwell's College in 1886.

T. Ross was the first of his family to pursue a profession other than farming. His dad, Thomas Ripley Sharpe, had encouraged him to leave the hard life of agriculture and seek his fortune elsewhere. Although he stood to inherit a good portion of the family's 191-acre farm in the 43rd Militia District of Toombs County, he wanted to follow his father's advice and pursue a career practicing law.

Everything was falling into place after he graduated and passed the bar. He had even gotten married in 1916 to Sara Carstarphen, who hailed from a wealthy family in Macon. He suffered a brief setback when the marriage failed soon afterward, and he had returned to Lyons seeking to establish a law practice there. Although he just had a modest home in Lyons and one automobile to his name, he had entered into a partnership with Enoch Giles and was now a part of a growing law firm. He felt his life was finally coming together.

His elation at his good fortune was interrupted when his secretary, Claire, stuck her head in his office.

"Mr. John Currie is here to see you, Col. Sharpe."

T. Ross had known John Currie for as long as he could remember and admired him greatly. Being raised in the Marvin Community, where John also lived, they both attended Marvin Methodist Church. T. Ross was only seven years older than Katie, John's youngest daughter. He remembered the Currie children playing and chasing other kids around Marvin Church during homecoming and other church events.

"By all means, send him in."

T. Ross was accustomed to people coming into his office with problems and a worried look on their faces, but he was taken aback at how dejected John Currie appeared as Claire ushered him in. He rose to shake his hand.

"John, it's great to see you. How are Lula and the family?"

As if unable to stand any longer with the weight he was carrying, John Currie briefly shook T. Ross' hand and then sank heavily into a chair, "Lula's fine. I wish I could say the same for the rest of my family."

T. Ross immediately thought about John's trouble-prone son, Lee. Likely he was the only thing that could trigger the level of concern permeating John's countenance.

"Tell me what's going on, John."

* * * * * *

"We've got a tough case here, Enoch," T. Ross told his senior law partner after John Currie had left his office.

"What has Lee Currie done now," Enoch asked, correctly guessing the reason for John Currie's long visit with his junior law partner.

"Looks like he's done murder, Enoch. They believe he killed a man from Vidalia by the name of Burley Phillips."

"Burley Phillips ... hmmm, I know that name. Isn't he a jitney driver or something?"

"One and the same, worked for old man, Wilson. They arrested Lee in Milledgeville with Phillips' car, a Baby Overland, in his possession. Found lots of blood in the car and the apparent murder weapon, with one bullet missing."

"Does he want us to represent Lee?" Enoch asked.

"He does. Paid me a retainer in cash," T. Ross answered.

"Oh, boy. You and I both need to clear our calendars. This is bound to take up a lot of our time over the course of the next few months. Any idea of what may have happened?" Enoch asked.

"John hasn't talked to his son yet and just shared with me the limited information Sheriff McLeod gave him. He is now headed over to the jail to see his son," T. Ross answered.

"Well, we need to do the same and make sure they don't talk too much in earshot of the jailers," Enoch said.

"I'm on it," T. Ross said as he grabbed his hat and quickly headed out of the door.

Chapter 27

"Whatcha got for me?" Walter asked as he strode into Sheriff McLeod's office with flair and sat down confidently.

Walter Grey had been the solicitor general of the Middle Circuit for a decade and had all the sureness of an elected official with several successful elections behind him. He lived in Swainsboro, just 30 miles north of Lyons, and was making a routine stop in the circuit to check with the sheriff about cases that might need to be prosecuted.

"Good morning, solicitor. It looks like we have a murder case on our hands. We have the suspect in lockup," McLeod said.

"Murder? Do I know the victim?"

"Jitney driver out of Vidalia, name of Burley Phillips."

"Don't know him. What makes you think it's murder?"

"The victim was shot and killed, and the perpetrator buried the body and took his car. If it's not murder, then I don't know what to call it."

"Murder sounds good to me. What with the plethora of petty squabbles, land grabs, bank frauds, and tiresome car thefts, I'm ready for a good ole murder case. Who's the shooter?"

"We believe it is a young man by the name of Lee Currie."

"Don't recognize that name right off, whose representing him?" Walter asked.

"Giles & Sharpe," McLeod answered.

"Giles & Sharpe? Oh, boy, that's some big guns. You have my attention. That name Currie sounds familiar to me. Who's his father?"

"He a prominent farmer in the lower part of the county. His name is John Currie."

"John Currie, now that's a name I know. Transplant from North Carolina, as I recall. Well, what do we know so far?" Walter asked.

"It's still early; we only discovered the body last Tuesday, but here is what we have been able to gather:

"Late last Thursday evening, we believe Lee Currie hired Burley Phillips to take him from Wilson's Jitney Service in Vidalia to his father's place down near Johnson's Corner. Somewhere on that trip, we believe he shot Burley at close range and then buried his body on John Currie's property on an old throwed-away road."

"Sounds routine so far," Walter said.

"It gets worse. It appears the victim was still alive when he was buried," McLeod said.

"Buried alive? Damn, that should inflame a jury. Did he suffocate?"

"I'm not a medical doctor, so it's hard to say. We did find dirt in his nose," McLeod answered.

"The defense will probably argue that he had a fatal head wound and couldn't have known what was happening to him. Still, it's good stuff. How old is this man Currie?"

"He's 22; he's been in and out of trouble all his life. So far, his father has been able to pay the damages and get him out of any mischief he has gotten into," McLeod answered.

"This one might not be so easy a rescue for dear old dad," Walter noted as he opened his briefcase and took out a notepad. He made some notes and then looked up at McLeod and said, "Tell me more ..."

"After burying the body, I think he walked a short distance to his Uncle David Wright's house around midnight to spend the night there."

"Didn't his uncle find that unusual?" Walter asked.

"Somewhat, but not really. Mr. Wright told me that Lee and his father were constantly arguing, and it was not at all uncommon for his nephew to show up on his doorstep after one of their arguments to sleep over," McLeod replied.

"So, David Wright is Lee Currie's uncle?" Walter asked.

"By marriage, his wife Nancy is the sister of the late Levency Currie, Lee's mother."

McLeod continued, "The next morning, Lee got up, was gone for a few minutes, and then returned driving the Baby Overland we believe he took from Phillips. He told his uncle that he was going to Reidsville. Wright told me Lee was acting kinda strangely."

"What do you mean, 'kinda strangely'?"

"The boy seemed distracted and in a hurry. His uncle urged him to stay for breakfast when he returned with the car, but Lee was in a rush to leave," McLeod explained.

"How'd they find the body?" Walter asked.

"Five days later, while hunting for a runaway cow, a neighbor named John Rushing came across some disturbed earth on an abandoned road. It appeared to him that something had been freshly buried there, which aroused his suspicions. Not wanting to dig up something on John Currie's land without his permission or at least other witnesses present, he summoned some other neighbors to help him investigate the site," McLeod continued.

"Mr. Rushing appears to have a bit more sense than those who usually happens upon a murder scene," Walter laughed.

"Don't I know it? But after a few neighbors arrived, Rushing's caution was overcome by the group's curiosity, and they decided to start digging. When they had dug down about six inches, they discovered a man's shoe heel. That's when their good sense kicked in, and they stopped digging to call me. We finished digging him up after I got there," McLeod said.

"Shot in the head and then buried alive on an old, abandoned road. Mighty disrespectful way to treat the dead. This is good stuff; I am going to enjoy telling a jury about this case." Walter looked up from his notepad. "Where's your probable cause to arrest Lee?"

"I'm getting to that. Lewis Edenfield, another neighbor of John Currie's, had spotted Lee on Tuesday morning driving the Overland near the burial site. Lewis told me that he knew Burley Phillips and that the car looked just like the one Burley had recently purchased," McLeod stated.

"Just because Lee was in the area doesn't mean he went to the gravesite. You need more than that," Walter voiced.

"I have evidence that Lee was there Tuesday morning. There were fresh car tracks at the gravesite. There was also sign that someone had tried to conceal the grave that same morning," McLeod declared.

"How you figure?" Walter asked.

"Well, it had rained the night before, and somebody had placed a log on top of the grave. It was wet underneath the log, which proved that it had been put there after the rain. We found the spot where the log had been, and it was dry where it had been laying."

"Hot damn! Good investigating, Sheriff. Where did you arrest him?"

"I had learned that he had gone that morning to Milledgeville, where he was working. I called the sheriff up there, and he had the Chief of Police at the Georgia State Sanitarium arrest him where he was staying."

"George, I'm impressed. You have made this very easy for the state to prosecute. Anything else?" Walter asked.

"One more thing. The car had bloodstains in it and Hawkins, the Chief of Police at the Sanitarium, found a gun in the car. One round had been fired."

"Slam dunk!" Walter exclaimed as he slapped his hands together jubilantly and stood up.

"Maybe, maybe not. We went to Milledgeville to transport Lee back to Lyons, and on the way back, he concocted a story that someone else had killed Burley," McLeod added.

Walter sat back down. "I can't wait to hear this," he scoffed as he picked up his pencil again.

"Lee admitted that he had hired Burley Phillips to take him home but said there were two men who rode along in the car from Vidalia to Johnson's Corner. He said that while going down the Dixie Highway, these men wanted some whiskey. He told them he knew where to get some and directed Burley toward an old colored man's house. They stopped a little piece from the man's house on account of Lee's belief that the man might shoot at them if they approached that late at night. Lee said he went to get the whiskey, but the colored man wasn't home. When he returned, he said Burley was lying dead on the ground, apparently shot by one of the men."

"And, of course, we don't know who these two mystery men are, right?"

"Right. Lee couldn't remember their names."

"How convenient," Walter glanced down at his notes. "Okay, what'd this, uh, Lee fellow do when he approached the men and the body of the victim?" Walter asked.

"Nothing. Oddly, Lee said he walked over to a branch and sat down on a log to think. After a while, he returned only to find that Burley's body was gone. The men were still there trying to start the car. After a while, they gave up, handed over the keys, and told him he could have the car."

"They GAVE him the car," Walter laughed. "He said that?"

"I'm telling you, Walter, the boy's mind ain't right. I guess it sounded reasonable to him that they had the right to take his car since they killed him. And once they took it, they had the right to give it to him. I know, I know, it's crazy. But here's the good part, he had told us earlier that he bought the car from a man in Reidsville."

"Can't keep his stories straight, huh? I don't believe this case can get any easier," Walter said, taking more notes.

"We reminded him of that contradiction, and he immediately changed his story back again. He reasserted that he had bought the car in Reidsville," McLeod said.

Walter laughed and made more notes. He put his pencil down and said, "I don't think we will have any problem getting a jury to convict him. I'm tempted to go for a capital murder charge. Any evidence it was premeditated?" Walter asked.

"Not sure about premeditation just yet, but he did try to cover his tracks."

"How's that?"

"It appears he drove to Claxton to send a fake telegram to Burley's wife indicating Burley had sold the car and would be driving down to Jacksonville, Florida for a few days to deliver it."

"That doesn't sound like something he would just think up after the fact. It could show prior planning to develop a complicated ruse to get the authorities to look for Burley in Jacksonville once it became clear he was missing. Hmmm," Walter said, writing down more notes. He looked up, "You got the telegram?"

McLeod handed Walter the telegram Tersia had given him.

"A poor effort to cover his tracks. Can you believe it? I can't figure out if this guy is dumb as a post or just unlucky," Walter exclaimed as he took the telegram and read it.

"Any more good stuff?" Walter asked as he put the telegram in his briefcase.

"One more, but let's start the documentation of the chain of custody here," The sheriff slid over an evidence tracking sheet, which the solicitor quickly signed and dated. McLeod retrieved a gun from the desk drawer and laid it on the table.

"This is the gun Chief Hawkins took from the Overland Lee was driving."

The solicitor took the gun and turned it over and around in his hands. "Colt 45?"

"Nope, Smith & Wesson Model 3."

"Looks like a Colt to me."

"Well, it's a Smith & Wesson, I can assure you. Look at it carefully. Notice anything strange?" McLeod asked.

The solicitor breached the weapon and took out a bullet. "Holy smokes!"

"Yeah, that's what I thought, too. The bullets were not made for it, and they have been filed off where the cylinder can spin unobstructed."

McLeod handed the solicitor the bullet removed from Burley Phillips' head. "Dr. Youmans removed this slug from the victim."

Walter took the bullet and held it up to the light as he spun it in his fingers.

The sheriff continued, "As you can see, even distorted as it is, it shows clearly that the tip was filed off, thus matching those remaining in this gun. It should be convincing to a jury that it came from the weapon found in Lee's possession."

"Hand me a case on a silver platter, why don't you, Sheriff!" Walter exclaimed. He handed the lethal slug back to the sheriff and returned the bullet to the cylinder before closing the breach. He started to put it in his briefcase.

McLeod extended his hand. "Let me hold on to that if you don't mind. I have some other witnesses I want to show it to. You can keep the slug." He slipped the slug into an evidence bag and handed it to the solicitor.

"Okay, George, but for heaven's sake, don't lose it. That is a key piece of evidence that links Lee to the victim." Walter handed the sheriff the weapon, and McLeod returned it to his desk drawer.

"There is a strong possibility that Lee also took some of Burley's things. We couldn't find a hat or wallet on the body," McLeod asserted.

"You need to find those if you can," Walter said.

"I'm already on it. We took a watch from Lee that we think was Burley's. James Mallard is going to take that to Mrs. Phillips and see if she can identify it."

Walter frowned, "Be careful with Mallard. He's not a trained law officer and doesn't know the rules of evidence."

"I've given him careful instructions of what to ask and what not to ask," McLeod said.

Walter closed his notepad and returned it to his briefcase. "What I've got here and what you have in that desk drawer should be sufficient evidence to take before a Grand Jury. But see if you can find those items you mentioned. Search his father's house and see if that sheriff in Milledgeville will search where Lee was staying up there. Talk to anybody who may have seen anything that day, his employer, his friends, and so forth," Walter instructed excitedly.

"I know how to do my job, counselor," McLeod said tersely.

"I know, I know, you'll have to forgive my enthusiasm. You've done a great job here, Sheriff. I leave it in your capable hands to gather me up all the evidence we will need to convict him. I'm going for capital murder on this one. Lee Currie is going to hang!"

As Walter practically skipped out of McLeod's office, the sheriff's spirits dropped. He had known John Currie for years. He was a good Christian man. This was an easy opportunity for the solicitor to put another feather in his hat, but for John Currie, it was a disaster about to happen.

He determined that his only course was to gather evidence, all the evidence, both incriminating and exonerating. He would do all within his power to see that the family of Burley Phillips got justice and that Lee Currie got a fair trial.

It was not going to be easy.

* * * * * *

"Good morning, Cap," McLeod said into the telephone.

"George, that you?" Bulloch County Sheriff Ben T. "Cap" Mallard asked. Cap Mallard was just 41 years of age but wise beyond his age. His parents died within a month of each other when he was 20, and he took on the role of the head of his family of five siblings.

McLeod had met the sheriff of Bulloch County four years earlier while attending a training seminar shortly after being elected. Cap was in the 4th year of his term as sheriff and was one of the seminar's lecturers. After the workshop, Cap had invited him to his home for dinner, where McLeod met his wife and children and became fast friends.

"The same, my old friend, how's the family? When last we were together, you had six little ones, as I recall," McLeod said.

"The same count so far, but not so little anymore, George. My oldest, Mary, has just turned 14."

"14! Already a young lady. Any suitors?"

"Now, do you think there would be any young man in this county foolish enough to want to date the sheriff's daughter?" Cap laughed. "No, they all know better, but there's a young man named Noah Deal who has been making a solid effort to sit by her at church. He's too scared to ask my permission to court her. Shakes every time I catch him close to Mary. Sometimes I'll just eyeball him, and he'll move a couple of seats over from her – it tickles me. He comes from a good family, but me and Eliza ain't in any hurry for her to get married, maybe when she's in her 30s!" Cap laughed.

McLeod joined in the laughter, "Poor Mary, having the big, bad Sheriff of Bulloch County for a father.

"So, tell me, how's Eliza?"

"I think she might be pregnant again," Cap said with a sigh.

"Well, you dog you. Number seven on the way. Now don't you despair; that's just another vote for Cap Mallard someday!" McLeod laughed.

"I hope I'll be retired by the time this one comes of voting age. That's enough about me; what about you, my brother still bugging you for a job?" Cap asked.

"James would love to come aboard, that's for sure, but the County Commissioners have been ignoring my requests to take on another deputy," McLeod said, trying to hide his concerns about hiring James Mallard. The man was just too eager to play lawman, and such eagerness often leads to the kind of mistakes that causes cases to be lost.

McLeod continued, "But he's been really helpful riding with me on a few occasions."

"Well, you just set good boundaries for him; I know he gets a bit over-eager at times, but he means well. He's given up on getting a job with me. He had to accept that I campaigned against nepotism. But enough of that; this call is costing you by the minute. Tell me about your case," Cap said.

McLeod was eager to comply. He unfolded his investigation in detail into the Currie case. He wanted another opinion and was desperate to get this case right. Discussing the particulars with a peer from another county, who faced the same challenges as he did, was so much more helpful than discussing it with the locals. He was not disappointed. Cap offered several valuable insights.

"I get the sense that you didn't just call me for information, George. Let's quit beating around the bush. What's really bothering you?" Cap asked inquisitively.

McLeod chuckled. "There's no fooling a seasoned lawman, is there? Okay, you are right; I could use your help."

"If I can be useful, I'm at your disposal, my friend; whatcha need?"

"Lee Currie married into the Corey family and has a few in-laws that live in your county," McLeod said.

"I know a bunch of Coreys. Which ones are you talking about?"

"Her maiden's name was Lilly Corey; the father is Solomon Corey," McLeod answered.

"Know him well, poor but honest farmer and one of the most upright men I know. I knew his first wife, Elizabeth Nevill, quite well. She had a big family in this county, but I haven't met his current wife, Jeanette. I think she's a Smiley, but I don't know much about her family. Been real sick, I hear."

"Cap, I have reason to believe that Lee may have visited his in-laws soon after the killing. I need to find out if he came a visiting and, if so, did he tell them anything or did they see anything unusual when he visited."

"I can go talk to 'em, iffin it'll help," Cap said.

"I'd be much obliged if you would, Cap. I'm covered up with gathering evidence locally, and with my meager budget, it would be unwise to go to Bulloch County if there's nothing to be gained."

"Not a problem, George. I know how it is with penny-pinching Commissioners. I'll go see Solomon and let you know what I find."

"I'm forever in your debt, Sheriff," McLeod said.

Following a few more conversational pleasantries, McLeod put the telephone receiver down. He felt better after talking to Cap Mallard. Only another sheriff could understand the challenges of a case like this. As the county's top lawman, all the deputies and even the solicitor looked to him for answers on gathering evidence. To maintain the respect his office needed to function, he had to give good direction to his underlings and have a good plan for the solicitor. Expressing any indecision or misgivings to either was unthinkable, so being able to talk candidly to another sheriff about his uncertainties with the Lee Currie case was therapeutic.

Reenergized, McLeod sent a deputy to scour the roads and look for the hat, the watch, or other personal items Lee may have dropped at the burial site or tossed out of the car while in transit to or from it.

He thought about revisiting John Currie to reassure him that he would be fair with his investigation, but it was too late for that. This was a capital murder case now, and any communications between him and the Currie family had to be strictly professional and related to the case. Further, he was too shorthanded and too invested in the outcome to leave the job of gathering evidence totally to his deputies.

McLeod took the gun from his desk, grabbed his hat, and headed out the door. There were only a few places in Lyons that sold ammunition. He was going to the Minter-Smith Hardware Store to see Mr. Bill Ivey, the manager. With a bit of luck, he might be able to link the filed-off bullets to Lee Currie.

* * * * *

"You're going to like this," Sheriff Cap Mallard told McLeod over the telephone. It had been two days since their earlier conversation, and McLeod could detect the excitement in his friend's voice.

"I've had a break in the case down here, too, but you first," McLeod said.

"I've got a hat and a pipe that might very well have belonged to your victim," Cap said.

McLeod took a deep breath. The case against Lee Currie was becoming as solid as a rock. He wanted to be happy about what Cap had just told him, but he found elation to be elusive.

"How in the world?" He asked.

"Turns out your perpetrator spent a couple of days after the killing over in my county visiting his in-laws, just like you thought. Solomon Corey says he came to his house in the Overland automobile and took him over to Glennville to see his wife at the hospital. Solomon said he saw the blood in the car, but Lee told him it was from a hog he'd run over and killed. Lee told Solomon that he had to pay the owner $12 for the hog and haul it off the owner's property in the Overland," Cap explained.

McLeod wrote some notes about what he was hearing. "Well, it looks like he's making up a story to account for the bloodstains. I didn't even think about a pipe. I just figured he had a hat."

"Bob Kerby, whose wife Anne is Lilly's Aunt, found the pipe in the floorboard of the Overland, and Lee gave it to him."

"I'll have to ask Tersia about whether the pipe ..."

"Tersia?" Cap interrupted.

"Burley's widow."

"Ah, of course."

"What about the hat?"

"He gave that to Jim Kerby, Bob's brother. Jim told me it had blood specks on it that he scraped off with a knife. Lee told him the blood was from the hog."

McLeod wrote 'blood specks on hat' on his pad. That evidence would be one more connection between Lee and his victim. McLeod found himself sketching a picture showing a stick man holding a hat with an arrow pointing to another stick man lying down.

"This is good evidence, Cap. Anything else?" McLeod asked.

"Bob Kerby said Lee had two purses on him, and he found that unusual."

McLeod frowned. It was clear now that this was not a case of Lee taking the car from two men or buying it from someone in Reidsville. Clearly, auto theft and robbery were the motive for the killing. Lee had gone to great lengths to conceal his crime, but his foolishly handing out key evidence to his family was further proof that Lee Currie was not in his right mind.

"I don't know how to thank you, Cap. I'll need to come to get those items and talk to the witnesses. Can you make the arrangements?"

"No problem. I know you will need to stay a couple of days and take some statements."

"I'm on a fixed budget, Cap. Any chance I can stay in an empty cell in your jail?"

"I'm not going to let you do that, George. We've got a hotel up here whose owner owes me a favor. I think I'll be able to get you a room at no charge. I'll also make the appointments," Cap said and hesitated. Then he continued, "I sense you are not all that enthused about what I've told you, George. Tell me, what's eating you?"

"No use my trying to hide anything from you, Cap. It's tough when you know the perpetrator's family. Lee's father is a good man and has done his best to raise a son that, as it turns out, was just destined to become a criminal. I just hate it for him, well, for both families."

"I've been there, George. There have been times I wish I wasn't the sheriff of Bulloch County. I even decided not to run for reelection after my first term because the burdens of this office began to weigh too heavily on me, but eventually, I came to realize that it's a job that somebody's got to do. I ran for office again, got elected, and took care of the people's business, just like they elected me to do."

"Thanks, Cap. That helps, really, it does," McLeod said.

"You said you had some news, too?" Cap asked.

"The word of the killing is spreading all over Toombs County, and people are coming forth with information. A farmer named Sutton came in to tell me Lee Currie deliberately ran over one of his calves last Friday, a day after the shooting, apparently trying to damage the car a bit and shore up his story that he had run over a hog."

"One of the other jitney drivers has placed Lee at Vidalia's jitney service on the night of the murder. I also have some witnesses that sold Lee the bullets he loaded the gun with," McLeod said.

"Bullets? How would that help you? They all look alike," Cap asked.

"The bullets he bought were too long for the gun, and the hardware store manager filed them off when the cylinder could rotate," McLeod said.

"That's hard evidence, George. It will be difficult for a defense attorney to explain that away. Look, I know you are torn up about this, but you have to carefully collect all the evidence and go where it takes you. I'm sorry about your friend, but it doesn't look too good for his son," Cap said.

"You're right, Cap. It is what it is. Let me know when you've made all the arrangements, and I'll drive up there."

"Will do. And George, don't worry too much about it. Just take care of the people's business. It'll all work out for the best. Good luck," Cap said.

McLeod hung up the receiver. Subconsciously he drew a hangman's noose down to his stickman holding the hat. Realizing what he had done, he wadded up the paper and threw it into the wastebasket. For the first time, he wished somebody else was the high sheriff of Toombs County.

Chapter 28

Early Friday morning, February 27, 1920, eight days after the killing of Burley Phillips, John B. Johnson was routinely distributing breakfast to the prisoners in the Toombs County Jail. Johnson was 52 and not where he had wanted to be at this stage of his life. He hoped to hear soon from a friend on the Board of Commissioners to get on with the Roads and Bridges Department – and now, things were looking up. With all the hoopla surrounding the Currie boy's arrest, working at the jail put him close to the big wigs he needed to impress.

Lee Currie frowned as he looked down at the tray Johnson had pushed through the food slot in his jail cell. "That the same slop y'all fed me yestade? And I thought the food was bad up there in the Milledgeville jail. Hell, you'd think my home county would treat me a little better. Can't ya bring me some of what you boys eat 'stead of this crap?"

"We all eat the same food you do, Lee. It's good food; now quit your bitchin'."

"Naw, that ain't good food. My step mama fixes good food. That jail food is crap, and if you've been eaten' it regular, it's no wonder you so skinny. What's ya name?"

"J. B. Johnson."

"Can't say as I know ya. What folks call ya?"

"John."

Lee took the tray and set it down on the little wooden table in the cell. "Lookie here, John. Tell the sheriff I need to see him right pronto like."

"I spec the sheriff's busy right now."

"That's not the answer I wanted to hear, John Johnson. Do you know who my pa is? If'n you want to keep your job, you best go fetch the sheriff fer me right now!"

Johnson didn't like this prisoner ordering him about, but neither could he afford to make this kind of an enemy while he was job shopping. He pushed the breakfast cart to the side and headed down to the sheriff's office, ignoring the shouted complaints of the other prisoners awaiting their breakfast meals.

* * * * * *

"Make it quick, Lee; I got things to do," McLeod said as he arrived at Lee's jail cell. Having retrieved the sheriff for Lee, Johnson continued passing out breakfast trays.

"Sheriff, you got to go arrest that negro that lives on my pa's place," Lee said as he pushed his face between two of the cell bars.

"And why would I want to do that?"

"I can't tell you that right now, Sheriff, but he's involved in the shooting of Burley Phillips, that's why."

McLeod raised an eyebrow.

"He knows about it, I tell you, and you got to arrest him right now before that sombitch skips out on ya."

"What's his name?" McLeod inquired.

"Frank McRae, that's the negro's name."

McLeod suspected that this was another of Lee's lies, but he had promised himself he would follow the evidence wherever it took him. He got the description of Frank McRae and the directions to his home from Lee and then left to arrest him.

* * * * * *

"Johnson ... Johnson!" Lee Currie called out. He had seen the sheriff returning with Frank McRae and leading him into the building in handcuffs.

"What you want, Currie," Johnson answered after walking down the corridor to Lee's cell.

"I need to talk to you."

"Let me have that tray if you're finished with it."

Lee passed the empty tray through the food slot.

"I see where the sheriff's got Frank McRae in cuffs. Where they take him?"

"He's locked up on the ground floor where they keep the negros," Johnson answered.

"Go get him and bring him up here. I wanna talk to him," Lee commanded.

"Don't think the sheriff's gonna allow that."

"Go ask him, dammit! I gotta talk to Frank!"

Johnson stared at Currie, who glared back at him. *This man is perfectly capable of killing someone*, he thought to himself. He had that "don't give a damn" look in his eye. However, Johnson decided to ignore this request. He turned and went downstairs, and said nothing to the sheriff, who had returned to his office after locking McRae up.

In a few minutes, Carl McLeod came down the stairs.

"Lee Currie is calling for you, John. I wish you'd go up there and see what he wants, if nothing else, just to shut him up. He's stirring up the other prisoners," Carl said.

"He's mighty uppity, Carl. Thinks I'm one of his pa's field hands. I ain't doin' his bidding."

"You might want to think about that a bit. You and I work for an elected official. If Lee complains to his pa, well, I need not remind you that John Currie is thought of quite highly in this county and controls a whole lot of the vote in the lower part of the county."

"Damn, the man's been accused of murder, and here we are giving him special treatment because of who his pa is."

"That's the way small county politics works, John. Better get used to it if you want to get that job over in Roads and Bridges."

"How'd you know 'bout that? Oh, never mind," Johnson said as he turned and went back up the stairs.

"Bout time you come back up here. Where's the negro?" Lee demanded.

"They are getting his paperwork straightened out," Johnson lied. "What you want him for nohow?"

"I got my reasons. Lookee here, you look like a smart fella. Let me ask you sumpin'."

"I'm listening," Johnson said.

"If I can get that negro to say he killed Burley Phillips, do you think it'd help me out?"

"Well, I speck it would. Why do you ask?"

"Like I told you earlier, old Frank's and his wife Novella looked after us kids since we was little. I'd be natural like for him to want to kill Burley if he thought he was about to hurt me."

"Are you saying that this Frank fella killed Burley? Is that the way it happened?"

"No, that ain't how it happened, but him saying he had him to kill would help me. You just said that."

"Look, Lee. If that negro had nothing to do with it, you better tell that to the sheriff so he can let him go back to work."

"Naw, him sayin' he done it will git me off, I'm sure of it. And iffin they don't buy it, well, I'd rather him hang than me," Lee said and laughed an evil laugh. "Now, go git 'im and bring 'im up here."

Johnson stared at Lee. Lee was callously trying to put the man who practically raised him into a noose to save his own skin. In his experience, he had found this behavior too typical of how rich folks looked down on the negros and even the county's poor folks. Johnson's instincts were to put him in his place, but his common sense made him more obedient. Like it or not, bucking the muckety-mucks did not make for a good career path.

"Well?" Lee asked.

"Well, okay, I'll go get him, but I'm going to have to be here while you talk to him – jail's rules."

"Fine by me. Now go git 'im."

Johnson turned and went down the stairs. He still wasn't sure this was the right thing to do, but the sheriff was away from his desk, removing any awkward explanations Johnson might have to provide. Frank McRae slowly stood up as Johnson unlocked his cell.

"Come with me, boy," Johnson ordered.

Being used to obeying without questioning the directives of white men, Frank dutifully followed Johnson up the stairs and down the hall to Lee's cell.

"Misser Lee, how come you had me locked up in heah?" Frank asked as soon as he spotted Lee.

"For your own good, Frank. What you been drinkin'?"

"I ain't been drinkin' nudin', Misser Lee."

"I'm in a fix, Frank, and I need you to help me git outn' it. These sonabitches gonna try to hang me for a killin',"

"Who dey say you done killed, Misser Lee?"

"That don't matter, Frank. I just need you to help me. Now listen up."

Lee unfolded what he wanted Frank to say about the shooting of Burley Phillips, that he had shot Burley to keep him from killing Lee. Johnson pretended not to listen to the conversation, but it was hard to ignore Frank when he would glance over his way, incredulous that Lee was telling this made-up story in front of his jailer.

Frank and Novella McRae had indeed looked after John Currie's children. Novella was an Indian woman John brought to Georgia from North Carolina. Shortly after arriving, she married Frank, who was from Tattnall County, back before that part of the county was combined with part of Montgomery and part of Emanuel County to form Toombs County in 1905. Even though Frank had helped look after Lee when he was coming up, he now lowered his head in deference to his former ward.

"Don't ax me to do dat, Misser Lee, iffin it was self-defense, like you says it wuz, den why don't you jes tell 'im dat? Dayd believe you lots quicker dan dayd believe me."

Lee turned red in anger but controlled it and said. "That ain't for you to decide, boy! Now you do like I tell you iffin you want to keep your job working for my pa, you hear me?"

"Yessir, I sorry. I do like you say." Frank lowered his head.

Johnson had heard enough. "Okay, you've seen him. Now I'm taking him back to his cell." The jailer grabbed Frank by the arm and led him down the hall.

"Don't you let me down, Frank McRae, you hear me? You do like I tell you, or you'll regret it!" Lee stretched his arm and fist out of the cell bars and shook them as Johnson turned at the hall's end to lead his prisoner down the stairs.

Johnson put Frank back in his cell and turned the key to lock the door. He stood for a moment as he watched Frank walk bewilderedly to his bunk. As soon as he sat on the bunk, he started staring at the floor. For a moment, he felt sorry for the man, who appeared as dejected as if he had indeed done what Lee wanted him to admit to doing.

Sheriff McLeod had returned to his office. Johnson knew he had to tell him about Lee's efforts to bring an innocent man into his scheme to beat this murder rap. He turned and nervously headed into the sheriff's office.

"The boys all quiet?" McLeod asked as Johnson entered.

"Yes, sir. I fed them all their breakfast."

"Good deal. Thank you, John," McLeod returned to his writing. Johnson continued to stand there in front of his desk. Finally, the sheriff looked up.

"Something on your mind, John?"

Johnson hesitated. He had not asked for the sheriff's permission to take Frank McRae to see Lee. Goosebumps, all up and down his arms, accompanied the doubts now overpowering him.

McLeod gestured to a chair. "Sit down before you fall down and tell me what's going on."

There was no way to escape the lawman's curiosity now. Johnson sat down and revealed to McLeod what he had just witnessed.

"He told you that Frank had nothing to do with it?"

"Yes, sir, he did."

"Damn. Alright. I can see where this is going. Let the negro go."

Johnson let a slight smile cross his face and then quickly hid it. He got up and left the office, elated that he had not experienced what could have been several bad outcomes of his actions.

That Lee Currie fellow was practically putting his head into a noose.

Chapter 29

Lee had been in Toombs County jail only two days before the rumor began spreading on Vidalia's streets that Burley's killer would walk because of John Currie's influence in the community and the powerful law firm representing his son. The mood of the family and friends of Burley and Tersia Phillips was getting ugly fast. The talk was especially ominous around the liar's table at Bob's Diner in downtown Vidalia.

Burley Phillips's brother Thomas was staring into his coffee, ignoring the talk around the table. Although they were trying to avoid eye contact with him, everyone at the table kept watching him discretely, no doubt wondering how he felt about his brother's killing.

Everyone hushed when he finally said in a low voice, almost a whisper, "You can't beat people with money. They can do murder and get away every time, but Lee Currie done kilt my big brother, and there ain't no way he's gonna walk."

The other men at the table looked at one another and then mumbled their agreement. Lawrence Pharr spoke on Phillips' left, "Surely, you don't think they gonna get him off, do you, Tom? After the horrible way he done shot your brother and buried him alive? I heard he's admitted he's the one what done the shooting."

Phillips winced upon hearing, "... buried him alive." He saw Eannus Smith touch Pharr on the shoulder and shake his head as if quieting him from discussing any further the details of Burley's gruesome death.

Pharr mouthed "sorry" to Eannus.

Phillips continued, almost in a whisper, "My brother wouldn't hurt a flea. I always had to look adder him, even though he was four years older'n me. He was real tender-hearted and wern't no fighter."

Thomas Clifton, an old Civil War veteran, listened quietly to the conversation. He finally spoke, and the others immediately stopped talking and listened respectfully to the old calvary man. "Thomas, yo pa fought by my side in the Great War of Northern Aggression. He was a part of the Georgia 25th just like me, only he was infantry, and I was calvary. He was one of the bravest men I ever knew."

The others nodded in agreement. Old man Clifton continued, "I was there when he killed three Yankees huddled behind a log after one of them shot one of his fellow soldiers whilst the two of 'em were charging a hill. I think that fellow was named Bowen, or something like that. Thomas, your pa shot one, bayonetted another, and strangled the third with his bare hands."

The men around the table stared at the old man and then looked at Phillips in awe. Nobody said a word.

"Yo' pa would've known what to do. If he was still living, that Lee Currie fellow would not see the light of another day for killin' one of his boys in cold blood like that."

As if they had gotten their marching orders from their commanding officer, the men shouted their agreement, and curses rang out in the diner's air. Other patrons curiously stared at the table of angry men with growing apprehension. Phillips could feel his blood boiling.

"He needs to hang," Eannus thundered.

"Damn right," Pharr added.

They looked at Phillips, seeking his confirmation. There was complete silence during the long moment that passed. For the first time since sitting down at the table, Phillips looked up. He was direct across from old man Clifton, who met his gaze for a moment and then nodded, as if confirming what Phillips was thinking. Phillips slowly stood up.

"Let's hang that son-of-a-bitch," Phillips growled.

Almost in unison, all the rest of the men stood up except the old man, Clifton, who kept his eyes fixed upward, proudly looking directly at Phillips, who was still looking back at him.

"Thomas, there's a rope in the back of my wagon just outside. Put it to good use, make your pa proud, avenge the killin' of your brother," Clifton said.

"Come on y'all. We need some more men in case the sheriff gives us any trouble," Eannus said, and the three of them hurried out the door.

* * * * * *

William E. Bugg picked up the phone and waited for the operator to pick it up, which she did almost immediately. "Dorothy Nell, get me Mack Wimberley!"

"I'll ring him right now, Mr. Bugg," Dorothy said.

After a moment, Mack came to the telephone, "Mack Wimberley."

"Mack, the Sheriff's got trouble comin' his way," William said anxiously.

"Who is this?" Mack asked.

"William Bugg."

"Oh, sure, William. Didn't catch your voice. What kind of trouble you talking about?"

William's answer came quickly and urgently, "I overhear a group of men talking just now over at Bob's Diner. They's aiming to form a lynch mob and go hang that fella Currie the sheriff has locked up."

"How many?"

"There were three of them that left here, but they said they were gonna go gather up some more men in case you gave 'em any trouble, and Mack ..."

"Yes?"

"Thomas Phillips is with them."

"Damn, well, thanks for telling me, William. I'll let the sheriff know right away."

* * * * * *

"Thanks for accommodating me on such short notice, Merritt; my prisoner should arrive there sometime this afternoon. I owe you one," George McLeod said into the phone before hanging it up. He had just made arrangements with Sheriff Merritt Dixon for a cell in the Chatham County jail for Lee Currie. Now he needed to get him out of town as quickly as possible.

"Carl, I need for you to go with Mack Wimberley and his son George to take Lee Currie to the Ohoopee Train Station," McLeod told his son.

McLeod's anxiety was not lost on his son, "What's up, Pa?"

"Just what I feared. Mack just got a tip that some men in Vidalia have gone and formed a lynch mob. I don't know how much time we have, so you will need to hurry."

Carl's brow furrowed, "You coming with us?"

"I'll take the train later. I need to stay here and delay the mob as much as possible and throw them off the scent. It will take them twenty minutes or so to get here from Vidalia with these roads. You need to leave in the next ten minutes."

Carl turned, and his father grabbed him by his arm. "Carl, I can't let Lee fall into the hands of a lynch mob. I could never face John Currie if I let that happen to his son. You get him out of here, and I mean pronto!"

"I won't let you down, Pa. Where is Mack now?" Carl asked.

"He's on his way here. Come with me. We got to get Lee ready to travel."

The sheriff bounded up the stairs of the jail, with Carl following close behind. He would need to call a few deputies and constables just in case the lynch mob arrived before his deputies got on the road, but right now, he needed to get Lee Currie ready for a long ride. He grabbed Lee's civilian clothes and held them out into Lee's cell.

"Lee, put these clothes on. You're going for a ride."

Lee stood up and took the clothes. "Hot diggedy dog, my pa's finally getting me out of this hell hole."

"Fraid not. We gotta move you to Chatham County. There's a mad bunch of folks from Vidalia coming this way, and they are aiming to string you up."

"The hell you say, what fer? I ain't done nothing."

"In their mind, you killed Burley Phillips, and they aim to set things right, vigilante-style."

"Well, you gotta protect me, sheriff!"

"That's what I'm aiming to do, Lee. Now get dressed. Carl will take you downstairs. I've got some calls to make."

Lee was frantically stripping off the prison whites and hopping on one foot while putting on his jeans. "I'm 'bout ready, sheriff; we ain't got time for no calls!"

"It's for your protection," McLeod called over his shoulder as he headed back down the stairs.

McLeod called John Johnson and appraised him of the situation.

"Be there in a jiffy," Johnson replied.

Four more calls and the sheriff had five men headed toward the jail. He felt confident that would be enough to hold off a lynch mob. It had been his experience that a mob's courage quickly dissipated when they had shotguns aimed at them. He unlocked the gun cabinet and started loading his stock of shotguns.

Carl came down the jail stairs holding Lee – still tucking his shirttail in his pants. McLeod looked up, but his calm demeanor did not assuage Lee; he looked worried. At the sound of gravel flying from a car outside breaking hard, Lee cowered behind Carl.

"Get me out of here, dammit! They've come to hang me!" Lee cried out.

McLeod anxiously went to the window.

"Calm down, Lee. That's your ride out of town. Carl, get him to Ohoopee as fast as you can. They won't know where he is. I'll meet you there later this evening. Now git!"

Carl took Lee by the arm and headed to the car.

McLeod watched dirt fly as Mack sped off in his personal vehicle, which he had offered to use to avoid being spotted while they were leaving town with Lee. McLeod went inside, got a broom, went back outside, and disguised the tracks where they wouldn't show that someone had just left in a hurry. He took the broom back inside and sat down to await the arrival of his backup.

* * * * * *

The sound of several cars arriving outside the jail caused McLeod to swallow hard. He breached his shotgun to verify it was loaded, closed the breach, and took a deep breath. *This is it*, he whispered to himself. Finding his courage, he stepped out onto the jail's front porch to a rapidly forming semi-circle of angry men, some armed. Despite his internal apprehension, the sheriff's expression was steely and did not change as the men stepped aside to open a path for Thomas Phillips to work his way to the front.

"Evening folks, yawl look like you might be a bit upset about something. Want to state your business?" McLeod said calmly.

"We ain't got no quarrel with you, Sheriff McLeod, but that man in there done killed my brother, and he's got a hanging coming," Thomas Phillips said from the apex of the semi-circle formed by the mob of twenty or so men now assembled at the front door of the Toombs County Jail. McLeod was standing before them defiantly but holding his shotgun across his waist in a non-threatening manner. McLeod wanted to keep the situation calm until circumstances dictated otherwise.

McLeod calmly said, "You must be Thomas Phillips."

"That's right. The man Lee Currie killed was my brother," Thomas said.

"I'm sorry about your brother, Mr. Phillips, and Lee Currie may indeed have a hanging coming, but not before he gets the fair trial that the law guarantees him."

Lawrence Pharr called out, "Burley didn't get no fair trial, Sheriff. That Lee Currie fella shot him in cold blood and buried him alive. The Bible says an eye for an eye and a tooth for a tooth. You'd do the same if it was one of your kin!" He moved toward the sheriff menacingly.

McLeod slowly pulled up his shotgun and aimed it right at Pharr's head, which froze him in his tracks. "The Bible might govern my actions when I'm off duty, Mr. Pharr, but when I'm wearing this badge, I'm sworn to uphold the laws of the State of Georgia, and I'm sure you don't want to test my commitment to my oath of office."

The men looked at each other, searching for crowd courage against the lone law officer.

"You can't shoot all of us before we overtake you, Sheriff. You might as well give him up," Thomas said.

Johnson and four other men came streaming out of the jail door, each chambering a round in their shotguns as they fanned out on the porch and aimed into the mob. Reactively, the men began to back up.

"Thomas," McLeod said calmly, but with that air of authority that demanded respect, "You and your family have suffered a great loss, but let's not create any more widows here today. The days of vigilante justice are behind us. Lee will be tried, and if convicted, he will be punished accordingly. Now go home and let the law take its course."

Lawrence Pharr and Eannus Smith, standing to the left and right of Thomas Phillips, looked at him as if waiting for his signal to fight or leave. For a long moment, Thomas stood there, glaring at Sheriff McLeod.

"Thomas, think very carefully about what you are doing. You need to go home now. These men are your friends, don't do something stupid and get some of them killed," McLeod said.

Eannus spoke quietly to Thomas, "Let's go, Thomas. There ain't a jury in this county that'll let Currie go free, no matter how powerful his pa is. Like the sheriff says, let's give the law a chance, and if they don't do right by ya, well, there will be another day for us to do justice."

Thomas looked directly at Eannus, who nodded to confirm that he would be there if vigilante justice was needed later. He turned back to face McLeod.

"Sheriff, I hate to see the taxpayer dollars wasted on trial for that no-good son-of-a-bitch. We'll do it your way for now. But mark my words ...,"

"Thomas, do like your friend suggests and go on home. Let the law take its course," McLeod said as he lowered the shotgun.

Phillips looked into the eyes of McLeod for another long moment, then turned. The mob again opened up a path for him and then followed him back to their cars, mumbling among themselves and looking back angrily over their shoulders at the sheriff and his deputies.

John Johnson lowered his shotgun but kept a wary eye on the receding mob as it dispersed. "We got lucky on that one, Sheriff. They think Lee's still in the jail."

McLeod also watched the mob as they got in their cars, cranked them, and drove away. "Let's keep it that way, at least, until I can get Lee safely tucked away in the Chatham County jail."

"You think they might try again?"

"I don't know what Thomas is capable of, and with that look of hate in his eye, I must tell you that I could feel ants crawling on my skin. We all need to be on guard."

The other men went inside, and McLeod stood for a few moments more on the jail porch. The last car drove slowly by the jail. Thomas Phillips glared hard at him from the passenger seat as the driver drove away.

I'd feel the same way if it had been my brother Lee killed, he thought to himself as he turned and re-entered the jail, continuing to struggle with his feelings for both men's families.

Chapter 30

It appeared to Carl McLeod that nobody was any happier than Lee Currie to be high tailing it out of Lyons. The town had become a dangerous place for him. As the dust rising behind Mack Wimberley's car swirled and dissipated, so, it appeared, did his concern for the lynch mob headed toward the jail behind them. The farther down the road the car went to Ohoopee; the chipper Lee seemed to feel.

"Hey, Carl, you get a chance to shoot my gun?" Lee asked him as if he now had no care in the world.

Carl was sitting at Lee's left in the back seat. He turned to him and asked, "Your gun?"

"Yeah, the Smith & Wesson Model 3. You know, the pistol that Chief of Police at the Sanitarium in Milledgeville stole from me and gave to your pa. I figured you'd be done shot it a few times by now," Lee said.

Carl saw Mack Wimberley turn his head slowly from his driving duties to look at his George beside him. George was already looking incredulously back at his pa. He knew what they were thinking. They were whisking Lee out of town to save him from a lynch mob, and yet the man was ready to make small talk about his gun – unbelievable! But Lee's gay mood might just evolve into an opportunity to gather more evidence against him.

Well outside of the City Limits with no sign of being pursued, Mack slowed down. It was only a short seven miles to Ohoopee, and it would be a while before the train left for Savannah. Carl knew what Mack was doing. He wanted to give Lee every opportunity to do what he liked to do best, brag about his exploits.

Being a trained police officer, Carl knew they had to carefully tread if they wanted anything Lee said to be admissible in court.

"Nope, my pa won't let me anywhere near it. But I would like to shoot it. Does it shoot well?" Carl asked Lee.

"Oh, hell yeah," Lee answered. "I could hit a telephone pole while driving that Overland at full speed!"

"You're kidding," George said, looking back from the front seat.

Lee's eyes sparkled. "Damned, if I'm lying. That's the same gun they issued soldiers in the Great War, and they ain't no fools. I bought it from the Minter-Smith Hardware Store, and I damn shore want it back after this mess is over," Lee said.

Carl saw his opening. "That might be a while, Lee. You've got yourself in a real pickle this time."

"Naw, my pa will get me off. He's hired the best damn law firm in the county to represent me."

George said, "Lee, I'm sorry they got you locked up for that killing. It ain't fair that you have to go through all this."

Seeking to appear sympathetic, Carl said, "Yeah, Lee, me, too – bad business, that is. I've known you for a long time. I can't possibly see how you could have done what they say you did unless Burley had it coming. It just don't make sense to me."

Lee went quiet, and Carl swallowed hard. Had they been too obvious?

"I don't mind telling you all about it, because I know you are my friends and won't tell it," Lee said after a long minute of silence.

"Yes, we are your friends," Mack quickly replied, trying to sound sympathetic.

Carl winced. He wished Mack had not said that. He moved quickly to mitigate the potential damage.

"You don't have to tell us anything if you don't want to, Lee. It's okay to keep it to yourself," Carl said.

"Nope, y'all my friends, and I don't mind telling you exactly how it happened," Lee said.

Carl gave Lee a small smile, hiding his glee and confidence that his statement telling Lee he didn't have to talk had removed any legal restrictions on using Lee's pending confession.

"I seen Burley Phillips driving one of the prettiest cars you ever saw around town – a Baby Overland – brand, spanking new. Now I figured on buying it from him, and I asked him to take me to my pa's house, giving me a chance to see how it rode.

"We took a different route down there, going down the Dixie Highway, because we wanted to go get some whiskey from a colored man what has a still down on Cobb Creek near J. S. Alexander's place. Onliest problem was when we come up uponst Cobb Creek; the water was over the bridge. Burley stopped, and I urged him to go on across, but he was too skeared to try it, so we turned around," Lee said.

"So, you didn't get the liquor?" George asked.

"Hell, no," Lee answered.

"What'd you do then?" Carl asked.

"While he was driving, I commenced bargaining with him for the car. I asked him how much he wanted fer it, and he told me he'd part with it for $1,150.

"Well, I told him I was interested if he could sell it to me on credit. I told him about my job in Hardwick with Mr. Harden at the barbershop and pressing club. But that son-of-a-bitch wasn't the least bit interested in letting me have that car on credit, said he weren't no damn banker. I didn't particularly like his attitude. My pa could probably buy his ass, cause he sho weren't no businessman, fer as I could tell. In fact, he was kinda insulting me, making out like I was some deadbeat or something. I decided right then and there that he didn't deserve to own a nice car like that Overland."

Carl couldn't believe what he was hearing. Lee was talking to three witnesses openly and freely, like he had nothing to hide. He had just admitted his motive for killing Burley Phillips, to steal his car. Solicitor General Grey was going to love this.

"Sounds like a stubborn fella, that's for sure," George said.

"Well, his insulting me cost him plenty. We come back toward Lyons for a little piece, and I told him that he needed to turn into the lane going up to Cobb Creek Church to get to my pa's house. I told him it was a short cut. He turned up the church road. I done made up my mind right then and there that I was going to have that car, and the only way to get it was to kill that sorry son-of-a-bitch. That's when I shot him."

Carl gasped. Lee had just admitted that he shot Burley Phillips. Goosebumps appeared on his arm. It was not only what Lee had said – it was how he had said it, so casually, as if bragging like he had bagged a deer or a wild boar and was telling his friends about his skill in making the kill.

Mack broke the long silence that followed Lee's startling revelation, "If Burley was driving the car, how'd you keep from having a wreck after you shot him?"

"Oh, we weren't a moving. He'd stopped at the church," Lee said.

"Why did he stop," Mack asked.

"Hell, I don't know," Lee answered.

"Could it be that he thought you had him driving on the wrong road?" Carl asked.

"Yeah, probably. The road was pretty rough, and it was late at night."

Carl realized they might need more evidence to convict someone like Lee, who liked to brag and make himself look important. The defense counsel could say it was just boisterous talk rather than a confession – full of Lee's visualizations. He decided to set a trap.

"How did you shoot him in the left side of his head if he was sitting on your left?" Carl asked.

"I didn't," Lee answered. "I shot him on the right side of his head."

Got him! Carl thought to himself. Only the killer and those who helped dig Burley up at the gravesite could have known where he was shot.

"I pointed off to the left and told him that was Cobb Creek Church, and we were on the right road to my pa's place. When he looked at the church, that's when I popped him. Here, let me show you. Carl, look off to the left," Lee instructed.

Carl turned his head as if to look out the window, and Lee made his hand into a fist with his index finger extended, and his thumb pointed up and bent as if imitating a gun. His handcuffs clanked as he placed the imaginary gun right behind Carl's right ear while George looked on in amazement.

"Bang!" Lee thundered, causing everyone in the vehicle to jump. Then he laughed at their reaction, drew his index finger to his lips, and pretended to blow smoke from the make-believe barrel. Carl turned his head back toward Lee, who was smiling broadly.

"So, Burley was looking at the church when you shot him?" Carl asked.

"Yep," Lee said, reveling in the interest this eager audience was showing for his story's details.

"What'd you do then?" George asked.

"I put him in the back seat and come on around and wound up heading for my pa's place," Lee said.

"How did you get him in the back seat?" Mack asked.

"I threw the son-of-a-bitch over," Lee said. It appeared to Carl that he was enjoying telling the story to his "friends." It seemed to make him feel special to have their undivided attention, with everyone hanging on every word. He continued performing for his seemingly captive audience.

"I drove back up and turned to the right on the road to Johnson's Corner. Drove by Mr. Gibbs' House and old Ed Parker's place. I needed to get rid of the body somehow, so I turned to the right in Johnson's Corner and went down to my pa's place to get a shovel."

"A shovel?" Carl asked.

"You know, to bury the son-of-a-bitch. I got a shovel and a hoe out of my pa's gin house and then drove out close to Novella McRae's house, where I turned on an old field road we had stopped using a couple of seasons ago."

"Novella McRae?" Carl asked, hoping he could remember all these details. He dared not take notes.

"Novella's an Indian woman my pa brought with him when he came to Georgia from North Carolina. She looked after us children, and pa gave her a place to live there on the farm."

"What did you do then?" George asked, not wanting Lee to stray from his account of what happened to the body of Burley Phillips.

"Well, I went out on that old field road, stopped, and just tried to figure things out for myself. I sat there for dang near two hours studying on what to do. While I was thinking, it come to me that a man named Bishop had told me Burley had a lot of money on him. I figured he had no more need of it, so I went through his pockets and found his purse."

Mack jumped in, "Well, he was a jitney driver that sold cars on the side. Everybody knew that. I'm sure he carried a lot of money with him for wheeling and dealing."

"I heard that, too. Did Burley have a bunch of money on him?" Carl asked.

"Why, hell no. He mighta had two dollars and fifty cents, or maybe two dollars and sixty cents was all. He had an old watch, but it didn't look like it had too many jewels in it, so I didn't figure it was worth much. I decided to go ahead and bury him."

"If I had been you, I would have carried him to somebody," Mack said.

"Where in the hell would I have carried him?" Lee asked.

"It wouldn't have made no difference. I would have carried him to somebody. I would have been crazy as a bat sitting there for two hours with a dead man. How'd you get him out of the back floorboard?" Mack asked.

"Just pulled him out," Lee answered nonchalantly. "I know this. I wasn't gonna bury him no six feet under. Didn't figure he deserved that, the way he talked to me like a dog. Dug a hole about thirty inches deep and rolled him into it."

Mack pulled up to the Ohoopee Train Depot and stopped the car. He set the brake and turned around in his seat.

"It will be a while before the train arrives from Lyons. Sheriff McLeod will be on it. We've got a little wait ahead of us."

"I gotta take a leak," Lee said.

"Me, too," George added.

"Can you take these cuffs off? They're hurting me and making it hard to do my business," Lee asked.

"Sorry, Lee, the cuffs gotta stay. Sheriff's rules," Carl said.

"Well then, I might need your help," Lee laughed.

"That's real funny, Lee. Now just step over there to those bushes and stay where I can see you," Carl said.

* * * * * *

The men relieved themselves, and all but Mack returned to the car. Mack went up the stairs of the depot to inquire about the train schedule.

As he entered the station, he noticed a fire in the negro's side of the waiting room. He recognized Dr. Kemp, who practiced medicine in the Lyons area, old man Smith, and another man he thought he had seen before but could not recall his name. All were sitting in the white's only waiting area. Also, the doctor recognized Mack and called out, "Why, hey, Mack, what brings you way out here to Ohoopee?"

"Transporting a prisoner from our jail to the one in Savannah," Mack told him. "We've got a lynch mob behind us that would like to dole out some vigilante justice rather than letting the man have a fair trial. I have come to ask you gentlemen for your help in protecting him."

"I don't want nothing to do with no lynch mob," Mr. Smith said.

"You think they may be following you?" Dr. Kemp asked.

"I don't think so. We left before they got there, and Sheriff McLeod stayed behind to try and throw them off on where we were taking him, but you never know."

The man Mack didn't recognize lifted his jacket to show a pistol on his hip. "I'm ready to do whatever it takes to protect your man, deputy. Name's A. W. Benton. I'm the Warden at the Brown Farm Prison in Savannah."

"You're just the kind of help I need there, Warden, and I appreciate it, good sir. Hopefully, there won't be any problems before the train gets here," Mack said.

Mack went over and spoke to the station agent to alert him to the possibility of trouble and then returned to his car outside.

After Mack reentered the vehicle, Carl asked, "Let's get back to your story, Lee."

"Can't we have something to eat?" Lee asked. "We left the jail before they fed me."

"I'm hungry, too, but they don't have any food at this depot. Besides, the sheriff's got the money to feed us. He'll be here directly to figure something out," Mack answered. "In the meantime, let's hear your story. It'll keep our minds off our hunger."

"Hard to think about anything with your belly growling at you, but okay. What do you want to know now?" Lee asked.

"What did you do after you buried him?" Carl asked.

"Well, I left the Overland there and walked over to my Uncle Dave Wright's place to spend the night," Lee answered.

"Why did you leave the car," Mack asked.

"Well, I was all dirtied up from digging; I was tired, and, quite frankly, I didn't want to have to deal with all the questions my uncle might ask about the car."

"Did your uncle think anything of you coming by so late to spend the night?" George asked.

"Naw, I stay there all the time when me and my pa gets to arguing. Uncle Dave's used to me coming round at all hours. I left early the next morning and got the Overland and drove it back to Uncle Dave's to tell him bye. He wanted to ask me about it then and tried to get me to eat breakfast, but I told him I had to go."

"Where'd you have to go?" asked Carl.

"I told him I had to go to Reidsville, but I drove to Claxton," Lee said.

"Claxton? What in tarnation for?" Mack asked.

To Mack, it was apparent that Lee enjoyed telling the story of his exploits to this eager audience. From what he knew about Lee, having killed a man must have commanded the respect he had craved all his life. Mack reasoned that Lee wanted these men's admiration for how clever he had been in how he had disposed of the body.

"Well, I didn't need for Burley's wife to come looking for him right away, so I rode over to the telegraph office in Claxton and sent her a telegram. I made it appear it was from Burley hisself."

"How'd you do that?" Mack asked. He had seen the telegram the sheriff had gotten from the station agent and knew what it said. Lee was about to prove he was the one who sent the telegram.

"I figured that I'd use the telegram to tell her that her husband had sold the Overland to a man in Jacksonville, Florida, and would be driving down there to deliver it. That way, when he didn't come back, they would go looking for him down there."

"Damn, if you ain't a smart cookie!" Carl exclaimed.

"I'm freezing my balls off," George said. "Can't we go inside?"

"There ain't no fire on the white's side of the waiting area," Mack said.

"Freezing will make you color blind," George said, opening his door. "Let's go inside and get out of this cold."

Everyone in the train station looked up when the four men walked in. The negros started whispering to each other when they saw Lee's handcuffs and chains.

"What the hell you darkie's looking at," Lee snapped at them and lurched forward until the slack in the chain Carl was holding ran out, and he was jerked back. "Y'all git on away from that stove and let your betters sit down!"

"Hush, Lee, this is their side of the station," Carl cautioned.

"Their side is wherever I tell 'em to sit, and my side is wherever I want to sit," Lee said intimidatingly, still glaring at the negros, who moved away from the stove, well-conditioned to subservience when white men spoke to them.

The four men sat down. Mack went to the station window closest to the road to Lyons and looked out. No cars were in sight. He looked down the train track going to Lyons. No sign of the train there either. He sighed and sat back down. They had all the information they needed to get a first-degree murder charge to stick against Lee. Now it was just a waiting game and waiting made him nervous.

* * * * * *

Lee jumped when he heard the whistle announcing the train's arrival from Lyons.

"What if that mob's on the train?" he asked Carl nervously.

"I'll check it out. Y'all stay near the other door till I make sure nobody but the sheriff is on the train," Mack said.

Carl quickly spoke up. "No, I've got my service weapon. I need to be the one to check it out. Mack, you stay in here with the prisoner. Warden Benton, since you're armed, you want to come with me?"

Benton nodded and joined Carl as he stepped out onto the platform to await the train, now plainly in sight. The train came to a halt with a screech – the steam hissing as the outlet valves released it from the pistons. Smoke billowed from the chimney. Both men stepped up from the station platform onto the train.

Sheriff McLeod met them halfway through the first passenger compartment.

"You alone?" Carl asked.

"Yep, the mob broke up pretty quickly when they realized five men with shotguns were guarding him. They think he's still back in town. Lee all secure?" McLeod asked.

"You ain't gonna believe all he told us, Pa. He laid it all out, plain as day, admitted to killing Burley for the car, burying the body, and even sending the telegram to Mrs. Phillips to throw her off his trail. It's open and shut," Carl said.

McLeod looked over at the Warden and then back at Carl.

"Oh, it's okay, Pa. This is the Warden at Brown Farm Prison in Savannah, and he volunteered to help me," Carl said.

"Evening, Sheriff. A. W. Benton, at your service," the Warden said.

"Much obliged for your help, Warden, but the danger's behind us, I'm pretty sure. The mob broke up quickly and headed back to Vidalia. We should be fine," McLeod said.

"Understand completely, Sheriff. Mobs are unpredictable, but most are pretty easily dissuaded from taking the law into their own hands in this day and time. If your prisoner is convicted, I'll be happy to house him at Brown Farm," Benton said.

"I'm afraid there ain't gonna be any need to house Lee Currie. If he's convicted, he's gonna hang," McLeod said.

Benton nodded and got on the train.

* * * * * *

The sheriff turned to his son and told him to get the other three men, who emerged from the train station soon after. Lee was looking about nervously.

"You're in no danger, Lee. The mob broke up and returned to Vidalia.

"George, would you please drive Carl back to the office? Carl, you go with him and look after the office till I return tomorrow. Don't tell anyone where we are going, and if anyone asks about Lee, tell them he's locked up safely. Mack, I'm going to need you to ride to Savannah with Lee and me," McLeod said.

"Got my bag in the car, Sheriff. I'll go get it," Mack said.

Mack soon returned with his luggage and boarded the train. The Sheriff and Lee were already on board. Only after they were safe inside and the train huffed out of the station did Lee finally calm down. He started smiling again, as if nothing had happened and he was on a fun trip to Savannah to go shopping or to the beach.

"I'm hungry, Sheriff. You are supposed to tend to my feeding, you know. How 'bout some vittles?" Lee asked.

McLeod nodded and walked down the aisle to where the conductor was standing. He ordered sandwiches from the dining car for him and his two companions. Mack followed him to get out of Lee's earshot and told him all he remembered about what Lee had said to the men.

"It just convinces me of what I've been suspicioning all along," McLeod said.

"What's that, Sheriff?" Mack asked.

"He ain't right in the head, Mack. No sane man would tell a deputy sheriff and two other witnesses all that. He seems to me to have the mind of a child. He is totally unaware of how much trouble he's in."

"You didn't offer him anything of value to get him talking, did you?" McLeod asked.

"No, Sheriff, he just offered it up freely. Once he got started, he wouldn't shut up. One thing's for sure, Sheriff, he did it, and no jury is going to let him go for not being right in the head. Heck, I could argue that anyone who kills another person ain't right in the head."

"I know, I know. An eye for an eye and all that. But I just feel sorry for John Currie. He's struggled all of Lee's life to make something of that boy, and now he will have to watch him swing. I just hate it for the Currie family."

"And I hate it for the Phillips family, Sheriff. Lots of folks are hurting, but Lee killed that man just to steal his car. There's no escaping that, and we have to serve justice, no matter who it hurts," Mack said.

George McLeod stared at the floor of the slowly rocking passenger coach. He glanced back at Lee, who was looking out of the windows like a child riding a wagon for the first time. He looked back up at Mack.

"It's times like this that I hate my job."

"I'm sure everybody on both sides appreciates the fact that you have this job, Sheriff. I know you will see that it is done right, and everyone is treated fairly and with compassion."

McLeod turned and walked back to where Lee was sitting. He sat down beside him and looked at the floor. Lee glanced over and then turned to look back out the windows again at the countryside flowing past the train window. Mack joined them. The two exchanged a glance and then just stared at the floor.

* * * * * *

It was only 30 miles from the Ohoopee Station to the Claxton Station, and they had hardly finished their sandwiches before the whistle announced the train's approach. Sheriff McLeod had telegraphed ahead to the station agent, asking him to meet the train and identify Lee as the person who sent the telegram from the Claxton telegraph office.

McLeod stood up and walked to the nearest exit. He signaled Mack to come over to him.

"I'm going to go in and bring out the station agent. When we come back inside, you wait for my nod and then ask Lee to stand up. Understand?"

"I got it, Sheriff," Mack replied and returned to his seat.

The station agent was waiting on the platform.

"Mr. Mulkey?" McLeod asked as he stepped off the slowly stopping train and walked in the station agent's direction.

"M. H. Mulkey, at your service. You Sheriff McLeod?"

"That's right," McLeod said as he shook his hand.

"Thank you for meeting me, Mr. Mulkey. I know it's probably past your quitting time, and I appreciate your staying over. As I wrote in my telegram, I need for you to identify whether the man in my custody is the man who sent that telegram to Mrs. Tersia Phillips a week ago," McLeod said.

"I'll do what I can, Sheriff. My eyes aren't too good, but I think I will know him if I see him."

The sheriff nodded, and the two men stepped off the station platform and into the passenger car. Lee was still looking out the window.

McLeod motioned for Mulkey to sit down and whispered in his ear, asking him if he saw Lee in the train car. The station agent immediately fixed his eyes on Lee and Mack, as they were the only other car passengers. They were seated about twenty feet or so away from Lee.

"I can't be sure, but that young man over there sure looks like the same man who came into the telegraph office last week," Mulkey said.

McLeod nodded at Mack.

"Stand up," Mack said.

"What for, we gitting off?" Lee asked.

"Just stand up, Lee."

Lee obliged and looked at Mack, puzzled. He then turned his gaze to the other end of the passenger car and squarely on Mulkey, who registered a chill and took a deep breath. Mulkey turned to the sheriff.

"Oh, that's him, all right. I'll never forget that face. He was in my office for probably a half-hour or so. I kept looking at him because he was taking so long to write that telegram; yep, that's him all right," Mulkey said.

The sheriff motioned for Mulkey to leave the passenger car and they both stepped out onto the station platform.

* * * * * *

Lee turned to Mack and asked, "What was that all about? Who was that man?"

"That's the fella that sent that telegram you wrote to Burley's wife to throw her off the scent, Lee," Mack answered.

"No, it ain't," Lee said. "He was there, but it was that little black-eyed, black-haired son-of-a-bitch that sent it."

"Thanks for setting me straight on that, Lee," Mack said as a slight smile appeared on his face.

* * * * * *

"Is it true that he killed that woman's husband, Sheriff?" Mulkey asked as the two men stepped back on the station platform.

"We are going to have a trial to find that out, Mr. Mulkey. Now, did you tell me that there was someone else in the office when the suspect came in to send the telegram?" McLeod asked.

"Yes, sir, Mr. D. R. Fussell was operating the telegraph key that day. He was suspicious about that man from the get-go, but I had no idea he was capable of murder," Mulkey said, shaking his head in bewilderment.

"I'm sure the Solicitor General Walter F. Grey or his assistant, George W. Lankford, will be sending you and your telegraph operator a subpoena to appear as a material witness in his trial," McLeod said.

"Well, you best not take too long, Sheriff. I'm moving back to Peoria, Illinois, during the latter part of June or early July to take on a job there. But Mr. Fussell witnessed it all, so he should be able to identify him."

"Is Mr. Fussell here right now?"

"No, I didn't know you would want to talk to him. I let him go earlier this afternoon when his shift ended. But I can send for him if you like. He doesn't live too far away."

"Not necessary; we can talk to him later. Thank you again, Mr. Mulkey. I appreciate your staying over," McLeod said.

The two men shook hands, and McLeod stepped back on the train.

"All aboard!" the conductor shouted as McLeod sat down in the seat opposite Lee and Mack Wimberley.

The whistle sounded, the steam hissed, and the train lurched eastward as the trio settled in for the fifty-mile ride to the sheriff's jail in Savannah, Georgia. McLeod watched Lee, who pressed his face to the window to look back at Mr. Mulkey, still standing on the station platform watching the departing train.

"He's a nice man, but I don't care too much for that other son-of-a-bitch that works at that telegraph office," Lee said as they pulled away from the station.

Chapter 31

Early Monday morning, March 9, 1920, John Currie and his wife Lula sat solemnly on the sofa in the plush waiting room of the law offices of Giles & Sharp. The elder Currie was spinning his hat in his hands, and Lula was trying her best to comfort him.

"Col. Giles and Col. Sharpe can see you now, Mr. Currie," Claire said as she motioned him toward the conference room.

"I'd like my wife to accompany me if you don't mind," John said.

"Certainly, Mr. Currie," Claire said as she escorted them into the room.

Enoch Giles and T. Ross Sharpe stood as the Curries entered.

"John, Mrs. Currie, it's good to see you both. I am so sorry to hear about Lee's being arrested," T. Ross said to his old friend as he shook his hand and gestured to two chairs.

"I can't imagine how the two of you must feel. Please, have a seat," Enoch said.

"Can I get you anything, Mr. and Mrs. Currie?" Claire asked.

"Nothing for me, thanks," John said.

"I'd like some water if it's not too much trouble," Lula said.

"No trouble at all. We have one of the new refrigerators, and I can offer you a cold Coca Cola if you would prefer that," Claire offered.

Lula brightened. "Oh my, we don't have electricity out in the county, much less a refrigerator. A Coca Cola would be a real treat, thank you."

"Bring me one, too, Claire," Enoch said.

"Col. Sharpe?" Claire asked.

"Coffee would be nice, Claire. Haven't yet had my limit this morning."

John looked up at T. Ross, "My son Lee has got himself in a mess of trouble that I can't get him out of this time. He's gonna need a good lawyer."

John choked up and dropped his head, spinning his hat again. Lula put her arm around him, "John has been worried sick about this. He has gotten Lee out of so many scraps before, but nothing ever like this," she turned to Enoch.

"Col. Giles, I'm sorry, we don't know you all that well, but my husband has known T. Ross all his life and his father Thomas before that. He has high regard for him, and if you and he are partners, I'm sure you must be a good lawyer, too," Lula said and then turned to T. Ross, "Ross, we had to come to you and Col. Giles for help. John wouldn't feel comfortable with anyone else representing Lee."

John softly sobbed while Lula rubbed his shoulder. Enoch opened a folder, and T. Ross flipped to a new page of his notepad. Claire returned with the sodas and coffee.

T. Ross spoke, "Lula, you know how I feel about your husband and his family. Of course, we will help you. And we are fortunate to have Enoch to help us with this. He was practicing law before I was old enough to go to law school and is one of the best criminal defense lawyers in Toombs County, if not the best."

"They want to hang Lee, Ross," John looked up and said. "They want to hang my boy. I know in my heart that he didn't mean to kill nobody. I mean, he's a braggart; he cusses like he's all big and bad, but he ain't never hurt anyone before," John was trying his best to regain his composure.

Enoch spoke up, "John, of course, we'll take the case and defend Lee with everything we have in us. Ross and I will do it together and keep you informed every step of the way." Enoch glanced over at T. Ross. He had seen frightened parents in his office before, but John Currie's pain was palatable, making him struggle for the right thing to say.

T. Ross spoke up, "We have both read the newspaper accounts of what happened, and I shared with Enoch what you told me Sheriff McLeod said about it, but he needs to hear it in your own words. Can you tell him what you know about what happened?"

John's gaze had returned to the floor. Lula broke the silence, "He has difficulty talking about it, Col. Giles. I'll tell you what we've heard.

"John and I went down to the jail right after they brought Lee back from Milledgeville, where they arrested him. John talked to Lee and Sheriff McLeod.

A little before they found the jitney driver's body on February 24, somebody saw Lee driving the man's car close by. They had Lee arrested up in Milledgeville, and he had the car with him, a Baby Overland, I think they said it was. According to the Sheriff, Lee told him that two men from Pembroke killed Mr. Phillips, but the bullets in the gun they found in the car Lee was driving matched the one they took out of the dead man, and, uh, they charged Lee with the murder."

Enoch looked up from his notes, "That's very helpful; please go on ..."

Lula looked at T. Ross, "I don't think you know about this yet, but I understand that a lynch mob formed up in Vidalia last Saturday to hang Lee, and the sheriff had his men take him to the jail in Savannah. When they were taking Lee to the Ohoopee train station to put him on the train there, Sheriff McLeod said Lee confessed to the killing and told his men exactly how the whole thing happened," Lula explained.

John had regained his composure and sat upright. "Col. Giles, the sheriff said that Mr. Phillips was still alive when Lee buried him. That ain't gonna sit well with no jury. I can't see a good ending of all this for my boy."

"John, let's don't give up just yet. The evidence against your son is certainly substantial, but there is always another side to every story. We don't know Lee's side yet," Enoch said.

Lula spoke up, "Lee told us at the jail that they tricked him into making that confession on the way to Ohoopee."

"How so?" Ross asked.

"He was so glad to be getting out of Lyons and away from that lynch mob, feeling like they had rescued him and all, that he just started babbling on when they started asking him all about the killing.

Lee doesn't always understand what people are thinking. He looks at things real simple like, when, in truth, they are not. He wants people to like him, and sometimes he exaggerates things to make him look, uh, brave, or bigger or better than he is.

He thought they were his friends and that he could talk to them about, uh, everything that had happened, and they wouldn't repeat what he said," Lula related. "Friendship means a lot to Lee. He hasn't got a lot of friends."

"What made him think they were his friends?" Enoch asked.

"They told him so," Lula replied.

Enoch was stunned. What Lee had said to the deputies was indeed damming, but it could be a flagrant violation of his rights if the deputies misled him to get him to talk.

"If they tricked him into saying something by promising him a reward, they won't be able to label it a confession. It might be what you call in law, an admission. By law, they may not be allowed to testify to what he told them while in custody because of how they induced him," Enoch said.

"A reward? I didn't hear him say nothing 'bout no reward," Lula said.

"For a man in as much danger as Lee was at the time, what with a lynch mob after him and all, their rescue of him and their accompanying offer of friendship would have been a great reward," Enoch explained.

"The Sheriff told me they charged him with 1st Degree Murder," John said.

"Well, to make that stick, they will have a tough row to hoe. The prosecution will need some evidence that it was premeditated, that Lee was preparing to kill his victim ahead of time," T. Ross said.

"All that man's family and friends in Vidalia are in an uproar. How can he ever get a fair trial with some folks in this county ready to lynch him?" John asked.

"We'll see if we can get a change of venue to another county. We can get more into the details later. You just leave it to Ross and me, Mr. Currie. We will give him the best defense possible," Enoch assured.

John Currie dropped his head in his hands, and Lula put her arm around him again.

"John, you know we'll do everything we can for Lee," T. Ross said.

John looked up directly at T. Ross, "You can't let them hang my boy, T. Ross; you just can't." He began to cry a father's tears for a son in grave danger.

T. Ross felt a lump in his throat. He had known John Currie all his life and knew full well of his struggles to raise Lee. It was harder than he had anticipated seeing this oak of a man, whom he had so long respected for his strength, reduced to tears like this. The fact that so little could be done to save his son from the hangman's noose made it difficult for him to maintain his composure.

Enoch broke the awkward silence and said, "John, we will do everything within our power to see that Lee gets a fair trial. We may not be able to keep him from prison, but Ross and I will do all within our power to keep him alive."

* * * * * *

Solicitor General Walter Grey was worried. Giles & Sharpe had not asked the sheriff to serve any subpoenas on witnesses, nor had the defense communicated with his office about a plea arrangement, given this appeared to be an open and shut case of murder one. They had not sent anyone out to question possible witnesses or gather their own evidence to his knowledge. He was entirely in the dark about their defense strategy. Assistant Solicitor General George W. Lankford read the concern registered on his boss's face.

"Giles & Sharpe have something up their sleeve, Walter. We've seen them in court before. When they have a weak case, they obfuscate, sow doubt, and use legal trickery to win the case," George said.

"True, and that strategy has worked for them time and time again. I don't like going into court as blind as we are in this case," Walter responded.

"Surely, they can't overcome the mountain of evidence and admissions we have against their client, can they? We have a motive, in that he wanted that Overland, we have a plethora of physical evidence, and we have Lee Currie's confession!" George said.

Walter threw his papers down on the table, "And what do we have if Enoch gets the confession thrown out? Not a single witness to the actual killing!"

"But Walter, they didn't offer him anything of value or threaten him in any way."

"They didn't?" Walter repeated loudly and walked over to within inches of George's face. "They didn't?" He turned and walked away, talking over his shoulder.

"You don't know the mind of Lee Currie, George. From everything I've heard about him, he's like a child desperately wanting attention and to be liked." Walter turned around to face his law partner. "Those stupid amateurs offered Lee the one thing he craves most in the world – friendship, attention, someone to listen to him and brag on him," Walter said and sat down.

George's brow furrowed. Walter had a point. A "thing of value" had different meanings to different people, but he wasn't ready to panic yet.

"Walter, the gun and the bullets were in Lee's possession when he was arrested. The bullets are unique in that they had been filed off. The slug taken from the victim was also filed off. How often do you see evidence that good? This is certainly manna from heaven. There is irrefutable evidence that Lee did the shooting, even if his admissions get kicked out."

George slid Burley's pipe across the conference table. It spun several times and came to rest in front of Walter. George then tossed over Burley's hat, and it covered the pipe.

"I mean, think about it, Walter. Lee went all about distributing his victim's hat and pipe, for gosh sakes, with Burley's bloodstains still on them! We caught him with Burley's car and Burley's purse. What more evidence do we need?" George's voice rose as he rattled off the facts and evidence.

"All circumstantial, all circumstantial. Nobody saw him shoot the victim. If his confession turns out to be non-admissible, that evidence is not worth a damn. He could claim he found it along the road.

"We are going up against the best, George, the best. You've seen the jurors crying after one of Enoch Giles' closing statements. And this hotshot new lawyer, T. Ross ...," Walter waved his hand in the air when his memory failed him, "... whatever is his last name, is just as good, I hear. If he catches us unprepared with one of his clever defenses, well, underestimate that law firm at your peril."

"Walter, I know they are the best defense attorneys around these parts, and I can attest to how sharp Enoch Giles is, having served on the Board of Directors at the Toombs County Bank with him, but you are the best prosecutor, and you've beaten him before. The fact that we don't have a witness to the actual shooting doesn't guarantee an acquittal with this overwhelming evidence. This case is rock solid. About all they can do is plea for life imprisonment rather than hanging," George said.

"And then there's the jury," Walter looked up and said. "What are the chances that none of the jury knows and holds John Currie in high regard? Limited to none, that's what! Burley Phillips didn't run in near as big a circle. Picking an unbiased jury in Toombs County will be damn near impossible."

George put his right arm across his chest, propped his left arm on top, and cupped his chin, "Well, then we better get started on finding twelve men who don't know John Currie that well." He stood up. "I'll get a list of the prospective jurors from Clerk of Court Dess Gray right away."

Walter nodded to George, who turned and left the conference room. Unfortunately, his assistant's assurances had not assuaged the Solicitor General. His experience with Giles & Sharpe had taught him to expect the unexpected when the evidence against their client was this strong. He nervously tapped his pencil on the legal pad and racked his brain over what strategy the defense would put up. Nothing came to him, and it was maddening. He pounded his fist on the conference table.

"I can't let Lee Currie get away with this heinous murder just because he comes from a prominent family and can afford the best of lawyers," he said out loud to an empty conference room.

Angrily, he flung the pencil across the room.

* * * * * *

T. Ross and Enoch began preparing a defense in earnest. They would need to talk to the sheriff and review the arrest record and evidence gathered. They would need to interview Lee Currie, and Enoch wanted a doctor to examine Lee to see if there was a medical explanation for his actions.

T. Ross heard Claire greet Sebe Hall, who had just come into the office.

"Col. Sharpe has completed that title search you requested," Mr. Hall, Claire said.

"Is that Sebe Hall out there?" T. Ross called from his office.

"Yes, it is, Col. Sharpe."

"Have him come into my office. I need to ask him something."

As Sebe walked into his office, T. Ross stood to shake his hand and gestured for him to take a chair.

"Sebe, don't you have two brothers who are doctors?" T. Ross asked.

"I sure do, my older brother John has been practicing medicine for over three decades now, and my younger brother Jim is in his 12th year as a doctor."

"Two doctors in the same family. How come you never took it up?"

"Doctoring never held much sway over me. Real estate is what gets me going. Why do you ask?"

T. Ross explained to Seaborn that he needed expert medical advice in a case he was handling. After the two men had talked for a while, he discovered to his delight that the elder Dr. Hall had even made a study of mental disease, and the younger Dr. Hall had treated the Currie family. He asked for Seaborn to help him secure their possible testimony in the murder case against Lee Currie.

"My sister is married to a doctor, too, Ross, if that will help you," Seaborn offered.

"It just might, Sebe. Please give Claire their contact information if you have it," T. Ross said.

"I do, and I'm happy to share that with you, Ross," Sebe said as he put his hat back on and was out the door.

* * * * * *

It was now time to talk to Lee. Being friends of the family and well known to Lee, the defense team agreed that T. Ross would lead the way and make the first trip on the train to Savannah to begin conversations with Lee at the Chatham County Sheriff's Jail. As soon as they could talk to Dr. John Hall and get his consent to be an expert witness in the trial, Enoch would take him to Savannah to examine Lee. Since neither he nor the doctor knew Lee Currie, he would ask John Currie to come with them to make the introductions and put Lee at ease around two people he did not know.

* * * * * *

T. Ross didn't particularly like trains, but they were faster and more reliable than automobiles, especially with the poor roads and recent rains.

The clickety-clack of the train's wheels created a rhythm that helped calm him and clear his mind of other distractions as he pondered a believable defense for his difficult client.

The evidence was a real problem, but there were places where holes might be poked. Lee had given his captors and others multiple versions of how Burley Phillips was killed, all of them inconsistent. He was coming across as a first-class prevaricator, but it didn't seem intentional. Lee appeared to be unable to separate truth from fiction.

The train conductor interrupted his thoughts, "Can I get you anything from the dining car, Mr. Sharpe? This will be the last call before we reach Savannah."

"Just coffee, please," T. Ross said, and the conductor moved on down the aisle, repeating the question to the other passengers on the train.

T. Ross' partnership with Enoch was still very young but had proven to be very successful. Together, they had garnered a reputation as the best law firm in Toombs County. A loss of this case would be hard to overcome. This was going to be his greatest challenge ever.

As he tried to relieve the anxiety of the case, he let his mind drift. Again, the long shot crept into his head – insanity defense. The gentle swaying of the rail car finally lulled him to sleep.

* * * * * *

Lee launched into a quick chatter as soon as he spotted T. Ross, "Bout time my damn lawyer showed up. Where have you been? I haven't seen a face I recognize the whole time I've been here. You would not believe how bad the food is in this place and I ain't got no business being locked up with the bunch of criminals they have in here. When you gettin' me out of this dump?"

He doesn't have a clue how much trouble he's in, T. Ross thought to himself. Lee Currie was accused of premeditated murder, and the prosecution had an ironclad case against him, and here he was gripping about the food and wanting to get out.

"Slow down, Lee. I'm here now. Your pa is concerned about you, and so are Col. Giles and me," Ross said as he pulled a stool that had been sitting next to the opposing wall up to the bars of Lee's cell.

"Pa should be concerned; I'm his boy, ain't I? Who's this Col. Giles fella?"

"He's my law partner. He's going to help us get you out of here."

Lee didn't appear to register the introduction and went right on complaining, "Now, Col. Sharpe, you have got to speak to the sheriff about my situation. That son-of-a-bitch in the cell next door must be crazy or something; he talks to himself all the time and whines all night long. And this place ain't clean. Hell, I found a bedbug as big as a roach in my bed last night ..."

"Lee," T. Ross cut him off. "We don't have time to talk about your living conditions here. You have been charged with premeditated murder. We need to build a strong defense, and that should be priority number one right now. Do you hear me?"

"Hell, I don't get it. All this commotion over a lousy jitney driver?" Lee quipped.

"Dammit, Lee, I'd be a bit more respectful if I were you. Killing that jitney driver could get you hung!" T. Ross said sternly.

If T. Ross meant to scare his client into realizing how much trouble he was in, it didn't work. Lee appeared unconcerned, looking as if he did not even hear T. Ross.

"Well, that's why my pa hired you, isn't it? Besides, we was neighbors and damn near growed up together. You know I wouldn't kill nobody; lessen they deserved it. Now, tell me how you are going to get me out of this damn place."

"We need to talk about the evidence, Lee," T. Ross said.

"What evidence do we need? That son-of-a-bitch came after me with a knife in his hand."

T. Ross' eyes widened. This was the first time he had heard anything about Burley coming after Lee with a knife, "What did you say?"

"Bout what?" Lee asked.

"About Burley coming at you with a knife?"

"Why? Is that important?"

"Of course, it's important – it's very important. Tell me exactly how it happened," T. Ross said as he took out his legal pad.

* * * * * *

On the train ride back to Lyons, T. Ross' head was spinning. He no longer had to think about how to develop an insanity defense. What Lee had described was a clear case of self-defense!

T. Ross began formulating all facets of this new strategy in his mind. Every man understood the concept of self-defense. When someone challenges you with a weapon, you have every right to use lethal force to defend yourself. He could also argue that Lee got scared afterward that people would not believe it was self-defense, which could explain some of his otherwise irrational behavior of disposing of the body.

He was glad to abandon the relatively new insanity defense. It would be much more difficult to prove and require months to gather witnesses and prepare testimony.

The winning trial strategy would be to make a light effort to cast doubt on the state's witnesses to keep the prosecution busy pursuing their goal of proving that Lee did the killing. The knockout blow would be calling no witnesses. Instead, they would have Lee make a statement as the last witness saying that he did indeed kill Burley Phillips, but he acted in self-defense and did some stupid stuff afterward when he got scared.

It could prove to the jury that the prosecution's theory about the case was wrong. Lee had killed Burley, which would be undisputed, but it wasn't for the car; it was self-defense. It could work!

And if it didn't, there was always the insanity defense. He and Enoch might need to go ahead and develop expert witnesses for that, even if they didn't have to use them, should the self-defense tactic prove successful.

T. Ross wanted as many arrows in his quiver as possible.

Chapter 32

Arch K. McGill took a deep breath and then exhaled as he looked at the daunting stack of telegrams on the spindle sitting on his desk. The requests for permission to reprint his Currie trial stories were coming from newspapers all over the state. With all this publicity and growing interest in this case, he had an opportunity, as the editor of The Lyons Progress, to elevate the local paper into a well-respected news outlet and increase circulation both in and out of Lyons. He had to be diligent to continue to be regarded as the best source of news of the case to his readers and other newspapers carrying his stories.

The first order of business would be to see if he could get an interview with one of the attorneys at Giles & Sharpe, who he had learned would be representing Currie. Their offices were just two blocks from his, and he decided he would go for it. He would do a cold call and see if he could get a statement.

As he walked down the Dixie Highway toward their offices, he mulled over what questions he would ask the attorneys defending possibly the most notorious client they had ever represented. By the time he arrived at the offices, he had a whole host of questions finalized in his mind. He stepped in, introduced himself to Claire, and told her he would like an interview.

To McGill's surprise and delight, T. Ross Sharpe came out and met him in the lobby, shook his hand, and invited him back to his office.

After the perfunctory greetings and inquiries about their respective families, he got straight to his call's purpose.

"I know you and Col. Giles have to be busy, so I won't take up much of your time, Col. Sharpe," McGill said as he took out his notepad.

"Call me T. Ross, Mr. McGill, and may I call you Arch?" T. Ross asked.

"Certainly," Arch answered.

"Arch it is then, and I welcome this opportunity to tell your readers about this case," T. Ross said. He lit a cigar and offered Arch one.

"No thanks, never acquired the taste," Arch said. T. Ross nodded, closed the cigar box lid, and placed it back on the desk corner.

"It looks like this trial is going to be sensational, T. Ross. It has garnered interest from across the state. Can't be hurting your firm's future business prospects to be representing Mr. Currie, now, can it?"

"Just trying to make sure he gets the defense that is his right and ensure that he gets the fair trial that the Constitution guarantees him, Arch, that's all. If we don't do a good job, it could hurt us as much as help us if we do."

"My sources tell me that he confessed to the murder, that true?"

"My client has signed no confessions, nor will he."

"But they say he admitted he did it."

"'They' say many things, whoever they are, but in court, we deal with facts and admissible evidence. The prosecution has charged my client with murder in the first degree, which involves premeditation and malice. They are going to have a hard time proving that."

"Was Burley Phillips buried alive, like some claim?"

"Mr. Phillips was shot in the head, and the bullet passed clean through his brain. Claiming that he was buried alive is just the prosecution trying to inflame the jury pool with wild speculation."

McGill made some more notes and then asked, "So, what is your defense going to be, T. Ross?"

T. Ross flicked some more ashes off his cigar, "It's still a bit early for us to know that Arch. We must depose the witnesses the prosecution has lined up, and we need to talk to our witnesses. It is another four months till the trial. Now, if you don't mind, I need to return to my preparations."

Arch got up and extended his hand, which T. Ross shook. "I thank you for your time, T. Ross. Good luck with the case, and feel free to contact me if there is something you would like the public to know about this case."

"I appreciate the job you do for the good people who subscribe to your paper, Arch. I'll keep your generous offer in mind," T. Ross said.

Arch donned his hat again and left the offices of Giles & Sharpe. On his way back to his newspaper office, he thought to himself; *this trial will put this city on the map. It won't hurt The Lyons Progress circulation one little bit, either.*

* * * * * *

"Dr. Hall?" Enoch Giles asked after hearing the voice on the telephone.

"Yes, this is Dr. Hall," the voice answered.

"Dr. James Knox Hall?" Enoch asked.

"Yes, that's right. How can I help you," Dr. Hall replied.

"Dr. Hall, I have been referred to you by your brother, Sebe, and I understand that you are the family physician to the Currie family near Johnson's Corner. Is that right?"

"I don't make it a habit of giving out the names of my patients to people I don't know, sir."

"I'm sorry, Dr. Hall, my name is Enoch Giles. I am a lawyer with the law firm Giles & Sharpe in Lyons. I have been retained by Mr. John Currie to defend his son, Lee Currie, who is accused of murder."

"Ah, yes. Well, if you are Lee's attorney, I don't mind talking to you somewhat; however, without authorization from the family, I can't reveal information protected by physician-patient privilege."

"I understand completely, Doctor. Are you aware that they have arrested Lee?"

"Lee's arrest has come to my attention, but I know nothing about the incident. How does this involve me?"

"We are interested in Lee's mental health and state of mind at the time of the shooting. I'm calling to ask you if you would be willing to provide expert testimony about Mr. Currie at his trial. We will also be contacting your brother, Dr. John Hall, to see if he will help us. We have not yet decided on the full nature of his defense, but I want to inquire if you would be willing to be called when we do."

"I don't mind helping the Currie family out if you think I can assist, but I have only limited expertise with the mind's diseases. My brother John is more familiar with this field and has studied mental illness extensively."

"That is what Sebe told us, and we definitely plan to call your brother, but as the Currie family physician, you may have additional insight into Lee Currie's behavior. We may need for both of you to testify."

"I see. I don't know how I could help, but if the family needs me."

"Excellent. Now, if you don't mind, I will put my secretary on the line to make an appointment to have Mr. Currie give you a call to verify that we are indeed in his employ and representing his son's interests. Please hang on for a moment for Claire."

Enoch handed off the call to his secretary and made a note to follow up with John Currie.

One down and three more doctors to go, he thought to himself as he hung up the telephone.

"Claire, see if you can get the telephone office to ring Dr. John Hall for me," he called through the open door.

* * * * * *

"Who was that on the telephone, honey?" Etta Hall asked as she placed a plate in front of her husband.

Dr. John Franklin Hall, II, did not answer, nor did he pick up his napkin and place it in his lap in his usual manner.

"John? Did you hear me?" Etta asked again as she sat his tea down before him.

"Huh?" Dr. Hall answered, nudged out of his thoughts by his wife's question.

"On the telephone, who was that calling you?"

"Col. Enoch Giles, attorney-at-law."

"An attorney? What in the world could he possibly want?"

Dr. Hall picked up his napkin and placed it across his lap, still lost in thought. "He says that Giles & Sharpe want to use me as an expert witness in a murder case involving Lee Currie. He wants me to go to Savannah first thing Monday of next week."

"Monday? Honey, that's when the grandchildren are coming to visit. You know how they will be looking for their papa as soon as they arrive."

"I know, I know. I don't like to disappoint the grandchildren, but this can't be helped."

"You don't have to be their expert," Etta said as she sat down and put her napkin on her lap. She dipped some mashed potatoes into her plate.

"Besides, I thought the Currie family were your brother Jim's patients. You don't know any of them; why do they want you to go?"

"Col. Giles says they have already talked to Jim and want both of us to serve as experts. I have Jim to thank for recommending that I go because I've made a special study of mental diseases for the past 15 years. They also want Jim to testify because he is Lee's personal physician. He's known Lee since he was seven years old."

"Are you going by yourself?"

"No, Mr. Giles is going with me to coordinate my visit with those holding Lee in custody, and Lee's father is going to introduce me to his son and, hopefully, make him more open to my examination."

"Why are they especially interested in your study of mental diseases?"

Dr. Hall took a sip of tea and wiped his mouth with his napkin, carefully returning it to his lap afterward. "They are interested in his state of mind at the time he is alleged to have killed that man."

"Having never met him before, how are you going to be able to tell them anything about that?" Etta asked.

"It will be just like any other new patient. I'll have to give him a thorough examination and develop a diagnosis."

"And how long is that going to take?" Etta asked.

"It could take several days."

"Several days? Oh, honey, no. You've got other patients, and the grandchildren will be so disappointed!"

"Jim could see my patients. And the grandchildren love their grandmother just as much as they do me. Make them some of your oatmeal cookies, and they won't even notice I'm not here."

"They won't notice until the cookies run out. Well, it sounds like you have your mind made up, and I guess there is nothing for me to do but pack you a bag," Etta said.

"Thank you, dear."

"Don't you stay any longer than you have to, John Hall. I need you here."

"I'll be back as soon as possible, Etta, don't you worry."

Dr. Hall picked up his copy of The Lyons Progress. There was an article about the discovery of the body of Burley Phillips, a jitney driver from Vidalia, on the front page. The report said that Lee Currie had been arrested and charged with the man's murder.

Putting the paper down, he opened a psychology text and turned to an essay written by the Russian Doctor Ivan Sechenov in 1873 entitled "Who Is to Develop Psychology and How?" The writer made an argument for a biological basis for mental disorders as measured by a person's reflexes. *In this case, this article might come in handy*, he thought to himself.

Looking at his bookshelf, he pulled out a newly acquired book written by Dr. Robert Howland Chase entitled 'The Ungeared Mind.' It was published on the first of January of the previous year, and he had read it from cover to cover several times. It was as good a compilation of all the other books he had read on the subject matter as could be found. He put it in his briefcase where it would be handy should he need it.

Chapter 33

As he was trying to read one of the psychology journals he had with him, Dr. John Hall was fighting back an attack of nausea brought on by the slowly rocking passenger car. He had no use for trains, and there was at least another excruciating hour to go before reaching Savannah. Not being able to read, Dr. Hall fixed his gaze on the night's blackness outside the train window, but that afforded precious little stimulation for his always-curious mind. Not working or having something to read during all his waking hours evoked a powerful sense of boredom and was a waste of time that he little enjoyed.

Enoch Giles had not allowed him to return to his offices in Alamo to get his examination bag, so it would be necessary to visit an apothecary in Savannah to pick up some tools needed to examine Lee Currie.

Of course, a good portion of what he had to do would require no tools at all, which was part of the beauty of psychology. Asking a bank of carefully constructed questions designed to evoke a specific response would allow him to observe Lee Currie's reactions and analyze their meaning.

He found psychology fascinating even while attending the Atlanta School of Medicine 31 years earlier. He had devoted as much as half of his medical career to developing a specialty in mental diseases. He was aware of no medical schools offering anything more than a few elective courses in the study of the mind. Many local doctors still considered psychology no more than pseudo-science and a useless preoccupation of European physicians. But a few American scholars were seeking to elevate psychology to a mainstream course of study, and Dr. Hall had amassed quite a library from those scholars.

It would be a welcome relief to vacate the infernal train he was riding and get to his room, where he could return to his reading. At least his accommodations would afford a comfortable respite from the train ride. When negotiating his fee for this trip, he was grateful that he had insisted on staying at the Marshall House on Broughton Street, which he knew to be among the best accommodations available in Savannah.

He was also comforted that Enoch Giles' secretary Claire had assured him that she would arrange transportation at the train station to take him to the hotel. Col. Giles and Mr. Currie would come in the morning and escort him to the Chatham County Jail to examine his patient. With any luck, a good night's rest would refresh him for the examination to come.

* * * * * *

Good restful sleep eluded Dr. Hall. The daunting task ahead and his distaste for being away from his practice had obviated the rejuvenating effects of a good night's rest. He found himself a bit grumpy upon the arrival of Enoch Giles and John Currie at the Marshall House mid-morning the following day to pick him up at the agreed-upon hour.

"Your accommodations were satisfactory; I take it?" Enoch asked as Dr. Hall entered the conveyance and greeted everyone.

"I suffer from the malady of too active a mind and unfortunately did not rest well; however, I have stayed at the Marshall House before and always found the staff most accommodating. They did not disappoint this time," Dr. Hall replied.

"Do you have everything you need?" Enoch asked.

"For today, I do. I just want to observe Lee talking to you and his father. That will help me formulate how the examination should proceed tomorrow. It is important that he be comfortable and motivated to reveal his thoughts," Dr. Hall answered.

"Just let us know what you need for us to do, doctor," Enoch said.

"It will be best today if I sit away from the two of you and Lee and just observe him without being introduced. I have a list of questions I want you to ask him, and if he knows who I am or why I am there, it may affect his answers. I don't want that to happen until I'm ready," Dr. Hall explained.

"I understand. You say you have a list of questions?" Enoch asked.

Dr. Hall removed a folded piece of paper from his coat pocket and opened it up. "Yes, I have them written on this piece of paper, Col. Giles," Dr. Hall handed the paper to Enoch, who unfolded it and began to read.

Dr. Hall continued, "Primarily, they are questions designed to impress upon him the nature of his offense and the enormity of the crime with which he is charged. I want you to explain why people consider what he did wrong and why public opinion is against him. You must make a conscientious effort to impress upon Lee that this is very serious, and the consequences of him not taking it so could be dire. It is important that you interact with him physically while talking to him. On this specific question here, I want you to put your hand on his shoulder and tell him that they want to hang him," Dr. Hall said.

Enoch looked up at the doctor, somewhat puzzled.

"It will be very revealing to me to observe if he is able to comprehend that he has committed a serious crime. Mind you, don't discuss the specifics of the case just yet; neither of you needs to do that; just talk about the consequences."

"What do you want me to do?" asked John Currie.

"Mr. Currie, you serve an important role in that you are a link to his foundation; that is, you were responsible for his safety as he was growing up, and your being there will likely put him at ease. Just make small talk, like you would engage in around the dinner table at home. Reassure him and make him feel comfortable," Dr. Hall answered.

He added, "Later, I will want you to introduce me and assure Lee that I am there to help him get through this. Certainly, I will need your help tomorrow when I give him a thorough physical examination."

"Thorough?" John asked.

"Very. I will need to examine all of Lee's body for malformation, mind you, which we find in people with ..." Dr. Hall hesitated and studied John's face before proceeding, "... a defective brain. I'll also need to see if he has any physical disease or disorders that might exacerbate his mental condition. Your being there and exerting that parental guidance that most of us continue to respect long after we have reached the age of maturity will hopefully increase his acquiescence to an outsider's intimate inspection of his person," Dr. Hall answered.

Enoch held up the paper containing Dr. Hall's questions. "And these will help you make your diagnosis?"

"Yes, disease of the mind is diagnosed primarily by observation."

Enoch folded the paper and placed it in his coat pocket just as they passed the old Colonial Cemetery on their way to the jail in Savannah, where Lee Currie was housed.

* * * * * *

Isaac Roos, the Assistant Sheriff at the Chatham County Jail, greeted the visitors from Lyons in the waiting room shortly after they had arrived. The Sheriff had advised that they would be coming to visit Lee.

Isaac liked Lee. He started working at the jail when Lee was transferred from Toombs County. Since then, he had handled a few hundred prisoners, but Lee was one of his favorites. It was not so much because Lee had a good personality, quite the opposite. It was because there was never a dull moment when Lee Currie was around.

When Lee was good, he was very good, and when he was bad, he was very bad, but what Isaac liked most of all was Lee's ability to wrestle.

The guards at the jail would pick out one of the prisoners as "their" guy and make bets on whose guy could win in a wrestling match. Lee's small size was deceptive, and Isaac had coaxed many a naive guard into betting against Lee when he was meeting a much bigger opponent. Throughout his incarceration, Lee had thrown down nearly every prisoner who had come to the jail, and some of them were big fellas. Yep, Lee was his guy.

Isaac invited them into a smaller room designed to allow prisoners to consult with their attorneys in a more private setting. In the room was a small rectangular table with four chairs on the visitor's side and one on the prisoner's side.

Glass panels allowed the outside guards an unobstructed view of the prisoners and their visitors.

After exchanging the usual pleasantries, Enoch introduced himself as Lee's lawyer and asked the jailer how Lee had adapted to his new surroundings.

"He sure as hell don't like being here, and he's been right unruly, so much so that we have had difficulty managing him at times," Isaac said.

John was disappointed but not surprised, "What do you expect? He's being restrained against his will, and he's away from his home."

"So is everybody in this jail, Mr. ...?" Isaac asked.

Enoch spoke up, "This is Lee's father, Mr. John Currie."

Isaac shook John's hand, "Please to make your acquaintance, Mr. Currie, and I'm sorry about your son being in this trouble, but as I said, everybody here is not happy about being away from their homes. Most accept their fate and are well-behaved, but Lee fusses with everybody pretty much continuously." He paused and continued, "I've already had to lock him up in solitary two or three times, and it was worse on us than it was on him, what with his hollering and screaming the whole time he was in there. But when he would see me making my rounds, he would quieten down and calmly ask me why he was locked up. When I'd tell him it was for breaking the rules, he would say, 'If you let me out, I will behave myself.' It seemed like he couldn't remember why he was in solitary or even in this jail, for that matter. Never seen one quite like that one, that's for sure."

"You haven't had to manhandle him, have you?" Enoch asked.

"We ain't hurt him if that's what you're getting at, but he's strong and knows some good moves to try and keep us from restraining him. Like I said, he's a pretty good wrestler. I've been encouraging him to wrestle with the other inmates to burn off some of his nervous energy during the yard time. He seems to like it – when he wins, that is," Isaac said, laughing.

Enoch asked Isaac to bring Lee into the visiting room. Dr. Hall moved a chair to the room's far side, away from the table. Enoch and John sat on one side of the table, with their backs toward the doctor, as was prearranged.

Dr. Hall was anxious to see Lee's first reaction to their being there. He observed as Lee immediately spotted his father coming down the stairs. Lee almost stumbled and yelled out, "Hey, Pa!" while accelerating his pace as much as the leg-irons would permit. He rushed into the room and attempted an awkward hug of his father while handcuffed.

"Are the cuffs necessary?" Enoch asked.

Isaac hesitated a moment and turned to Lee, "You gonna behave yourself if I take these cuffs off ya?"

"Hell yeah," Lee said excitedly and extended his arms out toward his jailer, "Get 'em off!"

Isaac produced a ring of keys and opened the handcuffs, which fell with a loud clang on the floor, still tethered to his leg-irons. Lee looked up at him expectantly. "I'm afraid those will have to stay, Lee." Then, ignoring Lee's arms outstretched as a sign of protest, he turned and went out the door, closing it behind him.

"Asshole," Lee said as he turned back to his father. "Pa, it's so good to see you." He hugged him again, unrestrained by the handcuffs this time.

Everyone sat down. Lee ignored Enoch and Dr. Hall, his dark eyes sparkling as he directed all his attention to his father.

"Has Lula had the baby yet?" Lee asked.

"The baby was born back on April 7th, Lee. A healthy baby boy. We named him Arthur Bascom Currie."

"Hot damn! I've got me a baby brother. And here I've been rottin' in this crap house and couldn't be there for the birth. How's Lula doin'?"

"Your stepma is doing fine, Lee, and she sends her love. They been treating you alright in here?"

"Alright, I guess. They been letting me wrestle the other inmates. I've been kickin' their butts! When you gonna get me out of here? I want to see the baby."

"As soon as possible, son. I've hired Col. Enoch Giles here and T. Ross Sharpe, too, to be your attorneys."

Lee looked at Enoch, "T. Ross is the best," Lee said excitedly, then turned to Enoch. "I don't believe I know you. Where's T. Ross?"

Enoch shook Lee's hand. "He couldn't come, but T. Ross and I are partners in this together to help get you out of here."

John took his son's hand from across the table. Pain and anguish went across his face, and Lee picked right up on it.

"What's the matter, Pa?"

John patted his hand. "Nothing's the matter other than I want you home, son. Now, listen to me; Col. Giles has some questions he would like to ask you. You pay close attention to him, you hear me?"

Lee couldn't take his eyes off his father.

"Thank you, John," Enoch said. "Lee, you need to understand that the Solicitor General has filed some serious charges against you with the court. You are charged with 1st Degree Murder," Enoch said.

Lee ignored Enoch's statement and asked his father, "Have you heard from Lilly?"

"Lee, you need to answer Col. Giles' questions. We can talk about Lilly later," John advised.

Lee turned to Enoch and stared at him so intently that a quiver ran down the lawyer's spine. "Okay, go ahead and ask your questions."

"They have charged you with murder; did you hear me say that a moment ago?" Enoch said.

Lee looked over Enoch's shoulder at Dr. Hall for a moment, then turned his head at the sound of another prisoner coming down the stairs.

"Lee?" Enoch said.

"What?" Lee said gruffly.

Enoch reached across the table and put his hand on Lee's shoulder, "Lee, you need to take this seriously; they are going to hang you!"

Lee brushed Enoch's hand from his shoulder and turned to look again at the prisoner coming down the stairs.

"Look at that damn red-headed son-of-a-bitch. He is in here for murder, too," Lee said.

Enoch and John looked at each other. Dr. Hall made a note.

Lee noticed Dr. Hall writing and turned to Enoch. He pointed toward Dr. Hall and said, "What does that damn long-legged rascal want in here?"

Enoch replied, "Dr. Hall has come down here to examine you, and I want you to do whatever he directs."

Lee looked at his pa, who nodded, then shouted to Dr. Hall, "How you going to do much examining or requesting sitting way over there, Doc?"

"I'm just observing right now, Lee. We'll get to know each other a lot better tomorrow," Dr. Hall said.

"Observing ... ha," Lee said.

For another thirty minutes, Enoch continued to ask Lee a series of questions with varying success at holding his attention, but it was like trying to herd cats. Lee seemed to favor small talk with his pa and talking about what was going on with the other prisoners. His perilous circumstances seemed of little concern to him. Enoch asked the last questions Dr. Hall had given him and stood up.

"Lee, we are going to leave now. We will be back tomorrow, and Dr. Hall is going to give you an examination. This is all for the trial and very important. It's going to help us get you out of here," Enoch said.

Lee smiled at the prospect of being released, "Well, now we are talkin'. Y'all just come on back tomorrow; that's just fine with me." He gestured down to his leg irons. "I ain't going nowhere, looks like. I'll be right 'cher waitin'."

* * * * * *

Dr. Hall's mind was racing. He was furiously making notes on the way back to the Marshall House while Enoch and John chatted about the defense Enoch was developing.

It was clear to him that Lee had no power of concentration. He would not stay on a subject for any length of time and was very easily distracted. Despite Enoch's best efforts to hold his attention, Lee jumped from one thing to another and could only concentrate on a single topic for a moment or two before he was off to something else.

Alarmingly, Lee showed no sympathy for his victim. It was as if there was no conscience controlling his actions, and he had no remorse for his actions at all. Even when his father tried to appeal to his sympathy for Burley Phillips' widow, Lee seemed utterly unmoved. Instead, he began to brag again about how he had beaten the other inmates at wrestling and wanted a crack at wrestling the guards.

This was not a case involving one of the three types of insanity most laypeople easily recognized: mania, melancholia, and dementia. This was paranoia, accompanied by a symptom for which he couldn't find a label in his medical journals just yet – a lack of power to resist.

Fishing out of his briefcase Dr. Robert Chase's book, 'The Ungeared Mind,' he thumbed through the index and then turned to the chapter on mind and body connections. The author had written that physical abnormalities in the body often accompany paranoia. When he was with Lee across the room earlier, Dr. Hall could detect nothing physically wrong. Still, his examination in the morning would better allow him to explore any causality between Lee's body and his paranoia.

"We need to go by an apothecary and let me purchase something. I will need to test his reflexes with a reflex hammer. I'll also need a flashlight and a few other things," Dr. Hall said.

Enoch nodded and began looking for an apothecary along his route.

"There's one," Enoch announced as he pulled to the curb.

"Let me pay for whatever you need," Enoch offered as he went into the apothecary with Dr. Hall. Soon they emerged with the needed items and were again on their way.

"What do you think so far, Dr. Hall?" Enoch asked.

"It is a bit too early for me to opine, but I can see indications of a mental defect. It would be premature for me to give a specific diagnosis before I give Lee a physical examination and conduct some more tests."

Enoch pulled up in front of the Marshall House and set the brake.

In the back seat, Dr. Hall saw John turn around to face him.

"You don't know how much I appreciate your coming with us to help out with this business. I have come around to accepting that my boy is in serious trouble, but he don't know no better, and it would be a mighty hurtful thing if they took his life when he couldn't help himself."

Dr. Hall smiled and nodded. He gathered up his notes and stepped out of the car. Turning back toward John, he said, "Mr. Currie, I can't imagine that any jury would allow someone to hang who is not responsible for their actions. I'm going to do all within my power to determine his mental condition accurately, I promise you. I will examine him thoroughly, and if he is sane, I will tell you. If he is insane, I will tell you that, too. I know that, as a father, either answer will be painful to hear, but I promise you I will, to the best of my ability, tell you the truth as I understand it about your son's mental state."

"Thank you, Dr. Hall, that's all I can ask," John said.

Dr. Hall tipped his hat, turned, and went into the hotel.

* * * * * *

Dr. Hall was relieved that, responsive to his urging, Enoch got the sheriff to arrange for them to use one of the places reserved for the prisoners' conjugal visits. It would afford a more private surrounding without windows for Lee's physical exam.

This will do fine, Dr. Hall thought to himself. It had two small windows that provided light but were high enough over their heads to obviate the need for curtains to preserve privacy. The solitary ceiling light would suffice to provide any additional illumination they might need.

Isaac patted down the three men for weapons or prohibited contraband as they entered the room.

"What's this?" Isaac asked when Dr. Hall handed him the small hammer, which the doctor had "muffled" by wrapping it with gauze.

"It is a hammer that I will use to test the prisoner's reflexes," Dr. Hall answered.

"His reflexes, what the hell for?" Isaac asked, turning the hammer over in his hands while carefully studying it.

"I use it to test if there are any defects in his brain," Dr. Hall answered.

"You don't need that little hammer for that, Doc. I can confirm that Lee Currie ain't right in the head," Isaac laughed as he handed the hammer back. "Just don't complain to me if he takes it from you and starts bashing you with it."

Dr. Hall took the hammer back and decided not to dignify the jailer's amateur prognostication with a reply.

Isaac brought Lee into the room. Unlike the day before, he removed Lee's handcuffs and shackles entirely. "Don't start any funny business, Lee. There is only one way out of this room, and it's through that door right over there. I'm going to be just outside, ready to throw your butt into solitary if you misbehave. You get me?"

"Yeah, yeah, tough guy, I get you. Why would I want to misbehave anyway? Unlike you, these men are my friends," Lee said and laughed.

"Aww, does this mean we're not friends anymore? See if I sneak you in another donut," Isaac said sarcastically and turned toward Enoch.

"He's all yours, Colonel; good luck," Isaac said as he stepped out, shut the door, and turned the latch, which sounded a loud click.

"That son-of-a-bitch is a real hoot, ain't he," Lee said. "But I kinda like his sorry ass. Okay, Doc, what we gonna do today?"

"We're going to check your reflexes, Lee," Dr. Hall answered.

The doctor explained the procedures to Lee, and Lee cheerfully agreed to cooperate. He was in a lighthearted mood and quite pleasant this morning. He didn't even object when the doctor asked him to strip down to his underwear and sit on the table where his legs could dangle over the edge.

Dr. Hall took the hammer and tapped Lee right under the kneecap. The doctor jumped back as Lee's lower leg immediately kicked out almost 90 degrees! The exaggerated reflex startled everyone in the room, including the doctor.

"Are you doing that on purpose, Lee?" Dr. Hall asked.

"Doing what?" Lee replied.

"Making your leg jump like that?"

"Nope, I ain't doing nothing," Lee said calmly. "You hit me, and my leg reacted all by itself. Kinda funny, ain't it."

"It is unusual. I need you to relax and don't try to help or hinder your reaction. You understand?" Dr. Hall asked.

"Yeah, I got it, Doc, but I didn't make it jump like that, I'm telling ya. My leg did that all by itself. Surprised even me," Lee said.

Dr. Hall tapped the other knee and got the same exaggerated reflex. After a remarkably identical reaction several times, the doctor concluded it was involuntary, especially after testing Lee's elbows and getting a similar outsized effect.

He moved on to Lee's back muscles and got more minor reactions, but it was still on the high end of the normal range. The effect was more pronounced in the extremities. Dr. Hall had never seen anything like it and noted it on his pad.

The doctor felt Lee's muscles and found them flabby, despite Lee and the jailer's earlier description of his wrestling prowess.

"Col. Giles, see if you can get something to cover up those windows. I need to make it darker in here where I can check the reaction of Lee's pupils to light," Dr. Hall said.

Enoch knocked on the door and, when Isaac opened it, requested covers for the windows. In a moment or two, Isaac reappeared with two blankets and a stool. John Currie held the stool while Enoch stepped up and hung the blankets over the two windows. John pulled the cord on the light switch to turn off the light, and the room descended into near pitch blackness. In a few minutes, their eyes adjusted, and they could see each other faintly.

Dr. Hall waited for about five or six more minutes and then took out the small flashlight purchased the night before.

He tilted Lee's head slightly backward and directed the light into his left eye.

Lee squirmed uncomfortably, and Dr. Hall said, "Lee, I know it's bright, but try to hold still." He flicked the flashlight away and aimed it into Lee's left eye again. The pupil constricted only slightly, which amazed the doctor. He made another note. Lee looked at the paper, trying to determine what the doctor was writing.

Dr. Hall put his hand under Lee's chin and raised his head again. He directed the light into Lee's right eye, and Lee jerked again, this time more violently.

"Damn, doc, you trying to blind me?" Lee said.

"Toughen up, son. The doctor must do this for his examination," John said.

Lee's pupil remained fully open and unresponsive. Dr. Hall again flicked the flashlight away and back into Lee's right eye. Again, there was no response other than Lee's squirming.

"You may turn the light back on," Dr. Hall directed, and Enoch pulled the light cord. Lee covered his eyes and drew back from the overhead light.

"Glad that shit's over," Lee said.

Dr. Hall was stunned. He had never seen a conscious patient have little to no pupillary reflex to light shining in their eyes. Something was wired incorrectly in Lee's mind. He made another note on his notepad.

"Please stand up, Lee," Dr. Hall directed.

As Lee stood up, unclad except for his underwear, it was now more apparent to the doctor that Lee was not structured symmetrically. The doctor inspected him closely, walking around him as he did. His skull base had an unusual shape, but he knew he could not read much into that, as phrenology had been debunked as a science long ago.

Dr. Hall had not noticed it before, but now it was more apparent to him that one of Lee's eyes was larger than the other. Clearly, there was a congenital defect in the young man's brain that had interfered with his normal symmetrical development. His diagnosis was becoming more evident. He pulled up a chair directly in front of him.

"I'm going to need to inspect your private parts, Lee. Please remove your underwear."

Lee laughed nervously, "I ain't gonna take my pants off for no man, thank you very much."

John Currie spoke up, "Son, he's a doctor, and he is trying to help you. Now, do as he says."

Lee looked about the room, and his eyes fell upon Enoch, who nodded and said, "Lee, I can't defend you properly if you don't abide by the doctor's wishes. He means you no harm and is just examining you to see if you have anything wrong with you."

"I ain't got nothing wrong with me down there, dammit," Lee protested.

"Well, then, Mr. Currie, you should have nothing to fear," Dr. Hall said calmly, knowing that these words would trigger Lee's defiant side.

Lee dropped his drawers.

Dr. Hall tried to hide his reaction to what he saw. Lee's private parts were filthy, and the smell that immediately greeted his nostrils was nauseating. His penis was smaller than average, and the prepuce was elongated. Additionally, smegma covered the prepuce. Cleaning his private parts was obviously not a part of his regular bathing hygiene.

"Col. Giles, would you please ask the guard if he has any examination gloves? Oh, and ask him for some soap and water and a towel," Dr. Hall said.

Isaac returned with the requested items in a few minutes and opened the door to pass them through. Seeing him try to peer around Enoch to see what was going on, John stepped into his sightline. Isaac handed the items to Enoch, who thanked him and shut the door.

Now wearing the protective gloves, Dr. Hall took Lee's penis in one hand and saw that it was infected with pus. He milked the end and got no discharge, but pus exuded from the end when he pressed on the penis base and milked forward. It was clear that Lee was infected with the gonococci germ and had a chronic gonorrhea infection.

Dr. Hall carefully washed Lee Currie's penis and dried it afterward. He stood up and removed his gloves, tossing them into the nearby trash can.

"You can get dressed again, Lee. I have finished my physical examination."

"They couldn't pay me enough money to do your job, Doc. Handling other men's private parts ain't my idea of a fun job," Lee said as he put his clothes back on.

"Lee, how long have you had this gonorrhea?" Dr. Hall asked.

Lee looked at his father, embarrassed that the doctor had revealed this in front of him. "I mighta picked it up when I was catting around in Milledgeville, but it had quit runnin' on me, and I thought I was shed of it."

"Well, you are not 'shed' of it, Lee, not by a long shot. It is in an advanced stage and could be fatal if not treated. We will need to get you on a regimen of merbromin right away," Dr. Hall said.

"What's that," John asked.

"Most people call it mercurochrome," Dr. Hall answered.

"Putting mercurochrome on his pecker ain't going to help cure the clap, Dr. Hall," John offered.

"We don't put it on the penis; we treat gonorrhea by injecting a one percent mercurochrome solution into the patient. About three to six doses, spaced a few days apart, should do it. New research out of John Hopkins Hospital in New York has shown this to be the most effective treatment."

Lee spoke up, "I don't see what all the fuss is about. It don't bother me none. They give me morphine for it."

Dr. Hall shot a look toward Lee. "They give you morphine?"

"He has a prescription," John spoke up. "Your brother, Dr. Jim Hall, gave it to him years ago to treat his recurring headaches. I gave the prescription to the sheriff when he was transporting Lee here."

Dr. Hall was aghast. This was a perfect storm of internal and external causes for Lee's aberrant behavior. It also made his diagnosis more difficult. Like his eyes' failure to constrict when exposed to light, some of Lee's symptoms could be caused by morphine instead of a defective mind.

"We won't do anything about that for now, but morphine is highly addictive and can have some bad side effects. Nevertheless, I am not here to treat Lee for his headaches or addiction; I am here to determine the state of his mind," Dr. Hall said.

"My mind? Ain't nothing wrong with my mind," Lee said.

Dr. Hall said nothing. Lee turned to his father.

"Pa, what the hell is he talking about?"

"Lee, don't you fret none about what the doctor says. He is here to help you in your trial. We are all here to do that. This is the best way to get you out of here," John said.

"Well, he better get off this crap about my mind, then. I ain't crazy, you know. I ain't crazy one little bit," Lee said.

"That's enough for today," Dr. Hall said.

* * * * * *

The three men returned to the jail the following day, and Dr. Hall continued his examination. He gave Lee the Stanford-Binet Intelligence test and asked him many questions about his family, friends, and everyday life. They were there for about four hours and even took dinner with Lee, as the doctor said he wanted further opportunities to observe him interacting with others.

On the way back to the hotel, Dr. Hall asked Enoch to stop by a bookstore. He wanted to order a copy of the latest edition of 'A Primer of Psychology and Mental Disease' by Dr. C. B. Burr and have it delivered to him at his office in Alamo. He had a copy of Dr. Burr's original work in 1894 but had heard a 3rd edition had been published in 1906 and wanted a copy of his latest book.

"Mr. Currie, I hate to ask this sensitive question, but it has a bearing on your son's diagnosis. Has there ever been anyone else in your family that has, er, had mental problems?" Dr. Hall asked as they drove back to the hotel.

John Currie hesitated for a long moment.

Seeing the awkwardness of his question, Dr. Hall said, "I apologize, Mr. Currie. I know some folks don't like discussing such matters about their family, but this could be relevant to proving that your son's insanity was congenital; that is, he was born with it, and it might have been inherited."

John's continued silence unnerved Dr. Hall, and he feared he may have gone too far asking him whether his family had a history of insanity. He might have to find that information another way if he used it at all. He was about to tell him that he didn't have to answer the question when John finally spoke up.

"It may have come from my side of the family. I have a brother that many folk thought was not right in the head, but there is nothing on his mother's side," John answered.

"Thank you, John," Dr. Hall said and made another note.

* * * * * *

On the train ride back to Lyons the following morning, Dr. Hall was lost in thought about Lee Currie's case. It intrigued him. The man had a plethora of medical and mental problems, and it was clear that his insanity was undeniable and well developed.

He had only appeared as an expert witness in a couple of other cases testifying as to the state of the defendant's mind. There was a Peterson man from Ailey and the Gibbs man in Lyons. Gibbs was a mail carrier being prosecuted for stealing, but Peterson had killed a man and was on trial for his life. In both cases, the jury had difficulty processing medical testimony and accepting the idea that insanity had anything to do with a man's guilt or innocence.

This case would be no exception. Dr. Hall's medical ethics did not allow him to choose sides in a murder, but as a doctor, he had a duty to convince the jury of the truth, that Lee Currie lacked the mental capacity to understand that what he did was a crime. He had to reduce a complicated idea to simple testimony a jury could understand.

Lee's concentration powers were minimal, yet it appeared that he might have planned the murder ahead of time. The prosecution's lawyers would ask him to explain that contradiction medically. He would also undoubtedly have to answer questions about why Lee seemed to feel no remorse for his victim or his victim's family. He already knew the answer to that line of questioning, should the prosecution pursue it to inflame the jury. Lee's inability to emote with others' suffering was, in fact, a symptom of the psychosis affecting his behavior.

In many ways, the paranoia affecting Lee was subtle. It had taken him, albeit trained in the mind's science, a considerable length of time to recognize that Lee was paranoiac. He was hopeful that Enoch would question him in a manner that allowed him to attribute Lee's actions to his disease.

It would be tough to reduce this complex medical diagnosis to everyday words that laypeople could understand. He closed his eyes and tried to rest his tired brain, but sleep eluded him again.

Chapter 34

Judge Robert N. Hardeman had ruled against the defense's motion for a change of venue. The June 22, 1920, appeal of that ruling to the State Court of Appeals was unsuccessful. The judge set the trial for August 16, 2020. Lee Currie was brought back to Toombs County from Chatham County by train. The trial of the century was about to begin.

* * * * * *

"All rise – the Special Term of the Superior Court of Toombs County is now in session, the Honorable Judge Robert Hardeman presiding," the bailiff loudly and officiously announced.

As he stepped into the courtroom, Judge Hardeman hesitated a moment, startled by the loud rustle and bustle of men and women standing up in unison at his entry. The courtroom was packed to capacity, something he had never seen before. He continued to his seat behind the bench and settled into his chair.

"You may be seated," he said and then marveled at the loud sound of the spectators all sitting at the same time.

It was an unusually hot August. Neither the tall windows nor the ceiling fans provided sufficient relief from the oppressive Georgia heat, which was now exacerbated by the body heat of the crowds of folks in the courtroom located on the 2nd floor of the Toombs County Courthouse. Looking through the windows from his high vantage point on the bench, he could see that a large crowd had also gathered outside. He spotted a man perched in a tree in the courtyard with binoculars looking into the courtroom and heard him shout, "The judge has just arrived!" The murmuring reaction that went through the assembled crowd of outside spectators was annoyingly audible. He frowned when he heard a popcorn salesman touting his goods. Other vendors, barking their wares, added to the annoying din outside.

"Bailiff, call the day's calendar," the judge directed.

"Your honor, today's only case to be heard is 'The State vs. Lee Currie,'" the bailiff responded pompously, feeling his importance in having such an official role in what was shaping up to be the trial of the century for Toombs County.

The onlooker perched in the tree outside the window yelled to those gathered below, "It's started!"

"Bailiff, kindly go outside and tell that songbird that if he disrupts my court one more time with his pronouncements, I will turn him into a jailbird. And tell those assembled to be quiet, or they will learn that they don't have to be in this room to be cited for contempt of court," Judge Hardeman ordered.

"Yes, sir, your honor," the bailiff said and quickly turned to go out of one of the doors in the rear of the courtroom.

"Are the attorneys ready for the trial?" the judge asked.

Solicitor Walter Grey stood and announced, "The State is ready, your honor."

Enoch Giles stood and announced, "The Defense is ready, your honor."

The judge nodded to them, and both attorneys sat down. Judge Hardeman studied the room. He had never seen so much interest in a case before. In the hot August heat, a low but audible hum was emitting from the handheld fans scattered among the spectators. Judge Hardeman sighed upon spotting Mr. DeLoach, the local funeral home owner, not missing an opportunity to pass out hand fans to the few spectators not already possessing one of these portable advertisement billboards. *Do these hucksters think for a moment they can make a mockery out of this trial?* He thought to himself, displeased at the commercial atmosphere that had developed in and about the courtroom.

"Sit down, Mr. DeLoach; you are distracting the court," he said. The funeral director quickly headed to his seat, handing fans to several outstretched hands along the way.

The heat was indeed stifling, and he made a mental note to thank his clerk for thoughtfully placing an electric fan discretely at his feet. Hidden from view by the bench, it provided some welcome relief as it blew gently up the obligatory robe he was wearing that would have been excruciatingly uncomfortable in the summer heat without it.

His gaze fell upon the defendant, newly transported back to Toombs County from Savannah. Judge Hardeman had been introduced to John Currie back in the fall of 1914 when he ran for the position of Middle Circuit Superior Court Judge. His supporters felt John could help garner votes in lower Toombs County for his candidacy, and they were right. His friendship with John had continued to develop through the years, and he had taken his two full-blooded Llewellyn Setters to the Currie Farm on several occasions during quail hunting season.

On none of these trips, however, had he met or learned very much about Lee Currie. Absent the notoriety he brought with him in the courtroom; he would have been deemed to be a rather handsome young man. Still, knowing what Lee was alleged to have done, those dark piercing eyes somehow unnerved him. He fought an involuntary impulse to prejudge Lee Currie as guilty of murder before hearing any of the evidence.

Judge Hardeman quickly looked away from the defendant. He had a legal duty to see that Lee received a fair trial, which would be difficult enough under the circumstances without his forming any opinions based on his appearance alone.

There were a lot of eyes focused on this trial. The man killed was very popular in Vidalia, and the accused was a member of the influential Currie family from lower Toombs

County. No matter how faithful he was to the law, this trial was sure to have a deleterious effect on his reelection chances. His scan of the room fell upon Sheriff McLeod, and he saw the same concern registered upon the face of his fellow elected official.

His gaze returned to Lee, who, it appeared to him, was gleeful. He was craning his neck, eagerly looking around the courtroom and waving at those he seemed to recognize. It seemed as if he was reveling in all the attention. Hardeman noticed T. Ross lean over and whisper something to him, after which Lee frowned and looked down at the table. No doubt, his lawyer was reminding his client that the jury was observing him, and he needed to guard his actions.

Contrasting Lee's excitement was the dejected look of his father, sitting right behind him. It hurt Judge Hardeman to see his old friend in this much obvious pain. What hurt even more, was his sense that John Currie's face did not show the indignation of having a son accused wrongly. Instead, he was showing the painful countenance of a man who feared his son would be found guilty.

The judge shifted his gaze to the people sitting behind Solicitor Grey. The lady dressed in black with a veil across her eyes was most likely the widow of Burley Phillips. Beside her sat a man, who, given the vengeance in his eyes and his incessant staring at Lee Currie, was likely Burley Phillips' brother, Thomas.

Sheriff McLeod had briefed Judge Hardeman earlier about the lynch mob Thomas Phillips had organized. Hardeman remembered Thomas. He had presided over a trial in the Fall of 1915 when Thomas was found guilty of stealing from the American Steel and Wire Company. Thomas' demeanor worried him then, and it was worrying him now. He made a note on his pad to tell the sheriff to beef up his staff and closely observe Thomas throughout the trial.

Hardeman rapped his gavel, and the conversational din in the courtroom immediately ceased, "I know this case has garnered much interest in the community. This is the people's court, and you have a right to be here and witness the mechanism by which justice is served in your county. However, I must put you on notice that I will not allow disorder or disruptions in my courtroom. I cannot allow my jury to become biased one way or another by your vocalizations of your support for or opposition to any arguments made or evidence submitted. During the proceeding, if I hear so much as an "oh" or an "ah" from this chamber, I will have the offending party escorted out immediately. Any outburst may earn you a day in Sheriff McLeod's jail with a contempt citation.

"During this trial, counsel for the State and the counsel for the defendant will present arguments and evidence to the jury for them to decide the guilt or innocence of the accused. You are spectators and not participants in this trial. The

ONLY persons who are authorized to speak in this courtroom are the attorneys, the witnesses, the court staff, and me. If anyone is not willing to abide by these simple rules, they may leave now and avoid the embarrassment of being escorted out later," the judge paused and slowly scanned the room from side to side and up to those seated in the balcony.

"Good. I will take from your decision to remain that you both understand and will abide by my rules. The prosecution may make its opening statement."

* * * * * *

Solicitor General Grey stood up. "May it please the court and ladies and gentlemen of the jury; my name is Walter Grey. I am the Solicitor General for this circuit, and I represent the people in this matter. I will be assisted in the prosecution of this case by Col. George W. Lankford, the Assistant Solicitor General."

The Solicitor knew that the State had the advantage with juries of being believed in most trials. He needed to solidify the jury's confidence in the State's case by showing a passionate desire for justice for the people harmed by the offense, respect for law and order, and a commitment to the general peace.

"This is a case of a murder in our county on February 19th of this year. We will prove that on that date, the defendant in this trial, Mr. Lee Currie, did, with malice and aforethought, murder one Burley Phillips, a human being, and a citizen of this county.

"Our evidence will show that the defendant carried out this heinous act merely because he coveted the automobile that his victim owned and was willing to kill him to get it. We will show that he planned this murder well in advance and afterward tried to carefully conceal his crime.

"We will present testimony that shows Lee Currie told other people days in advance of the killing that he was aiming to acquire a Baby Overland. The evidence we will present will show that the defendant stalked his victim at the business in Vidalia, where Burley Phillips worked as a jitney driver. As a ruse to his intentions, we will present witnesses that will attest to Lee's asking his victim to carry him to his father's home, knowing full well that he planned to kill him and take his automobile.

We will present to you the defendant's own words telling how he perpetrated this crime. He hired Burley Phillips to take him to his father's house, where he lived. Along the way, with the car stopped in the lower part of Toombs County, the defendant asked his victim to look at a church off to his left, and when his victim complied, he put a gun up to his head and shot him at point-blank range.

"We will show you the gun we believe he used to kill the victim and the bullet taken from his victim's head wound. We will also show you how the defendant had the pistol cartridges uniquely altered to fit that gun, so there is no question in your mind that the gun he had in his possession when he was arrested was the very same one he used to kill his victim and the bullet taken from Burley Phillips came from that same gun.

"The irrefutable evidence will show that the defendant drove his still-breathing victim to a remote area of the woods on the defendant's father's property. We will show that along the way; the defendant stopped by his father's house to get a shovel and a hoe to bury the victim and cover up his crime. The medical examiner will testify that Burley Phillips was still alive when Lee Currie buried him in a shallow grave."

The audience gasped and began murmuring among themselves. Some of the ladies seemed to almost swoon.

Judge Hardeman rapped his gavel several times. "Order, I will have order. Have you so soon forgotten my instructions? Do you not believe I will do as I have said if you do not remain silent during these proceedings? I will clear out this entire courtroom if necessary. Now, be quiet, all of you!"

Judge Hardeman turned to Walter, "You may proceed, counselor."

Walter smiled. Unlike the judge, he welcomed the courtroom reaction and wanted this last statement to sink in. He slowly looked at each juror, both trying to read their faces and with his own conveying to them the depravity of how Lee Currie had buried Burley Phillips alive.

"We will show that the next morning the defendant drove the stolen automobile to Claxton to send a telegram back to his victim's wife in a macabre attempt to mislead her so that she would not be alarmed when her husband did not return home. That telegram, which we will enter into evidence during this trial, had the lie written on it that her husband had sold the automobile to a man in Jacksonville, Florida, and would be gone a few days to deliver it. That ruse was designed to plant the seed in the mind of the authorities to begin their search for Burley Phillips in Jacksonville rather than in Toombs County, where Lee's victim lay buried in a shallow grave.

"We will further show that the defendant did purposefully run over and kill a calf, to deliberately damage his stolen automobile and bolster his lie that the blood in the car had come from a hog he had accidentally killed and hauled off the hog owner's property.

"We will show that the defendant not only took Burley Phillips' automobile but also took his hat and his pipe and distributed these items, with the blood of his victim still on them, to members of his wife's family in another county, just as the Roman guards divided up the garments of Jesus Christ after they had killed him!"

"Counselor," Judge Hardeman said in a warning voice.

"I'm sorry, your honor," Walter said and turned back to the jury.

"We will show that he took his victim's purse and all the money therein and paid off some of his personal debts.

"The evidence the State will present will show, beyond a reasonable doubt, that the defendant planned to murder Burley Phillips for his car, that he did, in fact, make good on those plans, killing him in cold blood, and afterward taking possession of the Overland automobile as if it were his own.

"We will show you all this evidence so that you will be able to conclude, beyond a reasonable doubt, that the defendant, Lee Currie, murdered Burley Phillips in cold blood. By carrying out your duty to see that Lee Currie faces justice for this terrible crime, you will send a powerful message to others in this county that nobody can take one of our citizens' lives with impunity. You will afterward go home to your own family, knowing you did your duty to make Toombs County a safer place by removing the likes of this murderer from our midst forever."

Walter slowly looked each juror in the eye, turned to look at Lee, who was glaring back at him, then turned to the judge and said, "Thank you, your honor."

"Thank you, counselor." Judge Hardeman said.

* * * * * *

"Col. Giles, you may make your opening statement," Judge Hardeman said.

Enoch gathered up his legal pad, flipped back to the beginning of the pages, and stood. He looked down at Lee Currie, whispering something to Col. Sharpe, then faced the judge. "May it please the court ..." He then turned toward the jury, hesitated a moment, and walked over to the podium, "Ladies and gentlemen of the jury: My name is Enoch Giles. I am here to represent the defendant in this trial. My law partner, Col. T. Ross Sharpe, will be assisting in the defense.

"It is a hallmark of our judicial system that every man is considered innocent until he is proven guilty beyond a reasonable doubt by a jury of his peers in a court of law. Despite what the prosecution has just told you, you must reserve any judgment of my client's innocence or guilt until he has had the benefit of a fair trial. He sits before you an un-convicted man; one you must presume at this point in these proceedings to be innocent. The only way he can have that fair trial to which he is entitled is for you to regard him as innocent until the State proves otherwise, which we believe they will not be able to do.

"You have heard it said many times that there are two sides to every story, and this case is no exception. What may seem straightforward and unequivocal when first presented by the prosecution may be found questionable and uncertain after we have had an opportunity to explain the other side of the story and show you evidence that the prosecution may have withheld from you. That is the nature of a fair trial, which the law affords every man, with attorneys on both sides trying to help you see the facts clearly. It will be up to you, the jury, being the reasonable men you are, to weigh the evidence and decide the guilt or innocence of the accused. Nobody but you can make that call, not us, not the prosecution, not the judge, not all the people sitting in this courtroom, assembled outside, or following these proceedings in the paper. Only you can decide the guilt or innocence of the defendant.

"I ask that you put yourselves into the defendant's shoes and ask what you would want a jury to do if it was your life on the line. Indeed, you would want the jurors to come into the jury box without preconceived notions about your guilt or innocence. Certainly, you would want them to have an open mind, listen carefully to all the evidence and accompanying arguments, make no assumptions that are not supported by that evidence, and weigh the evidence carefully before pronouncing a sentence that could take your life or liberty.

"Consider that last statement for a moment longer. Taking a man's life is a solemn act, and the law places the burden of proof upon the State to prove the defendant's guilt beyond a reasonable doubt. The defendant does not have to prove he is innocent. Where he sits right now, he is just a man accused, not a man convicted, and for you to convict him, the prosecution must convince you, the jury, beyond a reasonable doubt, that he is guilty.

"Let that sink in. Lee Currie doesn't have to prove his innocence; the State must prove his guilt.

"Now, you will hear the State, through its witnesses, present evidence they think proves his guilt. Our job is to question those witnesses, when necessary, to show you that their testimony may not be as determinative as the prosecution would like for you to believe.

"In your life experience, you will come across individuals and hear them say, 'so and so did this' or 'so and so did that,' and because the person saying it is your friend or someone you hold in high regard, you might tend to give their words greater weight than they deserve. As triers of fact, you must remove any tendency you may have to give greater favor to the testimony of someone you know or like. Instead, you must give fair consideration to all the evidence presented, even evidence that may challenge your previous notions about this case.

"The Solicitor has told you that the State hopes to prove the defendant's guilt by submitting evidence he thinks is irrefutable. We will be right here with you, listening to that evidence just as you will be and presenting to you the other side of the story, which the prosecution may not tell you because it will hurt their theory of the case. If we believe they have confused you about the facts and we need witnesses to clear up that confusion, we will offer them, but if they cannot prove the defendant's guilt, we will not try to prove his innocence. Their failure to prove his guilt will be enough to render a not guilty verdict.

"I will tell you this. After all the smoke has cleared, the defendant will be making a statement, which is his right, because he sincerely wants you to hear directly from him about what actually happened on the night of February 19th.

After you hear his statement, you will understand why he is not guilty of the murder of Burley Phillips."

Walter looked at George as Enoch Giles sat down as if to convey with his eyes, "I told you so." George signaled back that he understood the gravity of the revelation Enoch had just laid before the jury. Enoch had just revealed that the defense would likely be calling no witnesses. Presumably, that meant that he and T. Ross felt the evidence was so overwhelming there was no use rebutting it. But what tactic could they possibly use to convince the jury that Lee was innocent of this crime?

Walter was deep in thought. Enoch had indicated that the defense would let Lee "make a statement." That meant they were not calling him as a witness, and thus the prosecution would not be allowed to question him. What was Lee going to say that could overcome all the evidence they had against him?

* * * * * *

Walter looked down at the prosecution table at which he was sitting. He didn't like being in the position of not knowing what his opponents were going to do.

He wrote on his legal pad, "self-defense," and underlined it twice. He showed it to George, who looked at him with wide eyes. It was the only course of action the defense team could present that stood a prayer against the mountain of evidence they had amassed. Unfortunately for the prosecution, Lee's statement would come when no further evidence could be presented to refute it.

He knew that going up against Giles & Sharpe would be a challenge. The trial of Lee Currie was not going to be as open and shut a case as George had previously thought.

Chapter 35

"The State calls Lloyd Jones to the stand," Walter Grey announced from his seat. He turned his head to watch Lee Currie's reaction to this witness.

Lee's eyes followed the bailiff as he stepped out of the door to the judge's right. Lee started to wave when the bailiff returned with Jones right behind him, but Sharpe caught his arm.

The bailiff motioned for Jones to be seated in the witness box. Jones looked nervously about, holding his hat in front of him in both hands. Driving a jitney, he had carried passengers to and from the courthouse, but he had never had a reason to go inside before, and it was clear that he didn't like being inside now.

The bailiff held a Bible toward him, "Place your left hand on the Bible and raise your right hand." Jones complied. "Do you solemnly swear that the testimony you are about to give is the truth, the whole truth and nothing but the truth, so help you God?"

"I do," Jones said.

"You may be seated," the bailiff said.

Grey rose from the prosecution table and approached the witness. He could see Jones getting even more nervous, and he needed to try to calm him.

"Would you please state your name for the record?"

"Uh, Lloyd Jones."

"Good morning, Mr. Jones; I apologize for the heat. Would you like some water?"

"No, I'm fine, thank you," Jones replied.

"Okay, let me know if you change your mind. I won't take much of your time. I just have a few questions to ask you," Grey said.

"Can you tell us where you were employed in February of this year?"

"I was working for Mr. Wilson driving a jitney."

"Do you remember the time that the body of Burley Phillips was found in the woods out here south of Lyons?"

"Yes, sir."

Grey pointed at Lee Currie. "Did you see the defendant, Lee Currie, around that time?"

Jones swallowed, "I saw the defendant a few days before that."

"When was that, exactly?"

"I saw him on Thursday morning before the body was found. He rode with me from Vidalia to Lyons."

Grey walked over and stood near the defense table, looking at Currie, and asked, "What was said during your conversation with Mr. Currie?"

"He didn't have any conversation with me, only he told me that he was on a trade for an automobile, for a little Overland, and ask me how did I like it."

"Did he indicate he was going to purchase the automobile?"

"He said he believed he had saved up enough money since he had been working at Milledgeville to put on it."

"Did he ask you any questions?"

"He asked me was I going back to Vidalia anymore that day. I told him that I didn't know. He said he wanted to go back with me if I went."

Grey walked to the jury box and leaned on the rail, looking at the jury, "And was this the same day of the week they found the body?"

"I don't remember what day of the week the body was found."

Grey returned to his table and looked over at the defense table, "Your witness."

"I have no questions for this witness, your honor," Giles said.

Grey looked over at Lankford. It was telling that the defense did not cross-examine their first witness.

The judge turned to the witness, "You may step down, sir."

Jones appeared relieved, and he shook his head eagerly. He stepped out of the witness box, and the bailiff gestured for him to follow him through the witness door to the judge's right.

"Call your next witness," Judge Hardeman said.

* * * * * *

Lee had never been in a courtroom before; he was excited that all this fuss and bother appeared to be for him. Most of the people he knew in the world were there, and he enjoyed the attention. Nevertheless, he was eager to get it over with and return to his job in Milledgeville.

"The state calls Mr. Barney Brown to the stand," Grey announced.

That name didn't sound familiar to Lee, and he squinted to see who would be coming from the witness door. The man being sworn in looked vaguely familiar, but he couldn't place him.

"Please state your name for the record," Grey said.

"Barney Brown."

Lee listened while Grey asked a few questions about the last time the witness saw him. He wanted to know the answer to that himself to figure out who this was.

"Where did you see the defendant the day they found the body?"

"I saw him in the barbershop in the hotel building in Lyons. I was in there getting a shave, and after I got out of the chair, Lee Currie was standing side of the stove."

Ah, now I remember, that was the son-of-a-bitch in the Elberta Hotel Barber Shop the day I got my bullets, Lee thought to himself.

"And what did you see next?"

"When I got out of the chair and put on my collar and tie, some young man, I don't know who, came in and handed four or five pistol balls to Lee Currie."

"Did Lee say anything to the young man that gave him the pistol balls?"

"Lee said something back to him. He gave him a dime, I believe, I can't say. I believe Lee gave him a dime and says, 'Go get some more.'"

Lee leaned over to Sharpe and whispered, "Big deal, so I bought some bullets. That don't prove nothin'," he stared icily at Brown, who saw him and began fidgeting in the chair.

Grey turned to the prosecution table, "No further questions, your honor."

Brown started to get up. He was ready to get out of that courthouse.

"Just a moment, Mr. Brown, defense counsel may have a question for you," Judge Hardeman said.

Reluctantly, Brown sat back down.

Enoch Giles rose and spoke from behind the defense table, "Did you notice the cartridges' caliber?"

"I do not know what kind of cartridges those were or what size."

Giles sat down, "Thank you, Mr. Brown. No further questions, your honor."

Lee smiled. *They ain't got squat on me*, he thought to himself.

* * * * * *

"Well, this is a bunch of boring bullshit," Grey heard Lee whisper to Sharpe.

"Be quiet, Lee. Mind your composure and act interested in what's going on. The prosecution is allowed to present their case in their own good time," Sharpe whispered back.

"The State calls Mr. William Thomas Ivey to the stand," Grey announced.

Thomas Ivey walked smartly through the witness door and into the courtroom. He had a store manager's classical appearance, thin and with a very bushy mustache and a shock of black hair that at his age of 42 was beginning to show a wisp of gray around the temples. He took the witness stand and was duly sworn in.

"Please state your name for the record," Grey said.

"William Thomas Ivey."

"Were you employed in February of this year, Mr. Ivey?"

"Yes, I was working at the Minter-Smith Hardware Company in Lyons for my father-in-law, Mr. W. P. C. Smith, the president, and manager."

"Do you remember the time that they found the body of Burley Phillips out here in the country?"

"I do."

"Do you remember seeing Lee Currie at any time close to that?"

"I saw him a few days before that, about three days. He had come into the store to buy some cartridges, 38 cartridges, and at the time, I was out. I came in just as he was walking out."

"Who did Mr. Currie buy the cartridges from?"

"He bought the cartridges from Cecil, another clerk in there."

"And what happened after that?"

"In about 40 minutes, uh, 45 minutes, Currie comes back with those cartridges and wanted to exchange them for 32-caliber to fit a particular pistol he has."

"What type of pistol did he have?"

"He had an old model, look to be a Colt maybe, or an old-style Smith & Wesson. We found that a 32-Winchester cartridge would fit the pistol, except for possibly being 1/8 of an inch too long, possibly 1/16."

"So, the cartridges would not fit his gun?"

"Oh, they fit alright, but they were a bit too long for that model. They wouldn't let the cylinder revolve, and I told him I could cut the point of the cartridges off so as it would revolve in the pistol."

"And did he want you to do that for him?"

"Yes. He said he would be in the Hotel Barber Shop, and I had my nephew run them over to him after I had trimmed them."

Grey walked over to the prosecution table and picked up a revolver. He held up the pistol in front of Ivey. "Does this look like the pistol he had at the time?"

Ivey fiddled with his spectacles, craned his head to get a better look at the pistol, and after a moment, said, "Yes, I think so."

"The State would like to introduce this pistol into evidence as Exhibit 'A.'"

Judge Hardeman looked at the defense table for a moment, "Hearing no objection, I'll admit it."

Grey returned to the prosecution table and took four objects out of a bag. He walked over to the witness and dropped one of the cartridges into Ivey's hand. He held the others in the palm of his hand, "Do these look like the cartridges you trimmed?" He asked.

Ivey held one of the cartridges up to the light and studied it, "I wouldn't swear positively, but they look like the cartridges. I suppose any cartridges could be cut pretty near the same way."

"But the cartridges that you trimmed for Mr. Currie were trimmed similarly to these?"

"Yes. They were too long for the chamber in the pistol, and I trimmed them off for Mr. Currie."

Grey held out his hand, and Ivey returned the cartridge in him. "The State would like to introduce these pistol cartridges into evidence, marked as Exhibit 'B.'"

Judge Hardeman looked again at the defense table, "Hearing no objection, I'll admit them."

"No further questions, your honor," Grey said. He put all the cartridges back in the bag, handed it to the court reporter, and returned to his seat.

"Your witness, Col. Giles," Judge Hardeman said.

Giles rose and gestured to the bag holding the cartridges sitting on the prosecution's table. "Is it your testimony that these are the same cartridges that you trimmed?"

"I do not know whether these are the same cartridges or not," Ivey answered.

"Are you the only person that can trim cartridges in this manner?"

Grey noticed that Ivey looked offended. "I should think that anybody could trim those cartridges the way that I trimmed those."

"No further questions, your honor," Giles said and sat down.

The judge excused the witness. Grey was now confident that Giles was building a self-defense case. It is the only thing that could explain Giles' lack of aggression. The trimmed pistol bullets were hard evidence connecting Lee to the crime. New trials had been granted based on an inadequate defense, but the law firm of Giles & Sharpe was anything but incompetent. He sensed some creative lawyering at work and became even more determined not to let his case against Lee become the testing ground for an unorthodox defense.

"Call your next witness, Col. Grey," Judge Hardeman said.

* * * * * *

Grey stood up, "The State calls Mr. Nathaniel Haskins to the stand."

Lee sat up and turned his head toward the witness entrance. In a voice loud enough for Grey to hear, he said to Sharpe, "I know him, he's a jitney driver, too!"

Haskins spotted Lee as he approached the witness stand and quickly looked away, which bothered Lee. The bailiff swore him in, and he was seated. Lee remembered talking to Nathaniel the night he got Burley to take him to his pa's place. He couldn't figure out how this testimony had anything to do with the case and paid little attention as the lawyer asked the lead-up questions.

"Okay, so when you saw the defendant that afternoon, did the two of you talk?" Grey asked the witness.

"I had a conversation with him. I talked with him a little. I met him."

"What did the two of you talk about?"

"I told him that I had been around to Mr. Meadows, and I had a car broke down up there. Lee asked me where my car was, and I told him it was broke down."

Grey turned a couple of pages of his yellow pad.

"What type of business were you in at the time you had this conversation?"

"I was in the taxi business at the time."

Lee poked Sharpe and said, "See, I told you he was a jitney driver." Sharpe held his finger to his lips to silence him.

Grey looked at Lee as if he had heard him talking to Sharpe and then turned back to the witness, "Please continue."

"Lee asked me where my car was, and I told him, broke down, and I told him, don't ever buy any wire wheels, it would break down."

"Did Mr. Currie ask you to take him home?"

"There was not anything said by Currie about wanting me to carry him out home, not before me."

Grey returned to the defense table and looked over at Giles, "Your witness."

Giles said, without looking up, "I have no questions for this witness, your honor."

Lee frowned again. *This is a stupid waste of time,* he thought to himself. He began to doodle on the pad in front of him.

* * * * * *

"The State calls Mrs. Burley Phillips to the stand," Grey announced.

As Burley's widow rose from her seat and approached the witness chair, a general murmur rose among the spectators despite the judge's earlier warning.

"Let there be order," Judge Hardeman announced and rapped his gavel.

Sharpe knew that this would be a problematic witness. The men in the jury would no doubt be sympathetic to her loss and her status as a widow, newly made so by the killing of her husband. He whispered to Lee to be respectful and try not to look down as she gave her testimony, as the jury might interpret it as a sign of guilt.

The bailiff gestured to the witness stand, and Tersia Phillips sat down in the witness chair. She straightened her dress, pulled the black veil back to reveal her face, and placed her hand on the Bible the bailiff extended toward her. After being duly sworn, Tersia crossed both of her hands in her lap and looked up. She carried with dignity the loss she had suffered and the pain she was feeling.

Grey slowly approached the widow, "Are you comfortable, Ma'am?"

"I'm fine, thank you," Tersia responded.

"Please state your name for the record," Grey requested.

"Tersia Phillips."

"How are you related to Mr. Burley Phillips?"

"I am the wife of Burley Phillips."

"When was the last time that you saw your husband alive?"

"The last time I saw him living was on February 19th. That was on a Thursday."

"About what time might that have been?"

"It was on that day betwixt sunset and dark at home. It was after supper."

"Why did he leave after supper?"

"He left home to go to Johnson's Corner to carry a passenger down there."

"Are you familiar with Mr. Phillips' hats?"

"I am."

"Would you know the hat that he was wearing at the time that he left?"

"I most certainly would."

Sharpe watched as Grey retrieved the hat Bulloch County Sheriff Ben Mallard had gotten from Jim Kerby, one of Lee's in-laws. He walked over to Tersia and slowly handed her the hat. She caressed it gently, and tears appeared on her cheeks.

"Is this the hat he had on at the time he left home?" Grey asked softly.

Tersia continued crying and stroking the hat.

Judge Hardeman intervened, "Mrs. Phillips, do you need a moment?"

Tersia looked over at the judge and shook her head. Then she looked back at the hat, "Yes, this is Burley's hat."

"I know this is difficult for you, Mrs. Phillips, but can you tell me when was the next time you saw your husband after he left that night?"

Still clutching the hat with one hand and retrieving a handkerchief with the other, she wiped away tears, looked up, and said in a quiet voice, "The next time I saw him was on February 25th."

"The day after they found your husband's body," Grey said, directly at the jury.

Sharpe had been practicing law long enough to recognize this lawyering technique. Grey did not put the poignant statement in the form of a question. He was using an old trick to arouse sympathy in the jury. He looked at the jury and saw the men were reacting to the widow's grief just as the prosecution had hoped.

"No further questions, your honor," Grey said and returned to his seat.

Sharpe knew better than to question a grieving widow. Giles had his head down, and Judge Hardeman deftly sensed that the defense would have no questions.

"I am very sorry for your loss, Mrs. Phillips. You may step down now," Judge Hardeman said softly. Even the hand fans fell silent as Burley's widow rose slowly and accepted the bailiff's hand to help her down from the witness stand. There were quiet whispers in the courtroom as she returned to her seat in the courtroom, escorted by the bailiff.

"Call your next witness, Col. Grey," Judge Hardeman said sternly, and the whispering stopped immediately.

* * * * * *

"The State calls David Wright to the stand," George Lankford said as he rose to take over the questioning.

Lee set up straight again at the mention of his uncle's name, and Lankford heard him say aloud to Sharpe. "That's my uncle. What the hell is he doing testifying for the State?" Sharpe shushed him once again.

"Well, it ain't fair, calling my kin agin me like this, it ain't fair," Lee protested aloud.

Sharpe did his best to keep his client quiet.

Dave Wright was sworn in and settled into the witness stand. Lankford knew that he was a simple carpenter. During trial preparation, it was clear that Dave had few opportunities to interact with the judicial system. Despite their efforts to prepare him, he was uncomfortable, as evidenced by how he was nervously rolling his driver's cap in his hands.

"Please state your name for the record," Lankford said.

"Dave Wright."

"Do you remember when the body of Burley Phillips was found near your house?"

"I do."

"Did you see the defendant Lee Currie around that time?"

"I saw Lee a few nights before that."

"Can you remember the exact day of the week?"

"It was on Thursday night, and it was on Tuesday following that the body was found, yes, the following Tuesday."

"What time was that?"

"It was about midnight. I didn't see him until he come in the house."

"Whose house?"

"He came to my house. He just wanted to spend the night, and he spent the night there."

"Do you know what time he left the next morning?"

"I do not know exactly what time he got up the next morning. It was something like between daylight and sunup."

"And where did he go after he got up?"

"I don't know where he went. I saw him come back up here pretty quick."

"Back to your house?"

"Yes."

"From what direction did he come?"

"He come from right directly down in front of the house."

"In relation to where the body was found, where was that?"

"That was toward where the body was found."

"And how was he traveling when he returned to your house?"

"He was in an automobile. It was a new automobile."

"What kind of automobile was it?"

"I don't know what kind of a car it was. I did not notice."

"What is your relation to the defendant?"

"I am an uncle to Lee Currie by marriage."

"Thank you, Mr. Wright." He turned to Giles and said, "Your witness."

Enoch Giles got up from the defense table, looked at his legal pad, and then looked up at Dave Wright.

"How far do you live from where the body was found, Mr. Wright?"

"I suppose it was something like 5/8ths of a mile."

"What time did you go to bed that night?"

"I don't know what time I retired that night."

"Did you hear any gunshots or pistol shots that night?"

"Not at all."

"No further questions, your honor," Giles said and sat back down.

Lankford was perplexed. Giles's questions did not try to discredit Dave Wright's testimony, and he could make no sense of it. What was the defense up to? He rose, "Redirect, your honor?"

Judge Hardeman nodded. Lankford stepped over to the witness.

"Was Lee Currie driving an automobile when he first came to your house?" Lankford asked.

"Lee did not bring the automobile there to my house that night. He went after it the next morning."

"No further questions for this witness, your honor," Lankford said and sat back down.

"You may step down," Judge Hardeman said as he checked the wall clock. "It's about lunchtime, and we will take a one-hour recess. I cannot guarantee any of you in the courtroom that your seat will be available after your return. It will be first-come, first-served, and there are many people outside that may be anxious to come to take your place. If you leave, I ask that you take your belongings with you and not make a disturbance if you return and find your current seat is no longer available.

"Counselors, if you wish to confer with your client during the lunch break, just ask the bailiff to make a room available for that purpose. The county will be feeding the prisoner, and for your convenience, if you want to stay here in the courthouse to confer and don't mind eating the prisoners' fare, I will ask them to bring you a plate of whatever the jail has on the menu."

"Thank you, your honor, that is very gracious of you," Giles said.

"Thank you, your honor," Sharpe added.

"Court is in recess for one hour," Judge Hardeman concluded with a rap of his gavel.

* * * * * *

Sharpe could see that Lee was flummoxed about the court proceedings so far. He could tell that he relished the attention, but it was clear that Lee could not figure out how all of this would get him out of jail. Despite Sharpe's best efforts, Lee struggled to sit still and hide his emotions. Grey had given him the primary responsibility of managing Lee during the trial, and it was becoming a real challenge.

Lee, John Currie, and Enoch Giles gathered in the small conference room the judge had provided. Everyone eagerly ate the lunches that the bailiff had brought in, but Sharpe noticed that Lee seemed to have no appetite for any more jail food.

John Currie was the first to put down his fork, "Enoch, I don't understand why you are not asking the witnesses any questions. It seems this is going badly agin' my boy. I know you men have a plan, but for the life of me, I can't figure out what it is."

Giles wiped his mouth with his napkin and pushed his plate away from him, "John, don't be concerned about their case. They are trying to prove that Lee killed Burley, and we are not going to refute that. At the right time, we will argue that while he did kill Burley, he did it in self-defense, which is not against the law. Everyone has the right to defend themselves when someone attacks them."

"Hell yeah!" Lee exclaimed loudly.

"Quiet, Lee, they have a deputy posted outside," Sharpe said, holding his hand out, palm facing Lee.

"But aren't they also trying to prove that Lee planned the killing? Don't that make the killing, oh, what do you call it, premeditated? That Jones man that worked with Burley said that Lee told him he was aiming to trade for an Overland," John said.

"It's not against the law to want to trade for an automobile, John. Lee's a young man, and what young man is not clamoring to buy a car these days. Add to that the fact that he has a job in Milledgeville and is having to depend on others for transportation, and why wouldn't he want an automobile? He needs one; at least, that is what we may argue in our summation. Wanting an automobile is just not proof that you will kill to get one," Sharpe said.

"We are also not worried about Bill Ivey and Barney Brown's testimony. They helped the State prove that the gun Lee had was the one that killed Burley, but, again, we are not going to deny that. They are spending a lot of time proving facts that are not in contention, which is what we want them to do," Giles said.

Lee got up, walked over to a bookcase, and started pulling out books, appearing to have completely lost interest in the conversation.

"We've seen no indication that they know what our theory of the case might be, and we want to keep it that way. I don't think they know yet that we are going to contend that Lee killed Burley Phillips in self-defense," Sharpe added.

"Well, they will figure it out soon enough if you don't put up a little resistance to their witnesses, don't you think?" John asked.

Sharpe looked over at Giles, "He's got a point there, Enoch. We might ought to be a bit more aggressive with Walter's witnesses, or he will figure out our strategy."

Giles was unmoved. "Question the grieving widow? Not a good strategy, but don't worry. We're fine with what we have done so far. The first four witnesses were just foundational, and they threw the widow in there to get sympathy from the jury. Even Dave Wright did not hurt us, and if they had been smart, they would have called the widow as their last witness before dinner, where the jurors would have that tearful scene to think about while they ate. Putting Dave last, a hostile witness, was their mistake. The case is proceeding fine. We will be able to step it up with the next batch of witnesses."

Sharpe nodded as he weighed the logic of Giles's approach. He had much to learn from his senior law partner.

* * * * * *

George Lankford looked as if he had to force his dinner down. "It looks like you may be right, Walter. The ace up their sleeve might be that Lee acted in self-defense."

The two lawyers had retreated to the sheriff's conference room across from the courthouse to get away from the newsmen and curious onlookers.

Grey was not fazed, "It's not going to save Lee. It is a convenient defense based on the defendant's statement alone, but I'm confident the jury won't buy it. Lee is the only witness to the killing. They will not ignore our mountain of evidence and believe the killer's uncorroborated statement.

"And look, George, are you forgetting that on the way back from Milledgeville, while the sheriff was transporting Lee back to Lyons, that Lee told Jim Mallard two men from Pembroke killed Burley? That could surface as a defense," Lankford said.

"That was a long shot story Lee made up, and you know it," Grey said.

"Yeah, I know it, but the defense can use it as evidence that Lee makes things up. They could contend that the admissions Lee made to Mack Wimberley and the others on the ride up from Lyons to Ohoopee were made up, too," Lankford said.

"Well, if they go to a lot of trouble to prove that he makes up stories, it will undermine his statement when he claims he killed Burley Phillips in self-defense," Grey said.

"You're right; it could work to our advantage for them to prove Lee is a liar," Lankford said.

But Grey had to admit that he was worried about that strategy backfiring on them. It was true that Lee had lied profusely to his captors, and much of his theory of the case depended on the truth of Lee's admissions while in custody. If he went to great pains to prove that Lee's statements in that instance were trustworthy, would he not be establishing Lee as a credible witness? That would lend credence to any new story he might utter when he finally made his statement to the jury.

Further, arguing that what Lee said on the way to Ohoopee was true ran the risk of proving the deputies obtained the admissions illegally. If Lee sincerely believed the "promise" of Carl McLeod that those riding in the automobile with him were his "friends" and wouldn't tell on him, that promise became quid pro quo. The court might throw that testimony out completely or declare it an admission rather than a confession, which carries a lot less weight.

Giles had been cautious only to ask a few questions of the State's witnesses, none of which revealed his strategy.

Grey was still uncertain of the defense's approach, and it infuriated him.

But it was still early.

Chapter 36

"All rise, the Special Term of the Superior Court of Toombs County is now back in session, the Honorable Judge Robert N. Hardeman presiding," the bailiff announced.

Lord, give us some relief from this heat, Judge Hardeman thought to himself as he stepped up to the bench and sat down. "You may be seated," he said with a rap of the gavel. There were a few new faces in the courtroom, but he noted that most spectators had skipped their lunch or brought a box lunch to keep from losing their coveted seat.

"I hope everyone had a nice dinner. For those of you who are here for the first time, let me repeat what I have already said to those here this morning. I demand absolute silence from the spectators during these proceedings. Irrespective of what you hear this afternoon, if I hear so much as an "oh" or an "ah," I will have you escorted out. Do I again make myself clear?"

The judge scanned all the shaking heads in the courtroom, "Good. Let's proceed. Bailiff, please bring the jury back in."

The crowd was hushed as the jurors re-entered the courtroom. Walter Grey studied the jury members' faces to see if any glanced at Lee Currie, but all heads were down as if they were members of a chain gang moving to the next work site.

"Col. Grey, are you ready to continue?"

"The State is ready, your honor. We call David Robert Fussell to the stand."

David Fussell appeared to carry an air of confidence about him despite his young age. Grey suspected that came from being the station agent for the Seaborn Air Line Railway, the agent for the Southern Express Company, and a telegraph operator for the Western Union Telegraph Office, the youngest ever to hold all three posts. That confidence could work to his advantage.

Grey began his questioning in the usual manner. He had the witness identify himself, confirm that he was a telegraph operator in Claxton and working the day that Lee Currie came into the telegraph office to send a telegram to Burley Phillips' wife. He then walked over to the jury box and put his hand on the rail, "Please tell the jury what you remember about that occasion."

"I remember that the man took a long time composing the telegram. At one point, Mr. Mulkey even asked him if he needed some assistance."

"Clarify to the jury who Mr. Mulkey is."

"He was the station agent that I worked for at the time. He was there."

"Where is Mr. Mulkey now?"

"He's moved to Peoria, Illinois."

"Okay, you may continue."

"The man paid for the telegram and left, but he later returned and asked where we sent the telegram. Mr. Mulkey says to me, 'Where did you send that telegram?' I says, 'To Lyons.' Mr. Mulkey said that the fellow just said he wanted it to go to Vidalia. I asked Mr. Mulkey how to do it, and he says, 'Just ask Savannah to send a service message to Lyons to disregard the earlier message and then send the telegram to Vidalia.'"

Grey straightened, strolled over near the defense table, and looked down at Lee. "What was Mr. Currie wearing?"

"The best I remember, it seems to me like he had on an army overcoat."

Grey extended his finger and pointed to Lee, "Is this the man you saw in your office that day?"

Fussell looked intently at Lee, whose face was expressionless, "I couldn't swear positively whether he was the party or not, but he looks like the man that sent that telegram."

Grey was looking directly at Lee, who smiled, chuckled, and shifted back and forth in his seat until Sharpe put a hand on his arm to still him.

"What day in the week was it that the telegram was sent?" Grey asked and turned back toward the witness.

"I couldn't say the day of the week, but the date was February 20th."

"Do you still have the telegram that the party sent?"

"Right here." Fussell reached into his pants pocket and retrieved a telegram, which he unfolded. "This is the original that he handed to Mr. Mulkey," Fussell handed the telegram to Grey.

"The State would like to introduce this evidence as Exhibit' C.'"

"Hearing no objection, I will admit it," Judge Hardeman said.

Grey leaned on the witness stand and held out the telegram where both he and Fussell could see it, "What is this scratched out?"

"Lyons is scratched out, and it is changed to Vidalia."

"The handwriting appears to be different. Whose handwriting is this?"

"It is Mr. Mulkey's handwriting, I think. He changed Lyons to Vidalia."

"What time was this telegram sent?"

"The telegram shows it was filed at 9:50 AM and received in Savannah at 9:56 AM by the operator 'R' and sent by the operator 'R. F.' which is me."

Grey handed the telegram to the court reporter, who marked it and placed it on her table, "Your witness."

Grey watched in astonishment as Giles asked a few throwaway questions and sat down.

"Call your next witness," Judge Hardeman said.

* * * * * *

"The State calls James William Kerby," Grey announced.

Lee leaned over to Sharpe and whispered, "They're calling my in-laws now?"

"They are trying to show how you took some of Burley's things, but don't worry, we anticipated this and are not concerned about this line of questioning," Sharpe whispered back.

Grey approached the witness, "Please state your name for the record."

"James William Kerby," Kerby answered.

Jim Kerby was in his overalls, as might be expected for one who had farmed all his life and would probably die tilling the soil. He had a bushy beard that was totally gray, save the several dark streaks of tobacco juice.

"Good afternoon, Mr. Kerby, sorry to bring you out of the fields this afternoon. I know this is a busy time of the year for farmers. I only have a few questions. How do you know Lee Currie?" Grey asked.

"He's married to my sister-in-law's niece," Kerby answered.

Grey continued with a line of questions showing Kerby knew about the killing and had seen Lee in the Overland. Grey then got to the meat of Kerby's testimony.

"Do you remember Mr. Currie saying anything about a hat?"

"When I was walking by the car to get in the wagon, to get in with brother Bob, that is, he says, 'Fellows, here is a hat I found this morning. If one of you can use it, you may have it.' I asked him what number it was, and he said it was number seven, and I told him I could wear it, and I taken the hat and wore it at Claxton that day."

"What became of the hat?"

"I carried that hat back home, and the sheriff come and got it."

"The sheriff?"

"Mr. Mallard."

"The Sheriff of Bulloch County," Grey said, for the jury's benefit, and then handed the hat to Kerby, "Can you identify this hat as being the hat Mr. Currie gave you that day?"

Kerby took the hat and looked it over, "This hat resembles the hat he gave me." He turned it around and continued to study it, then returned it to Grey.

"You sure?"

"If that ain't the same hat, it is a hat similar to it, but it looks like the same one I turned it over to Mr. Mallard."

"The State would like to enter this hat into evidence as Exhibit 'D,'" Grey said as he handed the hat to the court reporter.

"Objection," Giles said, startling everyone. It was the first time the defense had objected to any evidence and caught the prosecution by surprise. "The witness just said he could not positively identify the hat as the one belonging to Mr. Phillips."

Grey countered, "I believe his words were '... it looks like the same one I turned over to Mr. Mallard.'"

Judge Hardeman stopped the argument, "Overruled. It is up to the jury to decide what value to place on the witnesses' characterization of the hat. I'll admit the hat."

Grey continued, "Thank you, your honor. Now Mr. Kerby, where did Mr. Currie say he found that hat?"

"He said he found that hat twixt Claxton and Pembroke."

"Did you happen to see a pipe in the car or on Mr. Currie?"

"Unh-uh."

"Please answer such questions with a 'yes' or 'no,' Mr. Kerby," Judge Hardeman interrupted.

"Sorry – I meant to say 'no,'" Kerby replied.

"Did Mr. Currie say where he got the car?"

"I didn't heared Currie say anything about where he got his car. I never talked with Mr. Currie but just a little."

Grey turned to return to his table, "Your witness."

Giles rose while still holding his legal pad as if studying it. Grey grimaced. He suspected it was time for Giles to resort to the old tried and true lawyer obfuscation method.

"Mr. Kerby, you swore under oath that this was the same hat. Are you sure?" Giles asked.

With its implied threat of perjury tacked on, this question rattled the old farmer, no doubt as Giles intended. It did not escape Grey's notice that Kerby was now frowning, and his face had flushed red.

"I did not say that this is the same hat. I said that it is one just like it. It was just like it, if it ain't the same hat."

"So, you can't say for sure that this is the same hat?"

Jim Kerby stammered, "I couldn't tell. You know it has been several months or something like that."

Giles pressed and leaned in, "In your direct examination, you said this was the same hat."

Jim began rambling, "I said it was just like the hat that he gave me, if that was the same hat. I did not say that it was not the same hat. I said, if it wasn't that one, it was one just like it if, it wasn't that hat."

Giles smirked and said, "Well, that makes perfect sense. No further questions, your honor."

Judge Hardeman said sternly, "Counselor, it is not your job to say whether the witness' testimony makes perfect sense or not. Let the jury do their job, please. You may step down, Mr. Kerby."

Jim Kerby did not move.

"Mr. Kerby?" Judge Hardeman asked.

Jim jerked his head toward the judge, "Huh?"

"You may step down, Mr. Kerby. They have no more questions for you."

"Oh, good," Jim got up and started walking toward the opening between the defense and prosecution tables, glaring at Enoch Giles.

The bailiff caught him by the arm and turned him around, "This way, sir."

John Currie leaned over to Lula and whispered, "Finally, they are defending Lee. It's about time."

"Well, that went well," Lankford whispered sarcastically to Grey, "Did you forget to ask him about the hat's bloodstains?"

"No, I didn't. Kerby doesn't sound credible. This is probably the first time he has ever set foot in a courthouse, and we should have prepped him better."

* * * * * *

"The State calls Robert Moses Kerby to the stand," an annoyed Grey said.

Sharpe was trying to hide a smile. His law partner had made quick work of the witness and probably thrown the Solicitor General further off the scent of their theory of the case. Ole man Currie was right about their needing to turn up the heat. Besides, destroying opposing counsel's witnesses was not only fun; it was their stock and trade and what had made their reputation as the best law firm in the county.

Grey composed himself and walked over to the witness stand, "Please state your full name for the record."

"Robert Moses Kerby, I go by Bob."

Bob testified that Lee had come to his house on Friday, February 20th, and spent the night there. Grey quickly moved to the blood evidence.

"When Mr. Currie spent the night at your house, how was he traveling?"

"He was driving a Baby Overland car."

"Did you ask him where he got it?"

"I heard him say he bought it. He didn't tell me whereabouts."

"Did you examine the car to see what condition it was in?"

"Well, I didn't examine it, so to speak, but I did see some blood in it. The blood was all about on the inside."

"Did the defendant tell you how the blood got in the car?"

"Lee said he killed a hog and put it in the car and carried it to the creek and threw it in there, that is how come it."

"Did Mr. Currie attempt to wash the blood off while at your house?"

"He didn't, but my wife helped him wash most of it off with some cornstarch."

"Did you have occasion to see if Mr. Currie had a pocketbook on him?"

"I did. He had more than one pocketbook there. He had two pocketbooks."

"Did you see him counting his money?"

"Nope."

"Did he have an extra hat with him or a pipe?"

"I saw him on Friday with two hats at my brother's, as I was on the way to Claxton. Lee didn't have nary hat while at my house. When I first saw him, I don't know whether he had nary hat or not. I saw him take one out of the car and he says, 'Here is a hat some of you can have that I found,' and my brother, he taken it. I did not see him at any time with a pipe."

Grey turned and returned to the prosecution table. "I have no further questions for this witness, your honor."

Judge Hardeman spoke up, "Col. Grey, you will need to be thinking about a stopping place for the day. It's hard for all of us to stay focused in this afternoon heat. How many more witnesses do you think you would like to call before we adjourn for the day?"

"Begging your indulgence, your honor, we just have two more for today," Grey said.

"Very well, call your next witnesses."

* * * * * *

"The State calls George Smith to the stand," Grey announced.

He needed all to go well with this witness, who was married to one of Lilly Currie's sisters. Lee had given Burley's pipe to Smith, and Grey didn't need for his testimony to blow up as Jim Kerby's had under cross-examination.

"Please state your name for the record."

"George Smith."

And he was not disappointed. George testified under Grey's questioning that Lee had driven to his house in the Overland at around two or three o'clock on the day after Burley Phillips was killed. Grey slowly moved his questioning to Burley's pipe.

"What did the two of you talk about when he came to your house?" Grey asked.

"Only just what me and him have always done, been jolly together, just like brothers-in-law will do that way, laughing and going on. He said he always wanted a new model Overland, and he said he got able to buy one," Smith said.

"Did he give you the particulars of how he acquired it?"

"He said he got it at Milledgeville and gave $1,150 for it, I think."

"Did I hear you say that you and Mr. Currie were brothers-in-law?"

"That's right."

"Did he give you anything on this occasion?"

"He gave me a pipe."

Grey retrieved the pipe from the prosecution's table and handed it to the witness, "Does this appear to be the pipe he gave you?"

"That's the pipe he gave me."

"You seem very sure of your answer. Why is that?"

"Because I put that there string around it."

Giles wanted to object to admitting the pipe into evidence, but the witness had been positive about it and had even altered it with a string. Judge Hardeman would likely overrule his objection, and he didn't want the jury to lose confidence when he used this tactic. Giles would have to obfuscate the connection of the pipe to Burley Phillips another way. He made notes on his legal pad.

"The State would like to admit this pipe into evidence as Exhibit 'E,'" Grey said.

"Any objections?" Judge Hardeman said expectantly while looking at the defense table. Giles shook his head. "Hearing none, I will admit it."

"Please tell the jury how Lee came to give you the pipe," Grey continued.

"He come over there and ask me the way to my wife's sister's and wanted to know where she lived. I told him across the creek, and he asked me how far it was. I says, about 7 miles, I suppose.

"He says, 'Let's go over there. I want to see her and haven't seen her in a good while.'

"I says, 'I haven't got time, Lee, I am trying to plow a little.'

"My wife, she insisted on me to go over there with him. I said, 'All right if you want me to go, I'll go over there with you.'" Smith hesitated as if he didn't know if he was supposed to keep talking or not.

"Go ahead and continue, Mr. Smith. Tell the jury what happened next," Grey said.

"I went over there, and I reckon we stayed about a couple of hours, I suppose, something like that, and come on back. I seen the pipe lying down in the foot of the car and a can of smoking tobacco. I smoke a good deal myself, and I says, 'I believe I'll smoke some.'

"Lee says, 'All right, help yourself.'

"I picked up the pipe and went to smoking. Before I got home, he says, 'If you want the pipe, you can have it.'

"I said, 'All right.' I taken the pipe and kept it and never thought anything about it and smoked it."

"Thank you, Mr. Smith." Grey turned to the defense table.

Giles had no questions for George Smith, and this unnerved Grey. Why would the defense challenge the identification of the hat and not the pipe? The defense's strategy still made no sense, and that bothered him.

"Call your next witness, Col. Grey," Judge Hardeman said.

* * * * * *

"The State calls Winfield D. Sutton to the witness stand."

Mr. Sutton was a rather stout man with a bushy beard and abundant stock of salt and pepper hair, except for a large bald spot on the back of his head that became visible when he removed his cap upon entering the courtroom.

Grey established that Sutton lived about a mile to a mile and a quarter from John Currie's home with his opening questions. On the same morning of the day they discovered Burley Phillips' body, Sutton had seen Lee in the Overland on his property. Grey wanted to put Lee near the body on that day.

"Where did it appear he was headed?" Grey asked.

"He was going down the big road, and I was going right down that little lane that joins with it, and he run over a calf down side of the road and killed it. I was looking at the calf there, and I knew it was him."

"Was the calf in the middle of the road?"

"No, he was out there by the fence. Lee quit the road entirely to run over the calf."

"Did you go up to the calf afterward and confirm it was dead?"

"I did."

"Did you see any blood on the calf?"

"There was no blood at all. I never seen a drop of blood, not a drop."

Grey turned to Giles, "Your witness."

Giles rose and approached the witness. He flipped a few pages on his legal pad. "Mr. Sutton, is it your testimony that Lee Currie didn't stop the car after he had run over the calf?"

"I know that he stopped just below my house there. After he hit the calf, he stopped."

"Why do you think he stopped then?"

"It looked like there was some little something the matter with the car."

"I have no further questions of the witness, your honor," Giles concluded.

Judge Hardeman glanced at the clock on the wall. It was almost 5 p.m., and he was tired and hot. The faces of the jurors reflected his own fatigue.

"Mr. Sutton, you may step down. Gentlemen of the Jury, we have arrived at a stopping point for today's proceedings. We will allow you to return to your homes for this evening;

however, I order you not to discuss this case among yourselves or with anyone outside this courtroom, not even your spouses. Nor should you allow the case to be discussed in your presence. Your verdict should only be based upon what you hear in this courtroom. You must close your eyes and ears to anything outside that might be related to this case. That would include any newspaper accounts.

"If you need transportation to or from your place of abode, notify the bailiff. We will reconvene at 9:00 a.m. tomorrow. Court is adjourned," Judge Hardeman rapped his gavel.

"All rise," the bailiff announced as the judge stood. A sheriff's deputy approached Lee, who turned to his father, and John Currie extended his arms to hug him. Lee accepted his embrace and said, "I'll be out soon, Pa. I just know it."

Tears appeared in John's eyes, "I'm praying for that, son. You stay strong now and don't give the deputy any trouble."

Lee turned around, and the deputy put handcuffs on him. Lee looked over his shoulder as he exited the courtroom, and his father forced a smile. John took Lula's hand, embraced her, and left the courtroom without speaking to Giles or Sharpe.

* * * * * *

Walter Grey and George Lankford returned to the sheriff's conference room. They found themselves walking several paces behind Lee Currie and several deputies, escorting him back to the sheriff's jail. Walter couldn't help but stare at the prisoner walking in front of him, trying to bring the puzzle pieces in his mind together sufficiently to reveal the defense's strategy. Still convinced that they were going to assert that Lee acted in self-defense, Walter was troubled that they seemed unconcerned that such a defense would rest solely upon the strength of Lee Currie's statement to the jury. After all, he had more than enough evidence to prove Lee Currie was a liar.

The story about the "two men from Pembroke" killing Burley was as full of holes as a flour sifter and would never stand up.

He was confident that the defense would try to throw out Lee's confession based on how the deputies handled Lee after arresting him. There indeed were some instances of bad judgment when they were transporting Lee. Particularly troubling were the deputies allowing non-officers to question him while in custody. They knew better than to allow that, and the defense would surely try to make it appear it was intentional. Still, he felt confident he could overcome the defense's arguments.

But this case could go anywhere. Grey's best bet was to stay the course and be on the lookout for any legal trickery from Lee's defense team.

* * * * * *

Giles and Sharpe returned to their offices and entered the conference room. Both men dropped their papers on the table and practically fell into their chairs. Sharpe could see that Giles was troubled.

"So, how do you think it went today?" Sharpe asked cautiously.

Giles was silent for a long moment and then said, "We will lose this case, T. Ross. I find myself looking for ways to appeal before we have even presented our side."

"It would be a victory if we can just keep him from the gallows, Enoch."

"I know, I know, and that would be the best outcome under the circumstances. But there is one thing that is troubling me."

"What's that?"

"That boy is not right in the head. I don't think he knows yet that he did wrong when he killed Burley Phillips. You've been around him, T. Ross, he ain't right, he just ain't right."

"I'm afraid the jury will be of the mind that being crazy doesn't excuse what he did."

"We don't put juveniles in jail for crimes because the law deems them too immature to know what they are doing. Why shouldn't the same rule apply to an adult who still possesses a child's mind?

"We apply the mature mind standard every day. It shouldn't be that much of a stretch to the jury to extend to him a child's immunity from punishment. How many times have you heard people say about another adult, 'He doesn't know any better,' and then excuse some mistake they've made?"

"This is not a broken plate a child has dropped on the floor, Enoch; they may think this man committed murder. Besides, even in those instances, when a child kills someone, they don't let him go because he is immature."

"They don't hang him either! They take his youthful nature into account, send him to reform school or something like that," Giles said emphatically.

Sharpe shook his head and was in deep thought before he spoke. "Do you know of a case where a murderer has been spared capital punishment because they were, I don't know, what would you call it, not guilty by reason of, what, insanity?"

"That's exactly what I would call it, and, no, I don't think it has ever been tried before, at least I've never heard of that type of defense being tried in the Toombs County court. But why should that stop us?"

"Do we have time? We can't just argue this new principle without evidence, and we haven't had sufficient prep time to develop Dr. Hall's testimony. Hell, we didn't even include him in the list of witnesses we gave Walter."

"Yes, I'm fully aware of that."

"Then what do you suggest we do?" Sharpe asked.

"We'll try to get Judge Hardeman to allow us to put Dr. Hall on the stand. If that fails, we can just hope the jury finds him innocent. If that doesn't work, we will try to get the guilty verdict overturned and start a new trial, one that plows this new ground. We'll throw a whole boatload of doctors at the prosecution."

"Sounds like a tough row to hoe to me, Enoch."

"What do you suggest we do, T. Ross, throw up our hands in defeat and let John Currie's boy hang? Our firm is known for managing our way through tough rows like these."

The two attorneys looked at each other. The course they were now considering could blow up in their faces, and they knew it. Or it could save a man's life and establish a new legal principle in the process.

"You stay focused on our current strategy, Enoch. I'll get started on the appeal and the research for this new approach," Sharpe said and headed for his office.

Chapter 37

Lee Currie was getting impatient. He was tired of all these bad things being said about him, and it did not appear to him that his legal team was defending him, not one little bit. This thing needed to be over with where he could go back to work before Mr. Harden fired him from his job.

* * * * * *

"The time to reconvene having arrived, this Special Session of the Toombs County Superior Court will come to order, the Honorable Judge Robert N. Hardeman presiding, all rise," the bailiff announced promptly at 9:00 a.m. on Tuesday, August 17th. The temperature had climbed to 80 degrees inside the courtroom, and most everyone in the packed group of spectators was already frantically waving their hand fan.

Judge Hardeman settled into his chair and seated the people present with a rap of his gavel. As the jury came in, he wondered how many of its members had remained true to his Order not to discuss the case overnight. The temptation had to be strong to divulge their thoughts so far on the trial, judging from the crowds outside and the growing hoard of out-of-town news reporters he had to wade through this morning.

Much to his chagrin, the State vs. Lee Currie case was indeed turning into the trial of the century for Toombs

County. Accounts of the crime and the trial were appearing in just about every newspaper in South Georgia, bringing even more massive crowds to the courthouse grounds. While it was a boon for local businesses, the risk of this trial sinking his reelection chances was looming large. It was more important than ever that he keep the case within due bounds and not give the losing side a basis for an appeal.

Again, he warned the spectators about the need for their silence during the proceedings, made sure the lawyers were ready, and then announced, "Mr. Grey, you may call your next witness."

"The state calls Mr. John L. Blackstone to the stand," Grey said.

* * * * * *

Grey knew that Lee Currie had taken John Blackstone and his family to Milledgeville in the Overland. He needed to show that Lee was deliberately trying to evade the authorities after the killing. He put the usual introductory questions to Blackstone and then got right to the meat of the matter.

"Did you see the defendant, Lee Currie, on the day Burley Phillips was found down in the county?"

"Yes, I did."

"Where did you see him?"

"I first saw him at the home of John Bell, my brother-in-law. The best I can recollect, it was about 8 o'clock in the morning, and we left there for Milledgeville."

"You went to Milledgeville that day with Lee Currie?"

"That's right."

"How were you traveling?"

"He was traveling in a car, an Overland car."

"Where does Mr. John Bell live?"

"He lives about two miles and a half or three miles from Johnson's Corner."

"In what direction did Mr. Currie drive to go to Milledgeville?"

"We went out from there by Marvin Church to Cedar Crossing, taking the Cedar Crossing Road to Alston. We went out close to Mount Vernon and then left Mount Vernon to the left a little."

"Did you go through Lyons or Vidalia?"

"No."

"Why not?"

"I think Superior Court was in session here at that time."

Lee could no longer contain himself. He stood up and blurted out, "That didn't have nothing to do with the way we went, and you know it, John!"

Judge Hardeman immediately responded, "Young man, you need to be quiet."

"What the hell for? I'm the one on trial here. Are you telling me that I can't say nothing when somebody lies about me?" Lee asked belligerently.

"Counselors, you need to explain to your client how this court works. Do you need a recess for that purpose?" Judge Hardeman asked.

Sharpe pulled Lee back down to his seat and began to whisper into his ear. Grey said, "Sorry, your honor, we are fine."

"Continue your questioning, counselor," Judge Hardeman said.

"When did you arrive in Milledgeville?" Grey asked.

"Tuesday evening about sundown."

"And whose idea was it to bypass Lyons?"

Blackstone swallowed hard. Lee's earlier outburst had rattled him. He didn't want to anger him further, but he knew what Grey wanted him to say, "Lee Currie is the one that suggested going that route around by Cedar Crossing instead of coming by Lyons."

"Because it was the best way to go, not because I was trying to avoid Lyons, you idiot!" Lee yelled out.

Judge Hardeman rapped his gavel and said sternly, "Silence, Mr. Currie! I'm in charge of these proceedings, and I decide when people get to speak. Your lawyers know how to properly challenge a witness's testimony. Let them do their jobs. You will get your turn to speak at the appropriate time."

Grey smiled at Lankford. Lee's volatility coming out in front of the jury played right into their case. He turned to Giles and said, "Your witness."

* * * * * *

Giles was also pleased with Lee's outburst, but for a different reason. The night before sleep had alluded him as he mulled over the new defense strategy that had come upon him earlier yesterday, that Lee was insane and not responsible for his actions. Unpredictable behavior, such as Lee had just exhibited, supported that theory. He was almost tempted to change his strategy mid-course, to ask for a continuance and secure some experts, but staying on a self-defense course was best for now. He rose and walked over to the witness.

"Mr. Blackstone, why were you and Mr. Currie going to Milledgeville together?" Giles asked.

"We were both working and living at Milledgeville at the time. We were working up there at a barbershop and pressing club."

"How long had Mr. Currie been working there?"

"Something like two or three weeks prior to that time."

"How had you been going back and forth to Milledgeville?"

"We normally rode in my car, but Lee had just acquired a new car of his own, and when I saw him the night before we went to Milledgeville, it was agreed that it was his turn to carry me back. He came here that morning in accordance with his promise and carried me and my uncle Math Bell and my family up there."

"Did Mr. Currie tell you why he went to Milledgeville by way of Cedar Crossing?"

"He said it was better roads, and it was near, and he knew that way better, the way he went, and it was the onliest way he had ever gone."

"So, it had nothing to do with the fact that the Superior Court was in session in Lyons?"

Grey stood up, "Objection, leading."

"Sustained. Rephrase your question, Col. Giles," Judge Hardeman said.

"Let me ask you this, Mr. Blackstone, did Mr. Currie appear to you to be avoiding Lyons or Vidalia or in any way trying to get away after this alleged murder took place?"

Blackstone was worried. He had been around Lee enough to know he was volatile, and now it appeared he was capable of murder. Should Lee beat this rap, Blackstone didn't want any part of his wrath. He tempered his answer somewhat, "He made no effort whatever to get away or to run away. I reckon he has been around there in the neighborhood practically ever since he come from Milledgeville."

"No further questions, your honor," Giles said.

"I have no further questions for this witness," Grey said.

"You may step down, Mr. Blackstone," Judge Hardeman said.

Blackstone rose and smiled weakly at Lee, who returned a blank stare. He was relieved that it was not that angry scowl he had witnessed before. He may have dodged a bullet. Leaving the courtroom, Blackstone was feeling relieved.

* * * * * *

"The State calls Mack Wimberley to the stand," Grey announced.

Grey knew Wimberley's testimony was going to be risky. Mack was a key witness and had gotten Lee to admit to the killing and much of what happened afterward, but the defense would no doubt try to get his testimony thrown out by proving that he and the other officers had coerced Lee's confession.

"Please state your name for the record," Grey asked.

"E. Mack Wimberley."

"Mr. Wimberley, do you remember when the sheriff of this county carried Lee Currie to Savannah?"

"Yes, I remember, and I went with him all the way there."

"Did the two of you talk about the killing?"

"We did."

"Were Mr. Currie's statements made freely and voluntarily and without any hope of reward or fear of punishment?"

"Of course."

Grey noticed that Giles made a note of his answer. "Why was Mr. Currie transported to Savannah?"

"The report came in that there was forming a mob at Vidalia to take him out and lynch him."

"Who gave the sheriff that report?"

"Mr. Bugg had told me about a bunch of men up there that he seen."

"Upon receiving this report, what did you do?"

"I told the sheriff about it, and I went on about some other business, but 'tirectly he came to me and ask me if I would go to Savannah with him, and I told him I would. To make it more inconspicuous, I proposed that I would take Lee in my car and go on to Ohoopee."

"Who went with you?"

"My son George and Carl McLeod."

"Not the sheriff?"

"He felt he needed to stay and deal with the lynch mob, if there was any truth to one forming up. Told me he would catch the train to Ohoopee that left later that day."

"What happened next?"

"Well, it was fixed for me to carry Lee that way, and I went on to the house and got George, and we taken Lee out and put him in the back seat with Carl. We drove right on down the front street, over the first crossing right there at Mr. McNatt's store. We drove on to the depot, and crossed the street, went on down to the drugstore, and crossed the next street again."

"And nobody saw you transporting the prisoner out of town?"

"Not with us driving my car."

"And so, you drove on to Ohoopee?"

"That's right."

"How did Mr. Currie react to being transported out of town?"

"Lee, I am satisfied, felt relieved."

"How so?"

"Well, he looked so, and he started to talking just like he was tickled to death to be out of danger and out of Lyons.

"He asked Mr. McLeod if he had ever tried his gun that they had taken from him, and I think he answered him, 'No.' Then Lee told him about how fast he could drive the car and hit telephone poles he was shooting at, and about it being such a good gun.

"Did Mr. Currie say he killed Burley Phillips?"

"He did. He said he killed him at a church just across the creek on this side of J. S. Alexander's. Burley turned around just this side or just the other side of Alexander's and come on back to a church."

"What road was he on?"

"I am not familiar with the roads, but he went just on the other side of Alexander's or just this side and turned around at a creek that was too high to cross. There is a church right at the creek and where the road bends."

Grey needed to make sure that he had proof the murder took place in Toombs County, to prove this court had jurisdiction, "Does J. S. Alexander live in Toombs County in the State of Georgia?"

"He does."

"How far is it from Mr. Alexander's place to the county line?"

"The nearest place to the county line from Alexander's would be the Altamaha River, and Mr. Alexander lives eight or ten miles from the Altamaha River."

"Then I asked him how was it, how did it happen, how could he shoot the man without having a wreck, and also how could he shoot him on the left side of his head."

Giles was furiously taking notes. These officers had been skating on thin ice, asking Lee Currie all these incriminating questions. If there was an element of threat or promised reward, the questioning was clearly illegal. He also noted the trick question Wimberley had asked about Burley being shot in the left side of his head when the coroner's report showed that he had been shot on his right side. They were trying to get Lee to admit to knowing details of how Burley was shot that had not yet been made public, and only the shooter would know. Those types of details would undermine his self-defense statement.

"He showed us how. He told George to turn his head to the left like he was looking off at something, and he would show him how it was done. George done so, and he showed him being shot on the right side of his head."

"On the right side, even though you had said the left?"

"That's right. He corrected me and said he shot him on the right side."

"Did he answer your question about how could he shoot him without having a wreck?"

"I think I ask him the same question again, and he said the car was stopped. Carl asked him, 'What were they stopped for? Did they think they were on the wrong road?' And Lee said, 'Yes'."

"Where did he say he went after he shot Mr. Phillips?"

"I understood him to say that he came through by Mr. Gibbs' place and Mr. Ed Parker's place and on through Johnson's Corner to Mr. Currie's. He said he stopped at a shed, somewhere near his father's house, and got a shovel, and I think there was another tool, maybe a hoe, I think it was a hoe, and went on to where he was going to bury him."

"Tell the jury what Lee told you about the burial."

"Lee said that he sit there in the woods something like two hours studying what to do with him. I think I asked him why he didn't carry him to somebody's or somewheres. He asked me where in the dickens would he carry him, and I told him I didn't know, but that I would have carried him to somebody because I would have been as crazy as a bat sitting there with that dead man for two hours."

"Is there anything else you can remember about what was said by Lee on the way to the Ohoopee train station?"

"I asked him about how did he get Burley over from the front seat to the back seat of the car. He said he rolled him over the back."

"Did he say anything else?"

"Not really. By that time, we had got to the Ohoopee station, and I didn't stay in the car very long with him. I needed to stretch my legs."

"Where did you go?"

"I got out and stayed on the outside. I seen Mr. Smith, the warden, and Dr. Kemp out smoking on the loading dock and told them what we were afraid of."

"The lynch mob?"

"Yep, and I told them that if anything happened, I wanted them to help protect our prisoner."

"So, you were just standing outside, waiting for the train to arrive?"

"That's right, till we got cold, and I went and got Carl and George and Lee and went to the waiting room. We found there was some fire on the negroes' side of the waiting room, and we went in there and stayed until the train came."

"What did you talk about while waiting for the train?"

"Someone spoke in regard to the lynch mob, worried that they might come down on the train. I told Carl and Lee not to go to the train until I seen whether anybody else came down on the train or not."

"What did you do when the train arrived?"

"Well, when the train stopped, Sheriff McLeod stepped out on the platform, and I called to him and told him we was all here."

"How was Lee reacting to the possibility of a lynch mob coming on the train?"

"Lee was worried up there at Ohoopee, all right, but when we got on the train, he was perfectly satisfied then. He felt that he was perfectly safe."

"Did the train make any stops between Ohoopee and Savannah?"

"We stopped at Claxton. The agent got on the train at Claxton to identify Lee."

"The agent? What was his name?"

"I don't know as I have ever heard his name, but the agent got on the train and identified Lee."

"Was Lee chained at the time the agent looked at him?"

"Yes, he had a chain on him, you know, and so many people on the train kept looking back there at me and him until I just hated to have the boy chained to me. I asked Mr. McLeod to take him, and he said, 'Just wait till we got to Claxton, that the agent was going to get on the train and identify him', and then the sheriff would take control of him."

"So, what happened when the agent came on the train?"

"Well, when we got to Claxton, I told Lee to stand up and he done so, and the agent stood there a minute or so looking at Lee, and 'tirectly he turned to Mr. McLeod and nodded his head and walked on out."

"Did Lee say anything as the agent was leaving the train?"

"He did. Lee asked me who that fella was, and I told him it was the station agent at Claxton, come in to identify him, but he said that wasn't the man. He said the man that sent that telegraph was a little black-eyed son-of-a-bitch."

Grey turned to the judge and said, "I have no further questions of this witness, your honor."

Judge Hardeman nodded to Giles, who approached the witness. Giles needed to establish that the officers' whole conversation with Lee was illegal.

"Mr. Wimberley, didn't you ask Lee Currie some questions just before he made the statement to you about the killing?"

"Well, Colonel, I don't know whether the first conversation started that way or not, or it may have been about the pistol."

"The pistol?"

"He asked Carl McLeod something about the pistol, just prior to the time that he made the statement to me about how the killing occurred."

"Do you remember Lee Currie making the statement, before he talked about how the killing occurred, that 'I don't mind telling you all, because I know you are my friends and won't tell it?'"

"If he made the statement to me, I don't remember it."

"So, you did not reply to that statement, 'Yes, we are your friends?'"

"No. In fact, why would I make that statement if he didn't say what you said he did?"

"Please let me ask the questions, Mr. Wimberley. Now, who did you testify earlier was sitting in the back seat with Lee?"

"Carl was sitting in the back seat with him."

"Who was driving the car?"

"I think I was sitting in the front seat driving; either me or George one was driving, but I think I was driving."

"You clearly remember that you did not tell Lee you would be his friend if he would tell his story, and you can't remember if you were driving or not?"

Wimberley appeared to be getting agitated. "Yes, I was driving, and my son, George, was on the front seat with me. Carl was sitting on the back seat by Lee."

"Now let's see if I have this right, you were concentrating on driving and were in the front seat with your back to the defendant, and you are confident that he did not make the statement that 'I don't mind telling you all because I know you are my friends and you won't tell?'"

"I do not recall about his saying that."

"And you did not remark back to him, 'Yes, we are your friends?'"

Wimberley was indignant. "No, I didn't."

"Mr. Wimberley, tell me again why the sheriff took the defendant to Savannah?"

"The word had come that there was a mob forming at Vidalia for the purpose of coming down here and lynching him."

"You testified that it was you driving the car that evening?"

"I think so."

"You're back to not sure?"

"I was driving. I'm sure of it."

"It's only 7 miles to Ohoopee. That sure was a lot of conversation to have in such a short drive."

"I did not drive rapidly going from here to Ohoopee because we had so long to wait. We didn't want to get there till just before the train time, and, in fact, we wanted to take it sort of slow because we didn't want to be there waiting long."

"Mr. Wimberley, are you sure it is your testimony, under oath, that Mr. Currie never said, before making his supposed confession, that he would tell you what happened because you were his friends and won't tell?"

Wimberley answered angrily, "It could have been said, and I would not have heard it, but I can sure testify that I did not say, 'Yes, we are your friends', because I did not say that, and I can testify that I did not hear anyone else in the crowd say that when he made that remark."

"Ah, so Lee did make the remark?"

"That remark could have been made, and I didn't hear it."

"After all, you were driving, and, of necessity, your attention had to be on the road ahead, right?"

"Right. I was keeping the car in the road."

"So, the statement could have been made?"

"Yes, that statement could have been made."

"Would you agree that, with you sitting in the front seat and with all the wind noise coming from the front of the car, that you could hear someone talking from the front seat to the back better than you could hear someone talking from the back seat to the front?"

"I suppose."

"You have testified that Lee said in that statement that he went down the road by Mr. J. S. Alexander's. How far the other side of Mr. Alexander's did he go?"

"If he said how far the other side of Mr. Alexander's he went I don't remember it, but it was somewheres near Mr. J. S. Alexander's house."

"That's not the way to his father's house. What were they doing down there?"

"He said they had started down on the river – I don't think he said what they were going down there for, no wait, I think he did, too. I think he said they were going after whiskey. I think that is what he said they were going after."

"Did he say why they turned back?"

"He didn't say."

"So, he did not state that they turned back at Mr. Alexander's because they were on the wrong road?"

"He said they came to the church, and that is where they thought they were on the wrong road, or where they stopped and where he done the killing."

"Were these statements made voluntarily, or were they made in response to questions asked Mr. Currie?"

"Well, of course, he answered the questions, but not all of the statements that he made about how it occurred were made in response to questions asked him; not all of them were. He was asked how the killing occurred, and then he told how it occurred, and then he was asked how would he kill him without having a wreck. That's when he told that they were stopped, then he was asked how he could shoot him in the back of his head, and then he answered how he shot him in the back of his head."

"And you offered him no inducement to make these statements?"

"None whatsoever, not a bit."

"No further questions, your honor," Giles said and returned to the defense table.

* * * * * *

"Mr. Grey, we are getting close to dinner time. Are you at a stopping point?" Judge Hardeman said. The fan under the bench was now insufficient defense against the heat, and the judge grudgingly had resorted to the indignity of waving a hand fan.

"If it pleases the court, I have one more witness I'd like to call this morning. It won't take long," Grey said.

Judge Hardeman sighed and said, "Very well, if you insist, proceed."

"The State calls Alex Hawkins to the stand," Grey said.

Hawkins was duly sworn in, gave his name, and told the jury he was the Chief of Police at the State Sanitarium in Milledgeville.

Grey asked, "After you received notice of the warrant on Mr. Currie, when were you able to arrest him?"

"It was on February 24th, on a Tuesday, I think, about sundown or somewhere about sundown."

"Please describe the circumstances of the arrest."

"He had just arrived at the Sanitarium in a car when I arrested him. I think it was an Overland car."

"What became of the car?"

"I turned that car over to Sheriff McLeod. I locked it up that night and our sheriff up here, Mr. Terry, wired Sheriff McLeod that we had the car and Mr. Currie. He came up the next morning after it."

"Did you find any weapons on Mr. Currie when you arrested him?"

"I found nothing on Mr. Currie when I arrested him, but he had a pistol in the car."

Grey retrieved the pistol from the court reporter's evidence table and showed it to Hawkins. "Is this the weapon you found in the car?"

Hawkins looked the gun over carefully, "If that ain't it, it is one just like it."

"Did you examine the bullets in that pistol?"

"I did."

Grey produced the bullets from the evidence table and showed them to Hawkins. "Do these appear to be the cartridges you examined?"

"Yep, that's them, or they look just like them. The balls had been cut off, trimmed off; they seem like. These balls are in the same condition those were in the pistol at the time I got it. They were cut off just like that."

"Your witness," Grey said.

Sharpe questioned this witness and asked, "Mr. Hawkins, you have testified that the defendant did not have any other type of weapon on him, is that right?"

"I searched the defendant when I arrested him. I did not find anything on him, but he gave me a pocketknife later."

This statement allowed Sharpe to display the peaceful side of Lee Currie. He looked directly at the jury and said, "He voluntarily gave you a pocketknife." Sharpe then turned back toward the witness and asked, "And how was it that you didn't discover the pocketknife when you searched him?"

"I don't know whether he had it in his pocket or in his hand or not. I didn't find anything on him. I just slapped his pockets around."

"So, you didn't put your hands in his pockets?"

"Not at all. I just felt to see if he had his gun on him, and I didn't find any gun, and I did not search him any further. I found nothing on him except a pocketknife, and he gave me that after I searched him."

"Mighty neighborly of someone the State is trying to prove wantonly just killed a man for a car, wouldn't you say?"

"Objection!" Grey stood up and said.

"Sustained. Counselor, save your summation for the end of the trial if you please," Judge Hardeman said.

"I withdraw the question and have no further questions, your honor," Sharpe said as he turned and winked at Lee, who was grinning broadly back at him.

"You may step down, Mr. Hawkins. Thank you for coming from Milledgeville to appear here today.

"Gentlemen of the jury, we are going to take a dinner break. I understand that the bailiff will take you to the Elberta Hotel. You'll find the fare there to be some of the finest in the county. The bailiff has reserved the entire dining room for your exclusive use, where you won't be disturbed.

"Remember that you are not to discuss this case until you have been given all the evidence and asked to deliberate and form your verdict. At the pace we are going, that will probably be sometime tomorrow. Please follow the bailiff. The sheriff has vehicles waiting to carry you to the Elberta.

"Court is in recess until 1 p.m.," Judge Hardeman said as he rapped his gavel and stood.

"All rise," the bailiff called out, and the judge whisked out of the side door and immediately shed his black robe. Damn this heat, he said as he headed to the judge's chambers and the cold jug of iced tea he knew would be waiting for him.

Chapter 38

Sheriff McLeod knew that testifying in the Lee Currie murder case was probably going to be a loser for him, and his mood darkened as his turn on the witness stand approached. The only good thing about the oppressive summer heat was the camouflage it afforded the sweat pouring from him, given the unwelcome prospect of being called to testify against his friend's son.

Being the county's chief law enforcement officer had its highs and lows. Before his wife Nancy died just over two years ago, she had been his rock through rough spots like these. She could read his every mood and had a way of calming him, helping him discover his strength and his courage during the hard times. He had not found a replacement for her companionship.

"All rise, the court is now back in session in the case of the State versus Lee Currie, Judge Robert N. Hardeman presiding," the bailiff announced.

McLeod's reactions were automatic as he heard his name called, entered the courtroom, was sworn in, and answered the usual introductory questions propounded to him. Only when Grey asked him about the body did he depart from his semi-attentive state and look directly up at the attorney.

"Where was the body found, Sheriff McLeod?" Grey had asked.

"Uh, right near Mr. Node Beddingfield's, in this county. I expect that is about 13 miles from Lyons, something about 3 miles, I guess, from Johnson's Corner."

"What day of the week was that?"

"It was on a Tuesday, to the best of my recollection."

"Tell the jury what happened when you arrived at the burial site."

"I saw the body dug up. Mr. Phillips's face was covered with dirt and kinder crooked about pretty badly, where it had been jammed into the grave. It was some little bit before we could recognize who it was. I don't suppose the body was buried over fifteen inches, that is, from the top of the body. The hole was deeper than that, of course, but I don't think there was more than twelve or fifteen inches of dirt over the body."

"Was there any sign of blood?"

"There was some, and the body bled after it was taken out."

"Did you examine Mr. Phillips's body to see if there were any wounds on it?"

"I did, and there was a wound right in the back of his head."

"Which side of his head?"

"Right at the back of his head, a little to the right side."

"How do you think he was wounded?"

"With a pistol ball."

Grey paused as he heard the soft sobbing of Tersia Phillips seated behind the prosecution table, and he turned for a moment to look in her direction, hoping to draw the jury's attention to the grieving widow. He turned back and continued.

"Did the pistol ball come out of his head?"

"Not there. Dr. Youmans removed it later."

"What else did you note about the condition of the body?"

McLeod looked straight at Tersia Phillips, who was still wiping tears from her eyes. It hurt him to know she was reliving all this.

"I'd rather not say with Mrs. Phillips sitting in the courtroom."

Grey turned to Tersia and said, "Mrs. Phillips has already had to endure her husband's loss. What will make those tears go away is for her to see justice done for her husband. Please answer the question, Sheriff."

McLeod lowered his head and said, "We found dirt in his nostrils, and it appeared he was still alive when he was buried."

The courtroom burst into a collective gasp, and hushed whispering immediately ensued. Tersia buried her head into her hands and let out a loud wail. Thomas Phillips put his arms around her to comfort her. Several of the ladies swooned while those beside them began to fan them vigorously.

Judge Hardeman rapped his gavel several times, "Order; I will have order!" The din soon died down, and the judge continued, "Ladies and gentlemen, I have already warned you about being quiet. This is a murder trial, and murder is never pretty or neatly done. If you cannot listen quietly to these proceedings, you will need to leave, or I will have you all removed; now settle down."

Except for the soft sobbing of Tersia Phillips, the courtroom slowly fell to dead silence. *The defense will have a hard time overcoming that searing testimony*, Grey thought to himself as he covered the lower part of his face to suppress a smile.

"Continue your examination of the witness, counselor," Judge Hardeman directed.

"Thank you, your honor," Grey slowly turned back to the witness, allowing as much time as possible for the jury to hear Tersia's soft sobs.

"Sheriff McLeod, when did you first see the defendant after that?"

"The next day. I left Vidalia the next morning and went to Macon and from Macon to Milledgeville. I don't remember the exact time it was."

"And what did you do when you saw the defendant?"

"I brought the defendant back here. I brought him in Burley Phillips' automobile, the Baby Overland, which I had picked up over at the Sanitarium from Mr. Hawkins, who had taken it from Mr. Curie. He had it in charge and turned it over to me."

"Where is the car now?"

"I turned that car over to Tom Phillips, Burley's brother, after Mr. O. D. Warthen examined it. That car was nearly a new car and had been used but very little. There was blood on the car, under the cushions, and on the curtains."

"Do you recall the occasion that you carried the defendant to Savannah?"

"Yes, I do."

"That was by train?"

"He rode with my deputy in a car from Lyons to Ohoopee and got on the train there to go on to Savannah."

"Did you make any stops?"

"I had wired Mr. Mulkey to meet the train at Claxton to identify Currie, and he got aboard the train and looked at Currie and said he was the man that sent the telegram."

"Did Mr. Currie make any statements about Mr. Mulkey?"

"Mr. Currie didn't say anything until the fellow turned and walked out, and then he said, 'That wasn't the son-of-a-bitch that sent that message.' He said it was a black-headed fellow that sent the message."

Grey handed McLeod the pistol from the evidence table, "Have you seen this pistol before?"

"I got that pistol from Mr. Hawkins."

Grey poured the bullets from the evidence bag into the sheriff's hand. "Are these the bullets that were in the gun?"

"I couldn't say that these bullets are the exact ones that were in the pistol, but they look like 'em."

"And where has this gun been before this trial?"

"It has been hanging up in my house all the time."

"Did Mr. Currie tell you how the shooting occurred?"

"Mr. Currie made two statements in my presence about it. They were made as we were coming from Milledgeville."

"And how did this conversation begin?"

"I told him that Mr. Phillips had been killed and that we were riding in Mr. Phillips' automobile, and I was bringing him back to stand trial for the killing."

"Did Mr. Currie say he knew Burley Phillips?"

"At first, he said he didn't know him, and he didn't know that he had been killed, but when we came down the road a little piece, he said, 'Yes, I know about it.' He offered details about it.

"He said Burley had been to Pembroke that day to carry two passengers, and when they got back to Lyons, he brought the two men with him. He got Burley to take him home, and they went with him, and when they got down there nearly to his home, one of these men wanted to get some whiskey. Lee told him that he thought maybe he might be able to do it, and he directed Burley to Ben Singleton's house, I think. I am not sure, but I think that is it. He said Ben didn't have any whiskey, and when he got back to the car, these men had killed Burley.

"I asked him, 'What did you do then, Lee?'

"He told me, 'I went down side of the branch and sit down on a log and stayed there a good while. After a while, I went back up there to where they were, and Burley was there dead, but the men were gone. They had left the car there."

"Did he tell you a different version of events after that?"

"He did. He told my deputy that he had bought the car for $100 and give a man a note for it. He couldn't remember the man's name."

"Did he tell you the first statement was not the truth, and the second statement was the truth?"

"I couldn't be positive about it, but I know he changed the statement."

"How long was it between the first and the second statement?"

"I don't know how far apart they were. I couldn't say. It was a good long ways this side of Milledgeville before he made the first one, and he told me the other one just before he got to Vidalia."

"So, he never told you that the first story was false?"

"I can't state whether he said he had told me the wrong tale the first time or not. I wouldn't be positive about that. I wouldn't say he did or he didn't."

"Your witness," Grey concluded. He looked over to the defense table to try and read the defense attorneys' faces. Grey still suspected that self-defense would be the only defense Giles & Sharpe would put up. With McLeod having just testified that Lee had told two different stories about how the killing took place, it would be easier for him to argue in the closing that Lee was a liar and was making up stories as he went along.

He walked to the prosecution table and sat down.

* * * * * *

Giles knew Lee's two versions of how Burley was killed were problematic. He also knew that the jury was naturally inclined to believe the testimony of Sheriff McLeod. Giles had to cast doubt on his credibility. He stood up and approached the witness.

"Sheriff McLeod, how do you know it was a pistol ball?"

"I am pretty sure it was."

"Did you see the ball?"

"No."

"Are there also some rifles that shoot 38-caliber bullets?"

"I suppose there are some 38-caliber rifles that would shoot the same bullets as some 38-caliber pistols."

"So, what makes you think it was a pistol ball?"

"The only reason why I say it was a pistol ball was the size of the hole, and there was just one shot."

"Are you such a ballistics expert that you can tell whether a ball came from a pistol or a rifle by the size of the bullet hole?"

"I wouldn't say positive about it being a pistol ball."

"Were you there when the bullet was removed?"

"I was in the examination room with Dr. Youmans, but I left before he probed the wound and took the ball out."

"So, you were not there, yet you have testified that you knew he probed the wound and took the ball out?"

"I don't know that as a fact, I didn't see it."

"So, any knowledge you may have about him probing the wound and taking the ball out is just hearsay, correct?"

Giles could tell that McLeod was trying to maintain his professional composure, but he could also detect the sheriff's rising anger. "It's not necessary that I witness the ball being extracted. This was a professional doctor operating as a part of a Coroner's Inquest."

"But, in fact, you don't know if it was Dr. Youmans that removed the bullet, do you?"

"He put it in his report that he did."

"But you don't even know if the ball came from Mr. Phillips's head, do you?"

"Dr. Youmans showed me a ball that he said came out of Mr. Phillips' head."

"But you didn't see it come out?"

"No, but Dr. Youmans, the physician, was there and attested to the fact that he took it out."

"Why was Dr. Youmans there?"

"I think he was called there to serve on the coroner's inquest."

"But you don't know that for certain?"

Giles had McLeod where he wanted him, and it was clear that he was now visibly annoyed. If he could make it appear that the chain of custody of the evidence had been broken by the sheriff's negligence while supervising the removal of the bullet, he could put doubt in the mind of the jury.

"No, I couldn't say about that. He was there, and my understanding is that he was called there to serve on the coroner's inquest. The body was under the control of the coroner. It wasn't my place to know."

"Did you search Mr. Currie on the return from Milledgeville?"

"I did."

"Where was he searched?"

"He was searched at Blocker's Mill, out from Vidalia."

"What did you remove from him during your search?"

"I took what money he had out of his pocket and counted it. I think he had $19.50 in money; I think."

"But you are not sure?"

"I am not sure about that."

"No further questions, your honor."

McLeod stood up and stepped down from the witness stand. His face was flushed red from his anger at being made to appear incompetent by Giles despite his efforts to remain professional. Just as he feared, this would reflect poorly on his political career. He left the courtroom dejected.

* * * * * *

"The state calls Mr. John Bert Rushing to the stand," Grey announced.

The reporters leaned forward in their seats upon hearing Rushing's name. Rushing was the one who found the body, and his testimony was expected to be riveting.

Grey approached him, "Do you remember the day that the body of Burley Phillips was found?"

"Yes. I am the first person to find that grave."

A general murmur went throughout the courtroom.

"What time did you find it?"

"I suppose it to be about 8 o'clock in the morning, maybe, or 8:30 when I found it," Rushing said, pleased to be receiving all this attention.

"What were you doing at the time?"

"I was going after a cow."

"What did you do when you saw the grave?"

"I stopped and looked at it, and it caught my attention, but I needed to go on and get the cow."

"What did you do next?"

"I called the Wolfe boys to come help me look for the cow, and they said they would. I went back to where I saw it, and I seen some automobile signs there right up to the grave."

"Was this fresh sign after the rain that day?"

"There might have been a little sprinkle on the sign, but it wasn't put out at all."

"What did you do then?"

"I rode up on the hill just off a piece, and I seen someone plowing off in the field there, across the woods. I rode on up there and called them to me and ask him about borrowing one of his field hands, and he said they would need the hand he had. I asked him did he know anything about any automobile being back there. I ask him did he know what that was buried down there."

"Did he know what it was?"

"He said he didn't, and he asked me if I thought there was anything buried down there. I told him, yes, I suppose there was, that there was a fresh hole had been dug and filled up."

"What did you say next?"

"I says let's go down there."

"So, you went down there right away?"

"I led my mule on back, and then we went down there. He said he didn't know what it was."

"What did you do after that?" Grey asked.

"I says, 'Go get on my mule down there and go across the branch there and get A. L. Wright and tell him to bring a shovel, and we would find out.' He got on the mule and went home and come back with Bud Wright and A. L. Wright. Mr. Wright took the shovel and dug down something like five or six inches and found the heel of the shoe."

"Did you dig the body up?"

"Of course not. We didn't go any further."

"What did you do?"

"We put the boy on the mule again and sent him after some of the neighbors. When they got there, there were three or four of them, or maybe half a dozen; we decided that we wouldn't go any further. I got on the mule myself and come back home and called for Sheriff McLeod. By the time McLeod got there, there was a pretty large crowd there, and McLeod then told us to dig him up."

"Was there any fresh sign at that grave where someone had been there right before you found it?"

"There was a chunk moved and put on the grave since that sprinkle of rain."

"Describe for the jury what you mean when you say chunk."

"The chunk was a back end of a log, and it had partly covered the grave, something like the length of the grave, and on top of that was a dead pine bough."

"So, is it your testimony that the chunk of wood was moved there after the sprinkle?"

"That's right."

"How would you know that?"

"There had been a sprinkle on the grave, and there had been a chunk moved, and we couldn't tell anything about any rain sign where the chunk was moved from. There came a sprinkle of rain that morning, and that night, just a light sprinkle."

"Did you see any tracks at the grave?"

"Yeah, there were tracks."

"What size were the tracks?"

"I couldn't say. It wasn't large tracks; they were small tracks."

"In what county was the grave, Mr. Rushing?"

"That was in Toombs County."

"In the state of Georgia?"

"That's right."

"Did you see the wound in Burley's head?"

"Yes, I did." Rushing turned his head around and held his finger on the back of his head on the right side. "The bullet went in here." He turned back around and looked at Grey. "I saw the sign where it went in, and I seen Dr. Youmans take it out up there over his left eye here – somewhere up in his forehead on the left side."

"You saw Dr. Youmans take the bullet out of Mr. Phillips?"

"Yes, I was one of the ones who carried Mr. Phillips into Dr. Youmans' office."

Grey looked at the defense table. Rushing was an eyewitness to removing the bullet from the victim and had just corroborated Sheriff McLeod's earlier testimony Giles had challenged during his cross-examination.

"Was there any sign around the wound that would indicate how far away the shooter was?"

"The hair on his head there in the edge of his hair, the hair was singed off and a powder sign in the skin."

"Your witness," Grey said and returned to his seat.

* * * * * *

"No questions, your honor," Giles said, hoping the jury would soon forget this witness' testimony. He involuntarily clenched his fists and then relaxed as quickly as he became aware the jury was watching him. The point-blank shot was not going to support Lee's statement to come.

* * * * * *

Judge Hardeman was again beginning to worry about the defense's placidity, but he knew it would soon be their turn to present their case, and he would hold his patience till then. "Call your next witness, counselor."

"The State calls Ober Dewitt Warthen to the stand," Grey said.

The electric fan at Judge Hardeman's feet was still losing the battle against the stifling afternoon heat. Again, ignoring the blow to his dignity, he picked up the hand fan and started fanning himself. He closely listened to Grey trying to establish that the Baby Overland Lee had in his possession was the same automobile Ober had sold to Burley Phillips.

"What was the last automobile you sold to Burley Phillips?" Grey asked.

"That was what they called a little Four Overland, known by most folks as a Baby Overland."

"Are you familiar with when they found Mr. Phillips dead?"

"Yes."

"Had you sold him a car just before that happened?"

"Just maybe a day or two over a month before that date."

"Have you examined the car in which Mr. McLeod and Mr. Mallard brought Lee Currie from Milledgeville?"

"I have."

"Is that the car you sold to Burley Phillips?"

"That is the same car."

Grey sat down, and Judge Hardeman looked over to Giles to see if he wanted to cross-examine the witness. Giles shook his head to indicate he didn't.

"You may step down, Mr. Warthen. Call your next witness, counselor," Judge Hardeman said.

* * * * * *

"The State calls Mr. John B. Johnson to the stand," Grey announced.

Grey needed Mr. Johnson's testimony to show a bizarre event that happened while Lee Currie was in custody. He hoped it would afford further proof of the lengths to which Lee was willing to go to cover his crime. Grey quickly got to the point after the witness was led in, sworn in, and asked the preliminary questions.

"When did you last have a conversation with Mr. Currie?" Grey asked.

"While he was in jail here," Mr. Johnson answered.

"During this conversation, did you offer him any hope of reward or fear of punishment?"

"No."

"So, what he told you at the time was freely and voluntarily made?"

"Spose so."

"While he was in jail, did the defendant ever ask you to arrest anyone?"

"Not me. Lee Currie had the sheriff to go and arrest a negro and bring him here."

"Why did he want the sheriff to do that?"

"I don't remember the conversation, but the sheriff arrested him. I went up to the jail to see the negro the same day."

"Did you talk with Mr. Currie that day?"

"I don't remember whether I talked to him at that time or not; however, I went downstairs, and he sent for me to come back upstairs."

"What did he say to you when you got back up there?"

"He wanted me to get the negro to where he could talk to him, but I told him that I couldn't do it, that the sheriff wouldn't allow it. Then I left him and went back downstairs. I actually went in to ask the negro about it, but he said he didn't know nothing about the killing. In about a minute or two, someone, I think it was Carl McLeod, told me that Lee wanted me again."

"Did you go back upstairs?"

"Yes, but the next time I went up, I got after him. In other words, I ask him if the negro had anything to do with the killing."

"What did he say?"

"He told me that he didn't; however, he still wanted to talk with the negro. I told him that if the negro wasn't guilty and had nothing to do with it, he had better tell the sheriff so he could let him go back to work. Then he asked me something most peculiar."

"What was that?"

"He asked me if the negro would make the statement that he had Phillips to kill; would that help him out? I told him that it certainly would, that if he had him to kill, it certainly ought to help him out of it, but then, I says, now, you told me that the negro had nothing to do with it, and the negro says that, too, then, how do you expect the negro to admit to the killing?"

"So, did he give you his reasoning?"

"He just said that he wanted the negro to say that he had Phillips to kill."

"Was anything else said about this cockamamie plan?"

From his seat, Giles said, "Objection."

"Sustained. Counselor, let the witness do any characterization of his testimony that he feels is warranted," Judge Hardeman said.

"I apologize, your honor. Let me rephrase, was anything else said about this plan?"

"No, that is about all," Johnson said.

"No further questions," Grey said.

* * * * * *

"The state calls Mr. Thomas Phillips to the stand."

Giles knew that the testimony of any family member of the deceased would be problematic for the defense, and he was not looking forward to the testimony of Burley's brother. However, he could attack Thomas's credibility because of his role as the lynch party's ringleader after the sheriff brought Lee into custody. And given his volatility, if he had an outburst on the stand, the jury might surmise that violence ran in the family, and Burley's alleged attack of Lee with a knife might carry more weight.

"Mr. Phillips, are you any relation to the deceased Burley Phillips?" Grey asked the witness.

"He and I were brothers."

Grey picked up the pipe from the evidence table, "Is this the pipe you presented to me before this trial, saying it belonged to your brother?"

"Yes, that is Burley Phillips' pipe."

"Where did you get the pipe?"

"I got that pipe from a fellow down here below Claxton named George Smith."

Grey took a distorted and twisted bullet from a small pouch and showed it to the witness. "Mr. Phillips, is this the pistol bullet you presented to me before the trial?"

Thomas choked up, "It is."

"The State would like to admit this into evidence as Exhibit 'F'."

"Hearing no objection, I will admit it," Judge Hardeman said.

"What is the significance of this bullet?"

For a moment, Thomas could not speak. A tear rolled down his cheek, and he finally composed himself and said, "The doctor gave me that bullet and said it was the one that killed my brother."

"I'm sorry to be having to ask you these questions, Mr. Phillips. I know this is not an easy memory for you. Did you say a doctor gave this to you?"

Thomas was regaining his composure. "Yes."

"Which doctor was that?"

"Dr. Youmans."

Grey took back the bullet, dropped it back in the pouch, and handed it to the court reporter, who marked it as an exhibit.

Grey held up a bloodstained tag with "For Hire" printed on it.

"Is this the tag that was on your brother's car?"

"Yes. Burley used that tag to advertise the car was being used as a taxi."

"The State would like to admit this into evidence as Exhibit 'G.'"

Judge Hardeman said, "Without objection, I will admit it."

"Mr. Phillips, where did you happen to acquire this tag?"

"I found that tag after I got the car back from Sheriff McLeod. It was under the back cushion in the toolbox."

Giles stood up, "Objection. Your honor, the sheriff gave the car back to Mr. Phillips months ago. How can we know that the sign came from the car?"

"The truth of the origin of the sign is up to the jury, your honor," Grey countered.

"Overruled," Judge Hardeman said.

"Mr. Phillips, was anything unusual about the sign?" Grey continued.

"I noticed blood on it."

"Where is the car now?"

"At my sister-in-law Tersia's house in Vidalia."

Grey took the tag back from Thomas and handed it to the court reporter, "No further questions."

Giles had nothing to gain from this witness, and he didn't want to antagonize him, but he had to challenge the pipe being introduced into evidence just as he had challenged the introduction of the hat. He decided to start slowly.

"Where do you reside, Mr. Phillips?"

"I live five miles north of Vidalia."

"What type of work do you do?"

"I work carpenter work most of the time."

Giles got the pipe and showed it to Thomas again. "You testified that this is your brother Burley Phillips' pipe, correct?"

"It's his," Thomas said belligerently.

"What peculiarity about this pipe makes you think so?"

"Well, I saw him smoking it all the time."

"And you were with him all the time?"

"I was with him very often."

"Is there a mark or anything about the pipe that you can identify? Perhaps it has some string or something else that is peculiar to it?"

"No, and I don't know anything about a string."

"The pipe did not have a string on it when you saw Burley with it?"

"No."

"So, how can you know this was your brother's pipe?

"My brother smoked a pipe just like that."

"Mr. Phillips, wouldn't you admit that there are a lot of pipes just like this one?"

"I suppose so, but if that ain't the pipe that belonged to my brother, it's one just like it."

"But would you agree that there are a lot of pipes just like it out there?"

"I guess I would."

"What was your brother's profession?"

"My brother ran a jitney."

"Thank you, Mr. Phillips; I'm sorry for your loss. No further questions, your honor," Giles said and returned to his seat.

Chapter 39

Sheriff McLeod was beyond alarmed at the growing crowds that had arrived in Toombs County as the third day of the trial commenced. The threat of a lynching still loomed, the local hotels had all filled up, and there were now tents beginning to pop up throughout Lyons and even on the courthouse grounds. Local citizens were taking in relatives and boarders. Hot dog vendors were working the crowds, and the litter was beginning to pile up. This Currie trial was turning into a circus and a big headache for him.

He welcomed the presence of the members of the Georgia Army National Guard Governor Dorsey had sent at his request to preserve the peace should it get ugly when the jury announced the verdict, probably sometime later that day.

"You watch things here. I'm going back inside," McLeod said to his son Carl.

Jim Mallard was already on the stand, and Grey was questioning him when McLeod entered the courtroom.

"Mr. Mallard, did you go with the Sheriff to Milledgeville to pick up the defendant and return him to Lyons?" Walter Grey asked.

"I went with him; I sure did," Mallard said.

"On your return with the defendant, did he make any statements with reference to how the shooting occurred?"

"He made two or three statements."

"Were those statements made freely and voluntarily?"

"They were, excepting one portion in regard to a telegram."

Grey stiffened. He needed to clarify that last answer. "Mr. Mallard, are you saying he made his statement about the telegram because of a reward you offered him or a fear you instilled in him?"

"Oh, I'm sorry, I misspoke. There wern't no fear said to him. The sheriff and myself had decided not to say nothing to him and to see if he would mention it."

"So did he?"

"After we had rode five or six miles without him saying nothing, the sheriff just up and ask him, he says, 'Lee, where did you get this car?' and Lee says, 'I bought it from some strangers.'

"Well, then I asked him, 'How much you give for it?' and the best of my recollection, he says, '$100'."

"Did the sheriff ask him whether he paid cash for it?"

"No, he didn't ask that ... not right then."

"What did he say next?"

"Nothing. He just hushed right then. We rode for some little piece, and finally, I ask him myself. I says, 'Did you pay cash or not?' and he says, 'No, I give a note.' And then I asked him, I says, 'Who did you make this note to?' He says, 'I don't know, it was strangers.'"

"Did you discuss the killing?"

"Well, we rode on for a good little piece then, two or three miles, before anything was said about it, talking about first one thing and another. I think the sheriff talked to him about something that happened down in our county, and Lee asked, 'What is it?' The sheriff said, 'The killing of Burley Phillips and taking his car.'"

"Did he answer the question?"

"Not right off. It seemed that he kinder went to pieces. You could tell there was a difference in his looks, kinder nervous, looked like. We rode on a little piece, and finally, he said he didn't know anything about that part of it."

"Did you continue to pursue the matter?"

"I did. I said to him finally, 'There ain't but one thing or nobody wouldn't of suspicioned you of knowing anything, but this morning a log was put on the grave, and a man hunting cows has seen it. If a man hunting cows hadn't seen you ...' He interrupted me and said, 'Who was that?' and I says, 'That man will come up later on.'"

"So, you are making this up to what, draw him out?"

"You're right. I didn't know anything about that. I hadn't heard anything of anybody seeing him, and the man hunting cows rode on without seeing anybody."

Grey knew he was walking a thin line with this witness. Although the sheriff deputized him for the trip, he was not a trained law officer, and his questions to the defendant were troublesome.

"How did he respond to what you told him?" Grey asked.

"He says, 'I know that Phillips was killed, but I didn't kill him.'"

"Did he volunteer any further information?"

"He went on to say about getting Phillips to take him home, and two strangers went along with them. He said that when he got down there, one of them said something about whiskey and ask him if he could tell him where to get some. Lee spoke to him about someplace over on the creek somewhere, that maybe they might get some, and they drove on over there. When they got to the creek, it was too full, and they couldn't cross. They turned back, and Lee then said he knew some man on this side of the creek that might have some whiskey."

"Some man?"

"I learned afterwards that the man was a darkie, and he said that they stopped pretty close to his house. Lee said he told them, 'You wait here, and I will step up there and see if I can get some whiskey.' He then said while he was gone that those men killed him, he reckoned, because when he got back, he said, 'I know he was dead.' He says, 'I saw him lying on the ground done dead, and I said to them, 'Well, what did you do?' and getting no answer, Lee says, 'I went off in the branch and set down on a log.'

"He hushed for a while, and finally, I says, 'Well, did you just keep setting on the log?' He say, 'No, after while I went back up there and when I got back up there Phillips had been moved.'"

"Did he say anything about where they might have moved Phillips?" Grey asked.

"He says, 'I don't know where they carried him to or anything about it. They was trying to crank up the car, but they couldn't.' Then he says, 'Finally they told me, 'There is the car, you can have it.'

"We rode on for a piece, and Lee finally says, 'I know this is Phillips' car.'"

Grey smiled. "So, he admitted that he knew the car he had in his possession was Burley Phillips' car?"

"That's right."

"Didn't you testify that he told you earlier that he had bought the car for $100?"

"Yes, and I mentioned it to him, I says, 'You didn't buy the car then?'

"It looked like my question kinda surprised him, and he says, 'Oh yes, I bought the car.' I says, 'Well, where did you buy it at?' He says, 'At Reidsville.' I asked him, 'When?' and he says, 'The next day.'"

"So, he returned to the first story he told you. And did you ask him what he paid for it?"

"Yes, and he went over that same $100, about giving the note for it and about how he did not know who it was to. I says to him then, I says, 'Well, didn't you go to Reidsville the next day in this car?'"

"Did he answer that?"

"Not right away, after we had rode on a piece again, he said, 'Yes.' I says, 'Where did you go to from there?' He says, 'To Claxton.'"

"So, he admitted going to Claxton the day after Phillips was killed?"

"Yes, and then it was that I mentioned him having sent the telegram to Mrs. Phillips. I mentioned that myself and went on to say something about what the telegram was. I says, 'That is the way you sent a telegram, just like it was Phillips sending it back to Mrs. Phillips, and told her you had sold the car and would be home in a few days.'"

"How did he respond to this direct accusation?"

"He says, 'No, not in a few days.'"

"Not in a few days? The telegram had said he would be home next week. So, did he say anything else?"

"I think that is about as far as he made any confessions or talked between us at the time."

"Let me show you State Exhibit' D', a hat that was turned over to you before this trial and allegedly belonged to

Burley Phillips." Grey picked up the hat from the evidence desk and handed it to Mallard. "Is this that hat?"

Mallard looked the hat over, "That looks very much like the hat that I got down there below Claxton."

"Who gave you this hat?"

"I can't think of the man's name, but I picked it up and brought it back and turned it over to Mr. Thomas Phillips."

"Your witness," Grey said as he returned the hat to the evidence table and got back to his seat.

* * * * * *

This was one of those times that Giles wished he had pursued the insanity defense instead of self-defense. Mallard's testimony clearly showed Lee was making things up as if he were a child caught with his hand in the cookie jar. Lee showed no evidence of an adult's cunning when telling a lie and was doing a poor job of getting his stories straight. It also showed he was foolishly unaware he was talking to law enforcement officials. That naiveté afforded Giles a perfect opportunity to ask questions that proved Lee was mentally unbalanced.

But it was too late to change strategies now. Giles had to lay the groundwork for the self-defense justification for the crime. He approached the witness.

"Mr. Mallard, have you related to this court all the confessions that Lee Currie supposedly made to you on the way from Milledgeville?"

"I think that is all."

"Did he say anything about Mr. Phillips not being agreeable?"

"Now, he did say something about that."

"What did he say?"

"I ask him if there was any trouble, and he said, 'No, not a bit.' He said everybody was peaceable, and there wasn't any fussing."

"And this was the only confession that he made?"

"I think that is about all he had to say."

"And where did all this talking between you and the defendant take place?"

"At different places between Milledgeville and here. He started, as I said a while ago, the first of it started about six or eight miles this side of Milledgeville. I expect when he told me about his going off and coming back and leaving the two strangers in the car, we must of been twelve or fifteen miles this side of Milledgeville."

"Who was driving the car?"

"Sheriff McLeod."

"Where was the defendant sitting in the car?"

"He sat on the back seat with me. Mr. McLeod was sitting in the front seat of the car doing the driving."

"From where you were sitting, could you easily hear the conversation between the defendant and the sheriff?"

"I think I could've heard any conversation he had with Mr. McLeod."

"Did the defendant tell Mr. McLeod that the way the killing occurred was that they got into a quarrel and that Burley Phillips came at him with a knife?"

"No, he positively did not."

"He didn't say that to you either? Are you positive about that?"

"I say positively he did not make any such statement to me."

"He didn't make it to you?" Giles repeated his testimony with emphasis on the word 'you.'

Mallard was indignant. "He didn't make it to me, and I was with him."

Giles wanted to remove any doubt that either Mallard or the Sheriff was lying. He continued, "But he might have made it outside of your earshot?"

"If he made any such statement that evening, I didn't hear it. If he made any such statement anywhere at all like that, I had never heard it up until now."

"Were you seated where you could hear it if it were said to Mr. McLeod?"

"I was in the car coming along. I was sitting on the seat with Lee Currie, and Mr. McLeod was sitting in the front seat driving."

"Do you have good hearing, Mr. Mallard?"

"My hearing is fairly good, but nothing extra. I heard what I have told you."

"So, it is your testimony that you heard everything said between the defendant and the sheriff?"

"I could hear that all right."

"So, he never said, where you could hear him, a statement to the effect that when he shot Burley Phillips, that Burley Phillips was coming on to him with his knife and that, as Lee threw his pistol on him, Burley dodged his head that way and he shot him?"

"I never heard him make such a statement like that in my life."

Giles decided it was time to discredit Mallard as a witness.

"You've taken a great deal of interest in this case, haven't you, Mr. Mallard?"

"I don't know whether you would call it that or not. I don't know, as I have taken so much interest, especially in it."

"Oh, but haven't you done some investigating of your own?"

Mallard began to get nervous, "I've done this much; I went down below Claxton hunting up where he went to."

"Were you a police officer at the time, Mr. Mallard?"

"I was not an officer."

"Yet, you went down below Claxton to hunt up witness statements and evidence down there, right?"

"I just said that I did."

"And did you not go around with the dead man's brother looking for evidence?"

"I went around with Mr. Phillips a day or two, I reckon."

Giles smiled. Mallard was proving to be a gold mine. He had just shown the jury how this group of amateurs mishandled the investigation from the start.

"You had not been officially deputized by the sheriff or trained in proper law enforcement procedures, and yet you went looking for evidence in this case? Don't you think that makes you an interested party?"

"I reckon you would call it that I took some interest in the case."

"Do you think Mr. McLeod also heard the statement you attributed to Mr. Currie that he had bought this car in Reidsville and paid $100 for it? Would he be able to corroborate your testimony?"

"No, I could not tell you that."

"How loud was Mr. Currie speaking when he was talking to you?"

"He was talking in just an ordinary voice."

"Mr. Currie normally talks in a thunderous voice; did you know that?"

"I don't know whether he usually talks rather loud or not; on that occasion, he talked just an ordinary voice."

"Was Sheriff McLeod driving the car pretty fast?"

"I think we were about four hours and a half coming from Milledgeville to here, and so, of course, we had to run pretty fast to do that."

"At that speed, with all the raring and bouncing and jumping about, first one way and another, do you think the Sheriff sitting upfront could have heard what Mr. Currie was saying in the back if Mr. Currie didn't talk in a loud voice?"

"Well, no, unless the Sheriff had been paying special attention to us."

Giles flipped a page of his pad, and Mallard shifted uneasily in the witness chair. It was easier than he thought to prove to the jury that Mallards' interest in the case was beyond professional. Giles could argue in closing that in his attempt to get hired on as a deputy, he allowed his over-enthusiasm to cloud his objectivity.

"Did you engage Mr. Currie in any casual conversation before you started asking him about the case?" Giles asked.

"I saw no disposition to talk until we began to question him and all."

"Did you attempt to talk to the defendant after they locked him up?"

"I came down to the jail and tried to talk to him a little, but I had very little to say to him."

"A little? You talked to him for about an hour, didn't you?"

"I didn't stay there about an hour. I reckon I stayed there about 20 minutes."

"You saw him several times at the jail, didn't you?"

"I don't think I went there but the one time. I don't think I went back. I don't think I went there, but the one time."

"Didn't you come to see the defendant another time to question him, and didn't you bring several parties along with you?"

Mallard was squirming in the witness chair, "I don't remember several parties. There might have been one or two along with me, but if anybody questioned him, I don't know anything."

"Did you bring the others along to hear what was said?"

"I couldn't say, there wasn't any understanding that anybody I brought in there was going to hear what he said."

"But you invited them to come with you?"

"They did not come at my invitation. I brought them at their invitation."

"At their invitation? Is it not true that you were having quite a time showing off your famous prisoner to curious onlookers, Mr. Mallard?"

"Objection!" Grey shouted.

"Sustained," Judge Hardeman said.

"I withdraw the question, your honor. Now, Mr. Mallard, when you went with Mr. McLeod to get Mr. Currie in Milledgeville, did you, at any time, search him?"

"I did not search Mr. Currie at all."

"Did anyone search the defendant?"

"Mr. McLeod may have, but I didn't search him."

"You never searched him at all?"

"I never did at all."

"Did you not, yourself, stop in the road after you left Milledgeville and search him?"

Mallard was growing irritated, "No!"

"So, if the defendant says he was stopped along the way and searched, he would be lying?"

"If he was searched, Mr. McLeod searched him. I didn't search him. I am positive I did not."

Giles believed he had discredited the sheriff's testimony that Lee was searched just outside Vidalia and found some money on him. It was time to show Mallard for the wannabe deputy he was.

"When the defendant was in jail, and you went there to take him out, did you handcuff him?"

"Of course, that is standard procedure."

"Describe how you handcuffed him."

"He was handcuffed, and there was a chain put in the handcuffs that was run through a ring."

"So, he was handcuffed and chained?"

"Yes."

"And who had hold of the other end of the chain?"

"Why, I did."

"Mr. Mallard, did you deliberately jerk on the chain while it was attached to the defendant?"

Mallard's facial expression revealed the honest answer. He turned scarlet and said, "I don't think I ever did jerk him at all, no sir. I don't think I am quite that rough with a prisoner."

"I have no further questions for this officer, er, witness, your honor."

"You got him good, Col. Giles," Lee whispered to Giles as he sat down.

Grey stood up and said, "The State rests, your honor."

"The defense may call its first witness," Judge Hardeman said.

"The defense calls Dr. John Hall, your honor," Giles announced.

"Objection!" Lankford stood.

"State your objection," Judge Hardeman said.

"Your honor, we have asked defense counsel for a list of their witnesses, as is our right, and they have not given us a single name. We have provided them with a list of our witnesses. How can we possibly prepare for trial without knowing who the witnesses are?" Lankford said.

"Your honor, we did not know that we could call this witness until recently. There was no time to submit his name to learned counsel. His testimony is critical to the defense of this case," Giles responded.

"Critical or not, your honor, the defense knows the court's requirements that each side must produce a list of their witnesses," Lankford protested.

Judge Hardeman thought for a moment and then asked, "Col. Giles, when did you first become aware of the criticality of this witness' testimony?"

Giles hesitated. His efforts to prevent the prosecution from presenting testimony proving Lee's sanity were about to backfire on him. "We were aware of his testimony back in March, your honor, but his availability was in question until just recently. He has a busy practice in Alamo."

"Four months is more than adequate time to arrange his patient load. The objection is sustained. Col. Giles, I'm afraid I can't let you call this witness."

"Your honor, we will need a recess to respond to your ruling and adjust our strategy," Giles said.

Judge Hardeman looked at the clock on the wall. It was only 11 a.m., but he needed a break from the heat. "It is almost dinner time, and I think this is a good time to take a break." He turned to the jury, "Gentlemen of the Jury, the State has finished presenting their evidence to you, and it is now the defense's turn to present their evidence. Where is my bailiff?"

"Right here, your honor," the bailiff spoke up from the judge's right.

"Send someone to the Elberta Hotel to see if they are prepared to feed our jury an hour early. If not, find them a cool place on the courthouse grounds where they can wait.

"Gentlemen of the Jury, you may wait in the jury room until the bailiff makes the arrangements for your noon meal. You are dismissed. Court is in recess till 1 p.m.," Judge Hardeman said and struck his gavel.

* * * * * *

As Giles was about to begin his dinner, Sharpe said, "Well, we will not be able to call the doctor to attest to Lee's mental state."

"We knew the insanity defense was going to be a long shot at this juncture, T. Ross. This is just a minor setback. And I think it will benefit our case," Giles said.

"Benefit our case? You know they are going to find him guilty, don't you?" Sharpe asked.

"It's likely they will, I agree," Giles said as he started eating his meal.

"You don't seem worried," Sharpe said.

Giles put down his fork and looked up at his law partner. T. Ross Sharpe still had a lot to learn about court procedures.

"We will make our case about Lee not being guilty by reason of insanity at his next trial."

"You're mighty confident that there will be another trial," Sharpe said questioningly.

"They haven't been able to prove this crime occurred in Toombs County, Ross, and most of their evidence is circumstantial. We will put Lee on the stand after lunch and let him make a statement, and then we will observe the judge when he charges the jury. He's going to slip up, and it will give us grounds for a new trial. Don't worry; the Supreme Court granting a new trial for a high-profile murder case like this one is almost automatic.

"We need to change our entire strategy. If one thing has come across during these last three days clearly, it is that Lee Currie is not right in the head. We will need more doctors than Dr. Hall. We will need to put Lee's teachers, friends, and family members on the stand to attest that Lee is insane. We will need several months to put this together, but it will work," Giles answered.

Sharpe nodded and started eating his dinner. He wished he could share Giles's confidence that Lee would get a new trial if the verdict went against him or that an insanity defense would work where self-defense failed, but he respected the old veteran's experience in such matters.

"We haven't spent that much time prepping Lee for his statement. Can you be sure about what he is going to say?" Sharpe asked.

Giles took a sip of tea, "It doesn't matter, as long as he asserts that he shot Burley in self-defense. Besides, we need to let Lee be Lee. It will help us in the next trial if we lose this first round."

* * * * * *

Spectators returning from dinner packed the hot courtroom, adding even more to the oppressive heat. This time, spectators lined the walls. Before calling the court back in session, Judge Hardeman motioned for the sheriff to approach the bench.

"What's going on, Sheriff? Who are all these new people?"

"I was getting complaints from all the local citizens that the out-of-towners and news reporters were taking up all the seats, your honor. I made anyone, who wasn't a local, give up their seats, but they wouldn't leave. I don't have enough room in my jail for all of them, so I just told them they could stand in the back if they were quiet," McLeod said.

"If the State Fire Marshall sees this, he will shut these proceedings down," Judge Hardeman said.

"I wouldn't worry about that. The Fire Marshall has a lot of territory to cover and was just here last month, but if you want to order those standing to leave, I'll get them out of here somehow. I do have the Georgia Army National Guard here. They can put up some type of barricade, if necessary," McLeod suggested.

"We'll try it and see how it goes," Judge Hardeman said.

Judge Hardeman rapped his gavel to quiet everyone down and then looked at the defense table. "Col. Giles, are you ready to present the defense's case?"

Giles rose. "Your honor, the defense has sat here patiently while the prosecution has gone to such great lengths to prove a lot of facts that were not in contention. We are sorry that this has taken up so much of the court's time and that of these good men of the jury. We are especially sorry that the taxpayers of Toombs County have been put to so much expense over a trial that should never have come before the court in the first place."

"I have already ruled on your Motion for a change of venue, Col. Giles," Judge Hardeman said.

"Yes, and we objected to that ruling at the time, your honor."

"Your objection is duly noted in the record, now move on."

"Since the court denied the defendant the opportunity to call his one witness, the defense has but one person to put on the stand. We call Mr. Lee Currie to make a statement," Giles announced.

Again, a din arose in the courtroom from the surprised spectators.

Judge Hardeman rapped his gavel, "I will have order!"

He looked at Giles, "That is the defendant's right." Then he looked at the jury. Most of them had puzzled looks on their faces. "Gentlemen of the Jury, the defendant has the right to make a statement in his defense. His lawyers may not prompt him or ask him any questions. Neither is the prosecution allowed to cross-examine him. You may give his remarks any weight you believe they warrant, given the other evidence in this trial and the arguments counsel may make to their validity during their closing. Bailiff, please swear the defendant."

Lee Currie smiled and walked defiantly to the witness stand. He nodded at the jury and turned to the judge, "How you doing, judge?"

"I'm fine, Mr. Currie. Please sit down. Bailiff?"

The bailiff extended the Bible toward Lee, and he placed his hand upon it.

"Raise your right hand. Do you solemnly swear that the testimony you are about to give is the truth, the whole truth, and nothing but the truth, so help you God?"

"I swear it," Lee said.

"Mr. Currie, you may now make whatever statement you want to make to the Jury," Judge Hardeman said.

"Do I have to do it from up here?" Lee asked.

"Feel free to make your statement from wherever you please, as long as you remain in the courtroom."

Lee got up and walked down in front of the jury. He looked at each juror intently. Giles noted that some jurors appeared to be drawing back from Lee in fear. Not a good sign.

Lee began, "Well, gentlemen of the jury, I killed Mr. Phillips.

"Me and Mr. Phillips was to go get some whiskey. I was to go with him and give him a quart of what we got. We were going to get a quart apiece." Lee turned and walked over to the prosecution table, glaring at Grey.

He turned back to the jury, "When we got to where we were going and couldn't get the whiskey, Mr. Phillips wanted me to turn around and pay him for the price of a quart of whiskey." He slowly approached until he was directly in front of the jury box. Several jurors squirmed nervously.

"I wouldn't do it, and so he says, 'God Dam your soul if you don't pay me, I will beat the hell out of you.'

Lee smiled, "And so I says, 'You big son-of-a-bitch, if you think you can do it, try it. If you think you can do it, just crawl out, and we will see.'"

Lee turned his back on the jury, and as he walked toward the judge, he said, "He got out of the car, and as he got out of the car, he run his hand in his pocket and got his knife."

Lee rapidly turned, crouched, and darted toward the jury while imitating someone taking a knife out of their pocket and holding it in front of them menacingly. Several jury members reeled backward in reflex, "As he got out of the car and come on me with his knife, I shot him."

Lee continued to act out the confrontation – imitating first himself and then Burley Phillips. "He turned his head to dodge the pistol when I shot him."

Lee straightened up and stood still for a moment. His countenance immediately changed from the aggressive stance they had just witnessed to a meek, humble expression, almost that of a child.

"I got scareder and scareder, and I didn't know what to do. I started to bring him home and tell it, but I didn't. I just got scareder and scareder, ..." he looked up at the juror closest to him, "... so I went into the woods and left him."

He turned and went back to his chair at the defense table. "That's all I got to say about that." He sat down and lowered his head. Sharpe patted him on his arm.

The courtroom spectators sat in stunned silence. Several of the reporters bolted out of the door to the nearby telegraph office to be the first to report Lee's testimony. *Lee got to them; I can tell it*, Giles thought to himself as he patted Lee on his other arm.

"I knew it," Lankford whispered to no one in particular. Grey heard him but said nothing. He was worried that Giles

& Sharpe had outflanked him once again. Throwing up this defense as the last bit of evidence submitted to the jury was masterful. He would have to be just as adept with his closing argument to remove its impression from the jury's collective mind.

"The court will be in recess for 30 minutes to allow counsel to finalize their closing arguments," Judge Hardeman said and rapped his gavel.

Chapter 40

"You may present your closing argument, Col. Grey," Judge Hardeman said after the court had reconvened.

Grey gathered several legal pads together, picked them up, and walked over to the podium in front of the jury. He arranged them for a bit, flipped up the cover for the first, and looked at the twelve men who were about to decide Lee Currie's fate.

"Gentlemen of the Jury. I realize it is sweltering this August afternoon, and you have been listening to testimony for the better part of three days now. I'm sure you are anxious to get home to your families. I don't want to hold you up any longer than is necessary to see the cause of justice done here today.

"Rarely does the Solicitor General's office have so much clear and convincing evidence as is present in this case. And the physical evidence we have shown you corroborates the defendant's confession of how he planned, executed, and covered up the killing of Burley Phillips.

"The defendant comes from a very prominent family and has lived a better life than most of you. Getting what he wanted in life was not difficult for him, whether clothes, a new pair of shoes, or a new horse. He is what we might call spoiled and used to getting his way.

"But then things changed for Lee Currie. He left the privileged, sheltered life he enjoyed living with his prosperous father and started out on his own. He got married and went looking for a job out of town, up in Milledgeville, where he could be his own man. Only working in a barbershop and pressing club was not as lucrative a profession as living on the prosperous farm his father had built up with years of hard work and dedication.

"The defendant discovered what so many of our children learn when they leave home, and their pa is no longer paying the bills. Life is hard, and success is not guaranteed. Lee Currie had not experienced his father's lean years. By the time he was born into the family, John Currie was already a successful farmer and wealthy man. Lee had never known hunger, worn second-hand clothes, or had to do without the good things of life.

"Lee also discovered the limitations of starting a new family in another city. He had no easy way to get back and forth from Lyons to Milledgeville or even to go to work. The wages he made at the barbershop and pressing club were meager and not nearly enough to enjoy the lifestyle his father provided back in Toombs County.

"You men are probably all husbands and familiar with the number one problem that can wreck a marriage – money – particularly the lack thereof. The man is the provider for the family, and his economic status is one of the most significant measuring sticks societies uses to judge his standing in his community. Yet here Lee was, having to rely upon John Blackstone for transportation, living in a rented apartment in Milledgeville, having no savings, and subsisting on a meager income washing and pressing clothes for a living. Is it any wonder that his marriage began to fail, and his wife initiated divorce proceedings against him?

"Lee Currie had gone from riches to rags, and he was unwilling to do the hard work necessary to turn things around gradually. No, he longed for the instant gratification provided by a father who indulged his every whim when he was coming up. There was a quicker way to prove his manhood to the world and a faster way to show his wife Lilly that he could be a prosperous husband and good provider. What he needed was something he wanted desperately, a token of his success, an automobile, and not just any automobile. His ego demanded one of the finest automobiles on the road today – a Baby Overland.

"How do we know that he wanted that specific car? Because he told Lloyd Jones several days before he killed Burley Phillips that he was in a trade for an Overland and thought he had enough money saved to put on it.

"The Overland is a fine, luxury vehicle. In Lee's mind, driving up in a car like that was bound to turn heads, bound to pave the way to a better job or even starting his own business, bound to earn him the respect he felt he deserved, and bound to convince Lilly to come back to him. No doubt, in his mind, at least, it was going to solve all of his problems.

"A burning desire to have a Baby Overland automobile began to grow inside of him. His heart leaped every time he saw the vehicle he coveted around town. There was just one problem, it belonged to Burley Phillips, and Lee Currie didn't have enough money to buy it from him. So, what to do?

"Just take it, he concluded. After all, he deserved it, and he wanted it badly.

"All Lee had to do was to get it from Mr. Phillips by whatever means were necessary. He made up his mind to have that beautiful automobile one way or another and began formulating a plan to make it his, even if it involved murder.

"Being summoned to court to stop Lilly's petition for divorce became the catalyst for putting his plan into motion. The thought of Lilly leaving him because he couldn't provide for her was more than he could bear and getting that car would quash her plans to leave him; he just knew it.

"So, Lee Currie set his plan into motion. He went to the Minter-Smith Hardware Store in Lyons and bought some ammunition for his gun. Only the ammunition wouldn't fit, and Lee didn't have the patience to wait for the right ammo to be ordered and delivered. He eagerly accepted Mr. Ivey's suggestion to file off a bit of the bullet tips to allow the pistol cylinder to rotate. A witness saw a clerk from the hardware store deliver the bullets to him. Lee liked what he saw and told the clerk, 'Here's a dime; buy me some more.'

"Those plain ordinary bullets became uniquely altered bullets, making it possible to identify them as being identical to the ones found in the pistol Officer Alex Hawkins took from Lee when he arrested him and identical to the one that Dr. Youmans removed from the victim's head.

"As his plan unfolded, Lee was seen at Mr. Wilson's Jitney Service in Vidalia asking his victim for a ride home. Burley's wife, Tersia, testified that when he came home for supper that fatal night, he told her that he had to take a passenger to the Johnson's Corner area. Little did she know when she kissed him goodbye that night as he was leaving to return to work – it would be for the last time.

"Lee Currie was proud of how clever he had been. He was practically crowing when he revealed his plans to police officers transporting him to the Ohoopee Train Station. He wanted to impress them with how the murder went down. His confession was more than just freely and voluntarily given. With no hope of reward or fear of punishment, he told the terrible story of how he killed Burley Phillips, down to the last precise detail, with pride. Lee Currie felt as if he had earned that beautiful car through hard work and meticulous planning."

Grey looked down at one of his legal pads and flipped through several pages. He again looked up at the jury.

"From the testimony of Mack Wimberley, we learn that Lee told him, his son George, and Deputy Carl McLeod, who were all riding in the car with him from Lyons to the Ohoopee Train Station, that he had killed Burley Phillips down by the Cobb Creek Baptist Church in Toombs County.

"Mr. Wimberley asked Lee how it was that he shot Burley in the back of his head on the left side, and Lee corrected him that it was on the right side of his head. He even asked George Wimberley to turn his head where he could demonstrate how he did it. How could Lee have known the bullet entry wound's location if not there himself? How could he have known these details of the bullet wound if it had not been him that pulled the trigger?

"After he shot him, he described to Mack Wimberley how he rolled the body over into the back seat, drove to his father's tool shed, got a shovel and a hoe, and went into the woods on his father's property to bury his victim on an old, abandoned road. These are his own words of how it happened.

"When Sheriff McLeod examined the body of Burley Phillips, he found something that was so heinous and so cruel that I hesitate to repeat his testimony with Mr. Phillips' family in the audience. Burley Phillips was mortally wounded but still alive when Lee Currie rolled him into that shallow grave and started shoveling dirt on top of him. There was dirt in his nostrils! Burley Phillips spent the last few moments of his life vainly gasping for air. What kind of a monster does that to another human being?"

Grey let his words soak in as he studied the faces of the jury members. He turned his head to the softly sobbing widow of Burley Phillips and held it there for a long minute. When he turned back to the jury, he noticed, as he had hoped, that several of the jury members had followed his gaze to Tersia Phillips.

"Now, gentlemen, after burying his victim alive, the defendant left the Baby Overland in the woods. He walked the short distance to his Uncle David Wright's house, getting there around midnight, according to his uncle's testimony. He left the next morning early, only to return a few minutes later, driving the Baby Overland. Then the lying started.

"He told his uncle that he was going to Reidsville, but that was a lie. David Fussell, the telegraph operator in Claxton, testified that Lee Currie arrived that morning posing as Burley Phillips wanting to send a telegram to his wife, telling her, and I quote, 'Sold my car to a man from Jacksonville, and going to drive through for him. Be home next week,' close quote. And while the defense may argue that Fussell didn't make a positive identification, when J. D. Mallard was riding with Lee Currie on the way back from Milledgeville, the defendant himself revealed intimate information about that telegram that conclusively proved he knew of its contents.

"Let's review J. D. Mallard's testimony," Grey said and then started flipping through his legal pads. "Here it is. Mallard testified that he told Lee the telegram said Burley would be back in a 'few days,' but Lee corrected him and said, 'No, not in a few days.' Lee knew that the telegram contained the words 'next week' and not 'a few days.' He knew it because he had written it.

"Lee Currie had a purpose in sending that telegram. He wanted to make sure Tersia Phillips would not worry when her husband did not come home that night. And by writing in that telegram that her husband would not be home till the following week, Lee meant to secure plenty of time for him to conceal the crime completely. Additionally, by making it appear her husband was driving the car to Jacksonville, Lee hoped that any search for her missing husband would start in Florida rather than in Toombs County, where her husband lay in a shallow grave.

"Now, let us follow Lee in the days after the murder. He left a trail of evidence behind him as he distributed the dead man's possessions to his in-laws in Bulloch County. Bob Kerby testified that Lee gave his brother Jim a hat Tersia identified as Burley's hat. Mr. Kerby also said he saw Lee with two pocketbooks. What man carries two purses? Lee's brother-in-law George Smith testified that Lee gave him a pipe, which Thomas Phillips identified as Burley's pipe.

"But the most incriminating evidence of all was Lee being in possession of the Baby Overland, the primary motivation for his crime. Ober Warthen, the Overland dealer, testified that it was the same car he had sold to Burley a month earlier.

"The Overland was what Lee had craved. He thought it would solve all his problems. He wanted it badly, and he decided to kill for it.

"And his excitement must have overwhelmed him because he could not get his stories straight about how he had acquired the car. He lied to Bob Kerby and told him he bought it. He embellished the lie when relating it to his brother-in-law, George Smith, by saying he paid $1,150 for it. Then, on the way back from Milledgeville, he told J. D. Mallard that he bought the car for $100 and gave a note to some unknown person for it. Later, on that same trip from Milledgeville, the lies continued when the defendant told Sheriff McLeod that two men from Pembroke killed Burley Phillips and gave him the Baby Overland. Lies, lies, and more lies.

"Lee Currie had a lie for every piece of evidence against him. When several people questioned him about the car's bloodstains, the defendant said he had accidentally run over a hog, carried it in his car to a nearby creek, and threw it in. Early on the same day Lee was arrested, Windfield Sutton testified that he saw him deliberately quit the road with the Overland to run over one of his calves.

"Lee got out of the car to examine the calf and note the damage it did to the Baby Overland, then got back into the car and drove away. Why did he do that if not to bolster his lie about running over a hog with the Overland?

"The evidence shows unequivocally that Lee Currie is a liar. Time and time again, he lied to all those around him. Then, as the only witness the defense has to offer in this trial, he stands before you and makes a statement, wanting you to now believe him, believe this lie that he killed Burley Phillips in self-defense!

"How convenient. Only two people witnessed that shooting, and one of them is now dead.

"The defense chose not to put the defendant on the stand and question him. No, they could not afford to do that. That approach would have allowed the prosecution an opportunity to expose his lies. By making a statement rather than taking the stand as a witness, the defendant could make up any story he wanted to tell you. But gentlemen of the jury, that is all it is, a convenient made-up story and a fabrication having no proof to support it.

"A liar abhors being questioned about their lies. With their clever use of the law, the defense has denied the people an opportunity to ask Lee Currie why he lied about buying that car. We can't ask him why he lied about running over a hog, why he lied about where he found the hat, why he lied about sending the telegram, or why he tried to get a negro to lie and take responsibility for the killing. Lee is a proven liar, albeit not a very good one, so why should you give any credence to his so-called statement now?

"But even if we were to give it credence for just a moment, think about what he is asking you to believe, that Burley Phillips tried to kill him with a knife over what, a quart of whiskey? He's asking you to believe that a jitney driver would demand his fare before they arrived at his rider's destination.

"The evidence shows that Lee Currie shot Burley Phillips in the back of the head, yet the defendant wants you to believe that when he pulled out his pistol, Burley supposedly turned and ran, and that is when he shot him. That statement ignores J. B. Rushing's testimony about the singed hairs and powder burns around the fatal bullet's entry point, showing that Lee shot him at point-blank range, not while Burley was running away. Even if that cockamamie story is remotely true, when is shooting someone running away from you called self-defense?

"No, it is not reasonable. It is not reasonable at all. The defendant wanted to make a statement rather than being subjected to questioning because he wanted to continue doing what he has done throughout his coverup of this crime – lie."

Grey turned and walked over to Giles. "Yes, I can understand why the defense didn't want us to be able to question the defendant..." He turned back to the jury, "... and you should understand why, too.

"This wasn't a case of self-defense, gentlemen of the jury. That is just more of the defendant's lies. No, Lee Currie had but one objective when he killed Burley Phillips. He wanted that beautiful Baby Overland automobile all for his own. The defendant dreamed about owning a car like that. He craved it. The only thing that stood between him and the fulfillment of his dream was Burley Phillips, and he killed him to make his dream come true.

"He planned to kill Burley Phillips, he did kill Burley Phillips, and he tried to cover up his crime and begin a new life, the proud owner of a new Baby Overland automobile, his Baby Overland.

"He almost got away with it, almost got away. If only that cow had not gone astray that day, and if only John Rushing, while searching for the wayward bovine, had not happened upon that freshly altered earth on that abandoned road. So close, so close. If only one more rain had fallen and obscured the tire tracks evidencing his return to the gravesite in the Baby Overland for one last look at his handiwork, he might have gotten away; he just might have gotten away – with murder.

"But providence intervened and brought the defendant before you twelve men of the jury where you could ensure that justice would be done for the Phillips family. The hat that Burley Phillips wore has been returned to his widow, the pipe in which he smoked his tobacco has been returned to his widow, and the Baby Overland which he drove has been returned to his widow, but nothing can return Burley Phillips back to his family. The only thing that can assuage this family for the cruel slaying of their loved one is that justice be done by your verdict of guilty."

Grey looked each juror in the eye while slowly collecting his papers.

"You must find the defendant, Lee Currie, guilty of murder in the first degree of Burley Phillips," Grey said and then walked back to the prosecutor's table, where he sat down. Lankford put his hand on his shoulder. Only the steady hum of the overhead fans broke the dead silence.

* * * * * *

Enoch Giles rose. Walter Grey had made a powerful closing argument for finding Lee Currie guilty. Giles turned and saw John Currie's eyes misting and pleading with him to save his son.

T. Ross Sharpe slid a paper over in front of him. On it, he had written one word, "venue." Giles looked up at his law partner and nodded. It would be a challenge to convince this jury of the legal points on which this case rested. That might be a better argument for the appeal that he suspected would be necessary to keep Lee from the hangman's noose. His task right now was to appeal to the jury's emotions. It wasn't going to be easy with the widow Phillips sitting just a few feet away.

He walked over to the podium and arranged his notes. Then he looked up at the jury and studied their expressions. Which ones were likely to vote for an acquittal, he wondered? An unease rushed over him because he still could not read the jury, yet his summation must be perfect.

"Gentlemen of the Jury, I, too, appreciate the time and attention you have afforded this case, and, given the oppressive heat, I also hope not to keep you unnecessarily long from your deliberations.

"Learned counsel's speculation that Lee Currie led a privileged life coming up, without any evidence to support that speculation, fails the test of common sense. Any of you can attest that money does not buy happiness. Many unhappy children have come from privilege. Wealthy parents have raised many unruly children.

"Being raised by a very successful and wealthy father can put tremendous pressure on a child's self-esteem. It can drive them to try to measure up by being an over-achiever or as happens in many cases, by building a false narrative of one's achievements using exaggeration or outright lying. But John Currie's parenting skills, or lack thereof, are not on trial here, nor are they relevant to Lee Currie's guilt or innocence.

"Lee's raising should not be the beginning of this case. So, let's move on to their relevant arguments.

"The prosecution gives you the testimony of George Floyd, a jitney driver taking Lee from Vidalia to Lyons as evidence of premeditation, that Lee was planning to kill Burley Phillips days before the shooting occurred, but is that reasonable? Is the mere mention of something we want proof that we are willing to kill to get it? If so, we should all guard our speech carefully and not mention our desires to acquire something, least our casual words make us suspect should something goes missing.

"And let's examine the defendant's so-called confession.

"The prosecution has put forth a herculean effort to convince you that Lee Currie is a liar. If I counted correctly, they used the words' lie' or 'liar' twenty-six times in their closing argument just now. But they don't want you to believe he lies ALL the time – heavens no. They want you to think that Lee Currie only lies when it is convenient for their theory of the case. The prosecution has been very selective in which of Lee's many statements made while in custody they want you to believe are confessions.

"When Sheriff McLeod was transporting Lee back to Lyons from Milledgeville and asked him about Burley's killing, Lee first said he didn't know anything about it. Was that a lie, or was that the truth?

"Lee told James Mallard that he bought the car for $100 from a man to whom he gave a note, but he couldn't remember the man's name. Was that a lie, or was that the truth?

"A little further down the road, he said he did know something about it and that two men from Pembroke had killed Burley Phillips and gave him the car. Was that a lie, or was that the truth?

"On the trip from Lyons to the Ohoopee train depot, Lee told his captors that he shot Burley Phillips and even demonstrated how he did it, was that a lie, or was that the truth?

"Earlier today, when he made his statement to you and told you that he shot Burley Phillips in self-defense when Burley pulled a knife on him, was that a lie, or was that the truth?

"All these different stories about how Burley Phillips was killed came from the same source, Lee Currie's mouth, but the prosecution wants you to believe only those statements that support their theory. They want you to believe, without any supporting evidence, that Lee Currie killed Burley Phillips to get the Baby Overland. What does that make the prosecution – mind readers?

"The prosecution cannot have it both ways. They cannot contend that Lee Currie is a liar, liar, liar, and then ask you to believe one of his many conflicting stories is a truthful confession and the other conflicting stories are all lies.

"The prosecution has a bigger problem in this case than trying to convince you which of the defendant's statements is the truth. They have not proven venue. In other words, they have not proven that this court has jurisdiction over this case.

"I know this sounds like a lot of legal mumbo jumbo, but the prosecution must bring a case for trial in the county where they maintain the defendant committed the crime. That is the law. Other than Lee Currie's admissions, they have no proof that Burley Phillips was killed in Toombs County. We know by direct physical evidence that Mr. Phillips was buried in Toombs County, but we don't know where he was killed by direct physical evidence.

"Do you remember my asking Dave Wright if he had heard any shots? That would have been more direct evidence the killing took place in Toombs County and would help their case, but the witness said he heard nothing.

"That is why they are trying so hard to get you to accept one of Lee Currie's admissions as a confession. You see, if what they heard Lee say was not a confession, then they have only circumstantial evidence that the killing took place in Toombs County, giving this court jurisdiction.

"Now, what is circumstantial evidence? Well, let me give you an example. Officer Hawkins testified that he found a gun in the Overland when he arrested Lee. Since Lee was driving the car, the inference is that Lee put it there, but that evidence is circumstantial. Nobody saw him put it in the car. Circumstantial evidence requires that you, as the triers of fact, make an inference whether it was reasonable to assume that Lee Currie had put the gun in the car.

"Now, if a witness saw him put the gun in the car, that would be direct evidence. Do you see the difference? Direct evidence can be relied upon more than circumstantial evidence.

"Also, the prosecution would like for you to believe that the gun Chief Hawkins found in the car is the same gun Lee used to kill Burley Phillips, but that, too, is circumstantial evidence. To conclude that Lee Currie used that specific gun to kill Burley Phillips, you must infer both acts: that Lee shot Burley Phillips and put the gun in the car afterward. That's two different inferences with no direct evidence to support either of them. That's what they call circumstantial evidence.

"Now, you shouldn't give the same weight to circumstantial evidence that you give to direct evidence, and that is the prosecution's dilemma. Unless the prosecution can get you to believe Lee's admission is, in reality, a confession, they haven't met their burden of proof that Lee is guilty of first-degree murder. And remember – this is the same prosecution that just went to great lengths to prove Lee is a habitual liar.

"Lee Currie stood up before you and made his statement of how this killing happened. He has freely admitted to you, the jury, that he killed Burley Phillips.

"But what the prosecution has not done, and what they cannot do by direct evidence, is prove that Lee was lying when he said he killed Mr. Phillips in self-defense. They did not even try to dispute that version of events. No, they want you to forget that story and instead believe the one Lee revealed on the way to the Ohoopee train station. Remember that story? It was the one where the law prohibits his captors from threatening or offering Lee any reward to get him to talk, the same one where they ignored the law and promised him they would be his friends, if he would just tell them what happened.

"Consider for a moment the eagerness of Sheriff McLeod and his men to prove Lee Currie guilty before this trial. James Mallard was the most egregious. He was not a trained law enforcement officer, nor was he even temporarily deputized. No, he was a lawman wannabe who took it upon himself to investigate this crime, and the sheriff, eager for a conviction, gave this untrained civilian free rein to go after evidence the sheriff knew was inadmissible if obtained by a law officer.

"James Mallard was so obsessed with this case that he asked the victim's brother, Thomas Phillips, to accompany him while hunting up evidence for a couple of days. Where I come from, they call that the work of a vigilante, not a seasoned law enforcement officer conducting a proper investigation. For all we know, Mallard could have planted the hat and pipe and convinced Lilly's relatives to lie about Lee giving them these items to ensure Lee would be out of Lilly's life forever.

"James Mallard even brought his friends to the jail to see Lee Currie, continuing to prod my client with inappropriate questions, amateurishly – no – illegally seeking a confession. James Mallard may have been involved in convincing Thomas Phillips to form that lynch mob that came to the Toombs County jail seeking their own style of vigilante justice."

"Objection, Mr. Mallard is not on trial here," Grey stood and said.

"No, but a mountain of the prosecution's evidence has this vigilante's fingerprints all over it," Giles retorted.

"I'm going to overrule your objection, Col. Grey, …" Judge Hardeman said, then turned to Giles, "... but I think you have made your point, let's move along," Judge Hardeman said.

"Okay, your honor, let me move to the so-called confession Lee made while on the way to the Ohoopee Train Station.

"Gentlemen of the Jury, Lee Currie has sought the approval of his friends all his life. He wants to be liked. That is very important to him, and Lee is prone to exaggeration to gain his friends' affection and esteem. He is also very keen on staying alive and was quite upset that a lynch mob was headed from Vidalia to Lyons to string him up.

"It is easy to understand his gratitude to his captors while being transported from Lyons to the Ohoopee Train Station. Mack Wimberley testified that Lee was 'in an excited state' to be leaving Lyons ahead of the lynch mob. These lawmen then decided to ambush him, illegally pelting him with questions about the killing of Burley Phillips.

"Carl McLeod testified that Mack Wimberley asked Lee how the killing occurred. When Lee decided to offer information because 'you are my friends and won't tell it,' Mack Wimberley eagerly reassured him, 'Yes, we are your friends.'" That statement, gentlemen, was a promise of a thing of value to Lee in return for his information, and that, gentleman, is against the law. Lee valued the friendship of these men who had just saved him from a hangman's noose. What he said shouldn't be considered a legally obtained confession. You shouldn't even view it as the truth.

"But I can imagine what you are thinking – Lee said it, right? What's all this mumbo jumbo about it being an admission or a confession?

"Well, let's examine the circumstances. Lee was relieved to be rescued from the hangman's noose and wanted to thank his captors. The prosecution has already gone to great lengths to prove he was a liar. Is it difficult to believe that the so-called confession was nothing more than a fabrication Lee made up to show off and gain the approval of his new 'friends'?

"It is a tragedy that Burley Phillips was killed on February 19,1920, but Lee Currie's malice was not responsible. Instead, Burley Phillips made a wrong choice when he drew his knife on another human being, who had every right to defend himself.

"Let that sink in for a moment. Lee had a right to defend himself. Some of you on this jury have family members that fought for our country in the Great War. When an enemy was coming at you on the battlefield, you knew what to do. You stopped him using whatever force was necessary. It was kill or be killed.

"Lee Currie has told you that Burley Phillips came after him with a knife because he wouldn't pay the jitney fare. And he did the only thing he could do – the same thing you would have done if you found yourself in his circumstances. He shot his attacker in self-defense.

"The prosecution says that was all a lie. But keep in mind that the burden of proof is on the prosecution to prove their version of events is the truth, and all they could come up with was circumstantial evidence against the defendant. They would also have you find him guilty in Toombs County when they cannot even prove by direct evidence that this is where the shooting occurred. They want you to go out on a limb with a noose hanging beneath it and proclaim Lee Currie guilty beyond a reasonable doubt. But can you live with yourself if you make a wrong call and cost a man his liberty, or worse, his life?

"It is regrettable that a disagreement broke out between these two men. It is regrettable that a man died due to that disagreement, but Lee Currie said he was defending himself against an attacker. The prosecution has no direct evidence to refute his statement. The only just verdict, in this case, is 'not guilty,' and that should be the verdict you return to this court.

Giles looked at each juror and, while looking at the last one, said, "Not guilty." He then turned about and returned to the prosecution table.

* * * * * *

Judge Hardeman breathed a sigh of relief. The trial's closing arguments were now over, and all that remained was for him to give the jury their charge. Then it would be in their hands.

"Gentlemen of the Jury, it now becomes my duty to charge you as to the law applicable to this case. There will be a one-hour recess while I confer with counsel on the content of that charge. It's hot in the jury room, and I will ask the bailiff to find you a cool spot out on the courthouse grounds to rest for a while. Remember not to discuss this case among you just yet or with anyone you might encounter inside or outside the courthouse.

"Court is in recess for one hour," Judge Hardeman said and rapped his gavel.

Chapter 41

Sheriff McLeod was not comforted by the raised voices in the judge's chambers as the lawyers argued over the charges to be put to the jury. The hour the judge predicted it would take had expired, and there seemed to be no letup. The bailiff had returned to the courtroom twice for instructions on when to bring the jury back.

Finally, the judge's chamber door swung open, and the attorneys emerged. From the expressions on their faces, Enoch Giles and T. Ross Sharpe lost the arguments about what to include in the final charge. Judge Hardeman followed them and turned to Sheriff McLeod, "Tell the bailiff to bring the jury back in and start making preparations to bring on some more deputies when the jury returns their verdict, in case this gets ugly."

When everyone was back in the courtroom, Judge Hardeman began his charge.

"Gentlemen of the Jury, the object of this investigation, the evidence introduced, and the rules of law concerning evidence I will give you; are all framed with one purpose, and that is the ascertainment of the truth.

"The State charges the defendant with the offense of murder. The True Bill of Indictment returned by the Grand Jury of the county of Toombs says and charges that the defendant now on trial, Lee Currie, killed one Burley

Phillips, in the county of Toombs, on the day and date named in the indictment and that such homicide was murder. And to that indictment, the defendant enters his denial and pleads not guilty," Judge Hardeman said.

Lee Currie looked around the courtroom as the judge continued charging the jury. He returned the smile his father offered him and reached his hand out to take the extended hand of Lula Currie, seeking to comfort him.

"No rumor, hearsay, nor things that may have come to your knowledge outside the court; nothing, save and except what you have heard in this trial, the sworn evidence, the defendant's statement, and such other matters as may be by the Court admitted for your consideration, should influence you in arriving at your verdict," Judge Hardeman continued.

Enoch Giles was already drafting his appeal. He peered over his copy of the judge's charge, looking for those portions he would include in his motion for a new trial.

Judge Hardeman continued with his charge, most of which was the standard language of which Enoch took little note while waiting for the critical part that would form the basis for his appeal.

"I charge you, gentlemen, that admissions generally refer to civil cases and confessions to criminal cases. A mere admission is not a confession. An admission, some incriminating statement, some incriminating admissions, is not a confession. I will give you my definition of a confession – a statement made by a party charged with an offense does not amount to a confession unless it is plenary admission of all the facts that go to constitute the offense with which he stands charged. Where a party makes a statement that is a plenary or full admission of every fact essential to fasten guilt upon him of the offense with which he stands charged, then that is a confession in law, but not necessarily admissible..."

T. Ross looked at the faces of the jury. There was no way these farmers and working people understood all that legal jargon coming from the judge. He had earlier slipped a note to Enoch containing the word "venue," which was, in his mind, the crux of this case. The prosecution hadn't proved that the killing took place in Toombs County. What they were calling "Lee's confession" was just an admission. It did not have the weight of a confession.

Additionally, the sheriff's men got the admission illegally by playing into Lee's need for recognition and feeling important when they claimed to offer him their "friendship" in return for his "confession." T. Ross turned to a clean sheet on his legal pad and wrote; *They must consider what Lee gave them as an admission, not a confession.* He slid the note over to Enoch, who looked up and nodded.

"... the law says that a confession may not be admitted unless freely and voluntarily made, without the slightest hope of benefit or the remotest fear of injury ..." Judge Hardeman continued.

Well, you got that part right, judge, so why did you allow it to be admitted as evidence when you knew Wimberley, Carl, and George were playing to Lee's desire to be befriended by them? Enoch thought to himself.

"... then you would be authorized to convict upon a confession thus corroborated, provided the evidence satisfies your minds beyond reasonable doubt of the defendant's guilt," Judge Hardeman paused to take a drink of water.

Enoch struggled to contain his anger. *It's not a confession, dammit!* Judge Hardeman was way off on this charge and was writing their appeal for them.

"... malice in law is the unlawful intent to take human life. That is all it is ..." Judge Hardeman continued.

You left out the part about the person doing the killing being of sound memory and discretion and that the killing must be with malice aforethought, judge, Enoch wrote on his legal pad. The judge continued reading the charge, and Enoch paid it scant attention. He already had enough for an appeal. His attention did not return to the judge's charge until he got to the part about manslaughter.

"... it must appear, in order to reduce the crime from murder to manslaughter, that the killing was the result of that sudden, violent impulse of passion, supposed, in law, to be irresistible, because if there should have been an interval between the assault or provocation given and the homicide, that you gentlemen of the jury find sufficient for the voice of reason and humanity to assert itself, then I charge you, gentlemen, the killing would be attributable to deliberate revenge, a killing for a past wrong, and it would be murder and the jury ought to so find ..." Judge Hardeman continued.

Ha, Enoch thought to himself; *the prosecution hasn't come close to proving that there was any length of time between when Burley came after Lee with a knife, and when Lee shot him*, Enoch wrote this on his pad. *They haven't proven any past wrong, either.* The judge's definition of malice almost screamed for a binary finding of guilty or not guilty, and there was no room for voluntary or involuntary manslaughter. Enoch was furiously writing while trying to listen to the judge. *This charge will not stand on appeal*, he thought to himself.

Enoch didn't know whether it was the legal jargon or the heat, but he could tell the jury members were no longer listening.

"...This jury, under the evidence, should bring in a verdict generally, either guilty or not guilty as you may find him to be. The form of your verdict will be 'We, the jury, find the defendant guilty or not guilty' as you find the case may be ..." Judge Hardeman said and lowered his notes. He looked over at the jury.

"Retire, gentlemen, and write your verdict."

* * * * * *

"What's happening? Why are they leaving?" Enoch heard Lee ask T. Ross.

"The judge charged them and sent them out to come up with a verdict," T. Ross answered.

"Then the trial's over?" Lee asked.

"It will be when they come back and announce their verdict."

"Then I can go home?"

"If they find you not guilty, yes."

"Well, the son-of-a-bitches better find me not guilty, then." Lee turned to Enoch, "What are you writing?"

"I'm working on your appeal, Lee," Enoch said, not looking up from his legal pad.

"My appeal? Hell, you already think they gonna find me guilty?" Lee snarled.

Enoch looked up at his client. "Lee, the judge didn't charge the jury correctly, and that gives us a good basis for a new trial. I have to be honest with you and tell you that, yes, the chances are they are going to find you guilty. But don't worry; we have a strong case for an appeal. They've made all kinds of mistakes."

John Currie leaned forward and rested his arms on the banner behind the defense table, "Did I hear you say they will find my boy guilty?"

Enoch turned in his chair to face the senior Currie, "I don't know for sure, John, but I wouldn't be surprised if they do. Don't ask me how I know. I've been in front of a lot of juries, and that's my sense of this one."

John Currie leaned back in his chair and turned to Lula, "They think the jury will find Lee guilty."

Lula clasped his arm, "John, they are good lawyers. They will figure out something."

* * * * * *

Less than an hour later, the jury's foreman advised the bailiff that they had reached a verdict. He advised Judge Hardeman, who rapped his gavel, "Court is back in session. Bailiff, bring the jury in."

The jury milled back into the courtroom. Only a couple of jurors looked up at Lee; one smiled.

"Has the jury reached a verdict?" Judge Hardeman asked.

The foreman stood, "We have, your honor."

"Will the defendant please rise and face the jury," Judge Hardeman said.

Enoch and T. Ross stood, and Enoch signaled for Lee to rise. He looked back and forth between the two of them and then stood.

"Please render your verdict. How do you find the defendant?"

The foreman looked at Lee and then over at the judge, "On the count of murder in the first degree, we, the jury, find the defendant Lee Currie … guilty."

Bedlam broke out in the courtroom. The doors swung open as all the reporters rushed out of the courtroom in mass. Lula hugged her husband, who, prepared for the worse just moments before by Enoch's prediction, sat stoically.

"Order, order," Judge Hardeman said, but his gavel raps were utterly lost in the courtroom's mayhem.

"Sheriff, I need order here."

The sheriff motioned to his deputies, who aligned themselves along the bar separating the spectators from the trial area. "Sit down, everyone, or I will have to remove you from this courtroom," the sheriff yelled. The din slowly died down.

The judge spoke somberly, "You have heard the verdict of the jury read. You have had a fair and impartial trial by twelve of your fellow-countrymen, and they have returned a verdict of guilty without recommendation, and it, therefore, becomes the solemn duty of the court to impose sentence upon you.

"This is indeed, a very unpleasant duty that I have to perform. It is the judgment of the Court that you, Lee Currie, be taken from the courthouse to the common jail of Toombs County or such other place as the proper authorities of Toombs County may direct for safe keeping and that you be kept there in close confinement, until Friday, the eighth day of October 1920, and that on said date, between the hours of ten o'clock a.m. and two o'clock p.m., at the common jail of Toombs County, in the presence of the Sheriff and such guard as he may deem sufficient, and in the presence of such of your relatives and friends as you may desire and designate, and in the presence of such minister or ministers of the gospel as you may desire and the physicians hereinafter named, otherwise in private, that you be, by the Sheriff of Toombs County, hung by the neck until you are dead, and may the Lord have mercy upon your soul.

"It is further ordered that Doctors G.T. Gray and I. E. Aaron attend said execution to determine when death shall have supervened."

"They are going to hang you for killing my brother, Lee Currie. They are going to hang you, you murdering son-of-a-bitch!" Thomas Phillips lunged forward and shouted as family members gabbed him and held him back.

Judge Hardeman banged his gavel as a deputy closed in on Phillips and ordered him to sit down. "Order, order, everyone sit down and come to order."

"Gentlemen of the jury, you have rendered the county a great service these last three days. You are dismissed and may return to your homes. Thank you for your service," Judge Hardeman said.

"Court is adjourned!" he continued, with a loud rap of his gavel.

* * * * * *

Sheriff McLeod saw right through the stoic look on John Currie's face when the jury foreman read the verdict, and Judge Hardeman passed sentence. He knew that his old friend was hiding great pain. He felt he should go to him to express his sympathy, but how could he engage in conversation with the father when it was now his duty to begin the task of building the gallows upon which to hang his son?

This job no longer holds any appeal to me, he thought to himself. Maybe it was time to explore other options before the general election in November. So far, his was the only name on the Democratic ballot, and no Republican had ever run for sheriff in Toombs County, much less won. But, if he pulled out of the race now, another candidate could easily be found before the election. It was another of those times that he wished Nancy was still alive to help him find a path forward.

Enough of this self-pity George McLeod, you've got a famous prisoner to manage and a gallows to build.

There was no urgent need to return Lee to Savannah. Judge Hardeman's death sentence by hanging should satisfy the lynch mob's blood lust that had prompted the transfer earlier. Of course, it might still be prudent to relocate him should Giles & Sharpe successfully get him a new trial. McLeod made himself a note to ask the Clerk of Court to alert him of any new filings in the case.

Looming large over him now was the distasteful task of building a gallows. To his knowledge, nobody had ever been legally hung in Toombs County since its creation 15 years earlier, and he had no idea how to hang a man humanely. In 1884, at the tender age of 12, he witnessed the lynching of a negro accused of looking at a white woman while she bathed naked in a creek. A rope was thrown across a tree limb and tied around his neck while he was standing in the back of a buckboard wagon. McLeod clearly recalled a man slapping the horse's rear, hitched up to the wagon, and seeing the animal pull away, leaving the man dangling. The man kicked and gagged for several agonizing minutes, during which McLeod tried to turn away, but his father turned his head back, forcing him to watch. He never wanted to see that sight again, but he had a painful duty to carry out, and he was not looking forward to it.

Perhaps a carpenter in town would know how to construct gallows. Mr. Garbutt owned the lumber mill and was likely to know several good carpenters. He would ask him for some names to contact.

McLeod left the courtroom and returned to his office at the jail. Hanging his hat up, he went into the storage room on the ground floor in the jail's SE corner and looked about.

The contents could easily be moved to one of the county storage barns, leaving sufficient room to construct gallows. Having a public hanging outside with hundreds of gawkers had absolutely no appeal to him, and the small room would only allow for family, friends, Lee's doctor, and a preacher. He found himself saying a little prayer that Giles & Sharpe would succeed in getting Lee a new trial. That might push the execution into next year, where it would be somebody else's concern.

* * * * * *

Giles & Sharpe went directly to the Clerk of Court and filed a motion for a new trial. Judge Hardeman set a hearing on the Motion for October 2, 1920.

Chapter 42

Arch McGill was already sitting in T. Ross Sharpe's office when the lawyer arrived at work the day following the Currie trial. The newspaperman rose, greeted T. Ross, and sat back down. T. Ross took off his coat, hung it up, and settled himself behind his desk. True to his usual routine, the first order of business was to light up a cigar.

"You are here bright and early, Arch. I guess people are eager to read about the Currie case in your paper," T. Ross said.

"You wouldn't believe it, counselor. This case has already increased my subscriptions by twenty-five percent," Arch responded.

"We certainly will look forward to receiving our commissions check for facilitating that new business growth for you," T. Ross said, laughing.

"Ross, I know you are busy with this case and your other work, and I don't want to keep you from all that, so let's get to it. I tried to listen to the proceedings as best I could, but could you help my readers understand why you think Lee is now entitled to a new trial?" Arch asked.

T. Ross took a long drag from his cigar and blew the smoke into the desk fan, which in turn blew it away from Arch, much to the reporter's relief.

"Well, there are many problems with how Judge Hardeman handled this case, especially with how he charged the jury."

"Oh? What exactly did he do wrong? Can you explain it to me where I can understand it?" McGill asked, taking his notepad out and preparing to write.

T. Ross leaned forward in his chair and put his elbows on his desk. "The main problem is that the judge erred when he told the jury that Lee's admission to his captors could be considered a confession. That profound misstatement of law made all the prosecution's circumstantial evidence a lot weightier than it merited legally.

"The judge made another error when he laid out a limited choice of verdicts before the jury. At worst, my client should have been convicted of voluntary manslaughter, but Hardeman effectively took that option completely off the jury's list of possible verdicts."

"Not sure I understand all that legal mumbo jumbo, but do you think Judge Hardeman will give the defendant a new trial?"

"Not for a minute. Judges don't like to admit they messed up a trial. No, we will have to go to the Georgia Supreme Court to secure that, but I am confident they will see things our way. Judge Hardeman just made too many mistakes in this case."

Arch was making a note and did not notice Claire stepping into the office. When she spoke, he jumped.

"Sorry," she said, "I didn't mean to startle you. Would you like some coffee?"

"No need to apologize; I'm a bit jumpy this morning. Coffee would be nice – add just a little cream and no sugar," Arch said.

Claire was back in no time with the requested coffee, which Arch sipped, and then smiled at Claire. "Just right – thank you."

Arch put the coffee cup on the corner of T. Ross' mahogany desk, carefully setting it on the napkin she had handed him.

"If you are successful in getting a new trial ...," Arch began his question.

T. Ross cut him off, "You mean WHEN we are successful in getting a new trial."

"I'm sorry; when you are successful in getting Lee a new trial, will you change your strategy? I'm sure Judge Hardeman will correct his charge if he is overruled by the Supreme Court, no?"

T. Ross needed the press on this case, but he had to walk a tight line. He did not want to alert the prosecution to their strategy going into the subsequent trial, should the appeal be successful, but the more important goal was to plant a seed in the minds of men from the county who would constitute the jury pool. The lawyer wanted to start folks thinking that Lee was not in his right mind when he killed Burley Phillips and was not responsible for his actions. T. Ross knew that virtually everyone in the county was talking about the trial and would be glued to whatever Arch McGill would be writing in *The Lyons Progress*. A plea of "Not Guilty by Reason of Insanity" had never been tried as a defense in Toombs County and would be a hard sell among men seeped in the biblical tradition of 'An eye for an eye and a tooth for a tooth.'

He needed to get prospective jurors to feel sorry for Lee. If telling this reporter a little about his strategy tipped his hand to the prosecution, well, he suspected Walter and George had already figured that out when they objected to the defense's efforts to introduce Dr. Hall as a witness.

"In preparation for and during this trial's progress, a new strategy did begin to manifest itself to Enoch and me. I'm not at liberty to reveal it all at this point but suffice it to say that our client has some mental issues influencing his actions. We believe those mental issues prevented him from fully comprehending the gravity of what he was doing."

"Are you asking me to tell my readers that Lee Currie is crazy?"

"I'm saying that Lee Currie has mental issues. Just exactly what those are and how they contributed to what happened is going to be the crux of the new trial we fully expect we will get."

"Is there a legal term for this type of defense?"

"There is – it's called the insanity defense."

"So, you ARE saying Lee Currie is crazy."

T. Ross took another puff and expertly tapped the ashes precariously perched on his cigar's end into a nearby ashtray. He again blew the smoke into the fan and looked up.

"Crazy is not, technically speaking, a legal term, and I don't find it very useful in explaining our position. The mind is a complex mechanism, but sometimes people come into this world with a broken one that doesn't work like it is supposed to, as a normal mind works. No doubt, you have seen idiots and morons who can't function like the rest of us. Well, with those poor souls, we go to great lengths to supervise them, train them in a useful craft, and care for them. We also make more generous allowances for them when they do something that an average person wouldn't do.

"Sometimes, when a mind malfunctions, it is not readily apparent. One might think the person manifesting the unusual behavior is 'quirky' or 'moody' or 'special.' But if you don't oversee them, they can suddenly break out and become lethal. Their mind is just not as capable as a normal person of reasoning things correctly and acting appropriately," T. Ross said.

"Not guilty by reason of insanity. Is there such a defense in law?" McGill asked.

"Well phrased, and indeed there is. The concept dates back to antiquity. People of all ages have had difficulty holding an insane man responsible for his actions. However, I don't believe we have ever seen it used in any local courts, and the state law concerning it is evolving. We hope to make some new precedent here in Toombs County."

The newly formed ash collapsed into a small pile in the ashtray as T. Ross expertly thumped his cigar again. He seemed to know, without looking, the exact moment to discard the ash.

"The study of the mind is a relatively new branch of medicine, Arch. They call it psychology, and it was formally recognized as a separate area of study in Germany in 1879, just over 40 years ago." T. Ross turned and pulled a book from the bookshelf behind him. He opened it to a place where he had previously put a bookmark.

"Most of the formal study has been done in Europe, a lot of it by an Austrian doctor named Sigmund Freud. The Georgia courts recognized the insanity defense several decades ago and generally followed what is referred to as the M'Naghten Rule," T. Ross said, head down while flipping through the pages. He was now on a roll, and Arch was having difficulty keeping up.

Arch made a note and then asked, "What's the M'Naghten Rule?"

T. Ross turned the pages to a marked place with a worn yellow tab. "The M'Naghten Rule states that every man is to be presumed to be sane, and to establish a defense on the grounds of insanity, it must be clearly proven that, at the time of the committing of the act, the party accused was laboring under such a defect of reason, from a disease of the mind, as not to know the nature and quality of the act he was doing; or if he did know it, that he did not know he was doing what was wrong."

McGill wrote disease of the mind on his notepad and looked up, "So, is it your intent to prove that Lee Currie had some mental disease when he killed Burley Phillips that kept him from knowing it was wrong?"

T. Ross closed the book and laid it on his desk with a thud. "By cracky, you should have been a lawyer, Arch. You hit the nail right on the head. Lee Currie is an immature boy in a man's body. If you are around him for any extended length of time, you can tell something is wrong with his mind. We aim to prove that he didn't know what he did was wrong and that his mental disease was responsible for him not knowing."

"I'm not sure you are going to be able to get twelve men in Toombs County to agree that Lee Currie didn't know what he was doing. I mean, he told people he wanted to acquire an Overland automobile, he stalked his victim, he lured him off to a remote area and killed him, buried him, took his vehicle all about, and then went to great lengths to cover it up. What crazy man, or insane man if you prefer, does that?" McGill asked.

"You have summed up the prosecution's theory of what happened well, but we think it happened differently. Oh, I won't argue that Lee didn't know what he was doing. The problem is that he didn't know that what he was doing was wrong! Or, he may have known it was wrong, but the part of the brain that tells you and I that we can't do something because it is against the law doesn't work in Lee Currie's brain," T. Ross said.

McGill thoughtfully tapped his pencil on his pad, "I'm just not sure you can make a jury understand that subtle difference, counselor."

"Maybe I can, and maybe I can't, but we will give it all we've got," T. Ross said.

Claire stuck her head in the door and said, "Col. Sharpe, Mr. Currie is here for his appointment."

"Thank you, Claire; tell him I'll be right with him." He rose and said to Arch, "Now, if you don't mind, I have to discuss my new strategy with Lee's father."

Arch rose and extended his hand to T. Ross. "I appreciate your giving me a moment of your time, Ross.

Good luck in your defense of Mr. Currie; I fear you are going to need it."

T. Ross shook Arch's hand. "And can I count on being able to read coverage of this case in The Lyons Progress that is fair and won't prejudice the jury pool against my client?"

"The reputation of our paper is of paramount concern to me, Ross. You can depend on our being fair. I can promise you that," Arch said.

"That's all I ask," T. Ross said.

Arch turned and left the office.

* * * * * *

Claire escorted John Currie into T. Ross' office, and Arch, on his way out, tipped his hat in greeting and said, "Mr. Currie."

John looked over his shoulder at the departing newspaper editor and then took a seat, "Isn't that the man from the Lyons Progress? What's he doing here?"

T. Ross didn't answer his question right away. He shook his hand and leaned out the door, "Claire, please tell Enoch that Mr. Currie is here."

He returned to his seat and said, "We need the press, John. Our strategy in this next trial is going to be plowing some new ground, and we are going to need some good coverage to try and get folks, and prospective jurors in particular, more accepting of it," T. Ross said.

Enoch Giles entered the room, and John Currie rose.

"Keep your seat, John," Enoch said.

They shook hands. Enoch sat down and said, "Glad you could make it so early. We've got a lot to share with you. You didn't bring Lula?"

"She's managing the farm, Enoch, what with this trial keeping me away from it so much. And I haven't been able to think straight since they found my boy guilty, and I heard that judge sentence him to hang. I know you tried to prepare me for the verdict, but that hurt me down to the very fiber of my being. It was a hard, hard thing for a father to hear," John said.

T. Ross spoke up, "We will try our best to ensure that doesn't happen, John. We've filed a motion for a new trial, and I think we will get it, if not from Judge Hardeman, then from the Georgia Supreme Court."

John looked encouraged, "A new trial, you say?"

Enoch responded, "Yes, and we are convinced we can get it. We have already contacted the Atlanta firm of Laurence & Abrahams, which is very experienced with appeals before the Supreme Court, and they have agreed to assist us with the case."

"That sounds expensive. Can't you and Ross handle it?" John asked.

"Trust me; you wouldn't want us having to run back and forth to Atlanta. It will be much less expensive for us to use a local Atlanta firm nearer the Supreme Court," Enoch answered.

"Now, let me tell you about our strategy going forward," Enoch pulled some papers out of a folder and spread them on the desk.

"You saw where they wouldn't let us put Dr. Hall on the stand, remember? Well, that signaled to us that the prosecution knew where we were going and wanted desperately to stop us from using the defense strategy we had in mind. So, in this next trial, we will put our total effort into plowing that field.

"What we are planning could save Lee's life, but you may not like it. Nevertheless, we are going to need your full support for it to work."

"What do you mean, I may not like it?"

"We are going all out for the insanity defense in the next trial, John."

"You mean, Dr. Hall ..."

"Yes, we received Dr. Hall's diagnosis, and he concluded that Lee's was insane when he killed Burley Phillips," Enoch said.

John Currie stared blankly at the two attorneys for a few moments as the gravity of what he had just heard sank in. He knew his son was different, but he believed he only needed guidance. John had dedicated himself to helping Lee live a normal life. Now, this doctor had decided that Lee might never be a normal person, that he was crazy. His son – a lunatic. A colossal sense of failure swept over him, and he lowered his head into his hands.

T. Ross and Enoch looked at each other. T. Ross finally spoke up, "Look, John, don't despair; we think this is a godsend. If we can prove that Lee was insane when he killed Burley Phillips, they can't hang him."

Enoch jumped in, "Legally, we want to prove that he lacked the mental capacity to stop himself from killing Burley Phillips, that, to use Dr. Hall's terms, he had no resistive power."

T. Ross quickly added, "And if we can prove that – the jury will have to find him not guilty by reason of insanity."

"Not guilty," John whispered as he slowly raised his head.

"That's right, John. It might not get him freed, but the state can't execute a man who has been adjudicated to be insane and not responsible for his actions. That's considered cruel and unusual punishment. In other words, executing someone for doing something when they didn't know any better is considered by the law to be inhumane and unconstitutional," Enoch said.

T. Ross jumped back in, "John, the worst they can do is send him to Milledgeville to be treated. He might even be released someday under limited supervision, perhaps even into your custody, if they think they have cured him. Certainly, you'll be able to see him while he's there."

John was circumspect. Finally, he said, "I have worried myself sick about this. I went along with hiring Dr. Hall because you told me it was the right thing to do legally, but I didn't understand why it was necessary. Now you are telling me that the doctor thinks my boy is crazy. I know Lee's different, a bit high-strung, maybe, but crazy?" He shook his head in disbelief.

"He's not exactly crazy, the way you and I think about crazy, but you know as well as I do, he's not normal, and it's the best chance we have for keeping the state from hanging him," T. Ross said.

John sighed. He got up and walked to the window, his eyes following a mule pulling a wagon by the offices of Giles & Sharpe. His heart was breaking. Without turning to the lawyers, he said, "No father wants to hear that his son is insane."

"No father wants to see his son hanged either," T. Ross said.

John turned and looked disapprovingly at T. Ross. Then his face softened, and he sat back down. "What do I have to do?"

T. Ross and Enoch looked at each other, conveying their mutual relief that they had just reached a milestone with the man paying the bills.

"The burden will be on us this time to prove Lee is insane by a preponderance of the evidence," T. Ross said.

"The State will have a much higher burden. They have to prove he is sane with clear and convincing evidence. I know it sounds like the same thing, but there is a decided legal difference in the level of proof needed, and we will have the advantage.

"We will need to find expert witnesses, more doctors, who can attest to Lee's mental state. We will need to find teachers, employers, neighbors, and others who know Lee or grew up with him, who can attest to his odd behavior," Enoch added.

Enoch saw John had looked down at his hands and appeared to be studying them for a moment. The lawyer knew what he was thinking, and John's next words confirmed his suspicions. "How much is this going to cost?"

"I'm afraid it is going to be expensive, John. Developing witnesses will take time, and the experts will cost us a sizable fee," Enoch said.

Now with the air of a businessman, John looked up, "How much?"

"It's hard to tell, but the best estimate I can give you would be around $7,500. Expenses might run a little more or a little less, depending on how far we must go to get the expert witnesses," Enoch said.

John's face went pale. "I paid you for the first trial from what I had saved up. That was the last of my cash on hand."

The two attorneys offered him no suggestions. The substantial financial commitment was something that John Currie would have to work out for himself.

Finally, John's countenance seemed to register determination, and he looked right at Enoch and said, "I've got 686 acres of land that is free and clear of any debt. It is easily worth $50 per acre. Enoch, you're the President of the Toombs County Bank. I can't see why you couldn't convince them to loan me that much on the farm."

Enoch nodded affirmatively. John continued, "Lee's my flesh and blood. If he's laboring with a defective mind, I'm as responsible as anybody because he came from me and his ma.

"Do what you have to do, but please don't let my boy hang." John rose, and both lawyers rose as well. He shook both their hands.

"Gentlemen," he said, put his hat on, turned, and walked out of the office.

* * * * * *

George McLeod saw the writing on the wall and decided not to run for another term as the sheriff of Toombs County. He felt sure there would be another trial, and the delay meant he would not have to hang Lee Currie. December 31, 1920 could not get here soon enough to suit him.

As soon as he announced his decision not to run again, several candidates threw their hats into the ring to vie for the office. He suspected his friend Charles Warren Culpepper would probably be elected to the post.

On October 8, 1920, Judge Hardeman denied the defense's motion for a new trial.

On November 2, 1920, Culpepper was elected without a runoff to be the new sheriff.

On December 15, 1920, the Supreme Court of Georgia ruled that Judge Hardeman erred and granted Lee Currie a new trial.

The next day Thomas Phillips drove the Baby Overland out to the North Thompson Baptist Church cemetery. He got out and stood at the foot of his brother's grave. With only the birds, insects, and the dead's spirits to hear him, he said aloud, "Them fancy lawyers ain't gonna save Lee Currie from the hanging that he's got coming, brother. You rest in peace now. As for me, I'm ain't gonna rest till that son-of-a-bitch swings."

Later that afternoon, in one of his last official acts as sheriff, McLeod carried Lee Currie on the train back to Savannah for his safety.

Judge Hardeman scheduled the new trial for the February 1921 term of court.

Chapter 43

"I think we have momentum on our side now, Ross," Enoch Giles said to T. Ross as they sat in the conference room of their law office.

"I don't disagree, Enoch. The talk in the county is that Lee got a bad rap, and the Georgia Supreme Court overturning Judge Hardeman's ruling against our motion for a new trial has increased the local chatter that Hardeman is handling this trial in an incompetent manner," Enoch said.

T. Ross eyed his partner, who was staring at the table. "Enoch, what are you thinking? Don't tell me you think he is vulnerable politically."

"He is vulnerable. He's been in that office for seven years, but this trial is hurting his reputation. I've been thinking about it for weeks now, and I've discussed it with Almedia. I'm going to run against him for Superior Court Judge next year. You know the popularity of the Currie family. Because of this trial, he's losing votes out in the county. I may not carry Vidalia, but the majority of Toombs County votes are in Lyons and the unincorporated portion of Toombs County. And if the newspaper accounts may be trusted, this trial is giving me lots of publicity in the surrounding counties of this judicial circuit, too."

"If you've got your mind set on that, Enoch, go for it. But the election is a year from now, and we have a new strategy to develop. Getting Lee acquitted is more important now, both for our client and your chances of prevailing in an election."

Enoch came out of his dead stare at the conference table and looked up at his junior law partner. "You're right, Ross. We need to focus on the present. What progress have you made?"

T. Ross breathed a sigh of relief to have his senior law partner's mind back in the game. "I've contacted just about everyone on the witness list we drew up. Claire was able to run down James Partin, Lee's school teacher, to get him to testify to Lee's unruliness during his school days."

"Good start. Let's get to plowing this new ground and fully develop this insanity defense," Enoch said as he spread out papers on the conference table.

They had lined up four doctors. Dr. John Hall would continue to be their main witness, and his brother, Dr. Jim Hall, who had been the Currie family physician for years, would provide some insight into how Lee had failed to develop mentally over the 16 years he had known him.

Enoch had told T. Ross that he wanted to find a doctor who would help him introduce evidence that Lee's insanity was inherited, given that John Currie had admitted to having a brother with mental problems. Dr. John Hall had told him that his brother-in-law, Dr. George Gray, would be willing to testify to the role inheritance played in insanity. Dr. Gray could also help build the legal theory that Lee had no resistive power even though he knew right from wrong.

He and Enoch had to overcome the problem of convincing a jury that Lee was insane even though he had periods of lucidity and seemed to be very clever in how he tried to cover up the killing. Dr. Joshua Collins would be his wrap-up doctor that would pull all the medical testimony together.

In the first trial, they had been somewhat confident that Lee's self-defense claim would carry the day. After all, there were no witnesses to the actual shooting, and everything the prosecution offered was circumstantial. Unfortunately, understanding the subtle difference between a confession and an admission had proven too much for the jury. They bought Lee's admissions hook, line, and sinker. This time around, they would welcome Lee's admissions as further evidence that he was not in his right mind to tell his captors every detail about how he had killed Burley Phillips. After all, what sane person would think that they could confess a crime to several sheriff's deputies and then expect those deputies to conceal that evidence just because they were his "friends?"

"Hopefully, with the medical, school, and family history, we might be able to convince at least one person on the jury to render a not-guilty verdict," T. Ross said.

"I'd settle for a verdict of manslaughter instead of murder to save Lee from the gallows," Enoch replied.

* * * * * *

Col. George Lankford was arguing for his boss to hold the course. The evidence was overwhelming, and the jury decided the case in less than an hour. The Supreme Court had overruled Judge Hardeman's denial of the Motion for a new trial. Their evidence was just fine – the high court decided on the technicality that the judge's charge was incorrect. Judge Hardeman would need to modify the charge, but they would prosecute the case just as they did before.

"It will be a piece of cake," George asserted confidently.

"I'm not so sure, George," Walter Grey said dubiously after hearing George's arguments. "You read the piece in the Lyons Progress from Arch McGill's interview of T. Ross Sharpe last week. They are going for an insanity defense on this next go around."

"And it will get them absolutely nowhere, Walter. Lee Currie is a dangerous, cunning man who planned that murder, killed that man in cold blood, and then meticulously tried to cover it up. That is not the irrational behavior of a crazy man. He's as sane as you and me, just mean as hell," George said.

"If you believe that, you're as crazy as he is, George. Let me play devil's advocate with you.

"Lee distributed the dead man's things to his in-laws. Is that something a sane man would do? No, a rational man would have buried his stuff with him, burned them, or tossed them into a swamp.

"He as much as confessed the crime to several law enforcement officers, for God's sake, thinking that they wouldn't tell on him because they were his friends? Are you kidding me? What sane man would do that?

"We argued that he bypassed Lyons and Vidalia when he returned to Milledgeville on that one trip to avoid anyone spotting the car. But the defense can argue that it was insane to do that after he had driven all over the county and adjacent counties with bloodstains all over the car, proudly showing the Overland to his friends and family and offering rides to relatives.

"And do you really think that a sane man would say that he ran over a hog, loaded it up in his car, and then just threw it in a creek? With the cost of pork being what it is, a sane man would have butchered the hog and put it in his smokehouse.

"Think about the stories he has told people about how he got the car. He tells the sheriff that two men from Pembroke gave it to him after killing Burley. He tells somebody else that he purchased it in Reidsville for $100 but couldn't remember the name of the person he gave a note. Do those unbelievable stories sound like something a sane man would make up to cover his crime?" Walter slammed his fist upon the table, and George jumped.

"Lee Currie is as crazy as a bed bug, and if we don't take that seriously and be prepared to prove he is sane at trial, he is going to walk, and I won't be able to be elected dog catcher in this county in the next election!"

George sat still for a moment to give his boss a chance to cool off.

"Walter, the best thing we can do to prove his sanity is to stay the course. We show how he told folks he wanted that car ahead of time, show how he stalked his victim, lured him off the main highway, killed him, buried him, came back later to check on the crime scene, and then sent that telegram to his victim's widow to keep anyone from finding his fresh tracks. I don't think we should get all excited about this new defense strategy. They know they can't defend what he did. This is just a desperate effort to keep him out of a hangman's noose."

"You forget that he is the son of one of the most prominent farmers in Toombs County, one who can afford to throw a ton of expert witnesses against us. I'm already over budget for this year. I don't have the financial resources to fight the army of expert witnesses that will be coming," Walter said calmly this time.

"We won't need any doctors, Walter. They will have an uphill battle trying to convince twelve men in this county that you can kill someone in cold blood and walk, no matter how high and mighty his father is or how many doctors his lawyers bring to trial. Hell, if those doctors start with their mumbo jumbo, you watch the jurors' eyes glaze over," George said.

Walter sat, thinking about what George had just said. George saw that his arguments were taking root. He continued, "We just need to counter that with religion, an eye for an eye and a tooth for a tooth. THAT the jury can understand."

Walter flipped his pencil and ran his fingers down the shaft, then he flipped it and did it again. He said nothing, lost in thought for at least a few minutes and nine or ten pencil flips. George did not interrupt him. He had planted the seed, and now he needed to sit quietly while the strategy he was advocating grew in the Solicitor General's mind.

"You're right, George. We do have a solid, robust case. There is nothing to be gained by deviating from the theory of the case pursued thus far.

"But we don't want to sit on our haunches and do nothing till time for the next trial. We need to shore it up a bit." Walter looked at his notes. "Find Moody Mulkey. We need him to positively identify Lee as the one who sent that telegram back to Burley's wife. Fussell was a weak witness. He was not able to identify Lee at all.

"We also need to get Lee's father-in-law, Mr. Solomon Corey, on the stand. Lee spent a good bit of time with him the day after the killing. We'll ask him to identify all the things Lee took from Burley: the hat, the pipe, the purse, the watch, and the car," Walter said. He looked again at his legal pad. George took advantage of the lull and chimed in.

"What about Math Bell? He was with them when Lee took that circuitous route around Lyons and Vidalia." he offered, glad that his boss had decided to stick to the same defense strategy.

"I think we have that covered with John Blackstone's testimony," Walter answered.

George countered, "I got the notion that John Blackstone might have been too close to Lee. Besides, Math is much older, and his testimony will carry more weight with the jury."

"Okay, you're right. We'll get him and coordinate their testimony, maybe let one testify to the route and the other to the blood in the car. By riding with Lee to Milledgeville, they were in the Baby Overland longer than anybody else," Walter said.

"I'll get right on it," George enthusiastically said as he got up and started for the door.

"And George, we need to meet with some of the witnesses and clean up their answers a bit, particularly Jim Mallard and Mack Wimberley. They were terrible in the first trial. If we can't get them to come across as more credible, we will lose Lee's confession, which makes everything Lee said to those officers on the way to Ohoopee merely circumstantial evidence. Enoch is going to go after them with both barrels, and we need to prepare them for the onslaught."

George nodded, turned, and left the conference room. Walter continued to make notes on the legal pad. He paused, put the eraser to his lips, and said aloud to the empty room, "You are not going to beat me on this one, Enoch Giles, neither you nor your new hotshot law partner, not this time."

* * * * * *

Lee Currie lay in his bunk in the Chatham County Jail, staring up at the empty bunk above. He had been sure that they would find him not guilty of killing that son-of-a-bitch, Phillips. This had not worked out as he wanted it to, not one little bit.

Damn that cow! If that dirt farmer Rushing hadn't been looking for it, nobody would have ever found Phillips. A stupid cow, for Pete's sake. How unlucky can a fellow be?

His father would get him out of this mess; he was sure of it. Heck, he was ready to go back home, and after all this, he was willing to work on the farm as his pa wanted. Milledgeville wasn't all that whoopee-damn-do a place to begin with, and he didn't need that crappy job at Mr. Harden's barbershop and pressing club.

He was ready to reconcile with his pa. After all, hadn't he quickly come to his aid? And Lilly might come back to him if he moved back into the Currie family home. He wouldn't need that Baby Overland to impress her anymore.

I hope they hurry up and get me free. I'm getting sick and tired of this damn place; Lee thought as he closed his eyes and fell right off to sleep as if he had not a care in the world.

Chapter 44

On Wednesday, March 2, 1921, just over a year from the day Burley Phillips was killed, the 2nd trial got underway. Judge Robert Hardeman again presided over another trial of Lee Currie.

* * * * * *

True to their plan, Solicitor General Walter Grey and his assistant George Lankford laid out the same basic case strategy as in the first trial several months earlier.

The entire morning was devoted to selecting a jury. The first trial was so notorious that they had to go through 273 members of the jury pool to find 12 men who were not intimately familiar with the case. Those selected consisted of Ben Harley Coursey, Duncan Odom, Samuel Johnson Bland, Sr., William Adam McNatt, Jr., James Alonzo Grace, Alexander Timothy Page, Herschel V. Lynn, Robert Lester McGill, James Louis Faircloth, Sr., Robert Abraham Kitchens, W. A. Dees, and William Hampton Partin.

After lunch, Grey began calling most of the same witnesses as in the first trial. He added a few new ones to drive home the point that Lee Currie planned his crime in advance, stalked his victim, lured him to a remote area, shot him, buried him alive, took his car, distributed his possession to his in-laws, and took several other steps to cover up his crime.

As methodically as before, the prosecution introduced its evidence through these witnesses. The pistol, the filed-off bullets, Lee's re-visiting the burial site and trying to conceal it further, and his attempt to damage the car by deliberately running over a yearling calf.

Grey introduced Lee's in-laws to testify how Lee gave them Burley Phillips' hat and pipe and linked how Lee had two purses and a lot of money on him.

Most damming was Lee's confession to police officers with all the gory detail of how he had killed Burley Phillips. The defense was much more aggressive this time and tried mightily to prevent Lee's admissions while in custody from being considered by the jury, but to no avail. Judge Hardeman was not having it and overruled objection after objection from the defense team.

Grey showed how Lee had been caught off guard by the officer's questions put to him and had come up with several different accounts of how Burley was killed, including one that claimed strangers killed Phillips and another that he had shot Phillips in self-defense.

Grey carefully painted a picture of Lee being so glad that he was out of the reach of a lynch mob that he finally decided to come clean and confess every detail of how he had shot Burley and buried him. From the testimony of one witness, Grey again established how it was clear that Lee sent the telegram to Burley's wife to throw her off. He characterized Lee's statement, "Y'all are my friends and won't tell anyone," as an example of Lee being naive and a braggart, not insane.

Grey's central theme in the testimony was Lee's obsession with the Baby Overland automobile. Had he not been caught in possession of the vehicle he craved enough to kill for, he might never have been connected to the crime, but Lee Currie could not resist the urge to show off the vehicle, bloodstains notwithstanding, to friends and family alike. When he was arrested in Milledgeville, having driven there from Lyons five days after he killed Burley Phillips, the gun he used was in the side pocket with the remaining filed-off bullets just like the one that killed his victim still in the chamber. The Baby Overland had undone him.

The case laid out by the prosecution was overwhelming, just as before. Grey and his law partner were confident they had offered proof beyond a reasonable doubt that Lee Currie had killed Burley Phillips, knew full well what he was doing, and even bragged about his actions. The defense was not going to be successful saving him from the hangman's noose this go around.

* * * * * *

It comforted John Currie that Enoch Giles seemed so calm. The lawyer showed no concern, much less the trepidation John was feeling, as he asked Judge Hardeman to adjourn for the day so the defense could present their case uninterrupted the following day. When the judge agreed to the accommodation and called a recess till the next day, John went straight to his son's lead attorney.

"Did you see the faces of the men in the jury? They were wearing the same expressions as his first jury, and I just know they have already convicted Lee in their minds. I can just read it all over them," John said as he watched the deputies carry his son out of the courtroom back to jail.

"Yes, that probably true right now, but they haven't yet heard our side of this case," Giles told him as he snapped the latches on his briefcase.

He put his hand on the old man's shoulder and said, "John, we know what we are doing. We have a strong defense laid out for Lee. We are going to try our best to get him declared not guilty by reason of insanity."

"Can you be sure this will work?" John looked pleadingly at Giles, a tear forming in his left eye.

"Nothing is for certain in a court of law, John, but we are going to do the best that we can. Go by the jail and see your son, then try to get some rest. Let this trial run its course and pray for a good outcome."

T. Ross Sharpe came over to John, "John, Enoch is the best defense lawyer in this county. I think this new course of defense he has chosen is solid. We're going to win this time; I just feel it in my bones."

Sharpe wanted to sound confident, but when John looked up at him through tear-filled eyes, his legs almost gave way, "I know you won't let them hang my boy, T. Ross, you can't, you just can't."

It was everything Sharpe could do to maintain his composure as John lost control of his emotions and buried his face in his hands, sobbing. Lula Currie put her arms around him.

"John, you need to compose yourself. We need to go see Lee, and you don't want him to see you like this," Lula said.

"She's right, John," Sharpe agreed.

Sharpe watched as John straightened his back and wiped away his tears. "You're right, Lula. I need to go see my son."

He looked straight at Sharpe, "I know you and Enoch will do all within your power to save Lee's life, and I thank you for your efforts."

John turned and began walking toward the exit that led to the county jail.

Sharpe watched him till he went through the door, sighed, gathered his notes into his briefcase, and turned to leave the courthouse.

* * * * * *

"Call your first witness," Judge Hardeman said to Enoch Giles shortly after the court was called back in session at 9 a.m. on March 2, 1921. Giles looked over at T. Ross Sharpe and gave him an acknowledging nod. The time had come.

They were about to present the first insanity defense offered in Toombs County. It was new ground, and the life or death of Lee Currie depended on what they were about to do.

"The defense calls Dr. John Hall to the witness stand," Giles announced.

Several reporters leaned forward in their seats almost in unison, including Arch McGill of the Lyons Progress, Jim Jacobs of the Savannah Morning News, and reporters from the Montgomery Monitor, The Milledgeville Union Recorder, The Thomasville Times Enterprise, and other publications, all drawn to the newspaper-selling trial of the century.

"Good morning, Dr. Hall. I appreciate your taking time away from your patients to be here today," Giles began pleasantly. Dr. Hall nodded.

"Dr. Hall, how long have you been a practicing physician?"

"For thirty-one years now."

"Where did you get your education?"

"I graduated from the old Atlanta school."

"Have you developed any specialties during your practice of medicine?"

"During this time, I have for the last fifteen years made a specialty of mental diseases," Dr. Hall answered.

Giles knew he was fortunate to find a local doctor this well trained in mental diseases, the formal study of which was still in its infancy. He had ruled out finding someone holding a degree in psychology. For that, he would have to bring them from New York or even Europe, which was in no way affordable, given John Currie's financial circumstances.

Having a degree or not, he hoped that the jury would accept Dr. Hall as an expert in the mind's diseases.

"Do you know the defendant, Lee Currie?" Giles asked.

"Yes."

"When did you first hear about him?"

"It was around the time that the body was found down there."

"The body that proved to be Mr. Phillips?"

"Yes."

"When did you first become acquainted with Lee Currie?"

"I saw him in the Savannah jail for something like two weeks after the homicide."

"And what was the purpose of your going there?"

"To examine Mr. Currie for mental diseases and to find out the state of his mind."

"What did you do while there?"

"I made an examination designed for testing the mental capacity of a party."

"Can you explain your examination?"

"Yes. I made the reflex test and observed his actions."

"And what did your examination reveal about Mr. Currie?"

"I found in him the most exaggerated reflex I ever saw."

"Please explain to the Jury what an exaggerated reflex is."

"You know there is a normal reflex and an abnormal reflex, but in this man, it was the most abnormal reflex I ever saw."

"Did you come to this conclusion by more than one test?"

"Yes, I tried out all of them."

"And which one did you find conclusive in making your diagnosis?"

"The muscular reflex. As compared to a normal man, I found him to be abnormal. His reflex was abnormal in every respect."

"Dr. Hall, can you explain that in layman's terms?"

"Whenever the reflex responds too much, it is called the exaggerated reflex. That is what I found in this party in all the instances, and there were quite a lot of them."

"Did you give him any other tests?"

"I also gave him the test of his eyes. In one of the eyes, there was no reflex at all, and in the other, there was a slight reflex."

"How did you conduct this test?"

"By using a flashlight in a dark room."

"Explain that a little further, Dr. Hall."

"I kept him in a dark room for about half an hour. If you take a person in a dark room and his pupils dilate, a normal person's eyes would react if you flashed the light in their eyes. If they are abnormal, you get no response."

"No response at all?"

"In some people, you may get some, and in others, you get none. Mr. Currie had none."

"I see. What other test did you give Mr. Currie?"

"I give him a physical test and found him a physical defect in size."

"Physical defect? What does that mean, doctor?"

"The boy is not symmetrically developed. The base of his skull is not normally formed."

"Did you find any other physical anomalies?"

"Yes, I found the boy suffering from gonococci in a chronic form or state."

There was a collective gasp in the room and murmuring as it dawned upon the spectators that Lee Currie had gonorrhea, a sexually transmitted disease never mentioned in polite company. The ladies in the audience fanned themselves furiously as if trying to blow away the words that had just assaulted their ears.

Judge Hardeman rapped his gavel, "Order." The murmuring immediately stopped.

"Having given him all these tests, and given your 31 years of experience, 15 of those specializing in the area of mental diseases, what, in your medical opinion, is your diagnosis of Mr. Currie?"

"It is my opinion of the defendant that he is a paranoiac, a mental defect."

Giles wanted to introduce his central strategy early, that Lee was insane and could not help what he did. He had coached Dr. Hall against using too many medical terms because the jury needed to hear this testimony using words with which they were familiar.

"What is paranoia, Dr. Hall?" Giles asked and swallowed hard, hoping the doctor remembered his coaching.

"Paranoia is a disease that grows in a person who is cognitively defective in nerve organisms."

"In English, Doctor, if you please," Giles said.

As if he finally remembered the coaching, Dr. Hall said, "Oh, I'm sorry, it is a disease of the brain, and the fact that it is congenital means that he is born in that condition."

"Having made your diagnosis that Mr. Currie is a paranoiac, what degree of resistance would he have to committing a crime?"

"That depends very much on how far it is developed. In this instance, Mr. Currie has no degree of resistance at all."

Giles turned to the jury, "No ability to resist." He let his words sink in and turned back to his witness, "How did you conclude that, Dr. Hall?"

"I tried his power of concentration and found he has none. I tried to draw his attention to things, but I could not get his attention to anything. It jumped from one thing to another. We would talk about one thing, and in a moment, he was off to something else."

Giles noticed that Juror number 3 was staring at Lee Currie, who was looking over his shoulder at the spectators as if looking for someone. He saw Lee turn, catch the juror's eye, and smile gleefully. Giles blithely moved between the juror and Lee, and the juror immediately turned his head back to him.

Giles was pressing his theory hard. He asked, "In the case of a paranoiac, is there automatically an inclination to commit crime?"

"The inclination to do things and to commit crime can manifest itself in different ways. In the paranoiac, it could cause him to be a kleptomaniac or set fires. And it could cause him to commit murder during the process of stealing or burning or something of that kind."

Giles pressed on, "Are most cases of paranoia usually proceeded by ill health?"

"Not necessarily. Some paranoiacs are born that way. It is a condition that exists in the brain at the time of birth, often unnoticeable until evidenced by some crime the paranoiac commits.

"Now, it can develop more rapidly due to injury or disease. Certainly, the impulse to commit crime in a paranoiac is easily excited."

"So, if it is in the nature of a paranoiac to commit a crime, what do you think would trigger the illegal activity?" Giles asked.

"The paranoiac is easily influenced into illegal activity by the instruments to commit the crime with, such as a gun. They will excite him. A person in that condition with a gun is easily carried away by temptations of money or property, or anything of that kind. Some of the paranoiacs have some resisting power; others have none. Mr. Currie has no resistive power whatever."

"When someone has no resistive power to control his criminal impulses, who is most likely to be the object of his intent?"

"The one that is nearest to him is the one he makes trouble with. It is generally some member of the family or some intimate friend. However, sometimes it is a person unknown to him or not intimately associated with him."

"Dr. Hall, what degree of intelligence is usually exhibited by a paranoiac in carrying out a crime of this kind?"

Dr. Hall had relaxed and was now on a roll. He became more animated with his answers as if he were lecturing to a college classroom.

"It is astonishing with what cunningness an insane person, especially a paranoiac, can form and design a plan to commit crime and to do it, and then it is astonishing all the things they leave undone, the evidence they leave behind in their efforts to cover it up."

Giles did not want to get into the specifics of what Lee had done to cover his tracks, and he quickly took his witness in another direction.

"Doctor, would an ordinary person, not trained as you are, be able to tell if a person is a paranoiac?"

"Paranoia is not ordinarily observable by the layman who is not trained in it. That form of insanity is never discovered by a layman and rarely by physicians, unless they are intimately associated with them or unless something is brought up to call their attention to the unusual behavior."

Giles wanted to turn Lee's confession against the prosecution. Instead of the confession being a "gotcha" moment, he tried to fashion it into further evidence that Lee was insane.

"Can a paranoiac who has committed a crime be easily persuaded by law enforcement to confess his deeds?"

"Well, you take many of those insane, especially in a paranoia form of it, will design and commit the crime and then surrender themselves without any sense of conscience. They will not make any effort to conceal their deed, while the normal man who commits a crime will make an effort to escape and keep his crime secret."

"Let's return to your statement that it is difficult for an untrained person to tell if a man is a paranoiac. Would someone with that condition exhibit some outward abnormal behavior or have violent traits?"

"They do not necessarily have to show any violent signs of insanity. It is possible for a man to be a confirmed paranoiac and still not exhibit to the ordinary layman any sign of his condition. It must be a man who is informed on mental diseases that can detect these things."

Excellent, Giles thought to himself. It was important for the jury to accept that they were not qualified to judge whether Lee was insane or not. It was time to move on to the planning aspect of this crime.

Giles knew the prosecution had to show premeditation to convict Lee Currie of first-degree murder. He needed to cast doubt that Lee had contemplated murder ahead of time.

"Does a paranoiac have the capacity to commit premeditated murder?"

Dr. Hall put his hand upon his chin and stroked his mustache, "A paranoiac does not necessarily have to have in his mind the intention of murder; rather, it comes by temptations. Sometimes the party doesn't think about it ahead of time. For example, where a normal murderer might enlist help to commit a crime, a paranoiac act by himself almost invariably."

Giles also needed to counter the heinous nature of Lee burying Phillips while he was still alive and the wanton way in which he described his crime to the deputies during his so-called confession. He also needed to counter any negative feelings the jury might have of Lee's continuing indifference during the trial.

"Would a paranoiac have the capacity to show remorse after committing a crime or murder?"

"After they have committed a crime, the paranoiac has no remorse of conscience at all. You cannot appeal to their sympathy. Sometimes they even get an idea that they have done something for which they should be honored, but you never find one who thinks with murderous intent."

Sharpe signaled for Giles to come to the defense table. Giles leaned over, and Sharpe said, "Enoch, these jury members are not responding to this line of questioning. They know what crazy looks like. You have got to help them know that their eyes are deceiving them where Lee is concerned."

Giles nodded and returned to the lawyer's podium. He looked through his notes and then looked up at Dr. Hall.

"Is there any type of insanity that is recognizable to a layman, doctor?"

"Why yes, the ordinary layman can identify only three phases of insanity, and that is mania, melancholia, and dementia. Those three degrees of insanity are very noticeable and observable by most anybody. However, the paranoiac state is not."

Giles noticed the jurors looking at each other. He had driven the point home. It was time to close with this witness.

"Dr. Hall, in a person with this type of insanity, a paranoiac, I mean, does that person have any special power to resist committing a crime of this type?"

"No, they would not."

"Then would a paranoiac like Lee Currie be responsible if he had committed a crime of this type?"

"In my professional judgment, they are not responsible because they have no resistive power."

"Thank you, Dr. Hall." Giles turned to the judge, "I have no further questions, your honor."

* * * * * *

Walter Grey nodded to George Lankford, who had been studying the insanity defense and would handle the defense witnesses' cross-examination. Lankford acknowledged his glance, stood up and approached the lawyers' podium.

"Good morning, Dr. Hall. My name is George Lankford, and I represent the state in this case.

"You testified that you have been practicing medicine for thirty-one years, correct?"

"Yes, I think thirty-one years this next Friday," Dr. Hall said and smiled.

"And how much of that time did you say has been devoted to a special study of insanity?"

"About fifteen years."

"Where all have you practiced medicine?"

"I have been practicing throughout this area."

"Throughout this area, you say. Including Toombs County?"

"Yes, my office is in Alamo, but many of my patients are from Toombs County."

"What was it that got you interested in the study of insanity?"

"It was because there was so much insanity around here."

"Lot of crazy people in this county, are there?"

Laughter rolled through the audience and in the jury box. Lankford would do his best to play to the skepticism he could see on the jurors' faces.

"Well, it was a disease that appealed to me, and I took it up in that way and became interested in it," Dr. Hall shifted uncomfortably in his seat.

"You get paid pretty well for your expert knowledge on insanity, don't you?"

"Of course. I am in the practice of medicine for remuneration. However, I do not find the study of insanity a well-paying job or profession in this county."

"I thought you just said we have a lot of insanity in Toombs County? How much money have you made by making a special study of insanity?"

"I suppose I have made in all about $1,500 to $2,000 since I have taken it up."

"Have you studied many people other than the defendant as to their sanity or insanity since you took it up?"

"Well, one especially was this man Peterson at Ailey. He was also charged with murder."

"Are there others?"

"I have quite a number of these cases in which I have been called in to treat them."

"Did you make any of the $1,500 to $2,000 appearing as an expert witness in cases such as these?"

"I did not make that much in the courthouses, to be plain about that."

"Is it not true that most of your study has been for cases of persons charged with murder, where you have examined suspects and testified, as in the case?"

"Well, I have in quite a number of them, but most of that sum has come to me through practice for mental troubles."

"Was the Peterson case that you were talking about an occasion where a fellow was charged with murder?"

"Yes."

Lankford had tried to plant the seed of doubt in the jurors' minds about Dr. Hall's motive for his testimony. He moved on to impeach his testimony.

"Where were you on the day they found the body of Burley Phillips?" Lankford asked.

"I was here in Lyons going down to Cedar Crossing."

"Did you know who Burley Phillips was?"

"No, I did not know who he was."

"After hearing about the body being found, what did you do?"

"I went on to Cedar Crossing to see my brother, Dr. Jim Hall. I was sick for two or three days after I was down there."

"How did you come to be hired by the defendant's attorneys to appear as an expert witness for them?"

"While I was sick, I received a telephone message from Sebe Hall, my brother, telling me that Giles & Sharpe wanted to see me."

"Did you go see them?"

"Yes. I went up to their office, and they asked me to go to Savannah to observe Mr. Currie. That same afternoon, I went down there with Col. Giles."

"How long did you stay in Savannah?"

"Three days and nights."

"Did Giles & Sharpe pay you for going?"

Dr. Hall was beginning to get visibly irritated at the inference that his motives for examining Lee Currie were financial.

"They certainly did pay me for going, or I would not have gone."

"How much did they pay you?"

"I got $25 for my expenses and $100 for my trouble."

"What examination did you make of Mr. Currie while in Savannah?"

"I made the general examination, that is to test out the reflexes of a person."

"What tools did you use for the examination?"

"I made the examination by observation, which is the usual way of testing out a man's mental capacity. I talked with the party and made the other examinations, which I have already mentioned."

"You said you went to the jail in Savannah with Col. Giles. Did anyone else accompany you?"

"Yes, Lee's father, Mr. John Currie, also accompanied us."

"Mr. John Currie?" Lankford repeated, looking at Dr. Hall inquisitively.

"Yes, let me explain that. When they told me they wanted me to go down there, I told them that I did not know the boy, and I did not know the officers down there, nor did I know if they would permit me to make the examination.

Col. Giles was to talk to the jail officers, and his father was there to make Lee feel more comfortable."

"During your three-day stay, how much time did you spend with the defendant?"

"I stayed in the jail the first day, something like an hour. The second time I stayed in the jail about three and a half or four hours, and the last time I stayed with Lee Currie about three or four hours."

"Okay, tell the jury how you conducted your investigation."

"I had given Col. Giles some questions I wanted him to ask the first day while I was in the jail. I sat a ways away where I could simply observe him."

"Did Lee Currie know why you were there?"

"The young man did not know until Col. Giles got ready to leave."

"So, Col. Giles didn't tell Lee Currie that you were there to swear he was crazy?"

Dr. Hall bristled. He glowered at George Lankford and said icily, "I know that Giles did not tell him that."

"So, it is your testimony that neither Col. Giles nor his father had told Lee beforehand that they were bringing a doctor to observe him?"

"There was no opportunity for that. There had not been an agreement between us until the evening of the night before, and we went the next morning."

"So, you are sure he did not know why you were there?"

"I'm quite sure he did not know because he turned to Col. Giles and wanted to know what that damn long-legged rascal wanted in there."

"He asked that right away?"

"I reckon he had been talking some ten or fifteen minutes."

Lankford turned a few pages in his legal pad, "What tests did you call yourself conducting by listening to him and Col. Giles talk?"

"The observation test."

"How did Col. Giles finally let him know who you were?"

"Col. Giles told him, 'Dr. Hall has come down here to examine you, Lee, and I want you to do as he requests and whatever he directs.'"

"Dr. Hall, did you go to Savannah for the specific purpose of ascertaining if Lee Currie was crazy where you could testify in this trial on his behalf?"

Dr. Hall stood up indignantly and glared at George Lankford. The bailiff came over and gestured for him to sit down.

"Answer the question, Dr. Hall," Judge Hardeman said.

Dr. Hall looked at the judge and softened his countenance, "That is a reflection on me, and I resent it. I went down there by request of these gentlemen to ascertain his condition and report it back. That is what I was paid for. If he was sane, I was to say so, and if he was insane, I was to say so."

"I apologize if you were offended, Dr. Hall; I meant no personal disrespect. If we can continue, please describe what a reflex is and how you do a reflex test."

Dr. Hall regained his composure and gestured to below his knee, "The reflex is when you strike a man here to test the action of the muscle. You can strike on the knee or patella or on the tendon. There are two reflexes there, one from the bone itself and another from the tendon above and below.

"If you hit a man there and get no response, you know that somewhere in that man's brain, there is decay. If you hit them there and get an exaggerated reflex, there are some abnormal conditions in the brain."

"How do you determine that a reflex is 'exaggerated'? Do his feet go flying up?" George asked sarcastically.

Sharpe stood up, "Objection, your honor, the prosecution is trying to ridicule Dr. Hall's testimony!"

"Sustained. Let's show the witness the proper respect, counselor," Judge Hardeman warned.

"I apologize, your honor. Let me rephrase. Dr. Hall, please describe an exaggerated reflex for the jury."

Pointing to below his knee, Dr. Hall said, "If you hit a man there in making that test, his feet have not necessarily got to fly up, but whenever I hit him, there was quite a good deal of response, what I termed and stated just now as an exaggerated reflex."

"And this 'good deal of response' reflex was not normal, in your expert opinion?"

"No, they are not normal; they are abnormal and exaggerated reflexes. When you hit him on the knee, the foot would indeed fly up. He also had an exaggerated reflex through the muscles of the back."

Lankford walked from behind the lawyer's podium and approached the rail in front of the witness box. He leaned in on the witness and asked, "Dr. Hall, is it not true that a champion boxer or wrestler, in good physical condition with the muscles well developed, would have greater reflexes than an ordinary person?"

"Not necessarily; it would be the normal reflex."

Lankford turned and walked over to the jury, "Would you say that Mr. Currie is a full-grown man?"

"I know that the defendant physically is a man in age."

Lankford asked his next question while still looking at the men in the jury, "Did you know that he could beat any man in the jail in Savannah in boxing or wrestling?" Lankford turned to the witness.

"I don't know anything of his capacity to box and wrestle with any man in the jail down there."

Lankford walked back to the witness, "You examined him carefully, and you can't say whether he is a strong man?"

"After examining him, I would not say that he was a normal man physically, but I consider him a fairly strong man for his size."

Lankford walked back to the lawyer's podium and consulted his notes, "You testified that you examined him all over his body. Did you remove his clothing to perform the reflex test?"

"Yes, I had him stripped myself."

"What instruments did you use to examine Mr. Currie?"

"I used one of these small hammers that are used for testing out muscles."

"A hammer? Does that mean you went to Savannah prepared in advance to conduct the reflex text to test Mr. Currie's sanity?"

"No, I went to a drugstore in Savannah and bought it. I used that on him muffled, in other words, wrapped."

"What other instruments did you use?"

"For the reflex of the eyes, I used that test with a flashlight in a dark room. That is all the instruments that I used."

"So, the only instruments you used were a flashlight and a hammer you bought in a drugstore?"

"That's right."

"How did you examine the base of Mr. Currie's skull?"

"Well, now, the only examination you can make of the base of the skull is from observation."

"You testified on direct examination that there was a formation at the base of the skull. Can you describe it in greater detail?"

"I did not say that. I said that the base of the skull was not developed like the normal head."

"It was not filled out like normal, you say. Do all normal people have skulls of the same shape and size?"

"There are not many people who have skulls of the same shape and size. Nearly every man has got a head of his own; if he ain't, he ought to have it," Dr. Hall said, and laughter broke out in the courtroom.

"It would be convenient, I'm sure," Lankford said sarcastically to more laughter.

"Order," Judge Hardeman said, rapping his gavel.

"Dr. Hall, tell us what you found wrong at the base of Lee Currie's brain that made you think the head he has is abnormal?"

"I could not say that there was anything wrong at the base of the skull there, but I do say that there was something wrong with his brain. I know from the examination that I made and from my knowledge of medicine and psychology and mental diseases, I know it is there."

"Did you not testify earlier that there was something the matter at the brain's base?"

"No, but there is something the matter with his brain."

"Did you x-ray his brain?"

"I did not have any x-ray."

"Wouldn't you agree that taking an x-ray might be part of a thorough examination of his brain?"

"I don't know how to handle an x-ray."

"Ah, so the only test you used to tell that his brain was abnormal was observation?"

"You are not listening, Col. Lankford. I observed him in the first test, and for the second and third tests, I used a hammer and flashlight."

"I'll try to pay better attention to your answers," Lankford said sarcastically. He looked up at the judge, who was frowning at him. Lankford knew he was getting close to the line, but he had to keep the jury from wandering off into this testimony. No, he wanted them to believe their common sense and not the doctor. "Now, how long did you say you were with Mr. Currie?"

"I was in there from three to four hours each day, the second and third day."

"You testified there were other physical defects you observed. What would be the nature of those?"

"I would not like to mention it here before the ladies."

Judge Hardeman spoke up, "This is a court of law, Dr. Hall, and we seek the truth." The judge spoke to those in the courtroom, "If any of you ladies are overly sensitive to such testimony about the male anatomy, you may leave the courtroom now."

Judge Hardeman paused for a long moment. No one in the audience moved.

"Very well, as you all have chosen to stay, I don't want to hear any more gasps if the testimony embarrasses you. A man's life is at stake here, and this is no time for modesty," the judge said and then directed the witness, "Answer Col. Lankford's question."

Dr. Hall took out a handkerchief and wiped the sweat from his brow. He returned it to his pocket and swallowed hard.

"There is a defect with the man's privates." A murmur went through the audience.

"One moment, counselor," Judge Hardeman interrupted. "Ladies, I am going to pause again for a moment to allow any of you who may be offended by medical testimony about a man's private parts to leave."

He looked out over the audience. Although there were a couple of dozen ladies in the courtroom, none got up.

"Okay, now that I have given you that opportunity, let me announce that I will not tolerate any more verbal reaction from those of you in this courtroom to the testimony you are about to hear. Dr. Hall, you may continue your answer."

Dr. Hall wiped his brow once again and continued, "For one, his penis is abnormally small, and he has an elongated prepuce. Also, his muscles are flabby. His muscles are not hard like a man who ordinarily had been at work."

Lankford noticed Lee Currie begin to squirm in his seat. Apparently, he did not like the direction this testimony was going.

"You testified on direct examination that Mr. Currie was infected with gonococci. Please explain that further."

"I found the boy suffering from gonorrhea, and the glands, I am satisfied, were infiltrated with the gonococci, which is the germs of gonorrhea."

"Does having gonorrhea mean that you will go crazy? Is that what you are trying to tell the jury?"

"I do not mean to say that a fellow who has gonorrhea and the other two things that I have mentioned stands the chance to be crazy. I certainly don't think that every man that has got gonorrhea would be crazy, for if I did, about two-thirds of these people in this house would be crazy ..." That drew both gasps and laughter from the courtroom. Judge Hardeman rapped his gavel but said nothing. Everyone knew what he meant, and the courtroom again became quiet.

"... but I mean, from the mental condition that Mr. Currie was already in, the gonorrhea would aggravate his mental condition."

"If having gonorrhea doesn't necessarily mean a person is going to go crazy, why have you concluded that the gonorrhea is relevant to the defendant's state of mind?"

"It is relevant in a case of this kind. The fact that he has not developed symmetrically shows there is some defect in the person and the gonorrhea simply exacerbates his disorder further.

"There is another thing I should mention here. In my examination of the prostate glands, I found a discharge that I was satisfied was the result of this gonorrhea."

Lankford noticed that the jury was beginning to show intense interest in Dr. Hall's testimony. He sensed he was losing them and needed to re-establish the absurdity of this line of testimony, "Would this discharge make a fellow want to kill people?"

"No, it might make him want to kill himself, but it doesn't make him want to kill anybody else."

"You are going to have to explain what you mean, Dr. Hall. Is it your testimony that the disease from which he suffered is responsible for his actions or not?"

"I mean this; I want to be as fair to you as I can. When a person is suffering from a mental disease, that mental trouble would be made more active from syphilis or gonorrhea or many other of these troubles I have been describing. I mentioned those as contributory to his mental condition, which is paranoia. He has a defective mind."

Lankford threw up his hands in exasperation. "Now we are back to paranoia. Okay, let's try to understand your diagnosis. You testified earlier that some people suffering from paranoia have no resistance to their actions, correct?"

"I said a while ago that some of them, to some extent, have no resistance to criminal acts. It depends upon the extent of the development of the trouble.

"There is a pseudo-paranoia which is curable, many cases of it, but if it is curable, it is not the true paranoia. In the case of a true confirmed paranoiac, there is no cure for it, and the true confirmed paranoiac is a person that has no resistive power. Their inclination to commit crime or do anything that they wanted is met with no resistance."

"And such a person, suffering from paranoia, has no regard for how many people he kills?" Lankford asked, confident that Dr. Hall had lost the jury with the complexity of his testimony.

"I don't mean to say that. When the opportunity presents itself, and they are left alone, they might kill one, two, or three persons. It depends on the situation."

"When the opportunity presents itself, and the paranoiac wants something, he acts, you say? Well, then, how is there any difference between the paranoiac and any other criminal with motive and opportunity?"

A snicker went up in the jury box. Lankford noted it. It was complicated for the doctor to explain this disorder in layman's terms, as the defense wanted. Yes, he was sure now the doctor was losing the jury.

"The criminal, the man who kills for game or robs, will rob anybody as a general thing. But with the paranoiac, he is not inclined to kill or rob everybody he comes in contact with, only that person he is with whenever the impulse to commit crime comes on him."

"That sounds like a distinction without a difference, doctor."

"Objection!" Giles stood up this time.

"Sustained. The jury will disregard the prosecution's characterization of Dr. Hall's testimony," Judge Hardeman said.

"Sorry, your honor, it was – a reflex." Lankford quipped. A snicker arose from the audience.

"Don't toy with me, Col. Lankford," Judge Hardeman said sternly.

"Sorry, your honor," Lankford said and turned back to the witness, "When you examined the defendant and gave him the reflex test and found that the reflex was greater than what it should be, could that not indicate that he was just of a nervous temperament?"

"He is indeed somewhat of a nervous temperament, but such a temperament does not mean your reflexes are going to be exaggerated."

"Doctor, under what circumstances is a paranoiac with no resistance likely to kill someone they come in contact with?"

"It depends upon the opportunity to commit a crime and having a weapon or lethal object to commit it with. That opportunity to commit a crime, the remoteness of the place where he is, and the possession of an instrument for committing the crime all come together to excite the inclination to commit the crime. Do you get that idea, counselor? I hope to make that clear to you."

The doctor was now feeling emboldened and was patronizing the attorney. Lankford was unfazed. He saw that the doctor was trying to match wits with him at a high level and had forgotten about the need to keep it simple for the jury. He pressed his advantage.

"But given your testimony about how a paranoiac has no resistive power, is it not true that such a paranoiac would be inclined to kill anybody they come in contact with?"

"No, that is not true. The inclination to kill has to present itself, along with the proper place and an instrument to carry out the killing. Under those circumstances, they are just as likely to kill a man on the street as anywhere else, or they may act with more cunning to lead their victim to isolated places where they can commit the crime undetected."

"Cunning, you say. Is it your testimony that crazy people can act with purpose and cunning?"

"It is astonishing with what cunningness many of these crimes are committed by insane people."

"Tell me, doctor, are you trying to tell this jury that a person who would lead their victim to a place and kill him and then go off and spend the night with somebody, acting perfectly okay and normal, is, in fact, not normal?"

"That's right; he would not be considered normal."

"Okay then, if the spell is on him, wouldn't he try to kill the next person he finds?"

"Of course not. The desire to commit crime is not present with a person suffering from insanity all the time. If it was, it would have been found out before he killed this unfortunate man."

Langford could tell from the expressions of many of the jury members that they were not buying the doctor's testimony. He wanted to press the idea that what Dr. Hall was saying was absurd. "Given what you have told the jury, that ordinary laypeople cannot detect a paranoiac, couldn't you say that almost anybody that commits a crime hasn't got his right mind?"

"No, a normal man can deliberately and premeditatedly plan a crime and commit it for revenge or for insult. Mr.

Currie is not cool and calm and in his absolute right mind like a person in average health committing a crime because he is a madman."

"Dr. Hall, what distinguishes a normal man committing such a murder from an insane person who does the same?"

"The insane person kills without any malice. He is no respecter of persons. He selects his party because that party is in possession of something he desires to have, that would be the design, the motive of it. He will lead his party away or slay him anywhere.

"I do not mean to say that every paranoiac is a murderer by any means, but in most cases, a paranoiac, after he slays and murders, takes it for granted that he is doing right, so he doesn't try to hide the crime. He doesn't make much effort, well, sometimes they do, but they generally do it in a bunglesome way which is easily discovered. Further, the insane man seldom ever makes an effort to escape where he does his crime."

It was time to wrap all this up for the jury and put it into the proper perspective. Lankford took a deep breath and laid it all out, "I'm having trouble determining the difference in culpability between when a paranoiac kills and when an ordinary murderer kills.

"Help me to understand this, Doctor; if a person goes to a store, gets some pistol cartridges, has them specially prepared so they would fit his pistol, gets a man that has a new automobile to carry him home, deliberately causes him to look around in the road, puts a pistol to his head and kills him, then drives back four or five miles to a house to get a shovel and hoe, goes out into the woods and digs a hole to bury him, goes back to the burial site in about three or four days to return to put a log on it to cover up the signs better, goes the next morning about twenty-five miles away and sends a telegram to the dead man's wife saying that he would be gone for some time, and signs the dead man's name to that telegram, do you believe that man was crazy?"

Sharpe leaned forward in his chair. This long, run-on utterance was not something they had prepared the witness to answer.

"I wouldn't say that all of them are, but there are plenty of them that are."

"Right," Lankford scoffed. "Well, then, Dr. Hall, if a man that does all that and then on the next morning takes the deceased's car, runs over a calf in the road while drawing no blood from the animal, goes on down the road to tell folks that he got blood on his car by running over a hog, killing it and putting it in the car, would you say that that man was crazy?"

"I would say that was the act of a man that was not mentally balanced because no normal man would do a thing of that kind."

"There are cases on record, Dr. Hall, plenty of murder cases where men have done that bad and worse. Would you have sworn in all of those cases that those men were crazy?"

"No, of course not. It is just as I have said, it might be the act of an insane man, or it might not. You will understand that you asked me to testify hypothetically to that question. Certainly, it would raise the suspicion of insanity in a situation such as you have just described."

Lankford knew he had been able to rattle the doctor. He was on a roll now and giving no credence to the doctor's answers to his hypotheticals.

"Do you believe an insane man who had killed another person and suspected there were people out looking for his victim's body would take an unusual route and go several miles around the dead man's neighborhood to dodge the town where the dead man lived?"

"It is perfectly possible."

"Possible? Is that your professional opinion that a crazy man would have sense enough to go around his victim's town?"

It finally dawned upon Dr. Hall that he was no longer talking to the jury. He remembered that Sharpe had told him to pause before he answered and not let the prosecution drill him with questions so fast, he might misspeak. He took a long breath.

"You must understand this; I hope to make myself clear that a person that is insane is not necessarily crazy. The form of insanity we are dealing with here might not cover every feature of a man's mind. There is a difference between the un-geared mine of a crazy person and the mind of a paranoiac which has begun to mentally decay."

Lankford did not react to the doctor's answer. He was confident that the jury had no clue what the doctor had just said. He continued, "Well, let me ask you this, Dr. Hall. Do you believe when Lee Currie was doing all these things that he knew right from wrong?"

"Well, I have stated all the time that this boy, in a sense, knew right from wrong."

Lankford got the answer he wanted. He turned to the judge and said, "No further questions, your honor."

Judge Hardeman looked over at Giles and raised his eyebrows to silently ask if he wanted to redirect. Giles stood, picked up his pad, and said, "I have a few more questions, your honor." In a sweeping motion, Judge Hardeman gestured toward Dr. Hall, indicating that Giles could proceed.

Giles had watched George Lankford ask the "if," "then," questions designed to introduce doubt into the jury members' minds about Lee Currie's actions being no different than those of any other murderer. He had to bring the jury back to thinking about Lee's mental state, and he had to restore Dr. Hall's credibility as a medical expert.

"Dr. Hall, you have described the test you made of Mr. Currie in Savannah. Are these standard tests for insanity?" Giles asked.

Glad to be facing a friendly lawyer again, Dr. Hall seemed to relax. He took out his handkerchief and wiped the sweat from his brow. "The tests that I made were thorough and exhaustive tests of insanity, and they are the test usually applied to cases in testing for a man's mental condition," Dr. Hall answered.

"Are these the tests that are usually used by a specialist in this line?"

"Yes, they consider them a thorough test."

"Dr. Hall, is it possible for a man's mind to be perfectly normal in a certain sense and devoid of reason or sympathy or sorrow or deranged in another?"

"Yes, but a man who is void of reason, who is void of sympathy, could not have a normal mind."

"You mentioned an 'un-geared mind' earlier. How is that different from a diseased mind?"

"They are the same."

"Is it possible for a man to have normal intelligence in one line of work and abnormal in another?"

"That is absolutely true. A man's mind is like a chain; it is only as strong as its weakest link. In other words, he could reach the top of the profession in one line of work and yet be mentally defective in another; but you get those cases coming in for treatment sooner or later; their minds go to decay. In other words, the mental condition shows a breakdown at some time or another."

Giles flipped a couple of pages in his legal pad, looked back at the witness, and asked, "What is the 'observation test' for insanity?"

"The observation test for insanity is one of the means of locating the trouble. In other words, you have to resort to that to confirm your diagnosis upon your examination. The observation tests are just as necessary to the process as it is to make the reflex tests."

"Describe how you conducted the observation test and what you observed Mr. Currie doing."

"Okay, the boy seemed indifferent in Savannah to what was being said to him. He had no power of concentration and paid no attention to Col. Giles when he was talking to him."

"Did you instruct Col. Giles as to what to say?"

"Yes. Before we went into the jail, I handed Col. Giles some questions and things that I wanted him to say. I says, 'I want you to tell him these things. I do not know whether it is true or not, but I want you to put it to him, just as I have written it and loud enough that I can hear it.'

"After he had talked to Lee in general terms for some time, he nodded to me that he was about to begin asking the questions and saying the things that I wanted to observe Lee's reaction to. When he told him these things, it made no impression on him at all."

"Can you give the jury an example of one of the things you ask Col. Giles to tell him?"

"Yes, one of the things was that I told Giles to state to him, or tell him, was that they were going to hang him. Col. Giles put his hand on his shoulder and says, 'Lee, they are going to hang you.'

"There happened to be a man coming up some steps adjacent to the room we were in at the jail, and when Col. Giles told him that, he pointed to this man, and he says, 'Look at that damn red-headed son-of-a-bitch. He is in here for murder, too.'"

Dr. Hall looked over at Lee, who was looking all about at the people present as if confirming the doctor's diagnosis that the defendant had no idea what was going on in the courtroom. He sighed and continued his statement, "It created no more impression on him then than this trial is impressing upon him now."

"How many times have you observed Lee Currie, Dr. Hall?"

"I have observed him from time to time. I saw him last court, and when I saw him in the Savannah jail. The next time I saw him was here in this trial."

"What would you conclude about Lee Currie's intelligence?"

"Based on my observations and tests, I would say that he has the intelligence of what we call a moron, on average, a person who is a child 12 to 14 years old. Yes, it would probably be that."

Lee bolted upright, "Did that son-of-a-bitch just call me a moron?"

Sharpe put his hand on Lee's arm, "Lee, you need to be quiet. Col. Giles knows what he is doing."

"I ain't sitting here and let him call me no moron; I can tell you that," Lee retorted.

John Currie leaned over the rail and put his hand on his son's arm.

"Lee, you steady down now. Let the lawyers do their job," John said and leaned back in his seat.

Lee calmed down, and Judge Hardeman breathed a sigh of relief. He didn't need an outburst in his court.

Giles continued, "How would you characterize the difference between Mr. Currie and a normal child 12 to 14 years old?"

"Because of his paranoia and the aggravating conditions also afflicting him, he has no power of resistance. That is the trouble with this young man. He is not mentally responsible for his acts."

"And how long would you say he has been suffering from this condition?"

"He was born with it."

"Could a person with this condition be cured?"

"It would not be possible to get paranoia out of him by training. There is just no cure for a paranoiac. Paranoiacs are born, they are not made, and a true paranoiac's condition is incurable, and it increases with age rather than decreases."

"Can a paranoiac live normally in society?"

"There is a lot of them that go out in life and make a success in business, but sooner or later, they break down. The undesirable behavior may be brought on from a disease or injury, things of that kind."

"When do they normally start to break down, Doctor?"

"Ordinarily, you find it in a man from 35 to 45 years old when the breakdown comes with him, but in this young man, it has been coming from his childhood."

"Col. Lankford asked you about the effect of his venereal disease on him. Could you clarify the effect this might have on his mind?"

"It would act as contributory because this is a serious mental condition. It will exaggerate the one already there."

"In other words, the venereal disease would serve to cause the mental breakdown to show up earlier, is that correct?"

"Yes."

"I have no more questions, your honor," Giles said and resumed his seat at the defense table.

"Dr. Hall, you may step down. Please remain in the courthouse in case you need to be called back up for further questioning.

"Ladies and gentlemen, it is not quite time for dinner yet, but I'm going to go ahead and call a recess. Court is adjourned until 1p.m. this afternoon," Judge Hardeman said and rapped his gavel.

Chapter 45

Giles was troubled all through dinner. Sharpe could see the concern on his partner's face.

"The jury isn't buying it, Enoch. George is making it appear that there is no real difference between Lee and any murderer," Sharpe offered as he took another bite of mashed potatoes. "And if I had to be honest, I'm not getting it either. Dr. Hall's testimony is a stretch for me, so I know the jury is struggling with it."

"I know, I know. I'm frustrated, too. Dr. Hall was our strongest medical expert, and he didn't come across as credible. George did a good job of ridiculing him, even over our objections. I almost laughed out loud myself when the doctor said that an insane person is not necessarily crazy. If he had not lost the jury before then, that statement undermined his whole damn testimony," Giles said.

Sharpe pushed his plate away from him. He had lost his appetite and had a sinking feeling in his gut that they had lost this case.

"Dr. Hall's brother is not going to be a strong witness either, I fear. George will tear him apart," Sharpe said.

"I'm just going to use him to show Lee had a long history of behavior that confirms Dr. Hall's diagnosis. I won't keep him on the stand long," Giles said.

The men sat for a few minutes more and had a smoke. Neither finished their dinner.

* * * * * *

The next witness, Dr. Jim Hall, had been the Currie family physician for years. Giles rushed through his testimony as he had forecasted to Sharpe during dinner, and mercifully, Lankford did very little in the way of cross-examination. Both lawyer teams knew that the good doctor was a throwaway witness who added little to the proceedings.

* * * * * *

Giles was worried. His next expert witness, Dr. George T. Gray, also added no real value to the case's strength. Giles had hoped that this doctor would give weight to Dr. John Hall's testimony by confirming the diagnosis and reiterating that Lee had no resistive power to prevent himself from killing Phillips when he made up his mind to have the Baby Overland, but George Lankford continued to ridicule the doctor's testimony effectively. He found himself mentally preparing to get another inevitable guilty verdict. He subconsciously began looking for a way to find an error in these new proceedings to get it overturned and prepare for a third trial.

The last of his medical experts was Dr. J. C. Collins. He was convincing in trial prep. Maybe he would be able to turn the tide.

* * * * * *

"Dr. Collins, for how long have you been practicing medicine?" Giles asked.

"I have been a practicing physician for twenty years."

"Where did you get your medical education?"

"I graduated at the Augusta Medical College, the University of Georgia."

"Do you know the defendant, Lee Currie?"

"Yes."

"Are you familiar with the word 'paranoiac'?"

"I guess that I know the word paranoiac; I have read it, the meaning of the word paranoia."

Giles felt a chill. His expert had just told the jury that he "guessed" that he knew about the disease that was central to the case. It was not a good start.

"Please describe your understanding of the disease, doctor."

"It is a non-development of an individual's mental conditions, a lack of development of the mind, of the brain structure. It is not a decayed mind; it is a diseased mind. It is not any decay; it is just a lack of organization of the mind."

Giles winced. Dr. Collins had just contradicted the testimony of Dr. John Hall, who testified that Lee's mind was decaying. He doubted the jury caught the contradiction and pressed on, "You are born with it?"

"Yes. Paranoia does not come on later along in life; it is a condition that existed there before birth."

Giles asked, "Can you learn to be a paranoiac?"

"Training would never develop that faculty. Sometimes it becomes more intense with age, but not always – I don't think."

Again, a testimony conflict between his experts. Dr. Hall had said the disease got worse with age. He chided himself for not preparing the witnesses better. "Can other diseases exacerbate the manifestations of paranoia?"

"In a case where a person is a born paranoiac and other diseases affecting the nervous system, such as gonorrhea or other venereal diseases, are present, it could bring on a spasmodic exhibition of it. Yes, yes, any disease of irritation in that body would have a tendency to bring about the development of paranoia more readily than otherwise."

"At what age would the paranoiac be most noticeable as to his paranoid symptoms?"

"Well, in middle age, paranoia would be increased by some of the diseases I have just mentioned."

"Does a paranoiac know right from wrong?"

"They would know right from wrong, but usually they have no fear about any punishment or anything generally."

"Do they have the power to resist their urges to do wrong?"

"They usually have no power to resist against doing any dangerous thing. When they fear a thing, they are willing to do it and take the consequences because they haven't got the power of resistance; that is usually the condition."

After a weak start, the witness was doing a great job of establishing what Giles had hoped, that Lee knew right from wrong but still had no power to resist his urge to kill to get what he wanted.

Sharpe gestured for Giles to come to the defense table, where he whispered, "I suspect George will lay out the actions of Lee before and after the killing and ask the doctor if those were the actions of a normal man. Let's use that tactic ourselves, only lay it out like we want it to sound."

Giles looked up at his law partner. It was brilliant. If he could lay out the entire scenario of Lee's actions and have the doctor verify it as being abnormal, it would make Lankford seem repetitive if he attempted the same thing.

"One moment, your honor, while I consult with my associate," Giles said. The two men collaborated on the question for several minutes.

"Counselor, the time to prepare your case was before we started. Now let's continue," Judge Hardeman urged.

"Sorry, your honor. I'm ready to pose my question.

"Dr. Collins, if a man should come to Lyons, buy some cartridges, go to Vidalia, try to hire one taxicab driver to take him out and couldn't get him, get another one to take him out 10 or 15 miles from town, kill him and throw him over in the back seat of his automobile, using very awful language, cursing at the time, and then should he go to a nearby shed, get a shovel, take his victim into the woods on a road that is not used, and bury him right side of the road," Giles walked over in front of the jury and continued.

"If that man then went to a home nearby to spend the night, get up the next morning, take the automobile which the dead man owned and which he had taken, drive up and down the community in which he had resided with blood stains on it and where everybody knew the defendant and the defendant knew everybody," Giles continued walking from one end of the jury box to the other as if asking the question to the men seated there instead of the doctor.

"Should that same man go over in Tattnall County, take the hat and pipe and various other articles of the dead man and give them to various people in the community, take his father-in-law and go down to Glennville and show him the blood signs and tell him that he killed a hog and threw it in the car and should come back and stay in the community in which he was known," Giles walked over in front of Lee Currie and continued asking his question.

"If that same man, four or five days previous to that time, send a telegram from Claxton, Georgia, to the wife of the dead man saying that he had gone to Jacksonville to sell his car and sign the name of the dead man to it," Giles walked back to the podium. He faced the doctor to finish his question.

"Should he go and get passengers out of the community that knew him and go down to a blacksmith's shop, and show the bloodstains to the owner, volunteering the information that he had killed a hog and this was the blood sign, and should go back to the grave and take the end of a log, drag it upon it, and then stay round there with his automobile, take these passengers and take the public highway and go to Milledgeville, from all that – would you say that man was not mentally right?"

* * * * * *

Dammit! George Lankford thought to himself. He turned and looked at Grey, who caught his glance and then diverted his eyes down to his legal pad and scratched through several of his questions.

* * * * * *

"Yes, I would consider him insane," Dr. Collins answered without flinching or pausing.

Giles noticed some of the men on the jury were leaning forward in their seats. "Do you also think those actions that I just described would reflect a want of precaution that the ordinary man would take when committing a crime?"

"Well, we usually don't find that in a sane person that would commit a crime."

"Tell me, doctor, what does it take to stimulate the imagination of a paranoiac?"

"Not much. When a person is a paranoiac, his imagination is easily aroused, and they are easily influenced to commit a crime."

"Can you give us some examples?"

"It could be anything they see that they want. If they see money or an automobile or even for the purpose of robbery, he will reach such a stage that he could commit the crime even though he knew right from wrong. Things of that kind easily influence them."

Excellent! Giles thought. Dr. Collins was doing great. Now, if he could just help establish that Lee's condition was difficult to determine in advance.

"Could this criminal intent be easily detected by someone not trained in medical science?"

"The condition of the paranoiac is usually not discovered by the ordinary layman. It is usually not discovered until some criminal condition has shown up."

"So, a crime would have to be committed before you could diagnose a paranoiac?"

"A paranoiac does not have to be attended with some violent act such as arson, murder, or larceny. It is possible for a paranoiac to be a confirmed paranoiac and even reach the middle-age life without the laity even knowing it."

"Thank you, Dr. Collins. I have no further questions," Giles said as he gathered his notes and sat down. He and Sharpe exchanged celebratory glances. Maybe they had this case back on track.

George Lankford was still furiously making notes on his legal pad. Grey was whispering to him as he wrote.

"Col. Lankford? Any time now," Judge Hardeman said.

Lankford continued to make a few more notes, "Sorry, your honor, I'm almost ready."

"Proceed with your cross-examination now, Col. Lankford. We'd like to get out of here at a decent hour if you don't mind," Judge Hardeman said.

Lankford walked to the lawyer's podium and spread out his notes. He needed to again appeal to the jury's common sense and point out the impossibility of what the defense was advocating. He looked up at the witness and smiled.

"Dr. Collins, are you saying that ordinary people can't tell if a person is insane until they commit a crime?"

"Well, not always, but it is often the case that the paranoiac is hardly ever found out until he commits some crime and is being tried."

"So, you or I wouldn't know he was capable of murder until he comes up and shoots one of us?"

"Objection!" Giles stood and said as a murmur of laughter rose in the audience.

"Overruled. You may answer the question," Judge Hardeman said.

"Well, it is very often the case that it is not known publicly; that is the general rule."

"Could it also be true that after someone has been indicted, the defense could claim that he is a paranoiac just to get him off?"

"Objection!" Giles stood again. "Counsel is impugning our integrity."

"Sustained. Rephrase your question, Counselor," Judge Hardeman said.

"Dr. Collins, is it then true that you can only diagnose a person as a paranoiac after he has committed a crime?"

"No, the general rule is that the paranoiac is only then found out. He could be a paranoiac and go on if he was not tried for some crime, and it might be overlooked, and nothing ever said about it."

"So, his folks, nor anybody would never know anything about it until he does something, and they try to convict him?"

"That is true."

"Let me ask you this, Dr. Collins, do you believe a man is insane that would kill another to rob him for his car and his money and then take him off in the woods and bury the body and cover it up?"

"Well, it is not always a man that is insane."

Despite Giles taking his approach from him, he had a foot in the door. Lankford pressed this approach.

"Forgetting this case, if any man goes and gets another and hires him to carry him home and he gets him out there and kills him and takes what he has got, his car and money and everything he has got, and he then carries him off in the woods and buries him, forgetting this case, is that man sane or insane?"

"Objection; the witness has already answered this question," Giles said.

"Overruled. I will allow the prosecution to ask the question in their own way. You may answer," Judge Hardeman directed.

"It would depend on the conditions what was connected with it."

"The evidence here shows that a man has killed for robbery and a car. He steals his victim's car and buries the body. Is he sane or insane?"

"Well, we find them both sane and insane when they do that."

"Let's add some more of those conditions you spoke of, Dr. Collins. The man that did the killing goes the next day, and to fool the wife of the deceased, sends a telegram to her, signing the dead man's name to it, telling her 'I will be gone about a week' to keep the fellow's wife from expecting him, so they would not be hunting for his body. Are these the acts of a sane or an insane man?"

"It might be in a case of insanity, as well as being sane."

Giles shifted in his chair. The doctor was characterizing the behaviors Lankford was describing as something a sane man might do, just as one that was insane. That was doubt the defense did not need.

"Doctor, why do you think Lee Currie sent that telegram to Burley Phillips' wife?" Lankford asked.

"Well, I suppose that was to keep her from expecting him."

"If a man was crazy, why should he do that?"

"Well, I suppose in a case of that kind, he would know her most likely reaction, but I do not know that Lee Currie wasn't crazy or that he was totally insane."

Giles winced. Lankford had rattled Dr. Collins, and his answer likely made no sense whatsoever to the jury. This was going badly.

"Forgetting this case, if a case like that was presented to you where a man kills another for robbery and he robs him and takes everything he has got and buries him and goes the next day twenty-five miles and sends the dead man's wife a telegram, and signs the dead man's name to it, that he would be gone for about a week, so as to keep the fellow's wife from hunting for him, would you say he was crazy and did not know what he was doing?"

Giles had to disrupt this line of questioning. "Objection! He has already asked the witness that question," Giles said.

"Overruled. Counsel is allowed to ask the same question more than once. You know that Col. Giles," Judge Hardeman said, then turned to the witness, "You may answer."

"Well, it still depends on the conditions connected with it. In some conditions, you would find it of an unsound mind. In other conditions, you might find it of a person that had a perfect mind."

"In most cases, would it be a sound or an unsound mind?"

"Objection – calls for speculation," Giles said, without any grounds, desperate to give the doctor time to think before answering.

"Your honor, this witness is an expert in diseases of the mind. We are relying on his experience in examining patients like the defendant. All I am asking about is his judgment based on his professional study of this type of disease," Lankford offered.

"Overruled. You may answer the question," Judge Hardeman ruled.

"I do not know which way it would be in most cases," Dr. Collins answered.

"Okay, let's try this then. Doctor Collins, is it not most likely, that a man who would kill a person, say, on Thursday night and on the next morning, rather than go through the town with the automobile that the dead man owned, through the town where the deceased man's family lived, instead choose not to go the direct route, the nearest route, to go through that town, but rather to take a circuitous route around? Is it not more likely that would be insanity?" Lankford walked over to the defense table and looked directly at Lee Currie. "Or is it just cunningness and shrewdness on that person's part to keep people from seeing the car?"

Dr. Collins shifted nervously in his seat, "It might denote some shrewdness."

"Some shrewdness ..." Lankford turned from Lee and walked over to the witness. "Let me also ask you this, Doctor, do you believe that a person who kills another for robbery and takes his car and everything he has got and buries him and then goes off and sends a telegram back to his wife in the dead man's name in order to fool her, do you believe that person knew right from wrong?"

Giles gripped the table. He knew where Lankford was going with this line of questioning.

"Well, in some instances, that could be where a fellow didn't know right from wrong. In others, they would."

Lankford turned his body and gestured to Lee, "In this case, if a fellow did not know right from wrong, why would he bury the body and conceal it?"

"Well, he buried the body to hide it away, to keep the crime from being detected."

Lankford was animated, "Then he did know right from wrong?"

"Well, he did, yes, in a sense."

"Is it true that in most cases, a paranoiac does not attempt to hide and conceal his crime?"

"Well, in most of the cases, they do."

"As does an ordinary murderer," Lankford said.

"Objection!" Giles practically shouted.

"Sustained. Save your opinions for your closing, Col. Lankford.

Lankford turned and sat down. "No more questions."

Giles stood. He had to remove Lankford's statement as the last impression the jury had of this witness, "One more question, your honor."

"Proceed," Judge Hardeman said.

"Dr. Collins, is it not true that very often a paranoiac is possessed of keen methods of chicanery and sharp tricks even though he is a confirmed paranoiac?"

"Often he is," said Dr. Collins.

"No more questions, your honor," Giles said and sat down.

"Col. Lankford?" Judge Hardeman asked.

George Lankford shook his head. He had done the damage to the witness he wanted to do.

******

"Call your next witness, Col. Giles," Judge Hardeman said.

"The defense calls Mr. James Bugg Partin," Giles said.

The doctors had not been as effective as he had hoped with the medical approach to showing Lee was not in his right mind. The jury's minds were full of medical testimony. Giles now turned to use his remaining witnesses to return the jury to ordinary thinking and show them that Lee was insane and had been so for a long time. If he could put enough doubt in the jury's minds or appeal to their sympathy sufficiently for them to recommend mercy, he might yet save Lee from the gallows.

"Mr. Partin, what is your profession?"

"For seven or eight years, my profession has been that of teaching."

"Do you know the defendant, Lee Currie?"

"Yes."

"How long have you known him?"

"I have known him some seven or eight years."

"Have you ever had him in your class?"

"He has been to school to me about six or seven months, I presume."

"During the time you had Lee Currie in your classroom, did you have a chance to become familiar with his actions and conduct?"

"Yes."

"Please describe those for the jury."

"I could use no power of persuasion over him whatever. Almost anything I wanted to get him to do, he would do the opposite."

"How successful was your use of verbal persuasion of your other students, as compared to Lee Currie, Mr. Partin?"

"Well, I generally got them to do what I wanted them to do, but as to the effect of it on him, it didn't seem to have any."

"Did you repeatedly try to use persuasion with Lee?"

"I had tried for a length of time to concentrate his mind on any one subject, and I had talked to him a few times, but I got no result."

"No results at all?"

"It did not have any results, whatever."

"Did you use punishment to coerce him into doing what you wanted?"

"No, I did not punish him."

"Oh? And why was that?"

"I did not inflict punishment on him because I never could make any impression on him or concentrate his mind at all. I decided there must be something wrong with him."

"Something physically wrong with him?"

"No, something wrong with his mind. If I could not talk it into him, I didn't think I could whip it into him."

"Did Mr. Currie learn his lessons while in school?"

"He didn't learn."

"So, he didn't acquire any benefit from school?"

"None that I was ever able to tell."

"Basing your opinion upon your association as a teacher with him as your pupil and your observation from then to now, would you consider him sane or insane?"

"I don't know as I know much about his sanity, but I have always been of the impression that there was something wrong with his mind. But as to what degree, I do not know. He just did not want to do what I told him to do. It seemed like I couldn't get him to understand hardly what the benefit was for his going to school."

"Mr. Partin, do you think Lee Currie knew the difference between right and wrong when you were teaching him?"

"I never studied medicine, and I'm not one of these experts."

"I'm just asking for your lay opinion as his teacher, Mr. Partin."

"From my observation of him, he knew right from wrong and what he was doing, I guess."

"No further questions," Giles said and sat down.

* * * * * *

Giles next called one of the Currie neighbors, that had known Lee most of his life, to the stand. G. B. Kirkland had also worked Lee and would attest to his work habits.

Kirkland was called to the witness stand and sworn in. Giles approached him.

"Good afternoon, Mr. Kirkland. Do you know the defendant, Lee Currie?"

"Yes, I know him."

"How long have you known him?"

"I have seen him; I have known him for about 18 years."

"So, most of his life. How far did you live from him during the time you have known him?"

"I live about two miles and a half from him. He stayed around my house some."

"For what reason would he stay around your house?"

"I kept him hired there some. I hired him along year before last."

"During those 18 years, did you have an opportunity to observe his conduct from time to time?"

"I 'spose so. He didn't do just like a boy ought to have done; I don't think. But I could get him to do things such as work."

"Was he a pretty good work hand?"

"I could get him to work sometimes, but I couldn't interest him in anything else much."

"Mr. Kirkland, basing your knowledge upon his working for you and your knowing him for the past 18 years, what would you say about his mind?"

"I would say that his mind was not good when he was with me."

"When was that?"

"That was the year before the killing of Mr. Burley Phillips."

Giles gathered his notes and turned to George Lankford. "Your witness."

Lankford gathered up his papers and walked to the lawyer's podium. He looked at the witness, then looked over at the jury.

"Mr. Kirkland, you just testified that Lee Currie's mind was 'not good.' Basing your opinion on your observations of him through the years, would you say he was crazy?" Lankford asked.

"Well, he has got crazy ways, I would say, at times while he was working with me."

Sharpe smiled, and Kirkland nodded at him. Lankford noticed and moved his body between the witness and the defense table.

"Why would you let a crazy man work for you?"

"I didn't say he was crazy; I said he had crazy ways."

"Okay, why would let a man with crazy ways work for you?"

Kirkland smiled and answered, "I had to get any kind of help I could get. I wasn't able to work myself."

"So, you were not able to work, and you had to resort to hiring a man with crazy ways to work for you. Is that what you are trying to tell this jury?"

"He had crazy ways, but he knew how to work, and I needed him."

"Can you give us some examples of those 'crazy ways'?"

"Okay, here's one: Sometimes, the dinner bell would ring, and he would be in the middle of the field. He would get on his horse and ride right through the field. He wouldn't go around the fence. He would go the nearest way to the house."

"And you considered that a crazy way to do it?"

"All people don't do that. I tell you; he hasn't got a good mind."

"Did he know when he got to the house?"

"Yep."

"Did he know right from wrong?"

Kirkland grinned and looked directly at the jury, "I couldn't tell you; I didn't ask him."

Lankford noticed some of the jury members laughing. He walked over to the jury box, and the laughter stopped, "Did you ever see him working, Mr. Kirkland?"

"I seen him do work."

Lankford turned around to face the witness, "Did he know how to work?"

"He would know how to work; he would work some."

Lankford casually walked back over to the podium, "Could he follow directions?"

"He would not know how to do it like you told him to do it all the time."

"So, he was forgetful, Mr. Kirkland?"

"At some things. At times he did not know how to fix his plows right and feed the horses. But he knowed how to cut wood and tote up wood and put out cottonseed."

"Not being able to fix his plows must have put a real strain on you, what with you not being able to work, correct?"

"Sometimes, I fixed his plows for him, and sometimes my boy done it."

"Your boy? Weren't you the least bit frightened to have a man with crazy ways around you and your boy?"

"He never offered to hurt me or him."

"Mr. Kirkland, have you ever been sworn in this case before?"

"No."

"Is it not true that you are a friend of the Currie family and have a personal interest in this case?"

Giles stood up, "Objection, your honor; half of the people in this county are friends of the Currie family and are interested in this case. The prosecution is trying to challenge this witness' integrity just for knowing the Curries."

"Your honor, I'm just trying to ascertain if this witness is in the half that knows him or the half that doesn't, your honor," Lankford retorted.

"Overruled. It's a standard question, Col. Giles; you've asked it yourself in dozens of trials before this one. The witness may answer," Judge Hardeman said.

"I'm not interested in this case. I'm not interested in the defense for Lee Currie."

"And you have never been subpoenaed to testify in the case previously?"

"No."

"How long did Lee Currie work for you?"

"Off and on, for two years there with me."

"Mr. Kirkland, you are under oath. Are you prepared to swear before this jury that, in your opinion Lee Currie is crazy?"

Kirkland's face reddened, "I didn't say he was crazy – how many times do I have to tell you that? I said he hasn't got his right mind at times."

"And at other times?"

"I guess he would have his right mind at times."

"You guess? The man worked for you for two years. Have you ever seen him when he has his right mind?"

Kirkland tried to look to Sharpe as if seeking direction on how to answer, but Lankford again blocked his view of the defense table.

"I don't know as I have seen him when he has had his right mind."

"So, is it your testimony that he has been crazy all his life?"

"Again, I didn't say he was crazy. He has just got crazy ways."

"Lots of people have crazy ways, but they don't go around killing people."

"Objection!" Giles shouted.

"Sustained, the jury will disregard Mr. Lankford's statement. Watch yourself, Counselor," Judge Hardeman said.

"Isn't it true that Lee Currie has got just as much sense as anyone else?"

"I don't know about that. He is not the craziest acting fellow that I have ever seen. I have seen people that was crazier acting than that."

"Have you seen plenty of people with less sense than Lee Currie?"

"I don't know whether I have seen plenty of people that had less sense than he had and go right along. He has just got crazy ways."

Lankford couldn't rattle this witness. He suspected that Kirkland was better prepped to be on the witness stand than the doctors. Score one for the defense, he thought to himself, but this is just a neighbor, and his testimony was unlikely to carry any weight with the jury.

"No more questions, your honor," Lankford said and sat down.

* * * * * *

"The defense calls Mr. Isaac Roos to the witness stand," Giles announced.

Lee smiled and waved at Isaac as he was brought into the room. He turned and said to Sharpe, "That's my friend from the jail." Sharpe shushed him.

Giles began his questioning, "Mr. Roos, where do you live?"

"I live in Savannah."

"What is your profession?"

"I am assistant sheriff in Chatham County jail."

"What are your duties at the jail?"

"Looking after prisoners. I have been jailer there for about two years now."

"During that time, have you handled a lot of prisoners?"

"I guess I have handled two or three thousand prisoners in the Chatham County jail; I couldn't tell you exactly how many."

"Do you know the defendant, in this case, Lee Currie?"

"Yes, I have known him, I guess – nearly a year now."

"Have you had very many opportunities to observe him over that time, Mr. Roos?"

"He has been under my constant observation since that time; I saw him day and night."

"Can you describe his actions while he was in your charge?"

"Well, he is a man that has been very unruly; you could not manage him at times. Sometimes, he was good. When he was good, he was real good, and he was really bad when he was bad."

"How was he bad?"

"He tried to fuss with everybody. I had to lock him up in solitary two or three times. He would go in the cell and holler and scream, and then I would go around and see him again, and he would ask me what I got him locked up for. He did not recall from time to time, and I would tell him it was for misbehaving. He would say, 'If you will let me out, I will behave myself.'"

"From your observation of him and his conduct since he has been in the Chatham County jail for the past year and comparing him to all the other prisoners you have observed, have you formed any opinion of whether Mr. Currie is insane?"

"In my opinion, I think he is insane; the way he acted, yep, his actions showed that he is insane."

"Your witness," Giles said and returned to the defense table.

Lankford had observed Lee waving to the witness when he entered the courtroom and overheard Lee telling Sharpe that he was friends with the witness. This could help discredit his testimony. He went right for the jugular.

"Mr. Roos, is it not true that you have a personal interest in this case and have become friends with Lee Currie?"

The question caught Isaac off guard, and he quickly glanced at the defense table. Lee was smiling at him and gave another small wave. Sharpe grabbed Lee's hand and pushed it down.

"I'm not at all interested in this case; I have no interest in Currie at all, nothing. I never knew him until we had him in jail."

"Have you not encouraged him to write letters to get something done for him?"

"No."

"You don't have a particular interest in him?"

"I don't feel any particular interest in him, only seeing him there and all, but nothing particular."

"Is it not true that while he has been in jail all this time, you have become very much attached to him?"

"No."

"Do you ever become attached to the prisoners you keep?"

"Well, we do sometimes when we have prisoners, but I have not become very much attached to him – no more than any other prisoner."

"Do you dislike Lee?"

"No, I don't dislike the boy. He is a very good man physically. He is a good wrestler."

"A good wrestler. Does he box too?"

"I don't know whether he is a good boxer or not, but he is a pretty good wrestler."

Grey gestured for Lankford to come over. He showed him a piece of paper, and Lankford picked it up. He turned to the witness.

"Is it not true that he has thrown down every prisoner that you have put in the jail with him?"

"I do not know that he has thrown down nearly every prisoner that I put in jail. I know that he has thrown down some pretty big ones."

"I'll bet he has. No further questions, your honor."

* * * * * *

"Your honor, the defendant wishes to make a statement," Giles announced.

Judge Hardeman spoke up, "Gentlemen of the jury, Mr. Currie is not being called as a witness in this case; however, every defendant has a right to make a statement in his defense. Neither the prosecution nor the defense may ask him any questions during his statement, and you may give what he says whatever weight you think it merits.

"You may make your statement, Mr. Currie."

Lee Currie looked at Sharpe, who smiled and gestured for him to take the witness stand. He did.

"Well, gentlemen of the jury, I am charged with killing Burley Phillips, and I can prove and tell why I killed him.

"I met him, me and him was going out in the country, and I was to give him a quart of whiskey for going out there, and we got out nearly to the place where we could get the whiskey, and we couldn't cross the creek.

Lee looked across at Sharpe, who smiled and gestured for him to continue.

"It had rained the evening before, and he wanted to turn around and go back, and he didn't want to go on and get the whiskey. So, I wouldn't agree to pay him what he wanted me to pay him without going on and getting the whiskey, and so me and him got in an argument.

"I was starting out in front of the car, had my hands on the radiator."

A couple of the jurors looked puzzled. Lee noticed and continued, "It was cold. So, me and him got into arguing, first one way and then another, and I wouldn't agree, and he wouldn't agree, and finally, he said he was going to beat hell out of me if I didn't pay him, and so I told him, 'You dirty son-of-a-bitch, if you can do it, crawl out.' So, he crawled out. He run his hand for his pocketknife. As he was opening his knife, I fired at him twice. The first time I missed him, and the next time I struck him, and that is the way that the ball wound up.

"There is one statement that Mack Wimberley made that was false. He absolutely never heard no such statement, and there was several others made that set right here in this chair, and it was made, and as far as the money matters, there never was a money matter spoke."

Lee looked at the jury and then around the courtroom. "I guess that is about all I want to state," he said and stood up. He looked at the judge, then the jury – nodded, smiled, and returned to the defense table.

* * * * * *

"How'd I do?" Lee asked Sharpe as he sat down.

The lawyer smiled, patted him on his arm, and said, "You did good, Lee. You did good."

"The defense rests, your honor," Giles stood and said.

"Gentlemen of the jury, we are going to adjourn for the day and then reconvene tomorrow to hear the closing arguments of counsel. Remember that you are not to discuss this case with anyone or among yourselves until it has been given to you for deliberation. You will be taken to the Elberta Hotel for supper and overnight accommodation. Let the bailiff know if you have any special needs. We will see you in the morning.

"We are in recess until 9 a.m. tomorrow morning," Judge Hardeman said and rapped his gavel.

Chapter 46

Back at his law office, Walter Grey felt there was no need to deviate from the closing argument that he and George Lankford crafted for the first trial. There was no new evidence, and even the new witnesses just collaborated with what other witnesses had said.

Walter suspected, and felt that George agreed, that the insanity defense put forward with great effort by Giles & Sharpe would not move this jury to a different conclusion. The jurors' faces told the story during the testimony of the defense's key witness, Dr. John Hall. They were not buying it. He was confident that each juror believed that Lee Currie killed Burley Phillips in cold blood and needed to be hanged for it.

"Here's what I think we need to add to the closing," George said as he slid a couple of pieces of paper across the desk toward the Solicitor General.

Walter picked it up and read it, sipping coffee as he carefully studied George's recommended addition to the first trial's summation. He could feel George observing him, looking for any sign of approval or disapproval. Walter slowly turned the page and continued reading without any expression. Finally, he laid the papers on the table.

"Brilliant," Walter said without emotion.

George let out his breath, "I'm open to any suggestions you think would improve it."

"Nope, I'm not going to change a thing. I think it will work fine. Let me test it on you, where you can see how it sounds," Walter said.

George sat back in his chair, "You have the full attention of this jury of one, counselor."

Walter stood up and walked to the practice podium to test their opening and closing arguments.

"The defense has a problem. There is clear and unmistakable evidence that the defendant killed Burley Phillips to steal his car, buried him afterward, and took extraordinary steps to conceal his crime. The defendant freely admitted as much to the law officers, who did not offer any reward or promise any punishment to get him to say what he did.

"And thus, their problem. How do you get a jury of twelve men to abandon their common sense and ignore everything they have seen and heard in this trial? Their solution to the problem? Convince each of you that Lee Currie is insane and not responsible for his actions. How convenient.

"Psychology is a new and relatively unknown branch of study. There are few diplomas offered for the study of psychology. Professors teach it as an elective course in most medical schools. A few books are available that certain doctors may pick up and read, but it is not a recognized discipline of medicine worthy of a degree being awarded, at least not in Georgia. Perhaps they might have specialists up north or across the ocean, but not here. The defense would like you to grant 'expert witness' status to men who took one of these psychology courses as an elective while pursuing their medical degree, but are they experts? Or are they perhaps lured by the growing demand for medical experts who can help get wealthy clientele a 'not guilty' verdict in court, despite their obvious guilt?

"Consider for a moment what the doctors are asking you to believe. The defendant had no resistive power to his urges. When he saw something he wanted, like that Baby Overland automobile, anyone standing between him and the object of his desires was doomed.

"Is this a paranoiac, or is it a spoiled child whose parents indulged him and never told him 'No'?

"The doctors have tried to convince you that the defendant suffers from a disease that ordinary people cannot detect until the paranoiac kills someone. But does that pass the smell test? Following that line of reasoning, defense lawyers could argue that ANYONE who murders or commits a crime is insane, if only for a moment. No one could ever be held accountable for their crimes ever again. We could just shut down the court system, abandon our laws altogether, and return to the chaos that existed before men adopted laws and societal norms to govern each other's behavior.

"No, what the doctor's testimony proved is that the defendant is spoiled and reckless. He contracted a loathsome venereal disease and gave it to his wife. Is that the actions of a paranoiac or an adulterer? He rode his horse straight for the fence across the crops when he heard the dinner bell ring instead of going around the field. Is that the actions of a paranoiac or a hungry man with no respect for property? He buries his victim alive. Is that a paranoiac's actions or a depraved man with no regard for human life desperately trying to conceal his crime?

"Use your common sense; how is the defendant any different from any ordinary murderer if there is such a thing? Don't most murderers try to conceal their crimes? And this was the worst kind of murder. This was not a crime of passion, where the emotions overcome the killer. This was not a jealous husband finding his wife in the arms of a lover and killing him. This was a cold, calculated, premeditated murder to obtain property that belonged to another person.

"The defendant did not have an immediate urge and act on it because he had no resistive power. He had been thinking about this long in advance of carrying out his crime. He told Lloyd Jones early in the day of the murder that he was '... on a trade for a little Overland.' He bought bullets for his gun that same day and had them filed off where they would fit his weapon because he didn't want to wait to order the correct ammunition. Yes, this was no passing urge that he couldn't resist. He planned this murder well in advance and carried it out as methodically as any murderer might have.

"You should have recognized this defense as a sham as soon as the doctor started telling you about the shape of the defendant's skull. Scientists discredited phrenology as a scientific theory in the 1840s! Dr. Hall even tried to tell you that the defendant was not 'symmetrical' or that his reflexes were exaggerated as evidence his brain was diseased. What kind of hocus pocus is that? Use your common sense.

"Think about what they are asking you to do. The defense wants you to accept that the defendant had a disease of the mind that nobody, but a trained expert could see. The defense wants you to accept that this disease could not be properly diagnosed until after the afflicted man killed someone. The defense wants you to accept that the diseased mind's possessor had no resistive power to stop himself from killing someone and should be institutionalized as a sick person instead of being held accountable for his heinous crime. They are asking you to abandon your common sense. Yes, that's what they want you to do, ignore all you know about justice and accept a cockamamie theory that defies logic and, yes, common sense.

"You might call this a Biblical defense. The defense has no proof that Lee Currie is insane, so they want you to take it on faith. Well, my Bible demands an 'eye for an eye and a tooth for a tooth.'

"This is not a complicated story. It's relatively simple. Lee Currie wanted a car that belonged to Burley Phillips; he methodically planned his murder, killed his victim, cruelly buried him alive, and then took elaborate steps to cover his crime.

"Don't be fooled by the doctors, or the teachers, or the neighbors. The defendant is a menace to our community – he killed one of our citizens – and he should be punished for his crime to the fullest extent of the law."

Walter looked up at his law partner. Chills ran over him. It was an excellent addition to their closing argument from the first trial.

"It sounds even better than it reads. I don't think we should change a word."

George stood up and shook Walter's hand. The two men grabbed their hats and headed for the courthouse without another word between them. Walter had his closing argument.

* * * * * *

Enoch Giles knew he had an uphill battle with this jury. During the prosecution's closing argument, he had seen several of the men shaking their heads in agreement as

Walter Grey delivered one of the most compelling arguments for a guilty verdict he had ever heard. But Enoch didn't need to instill doubt in all of the jury members' minds. He just needed to convince one to break from the others.

"Gentlemen of the jury, there are no winners in this trial. Two families have been devastated over what happened on February 19, 1920. Tersia Phillips lost a husband, Thomas Phillips lost a brother, the Vidalia community lost a prominent citizen.

"The Currie family has also suffered a loss. Throughout this entire ordeal, nobody has been more tormented than John Currie, the defendant's father. He has been living in pure hell, asking himself what he could have done differently in raising his son, blaming himself for the actions of a young man who was doomed from the day he was born.

"The signs were there from the beginning. As J. B. Partin testified, Lee Currie could not concentrate on his studies, incapable of being persuaded to do anything to further his education. The teacher ruled out punishment as ineffective against a student that couldn't associate his misdeeds with their consequences.

"Think about that for a moment. Effectively, Lee Currie had no formal education as a child. He probably never read the Bible, either. He was not able to absorb the wisdom that mine and your teachers drilled into each of us. He reached adulthood unpossessed of the general knowledge that serves each of us to mind our behavior and guarantees our success in the real world.

"Where do each of us learn what is proper and acceptable in our communities? Where do we master the rules of polite conversation, manners, and respect for others' property? We learn it at home, certainly, but much of it comes from our schools and churches.

"Lee Currie's inability to concentrate on his teachings left him with a set of rules of his own making. You've heard his language. Even in this proper court of law, with its high standards for decorum and respect, the defendant was unaware of the polite standards of speech and the inappropriateness of the profanity he used before you, the jury, while making his statement. Would a sane man, on trial for his life, stand up and curse like that before a jury of Lyons' finest citizens? Or does it show that his mind is so defective and diseased that he lacks the training in societal norms or force of will that restrain the rest of us from making such utterances?

"The limitations his mental disease imposed upon him were apparent when he tried to make a living as an employee for J. B. Kirkland, who testified that he could get him to work sometimes, but he could only keep him engaged in just a few simple chores. He even gave the example of the defendant's errant behavior when called in from the field to eat dinner, saying he would ride right through the field, damaging the crops instead of going around the fence. The prosecution would like you to think that odd behavior just proved Lee was hungry and had no respect for property, but the doctors' testimony should show you that this was another example of how the defendant could not correctly channel his behavior when going after something he wanted."

Enoch walked to the defense table and picked up a book. "One of the fathers of psychology, Sigmund Freud, in his work 'Project for Scientific Psychology,' published in 1895, described the mind as having three parts, the 'id,' the 'ego,' and the 'superego,' all developing at different stages in our lives.

"According to Freud's model of the mind, the id is the primitive and instinctual part. It controls our quest for food when we are hungry, our need for shelter, our sexual and other aggressive drives, and hidden memories. The superego operates as a moral conscience. The ego is the realistic manager of the mind that mediates between the id's base desires and the restraints of rules, laws, and norms harbored in the superego," Enoch said as he closed the book and returned it to the defense table.

"The first part of our brain to develop is the id. As babies, we cry when we are hungry, and our mother magically appears from out of nowhere and feeds us. We see food on the table and grab it with our fingers and gulp it down without concern for whether everyone else has been served. We see the id at work in children all the time.

"But as we get older, we learn appropriate behavior from our parents, teachers, and churches. The superego develops through training and experience to guide us to wait our turn in the serving line at the homecoming table, to not take a second piece of chicken until everyone has had some, and generally to become polite and mannerly members of a civilized society.

"What Freud likes to call the 'ego,' I prefer to call judgment. Our basic instincts, driven by the id's demands, are in constant conflict with the morals advocated by the superego. The ego must decide the realistic course of action between the two competing parts of our mind.

"But what if a disease of the mind prevented your superego from ever learning society's rules? What if your inability to concentrate prohibited you from learning those complex ideas of what constitutes acceptable behavior or patience? Your id, with which you were born, is making its incessant demands upon you, your ego can figure out how to satisfy those demands, but your superego is not there to guide you to use appropriate means.

"The defendant has no superego like you or me. The disease he was born with has prevented him from developing one while growing up. Dr. Hall said he was a moron with the intelligence of a 12 to 14-year-old. Do we hang 12-year-olds when they kill someone, not knowing any better?

"Col. Grey asked you to discount the medical professionals' testimony, medical professionals who have studied the mind's diseases for over a decade, but is that good advice? I know the nuances of paranoia and its manifestations are difficult to comprehend, but do you require your doctor to explain cancer's intricacies when you or someone you love has been diagnosed with that disease? Do you demand to know how he concluded you have diabetes, or your child has colic? Do you question his character because he charges a fee for his services? Or do you trust that his formal training and his Hippocratic oath bind him to give a proper diagnosis and give you the best advice possible to restore you or your loved one to good health?

"No, the prosecution would coax you into ignoring the doctor's diagnosis regarding what is wrong with Lee Currie and judge his behavior on your observations as a layperson. Think about that for a moment. Can you look at a person and tell his kidneys are failing or discern the cause of a rash on his body? No, for that, you go to your doctor and rely on his skill and knowledge to properly diagnose your ailment and the proper course of treatment.

"Remember what Dr. Freud said about the id and the ego. Just these two parts of your brain are perfectly capable of causing you to behave normally. Children for whom the superego is a work in progress can cover up their misdeeds. How often have your children broken one of their mother's fine China dishes and dumped the pieces in the woods to avoid their mother's wrath? How many brothers have blamed their wrongdoing on another brother to escape punishment? The lengths to which children will go to hide their misdeeds is an object of humor as well as scorn, and it demonstrates that individuals with undeveloped minds are still capable of cunning and deception.

"From birth, the defendant's mind has been diseased. It did not develop normally, and he did not develop those constraints of behavior that characterize mature men.

"J. B. Partin said discipline was ineffective on the defendant when Lee was one of his students in school. J. B. Kirkland said he could work, but I quote, '... he didn't do just like a boy ought to have done.'

"His jailer for the last year, Isaac Roos, said he would lock him up in solitary confinement, and Lee couldn't remember why he was being punished. When I told Lee that he would hang for killing Burley Phillips, it didn't faze him. Dr. Hall testified that Lee's being unconcerned about being hanged and being more concerned about a red-headed man who was in jail for murder like he was, proved his inability to understand the negative consequences of his actions.

"Dr. Hall has testified that the defendant has no powers of resistance. He also said the defendant had no remorse or conscience at all. This power of resistance, this lack of remorse, is controlled by the superego, which Dr. Freud describes, and which is absent from the defendant's brain because of the disease afflicting him.

"If a man allows a woman to fall off a train because he has only one arm and no means of grabbing her and holding on at the same time, is he guilty of negligence? If a poison is left where the sugar bowl is usually placed, and a blind man mixes it in his children's cereal by accident, is he guilty of murder? How, then, can a man with a diseased brain that has no superego restraining him be found guilty of malice murder?

"Certainly, the defendant should not be released back into society, as he is a danger to himself and others, but he deserves to be institutionalized, not put to death. He should no more be put to death than a child should be executed for picking up a gun and, thinking it to be a toy, accidentally killing a sibling.

"Lee Currie made a statement that he killed Burley Phillips in self-defense. I was not there, and you were not there. We will never know the truth of his account. Mack Wimberley testified that Lee told him that he killed Burley Phillips down by the Cobb Creek Baptist Church. I was not there when that statement was allegedly made, and you were not there. We will never know the truth of that statement, either.

"But irrespective of which statement is true, one thing is for sure – Lee Currie is mentally defective. Whether that mental defect caused him to shoot a man coming at him with a knife or shoot a man looking at a church, his actions were motivated by a mind inadequately developed to appropriately guide his actions, a diseased mind, and an insane mind.

"It would be unconscionable for you to find Lee Currie guilty of murder in the first degree, as that would imply that he was entirely in control of his mental faculties and responsible for his actions. It would be a travesty of justice for you to sentence a mentally handicapped man to the gallows. Put him where he belongs – in an asylum for the remainder of his life."

Enoch slowly scanned the jury box and looked at each juror, "I know you will do what is right."

* * * * * *

Judge Hardeman carefully instructed the jury. His first verdict had been overturned due to an improper charge, and he desperately did not want to see this case return to his court again. He had carefully crafted a new charge and reviewed it with both the prosecution and the defense. He was past ready for this case to be over and done with.

"Gentlemen of the jury, it is almost 5:00 p.m. You have heard my charge to you of the law applicable to this case. I know you want to get back to your everyday lives as soon as possible, but the court needs your services for a bit longer. The bailiff will take you to supper and your lodgings and then return you to the jury room by 9:00 a.m. to begin your deliberations.

"I will be here should you need my assistance regarding what the law is for this case. Do you have any questions?

"Hearing none, I leave you to your evening meal. Get some rest tonight and remember that you should not begin your deliberations until tomorrow morning when you have returned to the jury room. Bailiff, attend to our jurors. Court is in recess until 9:00 a.m. tomorrow."

* * * * * *

The jury convened at 9:00 a.m. on Thursday, March 3, 1921. Lunch was sent into the jury room at noon. At 1:00 a.m., after four hours of deliberation, the jury sent word to Judge Hardeman that they had reached a verdict. As they filed back into the courtroom, all eyes were upon them. Each juror was looking at the floor as he walked.

"Have you reached a verdict?" Judge Hardeman asked the jury foreman.

The foreman stood, "We have, your honor."

"Will the defendant please rise and face the jury," Judge Hardeman directed.

Enoch Giles and T. Ross Sharpe rose. At T. Ross' prompting, Lee Currie also rose, looked at each of them, and then at the jury. John Currie stood as well.

"On the count of murder in the first degree, how do you find the defendant?" Judge Hardeman asked.

"Guilty," the foreman said.

"So, say you all?" the Judge asked.

Every man in the jury box nodded in ascent. John Currie sat down heavily and began to sob. Lula put her arms around him to comfort him, but she also cried.

"Gentlemen of the jury, I thank you for your service to the community and this court. You are dismissed," Judge Hardeman said.

"Is it over?" Lee asked.

T. Ross answered, "Not yet, Lee, not yet."

"Court will be in recess for one hour. Bailiff, remand Mr. Currie to the county jail to await sentencing at that time," Judge Hardeman said.

* * * * * *

At 2:15 p.m., Judge Hardeman reconvened his court. "Will the defendant please rise," Judge Hardeman said.

Lee and his two attorneys stood.

"The jury, having rendered a verdict of guilty without recommendation, it is, therefore, the judgment of the Court that you, Lee Currie, be taken from the courthouse to the common jail of Toombs County or to such other place as the proper authorities of Toombs County may direct for safekeeping, and that you be kept there in close confinement, until Friday, the 22nd day of April 1921, and that on said date, between the hours of ten o'clock a.m. and two o'clock p.m. at the common jail of Toombs County, in the presence of the Sheriff and such guard as he may deem sufficient, and in the presence of such of your relatives and friends as you may desire and designate, and in the presence of such minister or ministers of the gospel as you may desire and the physicians hereinafter named, otherwise in private, that you be, by the Sheriff of Toombs County, hung by the neck until you are dead, and may the Lord have mercy upon your soul."

Chapter 47

On Friday, March 4, 1921, the next day, after a jury had found him guilty in a second trial, Enoch Giles filed a motion for a third trial for Lee Currie. Judge Hardeman set a hearing date on the Motion for March 30, 1921.

* * * * * *

Enoch had prepared his motion for a new trial when T. Ross walked into his office.

"Glad you're here, T. Ross. Let's go over these six grounds for our appeal that I've drafted. I want your honest opinion about how I have them framed and don't worry about critiquing your senior partner. You can't hurt my feelings on something as important as this," Enoch told his law partner.

"Let's hear what you've got," T. Ross said as he sat down across the conference desk from Enoch.

"My first ground for appeal is Judge Hardeman's failure to charge the jury they must acquit Lee if they find that he had a mental disease and didn't have sufficient willpower to refrain from shooting Burley," Enoch said.

"Didn't the judge cover that in other parts of his charge?" T. Ross asked.

"That's what he will no doubt contend, but I want to state it, nonetheless.

"My second grounds puts a finer point on it and says that, in order to constitute a crime, a man must have intelligence and capacity enough to have a criminal intent and purpose," Enoch said.

"He's not going to buy that argument, Enoch. Again, Judge Hardeman's general charge covered that."

"I know, but I'm not just aiming this at the judge. I fully expect that he will deny my motion for a new trial, and I want this language to be laid before the Supreme Court."

"Makes sense. What else you got?"

"My third ground for appeal is that Judge Hardeman told the jury their only choice of verdicts was to convict Lee of murder or to acquit him. With that, the judge effectively ruled out the jury's being able to find Lee guilty of the lesser charges of either voluntary or involuntary manslaughter. Being convicted of either of those charges would save him from the noose. It would be an expected verdict if the jury believes the story that Lee told McLeod while he was the sheriff. That is, the story that Burley came after him with a knife and he had to defend himself."

T. Ross pondered for a moment, "Yeah, I'm still puzzled about Judge Hardeman's refusal in both the first and the second trial to consider manslaughter as a possible jury option. A manslaughter conviction would take hanging off the table for sure. You think he'll go for it?"

"No, and I don't think the Supreme Court will either since they didn't during the first appeal," Enoch sighed.

"You might catch them in a better mood this time, so let's leave it in there. It can't hurt. What's number four?" T. Ross asked.

"I'm not real happy with this one, but I'm going to include it anyway unless you think I shouldn't. I'm going to maintain that Judge Hardeman should grant a new trial because he did not state in his charge that the evidence of insanity could be considered with the other evidence in determining whether or not the defendant was guilty beyond a reasonable doubt and that if considering all the evidence, including the evidence of insanity, the jury entertained a reasonable doubt as to the defendant's guilt they should acquit him."

"I'm not sure I even understand what that means," T. Ross said.

Enoch laughed. "It's called a 'kitchen sink' grounds for appeal. I'm leaving it in.

"For my fifth ground, I am hitting on that same theme and maintaining that Judge Hardeman erred in his charge that 'If the State shows that the defendant did the things that constitute murder, convict him unless he carries the burden then of showing, by the preponderance of the evidence, that he is not mentally responsible for the act that the State charges he committed.'"

"How is that any different than ground four?" T. Ross asked.

"Because Hardeman did not tell the jury that our evidence of insanity could show a reasonable doubt that Lee understood what he was doing. The judge effectively excluded all the testimony about Lee's sanity. We need that in the appeal for the Supreme Court to consider."

"I'm not sure they will buy that, Enoch. There are several places in the charge where the judge tells them to consider that evidence."

"You think I should take it out?"

"No, as you said, Hardeman will probably deny our request for a new trial, and we will appeal it to the Supreme Court. Our whole case revolves around proving Lee was not guilty by reason of insanity. We need to keep insisting that the judge didn't take our defense seriously and his attitude biased the jury against us. The insanity defense is a hard sell, we knew that from the beginning, but it must be an all-or-nothing argument. We are plowing new ground here, counselor. Let's do everything we can to keep that at the forefront of this case. Besides, if we win on appeal, Judge Hardeman will be forced to change his charge on the next trial to accommodate our insanity defense.

"Tell me what you have for your last grounds. I can't wait to hear that," T. Ross said.

"I'm going to maintain that Lee did not get a fair and impartial trial because jury member Wade Mitchum is the illegitimate third cousin of Burley Phillips."

T. Ross jumped out of his chair. "What? Where the hell did you get that information?"

Enoch held up a piece of paper by one corner and waved it, smiling broadly.

"What's that?" T. Ross asked as he sat back down.

"This, my good man, is an affidavit of M. M. Williamson."

"Quit teasing me and read the damn thing!" T. Ross demanded gleefully.

Enoch put on his spectacles back on and started reading. "I am 60 years old and a citizen of Toombs County, and I am a son of Lecy Williamson. My mother, Lecy Williamson, and Millie Phillips were own sisters; that Millie Phillips; was my aunt and was the mother of Ephraim Phillips; and that Ephraim Phillips was the father of Burley Phillips. That me and Burley Phillips are second cousins. That me and A. S. Williamson were brothers and that Lecy Williamson was A. S. Williamson's mother. That A. S. Williamson is the father of Wade Mitchum, and that Wade Mitchum was one of the jurors who tried the case of the State vs. Lee Currie, at the May adjourned term of Toombs superior court, 1922, charged with the killing of Burley Phillips, in which case a verdict of guilty was returned by the jury trying the same, against the same, against Lee Currie.

"It is common repute in the community that A. S. Williamson is Wade Mitchum's father, and that A. S. Williamson does not deny the same, in fact, admits it. That Wade Mitchum admits the same and calls A. S. Williamson Daddy and calls me Uncle; and I have attached hereto an order written by Wade Mitchum to me in which he addresses me as "Dear Uncle." A. S. Williamson is second cousin to Burley Phillips, and Wade Mitchum was third cousin to Burley Phillips whom Lee Currie was on trial for killing."

"Wow!" T. Ross exclaimed. "You were just teasing me with those other grounds. This is bound to get us a retrial!"

Enoch smiled and held up another piece of paper. "There's more. This is an affidavit of F. B. Williamson, in which he swears, 'That Wade Mitchum is the reputed son of A. S. Williamson. That the mother of Wade Mitchum swore that A. S. Williamson was the father of Wade Mitchum; and it is generally reputed in the community and is common repute therein that A. S. Williamson is the father of Wade Mitchum, and that A. S. Williamson admits the same. That Wade Mitchum resembles very much A. S. Williamson, talks and acts like him, and to the best of my knowledge and belief A. S. Williamson is Wade Mitchum's father.'"

"Enoch, you're a genius!" T. Ross exclaimed and slapped the conference desk.

Enoch held up the third piece of paper. "But I am not done yet; check this out. This is an affidavit of A. S. Williamson, who says, 'I am 54 years of age and a citizen of Toombs County, and I am a son of Lecy Williamson. That my mother, Lecy Williamson, and Millie Phillips were own sisters. That Millie Phillips was my aunt and was the mother of Ephraim Phillips, and that Ephraim Phillips was Burley Phillips' father. That Burley Phillips and I were second cousins. That I am the father of Wade Mitchum, or at least his reputed father, the mother of the said Wade Mitchum having sworn that I was the father of Wade Mitchum, and it being common repute in the neighborhood and generally recognized that I am the father of Wade Mitchum, which fact is admitted and recognized by me.'"

"By damn, we have an unreported filial relationship of one of the jurors to the deceased. If that won't get us a new trial, nothing will. How did you get these affidavits without my knowing about it?" T. Ross asked.

"I have my sources, my good partner," Enoch said and laughed.

"Come on, Enoch – spill," T. Ross pressed.

"Actually, John Currie brought this relationship to my attention. I've been busy all week getting the affidavits drafted, signed, and witnessed."

"That's why you are the senior partner in this firm," T. Ross said and smiled.

* * * * * *

At a hearing held on March 30, 1921, Judge Robert Hardeman denied Giles & Sharp's Motion for a new trial for Lee Currie. Enoch immediately filed an appeal with the Georgia Supreme Court. That filing automatically stayed the execution until the appeal could be heard. Again, they had bought Lee some more time.

Fearing the Phillips family and their friends might become impatient with these legal delays, Sheriff Culpepper transported Lee back to the Chatham jail for safekeeping.

* * * * * *

Lilly Currie could no longer carry the burden of being married to a man convicted of murder and sentenced to be hanged. Even more difficult was knowing that the whispers she could sense everywhere she went were that her husband had been characterized in court as a moron with the mind of a 12-year-old.

Aunt Sarah reminded her that she was married to that "moron," which was a poor reflection. Lilly had become resolute. Irrespective of the consequences of going back into society as a divorced and barren woman, she wanted nothing more to do with Lee Currie, or even Toombs County, for that matter. She now desired to leave everyone who knew her and move as far away from all this as possible.

Lilly was not running into resistance from her family this time for wanting to leave Lee. Solomon appeared to have accepted that she was about to become the widow of an executed murderer and would have little claim to the Currie estate. Thankfully, he now seemed supportive of whatever she felt she had to do.

So did Raymond Smith, and with both him and her Aunt Sarah now helping her, Lilly once more filed for a divorce.

Lee's divorce attorney had tried to forestall the action by representing to the court that Lee was suffering from the disability of not being able to appear in court to defend himself. However, this didn't impress the court, and on August 22, 1921, a jury found no need to "remove the disabilities" of Lee Currie and granted Lilly the divorce she wanted. She may be barren, but she was finally free of the disturbed man she had made the mistake of marrying.

* * * * * *

John Currie traveled to Savannah to give his son the bad news. He passed the divorce decree to Lee through the Chatham County prison bars. Lee gave a puzzled look to his father.

"Read the opening paragraph, son," the elder Currie said.

Lee looked down at the document and glanced back up at his father, his puzzlement still evident in his facial expression. He looked back down and started reading. His father braced himself for the inevitable reaction, which was coming up soon, judging from his son's lips that were moving as he read.

"Cruel treatment? Are you shitting me?" Lee shouted in disbelief. Lee's elevated voice caused the others in the sheriff's jail visiting room to stare.

"Watch your mouth, Lee," Isaac Roos said calmly from across the room.

Lee turned his head quickly to his jailer and said, "And what are you going to do about it, Isaac? I'll say what I please, and, besides, you'd cuss too if you just found out your wife is divorcing you and you were in this stinking place and unable to go stop it!"

This explanation got no response from Isaac.

Lee turned back to his father and pleaded, "Pa, you have to stop this. Everybody is abandoning me!"

John Currie took his son's hand, "Lee, not everybody. I will never abandon you if it takes every last cent of what I own. We will beat this thing, come one way or another. I know it in my heart."

Lee pulled his hand back. "Yeah, right, like those piss ant lawyers you hired are going to get me out of here. They have lost my case two times now. Hell, they are probably on the take from the prosecutor, and now my wife is leaving me. I'm screwed!"

"They are confident they can get this last case overturned in the Supreme Court, Lee, and we must be honest. It was just a matter of time before Lilly was going to leave you. She tried it once before when you cheated on her ..."

"Don't bring that crap up, Pa," Lee interrupted.

"I'm serious, Lee. You may have left her barren with your philandering, and now she is having to deal with the shame of all this trial mess. Her heart just wasn't in the marriage anymore, and she wanted out."

"Damn, Pa, whose side are you on? What about that till death do you part oath she took? Don't that mean nothin'?"

"She's a young girl, son, and having to deal with something that would be a struggle for women twice her age. Let her go. Besides, you don't need a wife that is not completely supportive of you," John said.

Lee turned and kicked the bunk bed in his cell, which elicited a stern look from Isaac, but John held his hand out to him as if pleading for forbearance since Lee was having a moment and needed to be left alone.

"She's a bitch, that's what she is; leave a man when he is down on his luck like this," Lee said.

"She's the least of your worries right now, Lee. Enoch and T. Ross are working hard to get you a new trial and get you out of here. Think about that instead of Lilly," John said.

"Okay, but when they get me out of here, Pa, I'm going to kill her," Lee said.

"And you would wind up right back in here if you did that, Lee. Now stop this crazy talk and tell me how you are getting along."

* * * * * *

By early February of 1922, it had been almost six months since Lilly divorced Lee. Isaac Roos had observed him growing so angry about his continuing incarceration and so disruptive that the sheriff had taken extraordinary measures to keep him away from the other inmates. His hostility toward everyone earned him a significant amount of time in solitary confinement, so he appeared beyond excited as Isaac approached his cell.

"Lee, you got company," Isaac announced.

"Pa was just here yesterday, and he's already back?" Lee asked.

"It's not your pa. It's a reporter from the Savannah Morning News. You want to talk to him?" Isaac asked.

Lee jumped up from his cell bunk and stepped so quickly over to the bars that Isaac moved back instinctively.

"Hell, yeah. I'll talk to him. I want people to know how badly y'all been treatin' me in this hell hole!" Lee snapped.

"Ain't nobody being mistreated but us poor guards who have to put up with your sorry ass," Isaac laughed.

"Sit tight, Lee. I'll get him for you. Now, don't you go bad-mouthing me while you are talking to him, or I won't let you wrestle anymore, you hear me?" Isaac said and laughed again as he turned to get the reporter.

Jim Jacobs was both pleased and apprehensive to have been selected by his editor to interview Lee. The Currie trial was being reported by practically every newspaper in Georgia, and, with Lee incarcerated in Savannah; his editor had insisted that his paper should be leading the coverage. Jim knew the pressure was on to get an interview with Currie, but he had also heard the tales about Lee's volatility.

The sheriff, enjoying the publicity that comes with housing such an infamous inmate in his prison, had agreed to allow Lee to be interviewed. The editor of the Savannah Morning News wasted no time assigning Jacobs the interview.

Jim began doing his research on Lee's background for the interview. Lee had lost in two trials, but the Georgia Supreme Court had overturned the first one, and Lee's lawyers were now appealing the second one.

The sensational nature of the crime attracted intense public interest in the trial. Currie had shot a jitney driver to steal his car, buried him alive, and, in an apparent effort to throw the authorities off the scent, had then sent his victim's widow a fake telegram saying her husband had gone out of state to sell the vehicle. Currie had been captured while still possessing the car and the gun he used to kill his victim. Adding to the drama was the fascinating fact that Lee was in the Savannah jail because he had been whisked out of town at the last minute by the Toombs County Sheriff to avoid being lynched by an angry mob. It was a riveting story that was just begging to be published in his paper.

Adding to the intrigue was the fact that the lawyers maintained that their client was insane at the time of the shooting. They were making the controversial argument that his insanity made him not responsible for his actions. This wild theory of people escaping judgment because they were nuts had created intense interest in the case and was helping to sell papers.

Jim followed Isaac to Lee's cell, intently listening as Isaac advised him not to get too close to the bars, as Lee Currie could get violent without warning. Jim could feel his heart pounding, and he began to sweat as he approached the cell.

"Lee, this here is Jim Jacobs. He's a reporter with the Savannah Morning News and wants to ask you a few questions. You behave now."

Isaac turned to the reporter, "He's all yours. Just walk to the end of the hall and tap on the door when you're done."

Jim nodded and continued to look nervously at the jailer as he walked back down the corridor. He turned to Lee.

"Good morning, Mr. Currie; how are you doing today?" Jim swallowed as he realized how silly his first question was.

Lee approached the bars and took hold with both hands, extending his face almost through them. His eyes were dark and sinister, almost black, and his stare unnerving.

"Oh, I'm just peachy, Mr. Jacobs; how the hell are you?" Lee answered sarcastically.

"I'm fine, thank you. I appreciate your willingness to see me today," Jim said awkwardly and swallowed again, his Adam's apple moving up and down nervously.

"Uh, my paper has reported a great deal about your legal situation, but that is not why I am here. My editor wanted me to inquire as to how you are faring, you know, what's it like being here in the Chatham jail," Jim said and looked intently at Lee. Not getting an immediate response, he reached in his shoulder bag for a pencil. Fumbling to get a pad out as well, he lost his grip, and the pad tumbled to the floor.

Lee smiled amusingly at the reporter, "How I'm faring, you say?"

Jim retrieved his pad and turned to an empty page, "Yes, uh, how you are feeling these days? If you don't mind telling me, that is."

Lee laughed out loud and then answered, imitating the reporter's careful speech, "Well, Mr. Jacobs, how I'm faring at this particular point in time is ..."

The reporter leaned in with his pencil at the ready, pencil point to the paper, eager to write.

"... not so goddamn good!" Lee shouted and reached out toward the reporter.

Jim jumped back and dropped his pencil. After a moment of reassuring himself that he was out of Lee's reach, he bent over to retrieve it and stood erect again, looking at Lee, afraid to ask anything more.

Lee laughed out loud and then turned serious, "Sorry, Mr. Jacobs, I didn't mean to upsot you, but how do you think I feel? They've had me locked up for two years for a crime I didn't do. How the hell would you feel?"

"But haven't you been tried twice now and found guilty both times by a jury of your peers?" Jim asked, scribbling away on his pad.

"And the Supreme Court overturned the first one of those damn trials and is going to overturn the last one too. Don't you read your own goddamn paper? Listen, you son-of-a-bitch; I'm innocent, I tell you!"

Jim backed away, holding pen and pad up against his chest, with a sheer look of terror on his face.

"Settle down, Mr. Jacobs. You look like you just shit yerself. Sorry, I didn't mean to cuss you. Being locked up for two years can make a man a little crazy," Lee said, returning to a calm voice.

Jim relaxed a bit and walked back over to the cell, being careful to say out of range of Lee's reach.

"Look, those lawyers have got it all wrong. I shot Burley Phillips because he come adder me with a knife. It's just as plain and simple as that, self-defense, I tell you, and the last time I checked, that ain't 'agin the law!"

Jim wrote some notes on his pad and said, "I'm not here to talk about the trial, Mr. Currie. My readers want to know how you are getting along in this jail. Let's – let's talk about that if you don't mind."

Lee relaxed and obliged. He and the reporter talked for several moments, and Jim began to relax, too. Lee Currie was interesting, and his interview would make a good story.

"Time's up," Isaac called out.

Jim looked off at the jailor and nodded. He closed his pad.

"I wish you good luck in your appeal, Mr. Currie, and I appreciate your seeing me today and letting me ask these questions," Jim said as he returned his pencil and pad to his pouch and started walking backward.

"You be sure and tell all your readers that those sons-a-bitches ain't gonna hang me, ya hear? My pa will git me outta here. He's got the best damn lawyers in the state working on my case. You just watch and see. You got all you need from me?" Lee asked.

"Yes, that will do nicely; you have a nice day, Mr. Currie," he said, and he turned and walked slowly down the corridor, glancing backward as he walked.

Lee called out after him, "You have a nice day too, Mr. Newspaper man!" He watched him leave. Then he pushed himself away from the bars and sat down on his bed.

"Damn reporters," he said, laid down, and put his hands behind his head.

* * * * * *

Jim Jacobs laid his article on his interview with Lee Currie on his editor's desk, who picked it up and slowly read it. Jim nervously shifted his position in his seat, but it wasn't the chair that was making him uncomfortable.

"Foul-mouthed fella, isn't he?" Tom Futch, the Savannah Morning News editor, said as he continued reading the story. Finally, he put it down and took off his glasses.

"Jim, you know we can't print this kind of language. We will have everyone in the community in an uproar. They will kick you and me both out of our churches."

"But that's what he said, Mr. Futch," Jim responded.

"I don't care what he said – we can't print it. It's a violation of the obscenity laws," Futch said sternly. "You need to revise it and use underlines when he cusses."

"That won't make any sense to the readers," Jim protested. He thought for a moment and then said, "Can I at least put the first letter of the cuss word?"

Futch did not answer immediately. It seemed to Jim that he knew he had a good story, and the profanity was a part of that story. He drew a circle around a couple of the words and pushed the reporter's notes back toward him, "Not for these, but you can for all the others."

"Thanks, chief!" Jim said excitedly, arose, and rushed out of the editor's office.

He returned with a new draft a few moments later and laid it before the editor. The headline read:

"LEE CURRIE WAITING IN SAVANNAH JAIL ON APPEAL."

"Lee Currie, convicted for the murder of a Toombs County man, here for safekeeping, also waiting for results of his appeal to the Supreme Court of Georgia, is remorseful.

"He has been in jail for two years, but he craves the great green outside. His confinement has caused him to curse and abuse those with whom he comes in contact, and he loathes the sight of jail, the jailers, and even the sheriff.

"'Food?' he said in answer to a query. 'If 'twasn't for the food we buy ourselves, we'd starve to death. This _____ stuff they give us here ain't worth a d_____. A _____ little piece of meat about the size of a walnut, some watery coffee, and they call it a meal.'

"When asked if his accommodations were clean, Mr. Currie replied, 'Yes, it's clean now. And the place is clean sometimes, but was just cleaned up now 'cause you were coming. Why this d_____ hole is so lousy sometimes, you can't stand it. I know I don't have any on me, but I see 'em often crawling up the wall. It's H_____.'

'To pass the time, I just sit around and talk and mix with the others. I'm tired of it, _____ tired of it, but' tain't no use. My lawyers say they're waiting on the appeal, an' I'm just waitin' too. Course, I didn't do it. I got a raw deal.'

"He hopes. He's not worrying much whether he gets his freedom or not. What the condemned man thinks about is strictly accountable to the man himself."

The editor looked up at his reporter and handed him back the article.

"Good job. Run it just like that."

Jim Jacobs smiled, took the story, and headed for the typesetting staff.

* * * * * *

On May 12, 1922, the Georgia Supreme Court overturned the conviction of Lee Currie and ordered a new trial to be held.

On June 15, 1922, the 3rd jury that heard the State vs. Lee Currie case informed Judge Hardeman they were deadlocked at eleven for conviction and one for life imprisonment. After 36 hours of deliberation, the foreman reported that they could not reach a unanimous verdict. Juror M. H. Clements, who stood out for a life sentence, said he absolutely would not agree with the other eleven men if they continued deliberating for 99 years. Judge Hardeman declared a mistrial and set July 17, 1922, as the date for a new trial to commence.

On July 18, 1922, the 4th jury was impaneled from a list of 147 county citizens. The 12-man jury, consisting of J. F. Murchison, foreman, Wade Mitchum, Fate Mosely, J. P. McNatt, P. G. Wheeler, A. H. Hardy, B. S. Alexander, F. L. McCollough, B. C. Anderson, M. C. Collins, M. J. Rattray, and Bill Murchison – again found Lee Currie guilty after only 15 minutes of deliberation. Lee appeared much weaker than in previous trials and almost collapsed when sentence was passed. Judge Hardeman sentenced him to be hanged on September 1, 1922, between the hours of 10 a.m. and 2 p.m.

Giles & Sharpe immediately entered a motion for a new trial based on one of the jurors being "an illegitimate third cousin" of Burley Phillips but nonetheless a relative. Judge Hardeman held a hearing on August 28, 1922. At that hearing, the judge said the law did not recognize illegitimate relationships, and even if it did, a third cousin was too remote to influence the juror's ability to render a fair verdict. He denied the motion for a new trial. He then issued an indefinite Stay of Execution to allow Giles & Sharpe time to prepare a Bill of Exception in their appeal to the Georgia Supreme Court.

The cost of housing Lee Currie in the Savannah jail had become prohibitively expensive. Sheriff Culpepper, believing tensions were still too high to house Lee in the

Toombs County jail, moved him to a jail in Richmond County that offered a lower housing fee.

On July 14, 1923, the Georgia Supreme Court disagreed with Judge Hardeman's reasoning. It asserted that the relationship of the juror to the deceased, however remote, was grounds for granting the defendant's motion for a new trial. They overruled Judge Hardeman and ordered a new trial to be held.

It would be the 5th time that Lee Currie would be tried for the killing of Burley Phillips.

* * * * * *

In the October Term of Court, 1923, the 5th and final trial of Lee Currie was held. The following jury was selected from the jury pool of 298 men: T. H. Sapp, H. C. Thompson, A. L. Osborne, C. A. Johnson, S. W. Hill, J. J. Anderson, T. J. Ainsworth, D. J. New, J. S. Banks, and W. H. Rollison. The jury again found him guilty of the murder of Burley Phillips.

Lee's attorneys immediately filed a motion for a new trial, as they had done on three separate occasions before. On February 28, 1924, Judge Hardeman denied the defendant's motion.

Lee Currie's attorneys filed an appeal with the Georgia Supreme Court to overturn the judge's decision.

Chapter 48

The messenger boy came bursting into the office of Toombs County Sheriff Charles Warren Culpepper with a telegram.

Culpepper had been elected sheriff in November of 1920 after George McLeod had decided not to run again in the aftermath of the first failed trial of Lee Currie. The taxpayers were upset about the cost of the trials and the continuing cost of incarceration of Lee Currie in Savannah. Additionally, the former sheriff's handling of the case had not sit well with many Vidalia voters. Some had told the new sheriff that McLeod was too close to the Curries and had botched the case investigation. Culpepper speculated that George had seen the writing on the wall and doubted his chances of winning reelection.

"Whoa, boy, what you got there?" Culpepper asked the panting messenger.

"It's a telegram from a law firm in Atlanta, Mr. Sheriff, and it's addressed to Judge Hardeman. Mr. Gibbs told me to get it to you where you could take it to him." He handed the telegram to the sheriff, who gave him a penny and waved him off. The boy turned and trotted out of the office.

Sheriff Culpepper unfolded the telegram. It was dated February 19th, 1925, and was from George M. Napier, the Attorney General, and read, "Hardeman affirmed by SC."

Culpepper exhaled slowly and ran his fingers over the telegram. The Supreme Court of Georgia had just affirmed Judge Hardeman's decision denying Lee's lawyers' Motion for a new trial. After five trials, it was finally over. Lee had exhausted all his appeals. The judge's order that he be hanged by the neck until dead now had to be carried out on May 21st, and he had to do it. He took a deep breath after realizing that he didn't even have gallows built.

Nobody had ever been legally hanged in Toombs County since the creation of the county by the Georgia General Assembly 20 years earlier. He had no idea how to hang a man. He would have to check with some of the other sheriffs and devise a procedure. He also had to construct gallows.

He stood up and grabbed his hat. Judge Hardeman would want to see this telegram right away, and he needed to find a carpenter.

* * * * * *

John and Lula Currie had gotten a telephone call that morning asking them to come to the law offices of Giles & Sharpe. The secretary told them the lawyers had received a telegram from Atlanta. The Curries arrived mid-morning and were shown into T. Ross Sharpe's office. He rose as the Curries entered.

"Good to see you, John, Lula. Please have a seat," T. Ross said as he shook the hand of the elder Currie.

The lawyer was stuck with how John Currie had seemed to age. His hair was thinner, pure white, and he had lost weight. Most of all, the shoulders of this formerly strong and imposing man had slumped, making him appear frail. Lula held his arm as if she sensed the burden he was carrying.

"I guess you've heard from Mr. Corbitt at that law firm up in Atlanta?" John weakly asked as if he knew why they had been summoned to the law office.

"I wanted to tell you in person, John. The Supreme Court has affirmed Judge Hardeman's decision to deny our Motion for a new trial," T. Ross said somberly.

John Currie stared at the floor. Lula spoke up, "What are our options now, Col. Sharpe?"

T. Ross exhaled. "Not many, at least in the local courtroom, but we have a few more options. I have affidavits from 20 of the 60 jurors who sat through the five trials urging the Prison Commission to recommend to Governor Walker that he commute Lee's death sentence to life imprisonment. Enoch knows Governor Clifford Walker very well and feels we have a good chance whether the Prison Commission recommends clemency or doesn't. Our only other legal option is to file an appeal with the United States Supreme Court if that's what you want."

John did not speak for almost a minute. When he spoke, he did so slowly, and his words were heavy, "Go ahead and have Enoch approach the Prison Commission and meet with the Governor, Ross, but I don't want any more appeals filed. I've lost most of my land to this trial. I can't take any more inheritance from my other children. It's not fair to them." He started to cry. Lula put her arms around his shoulders.

Seeing the old farmer quietly sob was proving difficult for T. Ross. He felt a lump forming in his own throat. "Nobody could ever say you didn't do right by your son, John. You have done more than most parents could or would have done. I completely understand your decision."

John looked up, "I don't blame you and Enoch, Ross. Lee lived five years longer than if any other firm had been representing him. I can't fault you for your handling of Lee's defense. I watched the faces of each member of those five juries and could tell they could not see letting Lee go after what he had done. For them, it was an eye for an eye."

"You know I did everything I could for Lee, John. I wish we could have had a different outcome, but you are right. No jury in Toombs County has ever found a person not guilty by reason of insanity. They couldn't accept the idea that Lee was not responsible for his actions," T. Ross said.

"Where will they do it?" John asked.

"We don't know yet. The sheriff has to build a gallows. I'll let you know as soon as I have the details. As his father, you will have every right to be there."

"Thank you, Ross. I appreciate everything you have done for this family," John said as he rose to his feet. Lula and T. Ross rose, too.

T. Ross embraced his old friend and then turned back to his desk to hide the tears that finally broke through his resistive power.

John turned and said, "Ross?"

T. Ross wiped his eyes and turned to face him. John continued, "All my life, I have firmly believed that God doesn't make a mistake when he brings a person into this world. Lee was born into this family for a reason. Maybe it was to punish me for my sins or to humble me, and if so, I take full responsibility for what has happened to him. But I will try to make sure that Lee does not die in vain and live out my life trying to be a better father to my other children, a better husband to Lula, and a better Christian."

T. Ross said, "You are a fine man, John Currie. Nobody can know the will of God or fully understand his purposes, but you did everything that any good father should have done and bear no fault in what happened to your son."

John Currie nodded to his friend, turned, took Lula by the arm, and left the law offices of Giles and Sharpe for the last time.

* * * * * *

"Tersia, I just heard some great news from the boys down at the cafe," Thomas Phillips said to his sister-in-law as he stepped into her living room.

"What news, Thomas?" Tersia asked.

"Lee Currie's luck has just run out. He lost his appeal to the Georgia Supreme Court. The Prison Commission didn't buy those shyster lawyers' attempt to get Lee's death sentence changed to life imprisonment. They have recommended to Governor Walker that they hang that murdering bastard!" Thomas snarled.

Tersia broke down into tears and almost collapsed. Thomas caught her and helped her to a chair.

"Thanks be to God," Tersia said.

Thomas held his brother's widow in his arms. The stress of the last five years and five trials had taken a toll on her, but he sensed that she would now get better.

"I'm going out to the grave to tell Burley about this. You want to ride out there with me?"

Tersia wiped her eyes on her handkerchief and looked up at him. "I need to go with you, I do. Can you get my coat from the hall closet for me?"

All bundled up, Tersia and Thomas left her home and drove to the North Thompson Baptist Church's cemetery.

* * * * * *

Solomon Corey watched his daughter read in the paper the account of Lee's losing his final appeal. He felt a tightening in his chest when he saw a tear fall from his daughter's right eye. Solomon had wanted the best for Lilly. He had worked hard all his life but could never escape the circle of poverty that had plagued the Corey's ever since they had everything taken from them by taxation and carpetbaggers after the south lost the war in the last century. Advice and love were all he had to give her, but his well-intended advice had brought her to this. She was barren and divorced from a convicted murderer about to be hanged.

He had pushed her into marrying Lee Currie even when the boy seemed a bit off, and his other daughters were warning him that Lee might be one of those men who mistreated women. Solomon reasoned that using the holy bonds of matrimony to tie her to a substantial family like the Curries seemed to be a way out of her poverty. After all, women were resilient and accustomed to abuse today. He felt she could put up with anything to be able to leap out of poverty. But there was no leap possible now. Even if she had stayed with Lee for his inheritance, it was clear the cost of five trials had reduced the Curries to near poverty.

He had talked her out of leaving Lee when he cheated on her and gave her that loathsome disease that would prevent her from ever giving him any grandchildren.

He did not intervene when she filed for divorce from Lee the second time while Lee was sitting in jail in Savannah, but she had not moved on. She was withdrawn and showed no interest in finding another spouse. Lilly seemed resigned to taking care of her father for the rest of his life.

That was not what he wanted for her, becoming an old maid looking after her widowed father, but he had lost all standing to give his broken daughter advice of any kind. Now all he had to offer her was love.

As he realized that love alone should have guided his advice from the very beginning, Solomon Corey also began to cry.

* * * * * *

"Lee, you have a visitor," the jailer called out.

"I don't want to see nobody," Lee shouted back from a reclining position on his bunk.

"It's somebody named Clarence James, Lee; you sure you don't want to see him?"

Lee sat up on his bunk. Whenever he was melancholic like this, his friend Clarence always made him feel better.

"Send him in."

John Currie had asked Clarence to deliver the bad news to Lee. He didn't have the heart to do it himself as he was all torn up inside. On the one hand, he had tried everything he could to save Lee from hanging, but in the process, he had brought the family into financial ruin, pursuing a lost cause.

He had first gone to the law offices of Giles & Sharpe determined to do anything to save the life of one of his children, but it was slowly dawning upon him that his extraordinary efforts to save one child had all but brought about the destruction of the financial security of his other children. None were complaining, but he now realized that what he had done for Lee was not fair to them.

Lee had been doomed from the start; John now realized. He was handicapped from birth by an abnormal mind, which led him to murder. There was no saving him after the way he had heinously killed that man from Vidalia. All John Currie had to show for his herculean efforts to save his first son was a broken family devastated emotionally and economically.

Yet John loved his son, and he knew that seeing him in that jail and having to tell him he was going to hang would force him to immediately return to T. Ross Sharpe with a directive to file that appeal to the United States Supreme Court. Yes, precisely that was what he would do, but he couldn't, in all fairness, do that to his other children. So, he turned to Lee's best friend, Clarence James, and asked him to tell Lee that his appeals had run out.

"Clarence, how the hell have you been?" Lee gleefully asked as he extended his hand through the bars of his cell.

Clarence took Lee's hand, shook it, and turned to the jailer to ask, "Can I go in there with him?"

The jailer nodded and unlocked the cell door. The two men embraced.

"Boy am I glad to see your sorry face," Lee said, smiling broadly.

"Hey, Lee," Clarence said.

Lee held Clarence by his shoulders, "Well, how are you?"

"I'm fine, Lee, but let's sit down. I have something important to tell you."

* * * * * *

On May 16th, 1925, Col. Enoch Giles traveled to Atlanta with Georgia State Representative Ernest Wimberly of Toombs County to meet with Governor Clifford Walker and plea for Lee's sentence to be commuted from hanging to life imprisonment.

After the first trial of Lee Currie, prosecuting attorney George W. Lankford was elected to the Georgia House of Representatives. There he had gotten close to the Governor, who was serving as a State Senator when George was elected. Learning that Giles would see the Governor, George also drove to Atlanta to argue against a grant of clemency.

On May 19th, 1925, two days before the execution was to be carried out; Governor Walker decided to follow the recommendation of the Prison Commission and deny clemency. Enoch immediately petitioned the Governor to form a special commission on lunacy to examine Currie. The Governor refused the request. That refusal sealed Lee

Currie's fate. He had a date with the executioner on May 21st, 1925, between the hours of 10 a.m. and 2 p.m.

Chapter 49

Most of the Currie family gathered at John Currie's home, along with many friends and well-wishers. Lula had prepared a large dinner early, and by 11:30 that morning, all had finished eating and were milling about. Small pockets of conversation created a low rumbling din. Everyone kept their voices down, sensitive to John Currie's somber mood as he sat on the front porch swing with his daughter Katie.

"We need to be leaving soon Katie. Are you sure you want to go with me? Your brother's execution is not going to be something that you can ever get out of your mind," John said as he squeezed his daughter's hand.

"I know you have been through a lot, Pa, and it has taken its toll on you. I can look at you and tell that. I worry about your health every day. I can't let you go through this alone," Katie answered.

"Lula will be there with me, Katie. I'll be fine."

"I know Lula has been very supportive, Pa, but you need blood kin with you. Lee is my brother. Lord knows he still doesn't know what all this is about. I need to be there with you."

John put his arm around Katie. As much as he didn't want her to see her brother put to death, he was glad she was determined to go with him. He stood up, "Okay, then, it's time to go."

Pratt, John, Jr., Sallie, and Lillian came over to hug their father. He bade each of them goodbye and made his way to the automobile sitting in the front yard. Lula and Katie got in, waved at the relatives and friends gathered on the front porch, and the three of them headed to town.

* * * * * *

Enoch Giles pulled out his pocket watch and flipped open the cover. They scheduled Lee Currie's execution at 1:30 p.m., and it was approaching time to head on over to the Toombs County Jail. He walked to T. Ross Sharpe's office door and stepped in. T. Ross was staring out of the window, a wisp of smoke from his cigar circling its way to the ceiling, disturbed only slightly by the movement of Enoch entering the office.

"You ready, Ross?"

T. Ross turned around to face his law partner.

"Not really." He thumped his ashes into the ashtray on his desk. "I know we can't win them all, Enoch, but this loss is hitting me hard."

Enoch sat down. The law firm of Giles & Sharpe was widely regarded as the best criminal law firm in the area, and they had just lost the trial of the century.

"Ross, when John Currie employed us to represent his son in this case, I was determined to see that he had a fair and impartial trial and not worry about what the outcome might be. I feel no remorse for having been recreant to my responsibilities in this case. I have discharged my duty to my client to the best of my ability, and so have you," Enoch said.

T. Ross took another puff from his cigar. "You have indeed done exactly what a defense attorney should do, Enoch. No one can fault you for your handling of Lee's case. Our defense was solid and well presented, and you shouldn't feel any remorse."

T. Ross stood and walked to the window and spoke, with his back to his law partner, "But you have an advantage over me, Enoch. To you, this was just another case. But John Currie is my friend, and I feel I have let him down." He turned back to face his law partner, "And now I must go down there and watch his son hang. I just can't share your sense of having done your duty. I'm sorry." T. Ross sat back down and inhaled again from his cigar.

The two men sat silently for several minutes, and T. Ross took out his pocket watch again and flipped open the lid.

"We best be going," T. Ross said.

"I'm going to sit this one out, Ross. You should be there to represent the firm. As you have stated, you are his friend, as well as his attorney. I am just his attorney. You go."

T. Ross did not argue with him. Enoch watched him as he got up and headed out to his automobile.

* * * * * *

"Lee, you are entitled to talk to a minister of your denomination if you wish. If you don't belong to a specific denomination, we have a chaplain here at the jail," Sheriff Culpepper said. Lee's jail cell was open, with deputies standing on each side of the door. The sheriff had brought two stools to his cell, anticipating the entitled visitors who would soon be arriving.

"No thanks, Sheriff. It's a bit late for me to be gittin' right with the Lord, wouldn't you say?" Lee said and chuckled.

Culpepper was a bit unnerved by Lee's calm and carefree manner. Since being elected, this was the sheriff's first execution, and he was nervous. It seemed that his prisoner would also be somewhat unsettled at least, but Lee acted as if this was just another day.

"My pa coming?" Lee asked.

"I haven't heard from him, Lee. I suppose so. Are you hungry? You're entitled to a last meal, and you can have whatever you want, even a steak," Culpepper said.

"Let me tell you what I would really like, sheriff."

"What's that?"

"An orange," Lee said and grinned.

Culpepper let out a nervous laugh and turned to one of the deputies, "John, go get Mr. Currie an orange." John Johnson looked at the other deputy and then back at the sheriff, not knowing if the sheriff was serious or not.

"Go on now, John. Mr. Currie wants an orange," Culpepper said.

"Where am I going to find an orange, Sheriff?" John asked.

The sheriff grew agitated, "I don't care where you find it, damn it, just find it, now go!" He made a sweeping motion with his arm.

The deputy turned and hurried down the stairs of the jail.

Lee laughed, "That's some booming voice you got there, Sheriff. Hell, you even scared me!"

Culpepper turned his head to the sound of more footsteps coming up the stairs. He looked at his other deputy.

"It's John Currie and his wife, Sheriff," the deputy said.

Culpepper got up and said to his prisoner, "I'll leave you alone with your folks, Lee." He stepped out and walked down the hall to greet the visitors.

"How's he doing?" Lula Currie asked.

"He is in surprisingly good spirits. He just asked for an orange as his last meal. He's asked about you. I can give you 15 or 20 minutes with him," Culpepper said.

"Thank you, Charles," John Currie said and walked on down the hall.

"Pa!" Lee exclaimed as he rose and gave his father a bear hug, then turned and hugged his stepmother. "I'm so glad you came. Wouldn't want to leave this world without saying bye to my folks."

John sat down, as did Lee and Lula. "Are they treating you alright, son?"

"Better than them sons-a-bitches treated me in Savannah and in Augusta, that's for sure. I ain't got no complaints, Pa."

John looked down at his hands, trying hard to choke back tears.

"Aw, Pa, don't you be frettin' none. You did all you could, hiring all them fancy lawyers and doctors and such. But they was out to get me and … and damned if they didn't. Although, I wish they had done it sooner. I think it's a damn shame for them to torture me for five years before hanging me."

"Lee, you have to know that if there was any way your father could have prevented that ..." Lula began saying.

"You don't have to defend my pa, Lula. I ain't begrudging him one little bit. He's been there for me from the beginning."

Lula smiled and put her hand on Lee's, "I'm glad you said that Lee, because he's been feeling like he let you down."

Lee reached over to his father and touched his hands, "Pa, I ain't blaming you one little bit. Them damn deputies set me up to go yapping my fool head off in that car 'bout what I done and led me to believe they weren't gonna' tell nothing I said. They lied to me. There's been a whole bunch of lying going on, but it ain't none of your doing. Don't you fret none."

"Lee, your sister Katie wants to see you if that's alright?" Lula asked.

"She here? Of course, it's alright; where is she?"

"They won't let but two of us in here at a time. I'll go get her," Lula said and got up to go and get Katie.

"Clarence James is here, too, Lee. You want to see him?" John asked as he wiped away a tear and composed himself. He suddenly found himself wanting to get out of the jail cell.

"Sure, Pa, good ole Clarence. He's been a true friend. It's only right that I should see him before I go."

John Currie stood up.

"You coming back?" Lee asked.

"I'll be there when they bring you down, Lee. I want you to spend some time with your sister and your friend."

Lee stood up and hugged his father. "Thanks, Pa. I love you."

John Currie could not remember when his son had ever told him he loved him. It was all he could bear, and the tears gushed forth. He hugged his son again and held him tight.

"I love you, too, son, and I'll see you on the other side where there will be no more tears and no more pain. You mean the world to me, and if I could go to the gallows in your stead, I would," John sobbed.

"I know, Pa, I know. It'll be alright. Don't you worry none." He pushed his father back to arm's length and held both his shoulders, "Now, Pa, there is no use to cry. I haven't wept yet, and don't intend to. It would only make matters worse. If you drop a glass of water, there is no use to cry, the glass is broken, and the water gone down.

"And I don't want no weepin' or cryin' stuff at my execution or my funeral, you hear me? Y'all have a party instead and make so much noise I can find you from the afterlife. That way, I can be there in spirit," Lee said.

John looked him square in the face. He managed a small smile, nodded affirmatively, and then turned to go. He took a step and paused, turning back to his son. "I know you have a good heart, son, and the Lord has a place waiting for you." And with that, John Currie turned and walked down the corridor.

* * * * * *

Two deputies walked Lee Currie from his cell down to the 1st floor, where the gallows ominously stood in the SE corner of the jail in a room formerly used for storage. Lee was calm and appeared to be in a good mood, much more relaxed than the two deputies escorting him, who knew of his volatile nature and were on high alert for any sudden moves or attempts to escape. None came. Lee even engaged Johnson in a conversation about the Pittsburg Pirates and asked him if he thought they would win the World Series later that year. Johnson said he thought the Washington Senators would win, and Lee laughed.

He was still talking sports with the guards as he walked calmly into the room enclosing the gallows. The guards paused, and Lee looked up to the top of the structure in front of him. Lee whistled.

"Boy, that's something, right there. That's not a sight you get to see every day," Lee said.

The gallows were made of fresh wood and had a cross beam supported by two posts, with a platform underneath. The noose hanging down from the crossbeam swayed gently from being recently held for a final inspection and then released by the sheriff.

Clement C. Moseley, Jr., who became the editor of The Lyons Progress newspaper in 1924, stepped up to Lee and asked, "Do you dread being hanged, Lee?"

The deputies paused to give Lee a chance to talk to the reporter.

"No, not really. My attorneys did all that could be done for me, but the judge wasn't fair. I got no justice. Every juror that went into the box swore that they would be impartial when they knew they were bitterly against me," Lee said.

Lee then looked out the window at the large crown assembled, smiled, and said, "Why are all those fellows running around out there? They act as if they are at a picnic."

Clement took out a pack of cigarettes and held it up to Lee, "Don't pay them no mind, Lee. Cigarette?"

"No thanks, them things will kill you," Lee said with a chuckle.

Clement laughed. He extended his hand, and Lee took it, "Goodbye, Mr. Currie."

Lee looked at him and smiled but said nothing. Clement stepped back in among the gathered spectators.

Looking around the room, Lee found the friendly faces of his father, stepmother, sister Katie, best friend Clarence, and T. Ross Sharpe standing behind the roped-off area. T. Ross offered a small smile that Lee returned with a slight wave.

There were others gathered that chased away his smile when Lee saw them. Solicitor General Walter Grey and his assistant George Lankford were there with faces that bore no expression other than gratifying anticipation of what was to come.

Lee's eyes finally fell upon Thomas Phillips, and a frown appeared. Thomas was almost snarling. Lee quickly turned his eyes back to his father.

At the guards' urging, he walked up the stairs to the gallows. Sheriff Culpepper pointed to a square in the middle of the platform, and Lee cautiously stepped on it.

Deputy Johnson tied a rope around Lee's waist binding his arms to his sides, while the other deputy tied a rope around his ankles. Sheriff Culpepper put the noose around his neck. The sheriff stepped back, and Johnson stepped over to the wooden handle connected to the trap door beneath where Lee was standing.

A large crowd gathered outside the jail, but only a few could see inside the room's windows where the gallows stood. Young Pearl Williams was standing in the back of her pa's buckboard and could see it well. She held her sister's hand with one hand and clutched a doll in the other.

"Is that him?" Pearl asked her sister.

"Yes, they are about to hang him," her sister answered.

Several people in the crowd without a good vantage point heard her and began to whisper to each other that the hanging was about to take place.

"Lee, do you have any last words?" Culpepper asked Lee.

"Yeah, I got something to say. You sons-a-bitches are about to hang an innocent man. I killed Burley Phillips in self-defense after he was coming at me with a knife, and youns what had a hand in my trial and this execution are going to burn in hell for whatcha doin' right now," Lee Currie said.

"Anything else?" Culpepper asked.

"Naw, that's 'bout it," Lee said.

Lee's words angered Culpepper. They had the chill of a curse, but he had nothing to do with Lee's arrest or alleged mishandling while in custody. George McLeod was responsible for how his deputies handled Lee Currie while in custody, not him.

The sheriff stepped forward and put a black hood over Lee's head, then stepped back and spoke up for all to hear.

"Lee Currie, you have been lawfully found guilty of murder by a jury of your peers and sentenced by a lawfully elected judge to be hanged by your neck until you are dead. May God have mercy on your soul."

He noted the time, 1:38 p.m., signaled Johnson to open the trap door and turned to walk away. He was done with the Lee Currie saga and would leave it to his deputies to dispose of the body. Lee Currie was no longer his concern, and this chapter was closed.

When the trap door was sprung, Pearl Williams turned her back to the jail. It was an image she did not want to be burned into her memory.

"Oh my God, they just dropped him!" her sister exclaimed, and the crowd picked up the announcement and spread it among those gathered.

Sheriff Culpepper had almost reached his office when John Johnson caught up with him all excited and out of breath, "You have to come back, sheriff; we got a big problem!"

John was tugging on his shirt sleeve, urging him to return. He followed his deputy back into the room only to discover that all bedlam had broken loose.

Lee was dangling at the end of the rope, making a blood-chilling gurgling sound as he writhed about. He had both hands on the rope holding it. Practically everyone in the room was shouting at the same time.

"Get his feet!" Culpepper screamed at John. He rushed under the platform to where Lee was dangling, but Lee had pulled himself back up by the rope to the gallows platform by the time he got to him.

"Go up there and secure him," Culpepper barked.

Some members of the crowd were beginning to approach.

"Get back, all of you!" Culpepper shouted as he rushed back up the steps to the platform where Lee had climbed up and was on his hands and knees, coughing and spitting. He took the noose off and removed the hood. Lee's face was red, and there were angry red rope burns on his neck, but he was alive. He turned his head toward the rapidly approaching sheriff.

"You dumb sons-a-bitches can't even get a hanging right," Lee said coarsely and coughed.

Walter Grey stepped up from the crowd and was quickly restrained by deputies. Anticipating what Grey was about to say, T. Ross Sharpe also stepped up.

"Judge Hardeman's order was to hang Lee Currie by the neck UNTIL HE WAS DEAD, Sheriff; you have to finish the job," Walter said sternly.

"You can't do that, Sheriff," T. Ross immediately injected, "God almighty himself has intervened to prevent this travesty of justice. You have to let him go! You can't hang a man twice!"

Grey grew red and practically shouted, "There was no divine intervention, you ass. The sheriff didn't place the hangman's knot properly to break his neck, and that fool of a deputy didn't tie his hands securely enough." He turned to the sheriff, "You must do it again and do it right this time. He has to be executed! The judge has spoken. It's the law!"

T. Ross shouted, "There is a higher law that is involved now. Sheriff, if you hang that boy after this divine intervention, you risk bringing the wrath of God down upon you and everyone involved in this hanging. Lee warned that you would burn in hell for what you were about to do. Do you want to risk your immortal soul?"

"String him up again!" Thomas Phillips shouted. "Hang the bastard!"

The sheriff saw John Currie move toward Phillips, but Lula and Clarence immediately restrained him. He heard Lula say, "John, let the law handle this; it is in God's hands now."

"Let him go!" Clarence shouted to the sheriff. He was joined by a cacophony of shouts from the crowd, moments away from becoming a mob.

Lee regained his composure from where the rope had momentarily cut off his wind. He coughed again.

"I guess a higher court has overruled your Judge Hardeman," Lee said, his voice now raspy from the swelling beginning in his neck. His laughter quickly turned into another cough as Sheriff Culpepper pulled him roughly to his feet.

"You gonna let me go now, Sheriff, or go to hell like Col. Sharpe said?" Lee asked.

"Sheriff, do your duty. Carry out Judge Hardeman's order," Walter shouted.

"Shut the hell up, Walter. I know my job. Now, y'all get back, get back, I say!" Culpepper shouted.

Lee could hardly stand on his feet but managed to stay upright.

"Dammit, Sheriff, you are making a profound mistake that you will regret for the rest of your life!" T. Ross yelled.

"Well, then, don't vote for me at the next election, Ross! Walter is right; Judge Hardeman ordered me to hang Lee Currie by the neck until he was dead, and he ain't dead yet." He turned his head to T. Ross, "And if God sees fit to punish me for following my oath, well, then so be it."

Everyone in the crowd was talking and shouting.

Culpepper shouted to his deputy, "Johnson, reset the trap now!"

Johnson reset the trap, and the sheriff practically dragged Lee to the trap door.

"Tie his hands behind him this time, dammit, and if they come loose again, by God, I'll string you up next!" Culpepper shouted to Johnson. His face was red with rage.

Lee was swaying and unsteady on his feet. "You sons-a-bitches couldn't hang a hog in a smokehouse," he laughed and then coughed violently again.

Johnson tied Lee's wrists behind him and then re-tied his ankles.

"Damn, deputy, that hurts. You gonna torture me to death or hang me?" Lee mumbled.

"Sorry," Johnson said.

The sheriff glared at him, "Get on the handle, now!"

Lee was standing under his own power, although he was still swaying. The sheriff put the noose around his neck and carefully stationed the knot behind his left ear. He took the hood from his back pocket and started to put it on Lee's head.

"You sure you don't need to go get somebody that knows what they are doing, sheriff?" Lee said with a grin.

"I'll manage, and may God have mercy on your soul."

"And on yours, lawman. Alrighty then, let's get on with it," Lee said.

Culpepper put the hood on and stood just outside the square hole on which Lee was standing to steady Lee should he falter. He turned his head to Johnson, who had both hands on the handle that would spring the trap door a second time.

"Do it!" the sheriff ordered.

Everyone in the room heard the loud crack when Lee Currie's neck broke as he reached the end of his rope.

* * * * * *

Katie's legs gave way, and she collapsed. Lee was pronounced dead by Dr. Ira E. Aaron at 1:45 p.m. The Sheriff of Toombs County, through torturous trial and error, had finally learned how to hang a man correctly.

Chapter 50

J. Frank Murchison had enjoyed his success as a carriage maker and the owner of the Vidalia Undertaking Company. He had built a prosperous business and currently handled most of the funerals in Toombs County. He had buried John Currie's wife Lavency when she died seven years earlier, so it was no surprise when he received John Currie's call to be present at the hanging to pick up Lee's body and prepare him for burial.

The embalming had gone well, and he was pleased with how he had been able to completely cover with makeup the rope burns on Lee Currie's neck. He was confident that Mr. Currie would be pleased.

However, it was disappointing to him that Mr. Currie had insisted that he use his old horse-drawn hearse for the actual funeral. Given the prospective turnout for Lee's burial, he had hoped to be able to use the 1924 Lincoln he had just acquired, which, using his carriage-making skills, he had modified into a beautifully carved panel hearse. There was nothing in all the surrounding counties to match it.

But he couldn't blame Old Man Currie for wanting him to carry Lee to his final resting place in the same ornate hearse that conveyed his mother, Lavency. The old hearse may have some age on her, but it was his best work of all the buggies he made over the years. Built from scratch a decade ago, it had served him well.

Sure wish I could have shown off my new Lincoln, he sighed to himself. He could handle more funerals in a single day with that car now that the roads were so much better. He had been promoting the Lincoln to future customers in recent ads in *The Lyons* Progress. The Currie Funeral would attract many citizens, and it would be an excellent opportunity to show off his new conveyance. Nevertheless, Mr. Currie was a prominent citizen, and it would be a good advertisement for his business, no matter which vehicle of the funeral car fleet he used.

He sent his two Negro boys to the livery stable to get his horses.

* * * * * *

"Pa, the hearse is coming," John Currie, Jr. announced as he ran into the living room of the Currie home. John got up and walked out to the front porch just as Frank Murchison pulled up in the front yard. Dozens of his relatives and guests spilled out into the yard and surrounded the funeral carriage holding the mortal remains of Robert Lee Currie.

The casket was already open, and Lee was visible through the glass panels of the hearse. He lay in a peace box made of mahogany, with beautiful white taffeta lining the interior. Murchison had fitted Lee with white gloves and crossed his hands at his waist.

John Currie smiled when he saw that Frank had not put too much rouge on his cheeks to remove the death pallor. John felt the rouge would have given his son a clownish appearance.

Frank stepped down from the coach driver's bench and walked over to where John Currie was standing, looking at his son.

"You did right by him, Frank. He looks very much like I had hoped he would. I don't know how to thank you," John said.

"I know this is a sad occasion for you, John. No father likes to bury his children. I'm glad I was able to help you through this difficult time," Frank said.

"Have all your guests eaten yet? It's time to head on over to the church," Frank continued.

"Yes, we're all ready. We have been awaiting your arrival," John said.

"Are the pallbearers here, too?" Frank asked.

"Yes," John said.

"Can you give me their names for the obituary?" Frank asked.

John looked over to Lula, who was standing beside him. She unfolded a piece of paper and began to read. "The pallbearers are J. P. Walker, S. E. Smith, Richard Sherwood Boyd, Clarence James, J. W. Moore, and G. L. Underwood."

Frank started to jot the names down on a pad when Lula said, "Here, you can have this list. I made it for you."

Frank nodded to her, took the list, and tucked it into his coat pocket. He shook John's hand and climbed back up on the hearse where he could be heard, "If everyone will please get into their automobiles and wagons, we need to head on down to Marvin Church. I will need for the vehicle carrying the pallbearers to fall in immediately behind me. Mr. Currie, you, and your family, please line up behind them."

John turned and went to the family truck, which the farmhands had cleaned to a shine he had not seen in many years.

Slowly the funeral procession, which stretched for a quarter

of a mile, made the three-mile journey from Mr. Currie's home to Marvin Church, near the Altamaha River.

Frank was astounded as he approached the church. He had never seen so many people attend a funeral in Toombs County. Parking places were difficult to find as people continued to arrive. Two of the church's stewards struggled to prevent people from blocking where the funeral procession would need to park.

Clement Moseley, who was there to report on the funeral in the Lyons Progress, estimated that a thousand people had gathered at the little country church. It was the largest funeral he had ever seen in the county.

When John Currie saw the assembled crowd as his vehicle neared the church, it took his breath away. At times, he had felt that he was fighting his son's legal battles all by himself, but practically everyone in the lower part of Toombs County had come to the funeral to show their support for him and his family. The tears started anew.

The pallbearers lined up in two rows behind the hearse. They moved forward to receive the casket just as Frank opened the rear door of the hearse. The stewards directed everyone to form a path from the hearse to the church's front door, and the pallbearers slowly brought the casket inside and placed it in front of the pulpit.

John and Lula followed.

* * * * * *

A chorus of twenty men and women sang sacred hymns as those attending the services came in a long line to view Lee Currie and pay their respects to the family. The chorus continued singing until those outside the church had an opportunity to come in and view the body. Finally, when the stewards had determined that everyone had seen the deceased, one nodded to Reverend H. J. Eason.

Reverend Eason stood and walked to the pulpit. He placed his Bible before him and opened it to a well-worn place.

"The Lord is my shepherd; I shall not want. He maketh me to lie down in green pastures: he leadeth me beside the still waters. He restoreth my soul: he leadeth me in the paths of righteousness for his name's sake. Yea, though I walk through the valley of the shadow of death, I will fear no evil: for thou art with me; thy rod and thy staff they comfort me. Thou preparest a table before me in the presence of mine enemies: thou anointest my head with oil; my cup runneth over. Surely goodness and mercy shall follow me all the days of my life: and I will dwell in the house of the Lord forever," Reverend Eason took a piece of paper from his pocket and spread it out before him.

"In my mind's eye, just like it was yesterday, I can see Lee Currie as a little boy running around barefoot on his pa's farm. He was as full of life and rambunctious as any boy you have ever seen, and it was all John and Levency could do to keep up with him," Reverend Eason hesitated, filled with emotion.

Mourners occupied every seat in Marvin Church. The stewards had opened all the windows to allow the people outside an opportunity to hear.

The preacher's evoking a memory of Lee as a little boy set Katie Currie Smith, dressed in black and seated beside her father on the front left row, to crying. Her father squeezed her hand.

"Every child of God is a blessing, even those who come into this world different from the rest of us. They are a blessing because they teach us humility and how to love our children deeply, whatever their limitations." He looked over at John Currie, "I can attest that John Currie loved his son very much."

* * * * *

Thomas Phillips pulled off the road as close as he could get to Marvin Church with all the other vehicles already there. He was driving the same Baby Overland that Lee Currie had killed his brother to get. He shut down the engine and sat quietly. Thomas couldn't explain what had made him want to attend Lee Currie's funeral. He looked at the massive crowd of people at the Marvin Church. Thomas' brow furrowed upon the realization that the overflow at Lee's funeral numbered into the hundreds, many more than had attended his brother's funeral.

He didn't know why he was there or how to interpret the strange emotions going through his mind. He took a swig from a bottle of moonshine, lit up a cigarette, and began to wait.

* * * * *

Preacher Eason continued, "In Job, Chapter 1, Verse 18, it says, 'While he was yet speaking, there came also another, and said, Thy sons and thy daughters were eating and drinking wine in their eldest brother's house: And, behold, there came a great wind from the wilderness and smote the four corners of the house, and it fell upon the young men, and they are dead, and I only am escaped alone to tell thee.

'Then Job arose, and rent his mantle, and shaved his head, and fell down upon the ground, and worshipped, and said, Naked came I out of my mother's womb, and naked shall I return thither: the LORD gave, and the LORD hath taken away; blessed be the name of the LORD.'"

For over an hour, Preacher Eason talked about the life of Lee Currie while never mentioning the events of the last five years. He alternated between eulogizing the dead and preaching the living into heaven.

"Lee Currie was born into this world without the same willpower that guides the actions of you and me. He lacked the mental restraint to know when his actions hurt others. But the good Lord created him and knew better than you or I could ever know the limitations of his mind to listen to his heart. Lee had a good heart. You know that, and God knows that.

"Our God is merciful; praise His mighty name. He has forgiven Lee for his transgressions, and there will be a great reunion in the sweet by and by where we shall meet on that beautiful shore and see brother Lee again. He will be whole and cleansed of his sins and his afflictions, and we will join in a great circle and sing praises to the Lord. A mighty band of angels will join us, and God shall wipe away all tears from our eyes; and there shall be no more death, sorrow, or crying, nor shall there be any more pain: for the former things are passed away. Let us pray.

"Lord, bless this family and all these friends that have suffered such a great loss. Place your loving arms around them and bring them peace and understanding and accept into your glory this humble servant lying before you. In Jesus' holy name, Amen."

* * * * *

Thomas Phillips watched the people leaving Marvin Methodist Church. He sat there while Lee's body was taken to the gravesite and lowered into the ground. He sat there, watching the men shovel the soil over the crypt. He sat there as he watched the stewards lock the church doors and drive away. He sat there as the sky took on an orange glow as the sun began to drop below the horizon.

When he was sure no one remained, he slowly drove to the gravesite of Robert Lee Currie, got out of the automobile that had cost the life of his brother, and walked over to stand before the grave of the man who had murdered Burley.

For five years, he had been consumed by hatred for Lee Currie and a lust for revenge for his brother's terrible and gruesome killing. Seeing Lee suffer as his first hanging was botched and hearing his neck crack the second time took a heavy load from his shoulders and felt good.

But now, standing before the remains of the man he had hated so long, another feeling came over him. The hatred and bitterness he felt on May 21, 1925, suddenly left him. Lee had paid the ultimate price for killing his brother, and somehow, now that he was dead, Thomas felt sorry for him and his family.

At every trial, Thomas had been there. He had cheered every verdict except the mistrial, yet a realization was slowly washing over him that Lee was indeed crazy and didn't know what he was doing.

He turned around and looked at the Baby Overland.

It was you; what did both my brother and Lee Currie in, he said to the car as if speaking to a living thing.

Thomas Phillips looked back at the grave. He turned up the bottle and took a drink; then, he poured a drink over the fresh soil covering the remains of his old nemesis.

Thomas took the keys to the Baby Overland and threw them down on Lee Currie's grave.

"It's yours, Lee, now and for all eternity," he said aloud.

Thomas Phillips turned and set out on foot, walking back to Vidalia.

The End

Epilogue

I'd like to offer a brief history of what happened to some of the main characters that appear in this book after Lee Currie was hanged for killing Burley Phillips:

John Warren Currie, Sr. lived four more years after his son's execution, never recovering financially or emotionally from the trial. He was 63.

George Bruce McLeod served as the sheriff of Toombs County from 1916 through 1920, replacing R. J. Partin and being replaced by Charles Warren Culpepper, Sr. He later moved to Emanuel County, Georgia, and became a United States marshal there, running down moonshine stills. The 1930 Census shows he had married Theodora Calhoun Courson and was a Deputy Marshal with the US Government living in Savannah. He died in 1959 at the age of 87.

Thomas Jefferson Phillips continued his trade as a carpenter. He died in 1938 at the age of 52.

Judge Robert Northington Hardeman, Sr., spent many more years on the bench. Immediately after the 5th trial of the State v. Lee Currie, he took a vacation with his two Llewellyn Setters. His Louisville Georgia home contained considerable evidence that the judge was a skilled performer with a gun and rod. He died on April 19, 1950, at the age of 77.

Enoch J. Giles lived for five more years after the trial. On December 9, 1930, upon returning from a day of hunting with his dog, he accidentally discharged his gun while trying to exit his vehicle and was shot in the abdomen. He died at his home. He was 67 years of age. His friends and fellow attorneys wrote a tribute, which read, in part, "He was a brilliant man. His powers of narrative and his portrayal in word pictures were marvelous. He held the notice and attention of crowds wherever he talked: his store of learning, his clean, clear analysis of facts, his fertile adjustment and assortment of incidents, and particularly, his bright, quick imagination and well-trained accent and delivery made him the wonder and magnetic source to hold entranced those who listened."

T. Ross Sharpe grew from his junior law partner status at Giles & Sharpe to opening his own law firm and becoming one of the most successful lawyers in Lyons. He began to write a series of stories for The Lyons Progress called "Tales from the Altamaha," which, starting in 2005, were made into community theater stage plays performed annually by the Lyons Main Street Program at the time of this writing. He died on January 28, 1968, at the age of 74. On his tombstone is written, "T. Ross Sharpe, Attorney, Farmer, Orator, Organized First Rural Electric in the South."

Walter F. Grey continued his law practice in Swainsboro, Georgia, as Solicitor General of the Georgia

Middle Circuit until he was taken ill on a trip with his wife to Savannah, Georgia. He died on September 15, 1926.

George W. Lankford served in the Georgia House of Representatives from 1925 to 1929, and was then elected to the Georgia Senate in 1929, serving two years. He was known "... to have owned the largest farm in Toombs County, Georgia, consisting of 1,000 acres of cotton, 80 acres of tobacco, and a large acreage in corn, potatoes, etc." At the time of his premature death on June 8, 1941, from a heart attack at the age of 59, he was the Chairman of the Toombs County Board of Education.

Lilly Corey Currie later married John C. Sumner and moved to Miami, Florida. None of her second family knew of her earlier marriage to Lee Currie. She died in 1979, childless. She was 79.

Now that you have presumably read this book, there are no more cats to be let out of the bag, and I can share with you some more details of how this story came to be.

As I related in the Prologue, my interest in Lee Currie began at a very young age while I was still in grammar school. My late uncle, Rev. James E. Boyd, told me the story about the only man who was ever legally hanged in Toombs County. My uncle was a great storyteller and, later in life, wrote a weekly column for *The Lyons Progress*, the local newspaper. His fascinating story stayed with me all my life.

One of the story components that piqued my curiosity at a very young age was his telling me that the killer buried his victim's body in a makeshift grave about a mile from where we were sitting on the banks of Cobb Creek in lower Toombs County, Georgia. The place he described was just a few hundred yards from the home of my grandparents, Richard Sherwood Boyd and Susie Hayslip Boyd.

When I was in the 8th grade in 1962, my English teacher, Mrs. Lottie Aaron, gave the class an assignment to write a short story about some famous event or popular family lore that had occurred in my home area. I immediately remembered the story of "the only man ever legally hanged in Toombs County" and called my uncle to get his name, which I had forgotten.

Uncle James told me his name was Lee Currie, and I could find a copy of the trial transcript down at the Toombs County Clerk of Court's office.

Little did I know when I entered the office of D. Q. Coleman, the Clerk of Court, that he was married to a member of the Currie family. When I told him that I was there to look up the trial of Lee Currie to write a report on it, he grew angry and told me, "That man has a lot of family still living in this county who wouldn't want you stirring up that case again! Now get out of here!" I left immediately.

My father, J. W. Griggers, Sr., was a prominent businessman in Lyons, being the local Studebaker Dealer, and when I told him of my run-in with the Clerk of Court, he loaded me up in his car and drove me downtown to the law offices of Col. T. Ross Sharpe, who was his attorney.

By the time we arrived at Col. Sharpe's luxurious office, I had begun to regret having told my father about the difficulty I was having with my writing assignment. There were a lot of adults now involved, and I was just a young whippersnapper. My dad was concerned, a prominent lawyer was about to get involved, and I had just tangled with the duly elected Clerk of Court of Toombs County. This had escalated far beyond what my young mind could handle, and I desperately wanted to go back home and find another topic for my writing project.

But Dad was insistent on my seeing this through. My heart was in my throat when we entered Col. Sharpe's office. His presence in the room was bigger than life, with his trademark bowtie, suspenders, and cigar.

"My son has a little legal problem and needs your help," Dad told his lawyer.

Col. T. Ross sat forward in his chair, "Oh? Well, then tell me how I can help you, young man."

His easy manner and big smile immediately put me at ease, and I told him what I had set out to do and how D. Q. Coleman had shooed me out of his office.

Col. T. Ross' eyes sparkled, and he sat back in his chair and put both thumbs beneath his suspenders, pulling them away from his chest a couple of inches and then releasing them, "Well, I just happen to know a little bit about that case as I represented Mr. Currie at trial."

He proceeded to tell me all about the case, how the killing occurred and how they had first tried to prove it was self-defense, then tried to prove Lee Currie was insane and not responsible for his actions.

Col. Sharpe told me how the sheriff and his deputies bungled their first attempt to hang Lee Currie and how he had vainly attempted to get the execution stopped after yelling out that "God Almighty himself has intervened and stopped this immoral execution!"

I was furiously writing as he related the details of a trial that had occurred over three decades earlier as if it had happened yesterday. After he finished telling me all about it, he called his secretary in and dictated a letter directing the Clerk of Court to show me the trial records. He continued to talk about it until she returned with the letter. He signed it and handed it to me.

"You give that to Mr. Coleman. Court records are public, and he must let you see them. If he doesn't, you come back to see me."

I asked my father to go with me to the Clerk's office; however, he wanted me to carry this project to its conclusion by myself. Nervously, I walked back into the Clerk of Court's office alone.

D. Q. Coleman was a large man with a commanding presence. He scowled when he saw me reenter the office.

"What are you doing back here?" he asked gruffly.

I handed him the letter from Col. Sharpe without saying a word. He read it and then threw it back down on the counter while loudly saying in a voice that scared the life out of me, "All right, you can look all you want, but I'll be dammed if I am going to help you!" Then he turned and returned to his private office.

I looked for the better part of an hour, but I did not know how to find what I was looking for. I found a lot of interesting cases and being an avid reader, I consumed them with glee, but I could find nothing about the trial of Lee Currie.

However, Col. T. Ross Sharpe's eyewitness account of the trial was better than any trial transcript I could have read, and I decided to go ahead and write my school report based on what Col. Sharpe had told me. It worked, and I got an "A," as I remember.

Years later, after graduating from Georgia Tech, I attended Woodrow Wilson Law School in Atlanta. Armed with a much better knowledge of how to research the law, I returned to Lyons in 1975 and went back to the Clerk of Court's offices. Sidney Dickerson had become the Clerk of Court, and I understood by then that I didn't have to ask for his permission to see the court records. Those records are open to the public, and in just a few moments, I had found the trial transcript. I made a copy.

I read the case with great interest and determined to write a book about it someday. I stored it away in my "round2it" file.

Forty-two years later, when I retired in 2015, I found the case and reread it. I noticed something that piqued my curiosity. In the trial transcript, some of the witnesses testified that they had forgotten their testimony "since the first trial." My excitement grew as I realized there was more than one trial!

I went back to the Clerk's office and, after a bit of research, discovered that there had been five trials to convict Lee Currie, possibly a State of Georgia record that still stands to this day! The 3rd trial was a mistrial, and they made no official transcript. I found the 1st, 2nd, and 5th trial transcripts. I could not find the 4th trial record; however, I discovered the 2nd and 5th trials were almost identical in how the case was presented. I discontinued my search on the assumption that the testimony from the 4th trial would not offer much that I didn't already know.

As I started researching the people mentioned in the trial record, a rich plethora of information about those whose lives were touched by this tragedy unfolded. My interest was intense because I knew many of the people involved personally and had gone to school with their children and grandchildren.

My attachment to the story reached a crescendo when I learned from a newspaper article that my granddaddy, Richard Sherwood Boyd, was one of the pallbearers at Lee Currie's funeral! Given they were about the same age, it was reasonable to assume that my grandfather and Lee Currie were friends.

Additionally, I learned that one of my mom and dad's best friends, Roy Taylor, who I remember as a fascinating man and fun to be around, was Lee Currie's nephew. Thus, I had several family and friend connections to the Currie family.

Researching this case, I learned that the prosecution of Lee Currie was indeed, as I wrote in the book: *the trial of the century*. The public was riveted, and during each of the five times he was prosecuted, the courthouse was packed, and the testimony was thoroughly covered by several Georgia newspapers. I read with delight the many stories that were published about the trials. The interview of Lee Currie in the Savannah jail published by the Savannah Morning News that I write about in the book is verbatim from the archives of that newspaper.

Researching court records and newspaper accounts further intrigued me. I interviewed people who could recall hearing about the trials to learn more about the people involved and the general history of Toombs County when the crime occurred. Eventually, I gathered enough background material to write a documentary of the events; however, that was not my goal. Instead, I wanted to create a novel based on a true story that would provide me with the freedom to use my imagination to add dialogue and characters that would fill in the gaps in the trial record. My goal was to take my readers back to that era and into the lives of people affected by the event.

I have striven to remain faithful to the facts drawn from historical records, using real names, when known, of the people involved. I have drawn a few characters from my imagination and made up some dialogues to supplement the direct quotes taken from the court transcripts and news accounts. I have tried diligently to make the content from my imagination plausible, given what I had read about the case.

Despite the heinous nature of the crime, I found myself feeling empathy for the killer, who had a mental condition that today would likely have rendered him not guilty by reason of insanity. However, in the 1920s, psychology was in its infancy, and I could not find a case where the insanity defense had previously been attempted in a courtroom in Toombs County. It was clear that it was an uphill battle for the defense attorneys to try and convince a jury that the insanity defense should trump the old Biblical directive of "An eye for an eye and a tooth for a tooth."

But by the time I began to write this book in 2015, everyone directly involved in the story had passed. The closest living relative to Lee Currie was Vinnie Jo Currie Frost Stanley, Lee's niece and the daughter of John Currie, Jr., Lee's brother. She went by the name of "Judy."

While he was still living, my Uncle James and I visited Judy and told her about my project. She said her parents did not like to talk about the trial, but everyone immediately connected to Lee had died. She was very supportive of my writing the book.

Judy clearly remembered where her family had told her Lee had buried the body of Burley Phillips, and we rode out to the spot. This helped me put together the sequence of events and the burial spot's relationship to the people Lee interacted with on the fateful day of the shooting. I cherish the recordings I made of her describing what she knew about her uncle.

Judy was anxious to read the book and asked me for a copy when I finished it. I promised her that she would get an autographed copy as soon as it was published, but she died unexpectedly on January 3, 2018.

They say that every person living has at least one book in them. This one is mine. I fell in love with the story as a little boy, and I've now written a book about it. I got an "A" on my 8th-grade rendering of the story "The Only Man Ever

Legally Hung in Toombs County." I hope this book has earned similar approval from you.

Larry M. Griggers
Lyons, Georgia
December 30, 2022

www.ingramcontent.com/pod-product-compliance
Lightning Source LLC
Chambersburg PA
CBHW050254010526
44107CB00003B/319